INDUSTRIAL DEVELOPMENT IN AFRICA

Industrial Development in Africa critically synthesizes and reframes the debates on African industrial development in a capability-opportunity framework. It recasts the challenge in a broader comparative context of successive waves of catchup industrialization experiences in the European periphery, Latin America, and East Asia. Berhanu Abegaz explores the case for resource-based and factor-based industrialization in North Africa and Sub-Saharan Africa by drawing on insights from the history of industrialization, development economics, political economy, and institutional economics.

Unpacking complex and diverse experiences, the chapters look at Africa at several levels: continent-wide, sub-regions on both sides of the Sahara, and present analytical case studies of 12 representative countries: Egypt, Tunisia, Ethiopia, Kenya, Tanzania, Mauritius, Zimbabwe, South Africa, Ghana, Nigeria, Senegal, and Cote d'Ivoire.

Industrial Development in Africa will be of interest to undergraduate and graduate students studying African development, African economics, and late-stage industrialization. The book will also be of interest to policymakers.

Berhanu Abegaz is Professor of Economics and Public Policy at the College of William & Mary, USA.

INDUSTRIAL DEVELOPMENT IN AFRICA

Mapping Industrialization Pathways for a Leaping Leopard

Berhanu Abegaz

LONDON AND NEW YORK

First published 2018
by Routledge
2 Park Square, Milton Park, Abingdon, Oxon OX14 4RN

and by Routledge
711 Third Avenue, New York, NY 10017

Routledge is an imprint of the Taylor & Francis Group, an informa business

© 2018 Berhanu Abegaz

The right of Berhanu Abegaz to be identified as author of this work
has been asserted by him in accordance with sections 77 and 78 of the
Copyright, Designs and Patents Act 1988.

All rights reserved. No part of this book may be reprinted or reproduced or
utilized in any form or by any electronic, mechanical, or other means, now
known or hereafter invented, including photocopying and recording, or in
any information storage or retrieval system, without permission in writing
from the publishers.

Trademark notice: Product or corporate names may be trademarks or
registered trademarks, and are used only for identification and explanation
without intent to infringe.

British Library Cataloguing-in-Publication Data
A catalogue record for this book is available from the British Library

Library of Congress Cataloging-in-Publication Data
Names: Abegaz, Berhanu, author.
Title: Industrial development in Africa : mapping industrialization pathways
    for a leaping leopard / Berhanu Abegaz.
Description: New York, NY : Routledge, 2018. | Includes bibliographical
    references and index.
Identifiers: LCCN 2017040346 | ISBN 9781138059702 (hardback) |
    ISBN 9781138059719 (pbk.) | ISBN 9781315163413 (ebook)
Subjects: LCSH: Industrialization—Africa. | Economic development—
    Africa. | Africa—Economic conditions.
Classification: LCC HC800 .A5198 2018 | DDC 338.96—dc23
LC record available at https://lccn.loc.gov/2017040346

ISBN: 978-1-138-05970-2 (hbk)
ISBN: 978-1-138-05971-9 (pbk)
ISBN: 978-1-315-16341-3 (ebk)

Typeset in Bembo
by Apex CoVantage, LLC

For Fernus and Abinnet

CONTENTS

List of figures	*ix*
List of tables	*x*
List of boxes	*xiii*
List of acronyms	*xiv*
Preface	*xvi*
Acknowledgments	*xvii*
Introduction	1

PART I
Industrialization and growth   13

1 Growth, structural transformation, and industrialization	15
2 Industrialization: why and how?	48

PART II
Theories of industrialization   63

3 Theories of industrialization	65
4 Theories of late and very-late industrialization	83

viii Contents

PART III
Waves of globalization and industrialization 109

5 Production and trade under the first unbundling 111

6 Production and trade under the second unbundling 132

PART IV
Africa's postcolonial industrial experience 151

7 African industrial development 153

8 Resource-based industrializers 175

9 Labor-based industrializers 215

PART V
Rethinking industrial strategy 253

10 New industrial policy for Africa 255

11 Africa's industrial future 288

Appendix on data sources *292*
Glossary *296*
Index *301*

FIGURES

0.1	Africa at night	6
1.1	Real per capita income: Africa versus the world, 1950–2010	17
1.2	Convergence rates to "revealed" steady-state per capita incomes, 1970–2010	18
1.3	Growth of GDP per capita in Sub-Saharan Africa, 1966–2014	28
2.1	Venn diagrams of three dimensions of industrialization	56
4.1	Pathways of latecomer industrialization	94
4.2	Pathways of business diversification and control for latecomers	97
5.1	IS: incentives versus capacity	117
5.2	IS and ES: incentives versus market choice	119
5.3	Evolutionary ladder of an IS-biased industrialization strategy	124
5.4	Alterative paths of catchup industrialization: autarkic, integrationist, neutral, and alternating	125
6.1	The twin unbundling of production and consumption	134
6.2	Industrial capability and catchup under two regimes	144
7.1	Two African pathways of industrialization	170
8.1	Real annual indices for major commodity groups, 1960–2015	176
8.2	Real GDP per capita for the resource-based industrializers, 1960–2011	177
8.3	Real GDP per worker, 1960–2011	178
9.1	Real GDP per capita for the factor-based industrializers, 1960–2011	216
9.2	Annual GDP growth rates for the factor-based industrializers, 1990–2014	217
10.1	Policy framework based on the common characteristics of successful developers	256
10.2	A capability-opportunity-performance (COP) perspective on African industrial development	273

TABLES

0.1	Sub-Saharan Africa as a world economic region, 1990–2014	5
0.2	Recent notable publications on African industrial development	7
1.1	Decomposition of the sources of growth, 1990–2014	21
1.2	Patterns and speeds of catchup growth since 1946	26
1.3	The structure of production of African economies	37
1.4	The structure of demand of African economies	38
1.5	African GDP, employment, and relative sectoral productivity, 1975–2010	39
1.6	Growth and structural change at four income levels	40
2.1	National and regional distribution of persons engaged by sector, 1971–2009	50
2.2	Measures of industrial development for selected latecomers, 1980–2010	57
3.1	Three industrial revolutions, 1770–2016	67
3.2	A stylized characterization of early and late industrializations	68
3.3	A stylized characterization of late and very-late industrializations	72
4.1	Distribution of GMVA by development group and region, 1990–2014	84
4.2	Profile of globalized manufacturing under IR3, circa 2010	85
4.3	Competing perspectives on dynamic comparative advantage	88
4.4	Notable attributes of leaders and followers in industrialization	95
4.5	Three stylized strategic sectoral foci for industrialization	99
5.1	A stylized demography of manufacturing industries	115
5.2	A taxonomy of manufacturing industries by factor and technology intensities	116
5.3	Product life cycle and trajectories of technological diffusion to latecomers	127

6.1	The changing nature of manufacturing production and sales	133
6.2	The three C's for African and selected comparator economies	142
6.3	Flexible industrialization under NVC and GVC	143
7.1	Economic profiles of the case-study countries, 2014	169
7.2	Human development indicators for the case-study countries, 2014	170
8.1	Economic profiles of resource-based industrializers, 1990–2014	179
8.2	Manufacturing in resource-based industrializers, 2014	180
8.3	Firm characteristics and business climate in resource-based industrializers	181
8.4	Quality measures of African economic institutions and policies, 2005–2014	182
8.5	Global competitiveness index for resource-based industrializers	186
8.6	Structural change in manufacturing output for resource-based industrializers	187
8.7	Structural change in manufacturing employment for resource-based industrializers	188
8.8	Cote d'Ivoire: competitive industrial performance, 1990–2012	189
8.9	Ghana: changes in sectoral economic structure, 1970–2010	192
8.10	Ghana: competitive industrial performance, 1990–2012	194
8.11	Mauritius: changes in sectoral economic structure, 1970–2010	196
8.12	Mauritius: competitive industrial performance, 1990–2012	198
8.13	Nigeria: changes in sectoral economic structure, 1970–2010	200
8.14	Nigeria: competitive industrial performance, 1990–2012	202
8.15	South Africa: changes in sectoral economic structure, 1970–2010	206
8.16	South Africa: growth performance of three-digit manufacturing industries, 1965–2004	207
8.17	South Africa: efficiency of three-digit manufacturing industries, 1963–2009	208
8.18	South Africa: competitive industrial performance, 1990–2012	209
9.1	Economic profiles of factor-based industrializers, 1990–2014	218
9.2	Manufacturing in non-resource-based industrializers, 2014	219
9.3	Firm characteristics and business climate in factor-based industrializers	220
9.4	Global competitiveness index for factor-based industrializers	221
9.5	Structural change in manufacturing output for factor-based industrializers	222
9.6	Structural change in manufacturing employment of factor-based industrializers	223
9.7	Egypt: changes in sectoral economic structure, 1970–2010	225
9.8	Egypt: growth performance of three-digit manufacturing industries, 1965–2004	226
9.9	Egypt: efficiency of three-digit manufacturing industries, 1967–2006	227

xii Tables

9.10	Egypt: competitive industrial performance, 1990–2012	228
9.11	Ethiopia: changes in sectoral economic structure, 1970–2010	231
9.12	Ethiopia: efficiency of three-digit manufacturing industries, 1990–2009	232
9.13	Ethiopia: competitive industrial performance, 1990–2012	233
9.14	Kenya: changes in sectoral economic structure, 1970–2010	236
9.15	Kenya: growth performance of three-digit manufacturing industries, 1965–2004	237
9.16	Kenya: efficiency of three-digit manufacturing industries, 1967–2002	238
9.17	Kenya: competitive industrial performance, 1990–2012	239
9.18	Senegal: changes in sectoral economic structure, 1970–2010	241
9.19	Senegal: growth performance of three-digit manufacturing industries, 1965–2004	242
9.20	Senegal: efficiency of three-digit manufacturing industries, 1970–2009	243
9.21	Tanzania: changes in sectoral economic structure, 1970–2010	245
9.22	Tanzania: competitive industrial performance, 1990–2012	246
9.23	Tunisia: growth performance of three-digit manufacturing industries, 1965–2004	248
9.24	Tunisia: competitive industrial performance, 1990–2012	249
10.1	African industrial development plans, 1990–2030	265
10.2	Measures of financial depth for the case-study countries, 1980–2010	275
10.3	Disbursement of ODA to Africa, 1980–2014	277
10.4	Foreign exchange receipts from exports and official aid, 1980–2013	278
10.5	Foreign exchange receipts from FDI and remittances, 1980–2013	279

BOXES

4.1	Productive industrial capabilities	90
6.1	Value chains and supply chains	136
6.2	Special economic zones, industrial parks, and industrial districts	140
7.1	The developmental state	167

ACRONYMS

Organizations

ACET	Africa Center for Economic Transformation
AfDB	African Development Bank
BRICS	Brazil, Russia, India, China, and South Africa
COGD	Commission on Growth and Development
EAC	East African Community
ECOWAS	Economic Community of West African States
ILO	International Labour Organization
IMF	International Monetary Fund
NEPAD	New Partnership for Africa's Development
OECD	Organisation for Economic Co-operation and Development
SSA	Sub-Saharan Africa
UNCTAD	United Nations Conference on Trade and Development
UNECA	United Nations Economic Commission for Africa
UNIDO	United Nations Industrial Development Organization
WBG	World Bank Group
WTO	World Trade Organization

Concepts

ADLI	Agriculture Development-Led (Demand-Led) Industrialization
AEO	African Economic Outlook
ALI	Agriculture-Led Industrialization
ASLI	Agriculture Supply-Led Industrialization
ATI	African Transformation Index
CPIA	Country Policy and Institutional Assessment (World Bank)

DS	Developmental State
EPZ	Export Processing Zone
ESI	Export Substitution Industrialization
FB	Factor-Based (industrializers)
FDI	Foreign Direct Investment
FGM	Flying Geese Model
GDP	Gross Domestic Product
GNI	Gross National Income
GPT	General Purpose Technologies
GSC	Global Supply Chain
GVC	Global Value Chain
HDI	Human Development Index
ICT	Information and Communications Technologies
IDS	Industry Development Strategy
IE	Industrial Estate
IP	Industrial Policy
IR	Industrial Revolution
ISI	Import Substitution Industrialization
ISIC	International System for Industrial Classification
IVA	Industrial Value Added
IZ(D)	Industrial Zone (District)
LIT	Learning, Industrial, and Technology
LPA	Lagos Plan of Action
MDGs	Millennium Development Goals
MSSE	Medium and Small-Scale Enterprise
MVA	Manufacturing Value Added
NSE	New Structural Economics
NSC	National Supply Chain
NVC	National Value Chain
ODA	Official Development Assistance
OEM	Original Equipment Manufacturer
PCM	Product Cycle Model
PPP	Purchasing Power Parity
R & D	Research and Development
RB	Resource-Based (industrializers)
SDGs	Sustainable Development Goals
SEZ	Special Economic Zone
SME	Small and Medium Enterprises
TFP	Total Factor Productivity
U(L)C	Unit (Labor) Cost
ULI	Urban-Led Industrialization
URI	Urban-Rural Industrialization

PREFACE

Africa is the proverbial last frontier of late industrialization. Industrial development can be analyzed from three complementary vantage points. The first, at the macro–level, pertains to the appropriate macroeconomic environment to foster industrialization – competitive real interest rates and real exchange rates, and effective tariffs. The second, at the meso-level, focuses on changes in industry structure. The third, at the micro level, concentrates on interconnected and fast-moving firm dynamics. This book is devoted primarily to issues at the meso (industry) level with an accent on the drivers of Africa's industrial performance and its prospects.

I provide a historically informed *tour de force* on an industrializing Africa on both sides of the Sahara. Employing a unifying theoretical framework that is built around the capability-opportunity-policy nexus, *Industrial Development in Africa* seeks to explain the puzzles that are discernible from the economic and political stylized facts of African development since 1970. I draw heavily on internationally comparable data for mostly three-digit manufacturing industries. The cross-country evidence is buttressed by analytical case studies of 12 representative African countries which together account for 75% of the continent's industrial output.

The book pays special attention to the implications, for a very-late industrializing Africa, of the second global unbundling currently in full swing. I argue that, to telescope the process of industrial catchup, Africa needs to build up its productive industrial capability and to synchronize it with the opportunities offered by the expanding home market and the new production-cum-sales gateways provided by global value chains.

ACKNOWLEDGMENTS

This book is a product of a longstanding interest of mine in catchup industrialization of the capitalist and the socialist types. For the past ten years especially, I was preoccupied with the intriguing question of whether there exist feasible pathways for telescoping African industrialization. This thinking has meant taking two considerations seriously. One is radical, if not revolutionary, changes in the international economy that are being opened by the digital revolution. The other is the combination of Africa's limited technocratic capability and inadequate infrastructure, and the distracting lure of periodic booms in commodity prices.

As I started to write, I was struck by the lingering paucity of long and consistent time series data to provide credible structural profiles of African economies even though the supply of micro-level and macro-level data has recently increased quite remarkably. I also noticed that Africa's incipient industrial development, on both sides of the Sahara, cannot be properly contextualized without a discussion of the multi-sectoral growth experiences of its leading economies and the rapidly changing global environment in which the continent has found itself since independence. This means I had to provide a broader coverage of issues than is commonly expected from a book whose primary concern is the industrial sector.

I tend to be a loner in my research endeavors, but I did benefit from the comments and questions posed by the external reviewers of the prospectus. I am also grateful for assistance in data work and feedback on early drafts from my graduate students: Timothy Planert, Troy Wiipongwii, Joshua Klein, Vahid Dejwakh, Kiel Kinkade and Andrew Weidman. I also wish to thank the University of Chicago Press for permission to incorporate copyrighted material into Figure 6.2.

My debt, however, is mostly institutional. The first is to the Department of Economics of the College of William & Mary which allowed me to teach a variety of development-oriented courses and seminars. The unusually bright students in

xviii Acknowledgments

my classes challenged me to refine my ideas. The Department also paid for various industrial data sets. Credit is also due to the university's research leave program which afforded me a large block of time to think through many of my tentative ideas and judgments on the subject. Finally, my special thanks go to Leanne Hinves, the acquisition editor at Routledge, for her patience in overseeing the whole process, and to Kate Fornadel of Apex CoVantage for the wonderful support in the copyediting and production stages.

Berhanu Abegaz
Department of Economics
The College of William & Mary
Williamsburg, VA (USA)
October 2017

INTRODUCTION

Around 1750, English, Dutch, and Swiss entrepreneurs showed the world how marshaling the stored energy of coal and steam could revolutionize production (through factories) and transportation (through railroads and steam engines) of previously hand-crafted and cottage-processed goods. This is indeed why "industrial activity" is defined as the energy-intensive mechanical or chemical transformation of primary materials, substances, or components into new goods.

Known as industrialization (manu-facturing and machino-facturing), these bundled organizational, product, and process innovations continue to diffuse both to other sectors of the economy and to the economically laggard parts of the world. The core of this process is the conscious application of increasingly sophisticated technologies and machinery for the enhancement of factor productivity, product quality, or product variety.

The industrial sector, broadly construed, includes manufacturing, mining, construction, and modern utilities. Lately, it has also blended with segments of business services where product design, financing, and marketing are decoupled in country-space from fabrication. Industrialization is a historically variable and complex set of economic, social, and political *processes*. It has historically induced several associated changes in the behavior of firms and households, including changes in the propensities to save, invest, procreate, engage politically, or migrate.

The modern industrial economy has a direction as well as a growth trajectory. The "industrial revolution," and the "industrious revolution" of proto-industrial activities that paved the way for it (de Vries, 1994), turned out to be one of the most transformative directions in economic history.[1] Industry-driven economic diversification enhances productivity, and hence income, precisely because it lies at the core of technological learning. This fact would explain why industrialization has historically served as a major vehicle for nurturing a national as well as a transnational middle class while enhancing the ability of elites to support poverty reduction whenever they find it politically expedient to do so.

2 Introduction

Economic historians continue to debate the genesis and nature of the industrial revolution. As Gregory Clark (2007: 8–9) puts it,

> The term "Industrial Revolution" has come to mean two very different things: first, the transformation the British economy experienced between 1760 and 1850, to become the first modern industrialized, fast-growing economy; second, the general switch between the pre-industrial world of slow technological advance, high fertility and little human capital to the modern world of rapid efficiency gains, low fertility and large investments in human capital.

Some economists, in fact, define development as a process that links learning at the micro level, accumulation of technological capabilities at the macro level, and industrial policy at the meso level (Cimoli et al., 2009). Agriculture, save a handful of subsectors, is relatively self-limiting in the sense that it is prone to ecological limitations and subject to the boom-bust cycles of commodities (Amsden, 2001; Williamson, 2011). Manufacturing, the learning center of industry, is special precisely because it is income-elastic, linkage-rich, and technologically progressive. Manufacturing and high-end services are high-productivity sectors. Manufacturing is one of the easiest industries to mechanize, and it has, in turn, mechanized agriculture, construction, transportation, communications, and mining.

Industrialization and urbanization are at the heart of what turned out to be the great divergence in average living standards between the West and the rest of the world (Findlay and O'Rourke, 2009). The momentous transformation wrought by the spread of industrialization outside of Europe and its offshoots has been quite remarkable. The West accounted for 29% of global manufacturing value added (MVA) in 1800, 87% in 1900, and 55% (and about half global GDP) in 2015. If current trends continue, the West may very well account once again for just 29% of global MVA and GDP by 2050 (Baldwin, 2016).

While we have numerous examples of resource-rich countries which have attained high income through a combination of resource rents and resource-induced growth, countries almost invariably grew rich using the most robust form of economic diversification – industrialization. That some contemporary developing countries have prospered based on niches of modern agriculture and services does not change the fact that a broad-based and technologically receptive industrial development has been the pathway to prosperity for most successful developers. Despite the halting deindustrialization of economies at both ends of the per capita income spectrum and the concentration of recent industrial output in East Asia, there is little evidence that manufacturing has ceased to be the leading growth engine (Haraguchi et al., 2017).

Industrialization may therefore not be everything, but it is almost everything. Africa's 1.2 billion people and South Asia's 1.5 billion people live in the two major world regions which have yet to mount a robust industrialization drive. Africa especially continues to be a nagging challenge for development theory and policy since it currently lags in nearly all measures of economic well-being.

Introduction **3**

Why, some 250 years later, such large income gaps and structural differences persist between the top billion and the bottom billion remains poorly understood. This puzzle needs to be explained if Africans and South Asians are to chart an appropriate industrialization and growth strategy. That Africa and South Asia remain poor and only partially industrialized clearly suggests a gigantic market failure globally and political failure nationally.[2]

Among the stylized facts of industrialization, four stand out. First, early industrial development entailed a transition from traditional agriculture and crafts to light industry. Second, deeper industrial development was characterized by a transition from light industry to capital-intensive or heavy industry and then to technology-intensive activities. Third, overcoming persistent industrial dualism entailed a supportive environment for high firm entry and growth, and export orientation. And fourth, the post-1990 phase of globalization has made it less necessary for latecomers to develop a broad-based industrial capability to launch a viable industrialization drive.

The impediments against and the opportunities for industrializing are, therefore, profoundly shaped by changing international environments, varying levels and congruence between national capabilities and institutions, and the extent to which industrialization strategies recognize these realities. Africa, as a very-late industrializer, faces momentous challenges emanating from a deeply integrated global economy, the unbundling of not just production from consumption but production itself across international boundaries, the over-crowding of the world market by highly competitive recent industrializers, and the formidable prerequisites for international competitiveness that include massive investments in skills, infrastructure, and a threshold of national manufacturing capacity.

The debates on latecomer industrialization are usually centered on three sets of issues about changes in organization and technology (Sutcliffe, 1984; Amsden, 2001; Adelman and Morris, 1988). The first is concerned with sectoral priorities for the generation of savings, the allocation of investment, and the scope for technological progress – issues which go back to the German and later the Soviet industrialization debates. The second deals with the reaction of rural households to proto-industrial opportunities created by expanding markets which may take the form of diversification into non-agricultural activities (the Japanese road) or greater specialization within agriculture (the Anglo-American road). The third concern deals with the growing intricacy of cross-border fragmentation of production of whole products into distinct, sequenced tasks and components. The fourth issue speaks to the oft-neglected balance of political forces in favor of or against industrial development as the nascent industrial class and powerful agrarian interests contest costly import substitution or the consequential changes in the balance of political power.

Nevertheless, the remarkable industrial achievements by such very-latecomers as China, India, Vietnam, Ireland, Bangladesh, Tunisia, and Mauritius as well as new opportunities being opened by the intensively globalized management of components and tasks have made it easier to imagine an industrial Africa within two or three generations. The larger countries in the continent have, over the past two

4 Introduction

decades, attracted sizeable FDI and domestic investments in infrastructure, ICT, basic education and health, resource processing, and lately commercial agriculture. In search of low wages, growing local markets, and preferential access to the markets of the EU and the U.S.A., such upstarts as Brazil, Russia, India, China, Turkey, and South Korea have been building manufacturing plants in the more promising African countries.

A couple of vignettes illustrate these intriguing trends. The Hualien Group, a Chinese shoemaker, based in the south China hub of Dongguan, plans to invest as much as $2 billion in Ethiopia over the next decade to make the country a base for exports to Europe and North America. In response to a $100:$500 monthly wage ratio between Ethiopia and China, Huajian opened its first factory in Ethiopia in 2012. Mr. Zhang Huarong, the owner, expects to create 30,000 jobs in Ethiopia by 2020 along with up to $1.5 billion in exports when his industrial park on the outskirts of Addis Ababa becomes fully operational.[3]

Chinese factory owners have found themselves squeezed between the demand for higher wages and falling growth at home, and they are beginning to export as many as an expected 85 million jobs to Indo-China, South Asia, and Africa. Chinese companies are also investing in upper-end manufacturing with productivity-adjusted unit labor costs.

The Hisense Co. factory in Pretoria produces televisions and refrigerators. Facing a shortage of engineers and technicians, it has been providing on-the-job training opportunities for native workers. Hisense, which is based in Qingdao (China), offers about $580 a month for entry-level technicians – much less than the average of $800 at its 20 factories in China.

"China is a resilient investor," says Martyn Davies, chief executive of Frontier Advisory, a consulting firm that does business in China and Africa. "You see it in Ethiopia at the bottom end and in South Africa in the higher-end stuff."[4]

This reminds one of the fairy-tale-like beginning of the brilliantly successful ready-made-garments (RMG) industry in Bangladesh. The Desh-Daewoo joint venture sent some 130 Bangladeshi garment workers for a six-month training program in 1979 to the state-of-the-art factories in Pusan, South Korea. They formed the initial human capital base for RMG exports beginning in 1980. Today, Bangladesh is the second biggest garment exporter in the world (Heath and Mobarak, 2015) Catchup is indeed possible but not probable in the absence of a tenacious and focused national effort.

Catchup industrialization for Africa

In 2014, Africa accounted for almost 16% of the world's population, but for only 5% of the global economy and just 2% of global trade. The African economic landscape is also strikingly non-industrial, accounting for less than 4% of global MVA.

Furthermore, during 1990–2014, an inter-regional comparison shows that Sub-Saharan Africa (SSA) has the slowest real per capita income growth compared with

TABLE 0.1 Sub-Saharan Africa as a world economic region, 1990–2014

Indicator	1990	2014	2014/1990	GDP
GDP per capita, 2011 PPP $:	*(actual)*	*(actual)*	*(ratio)*	*(trill. ppp$)*
Australia	28,572	43,219	1.5	1.0
China	1,516	12,599	8.3	18.0
India	1,773	5,439	3.1	7.4
SSA	2,500	3,352	1.3	3.4[a]
World	8,813	14,287	1.6	108.6
Population, in millions:				
Australia	17	23	1.4	na
China	1,135	1,364	1.2	na
India	871	1,295	1.5	na
SSA	509	974[b]	1.9	na
World	5,283	7,261	1.4	na

Sources and notes: World Bank, *World Development Indicators 2015.*
SSA = Sub-Saharan Africa
a When added to North Africa's GDP of $2.0 trillion, total African GDP was $3.4 trillion in 2014. See Table 0.2 for country breakdowns.
b When added to North Africa's population 180 million, total African population rises to 1.15 billion in 2014.

Australia, China, or India (Table 0.1). Every year, 13 million young Africans join the labor market, one-eighth of them in formal wage employment. Africa's total labor force is projected to reach 1 billion by 2040 to make it the largest regional "reserve army of labor" in the world, surpassing China or India (AfDB, OECD, and UNIDO, 2014).

Africa, China, and India have comparable population sizes (about 1.2–1.3 billion each). And yet, compared to a global GDP of about $106 trillion in 2014, China's GDP was $18 trillion (or $13,000 per capita), India's was $7.4 billion ($5,700 per capita) and Africa's was $5.5 trillion (or $7.2 trillion if GDP is entirely rebased) equaling $4,700 per capita. One clue to recent growth rate rankings among the three (China, then India, and then Africa) lies in the relative weight of manufacturing in the economy. While the GDP share of manufacturing value added in China is a whopping 44%, India boasts 25%, and Africa's is a measly 11%. Africa's failure to industrialize is, in fact, visually dramatized by the NASA satellite map of Africa at night, reproduced here as Figure 0.1, which evokes the ill-willed metaphor of the "dark continent."

Charting a tailored path of structural transformation requires identification of the economically significant peculiarities of each sub-region and each African country regarding its economic assets and liabilities. African assets which hold immense economic promise for industrial development include: a young, reasonably educated, and growing labor force; emerging lower-middle-class consumers; abundant

FIGURE 0.1 Africa at night

Source: NASA, http://eoimages.gsfc.nasa.gov/images/imagerecords/79000/79793/city_lights_africa_8k.jpg.

and processable natural resources (with an estimated 10% of the global reserves of oil, 40% of gold and 80–90% of chromium-platinum group metals); and a quarter of the world's arable land of 600 million hectares (AfDB, 2011; AEO-AFR, 2015).

The new globalization and the associated new technologies have enhanced the productivity of manufacturing-based development while denting its ability to generate lesser-skilled jobs – at least directly. This pattern is encased in important global megatrends. These include radical changes in the geography of production and consumption, in the rapid aging of the populations in high-income and certain middle-income countries, in the youth bulge and the implied demographic dividend in low-income countries particularly in Africa, rapid urbanization led by low-productivity services, expansion of educational opportunities for the youth despite quality problems, and greater appreciation for green technologies among consumers in the developed countries (Hallward-Driemmeir and Nayyar, 2017; World Bank, 2018). The brightening prospects of African industrialization, given especially the 85 million jobs expected to be shed by China alone because of rapidly rising wages and steady gains in human and public capital in Africa, have induced international development institutions to issue research reports which make a case for light industry at least for selected parts of the continent. Some leading development economists have also revived the debate on smart industrial policy for Africa (see Table 0.2).

TABLE 0.2 Recent notable publications on African industrial development

A. Micro-level and comparative research reports:

1. Mazumdar, Dipak, and Ata Mazaheri. (2003). *The African Manufacturing Firm: An Analysis Based on Firm Surveys in Seven Countries in Sub-Saharan Africa.* London: Routledge.
2. Sonobe, Tetsushi, and Keijiro Otsuka. (2011). *Cluster-Based Industrial Development: A Comparative Study of Asia and Africa.* New York: Palgrave Macmillan.
3. Dinh, Hinh, et al. (2012). *Light Manufacturing in Africa: Targeted Policies to Enhance Private Investment and Create Jobs.* Washington, DC: World Bank.
4. Whitfield, Lindsay, et al. (2015). *The Politics of Industrial Policy in Africa: A Comparative Perspective.* New York: Cambridge University Press.
5. Newman, Carol, John Page, John Rand, Abebe Shimeles, Mans Soderbom, and Finn Tarp. (2016). *Made in Africa: Learning to Compete in Industry.* Washington, DC: Brookings Institution Press.
6. Oqubay, Arkebe. (2015). *Made in Africa: Industrial Policy in Ethiopia.* Oxford: Oxford University Press.
7. Kelsall, Tim. (2014). *Business Politics and the State in Africa.* London: Zed Press.
8. Handley, Antoinette. (2014). *Business and the State in Africa.* Cambridge: Cambridge University Press.

B. Theory and policy-oriented edited books:

1. Stiglitz, Joseph, Justin Yifu Lin, and Ebrahim Patel, eds. (2013). *The Industrial Policy Revolution II: Africa in the 21st Century.* New York: Palgrave Macmillan.
2. Noman, Akbar, and Joseph Stiglitz, eds. (2015). *Industrial Policy and Economic Transformation in Africa.* New York: Columbia University.
3. Newman, Carol, et al., eds. (2016). *Manufacturing Transformation: Comparative Studies of Industrial Development in Africa and Emerging Asia.* Oxford: Oxford University Press.

C. Reports by international organizations:

1. World Bank. (2010). *Industrial Clusters and Micro and Small Enterprises in Africa: From Survival to Growth.* Washington, DC: World Bank.
2. U.N. Economic Commission for Africa (UNECA). (2017). *Urbanization and Industrialization for Africa's Transformation.* Addis Ababa.
3. United Nations Industrial Organization (UNIDO) and United Nations Conference on Trade and Development (UNCTAD). (2011). *Africa Report 2011: Fostering Industrial Development in Africa in the New Global Development.* Geneva.
4. African Development Bank (AfDB). Organisation of Economic Co-operation and Development (OECD), and United Nations Industrial Organization (UNIDO). (2014). *Global Value Chains and Africa's Industrialization.* Abidjan.
5. African Development Bank (AfDB). Organisation of Economic Co-operation and Development (OECD), and United Nations Industrial Organization (UNIDO). (2017). *African Economic Outlook: Entrepreneurship and Industrialisation.* Abidjan.
6. United Nations Economic Commission for Africa (UNECA). (2016a). *Economic Report on Africa 2016: Greening Africa's Industrialization.* Addis Ababa.
7. United Nations Economic Commission for Africa (UNECA). (2016b). *Transformative Industrial Policy for Africa.* Addis Ababa.

D. Older overview, or country case studies:

1. Riddell, Roger. (1990). *Manufacturing Africa: Performance & Prospects of Seven Countries in Sub-Saharan Africa.* London: James Currey.
2. Wangwe, Samuel, ed. (1995). *Exporting Africa: Technology, Trade, Industrialization.* London: Routledge.

8 Introduction

Unfortunately, there is no single book in the market that provides a unified treatment of the theoretical, empirical, and policy dimensions of African industrial development. *Industrial Development in Africa* fills this gap by critically synthesizing and reframing the thin but growing literature on African industrialization in a capability-opportunity framework. It also aims to recast Africa's prospects in a broader comparative context of successive waves of catchup industrialization experiences in the European Periphery, Latin America, and East Asia.

The book addresses a series of vexed questions about African development prospects. How has the nature of industrialization changed, and is it still a viable engine of growth for very-latecomers such as Africa and South Asia? What useful lessons can be learned from European and East Asian successes and Africa's stint with industrial development, albeit in a highly competitive global environment? Will spatial clustering and economic geography become more important in the future? Are the boundaries between manufacturing and related sectors disappearing, say, as agriculture itself and business services become industrialized? What are the new forms of interaction between firms based in the successful cohort of late industrializers (so-called born-globals or micro-multinationals of Korea, Taiwan, China, India, and Brazil) and the budding ones in Africa and other would-be industrializers?

These questions beg a deeper inquiry regarding the role of institutions, organizations, and industrial entrepreneurs. What are the appropriate forms of industrial policy for a very-late industrializing Africa to foster an industrial class? What is the relationship between state entrepreneurs and private entrepreneurs in industrial development? How can we measure the type of entrepreneurial activity most needed for an industrial transition in societies dominated by merchant capital or comprador capital? How do the changing international division of labor, a social-spending focused aid regime, and the less supportive WTO (World Trade Organization) rules shape the evolution of comparative advantage for very-latecomers? What drives the competitive balance among industrial, state, and finance capital in the age of vertically integrated but spatially disintegrated transnational production chains?

Another set of questions focuses on the process of innovation, employment, and environmental sustainability: Are there cleaner and more energy-efficient forms of industrial catchup today than in the twentieth century? Can industrial development generate the well-paying jobs that can absorb the rapidly growing and better-educated labor force? Will the vast reservoir of labor keep wages low for a long time thereby accentuating income inequality? What are the mechanics of technological learning for productivity-driven industrial development?

As noted earlier, one striking feature of the typical African economy is its shallow and self-limiting industrial base. Another is the prevalence of patrimonial political institutions that provide stronger incentives for "costly acts of redistribution" than for the creation of wealth. The circumstances (adverse initial conditions, weak institutions, structural shocks, and distorted endogenous policies) under which Africa is integrated into world markets (as a low-wage, primary-good exporter)

Introduction **9**

have imposed significant legacy costs. However, countries once considered basket cases (such as South Korea and Bangladesh) have managed to overcome comparably unfavorable initial conditions to mount vigorous industrialization.

A recently published synthesis volume for the Learning-to-Compete research project (Newman et al., 2016) is especially insightful for its evidence-based advice concerning a new set of "normative" African industrial policies. Based on eight country case studies and econometric evidence from firm-level data, they argue that African industrial policy should put renewed emphasis on export-oriented industries to take advantage of domestic market growth and to accelerate the divestment from labor-intensive manufactures by East Asia. Accentuating the need for competitive discipline, they recommend improving infrastructure, human capital, and the business environment to attract the investment necessary to underwrite industrial densification and clustering.

Distinctive features of the book

There are many good books on African industrial development that have appeared since 2000, most of which are edited volumes that deal with theoretical and policy issues framed in a comparative framework. The growing number of country and industry case studies and econometric analyses of firm behavior based on recently available data have also enriched our knowledge of the challenges facing an industrializing Africa. What we still lack is a comprehensive, historically informed book-length treatment of the experiences and prospects for African industrialization under the new globalization.

Industrial Development in Africa is primarily a synthetic work that reframes the theoretical, empirical, and policy challenges of industrializing very late. More specifically, the book:

- provides a consistent theoretical framework to tie together the various interlocking economic (and where relevant, political) strands that define African industrial development,
- presents key stylized facts drawn from the economic profiles of the continent and its key countries using internationally comparable data,
- situates the industrial development challenges facing the various countries and sub-regions in the broader context of global history, and
- frames industrial policy regarding bridging built-up productive capability and market opportunity, mindful of the fact that the politically feasible may trump the theoretically first-best.

This book is, therefore, distinctive in at least two respects. First, it provides a unifying framework of our own that is informed by development theory, economic history, institutional economics, and a comprehensive series of internationally comparable data since 1970. Second, it looks at a diverse Africa from several vantage points:

10 Introduction

continent-wide, the sub-regions on both sides of the Sahara, 12 representative case-study countries, and manufacturing industries at disaggregated levels.

The analytical case studies draw on representative countries (Egypt, Tunisia, Ethiopia, Kenya, Tanzania, Mauritius, Zimbabwe, South Africa, Ghana, Nigeria, Senegal, and Cote d'Ivoire). These 12 countries represent half of Africa's 1.2 billion people, 60% of its US\$1.7 trillion continental markets, and over three-quarters of its US\$215 billion of manufacturing value added in 2014.

In the realm of policy, we critically examine two competing perspectives on industrial policies to accelerate late industrialization. The "capability identification" approach, true to its Neoclassical roots, focuses on static comparative advantage favoring the non-discretionary industrial policy that is limited to the timely provision of key public services, including regulation. The "capability accumulation" (or capability cultivation) approach, true to its structuralist bent, recognizes the protracted nature of market formation and state formation to nurture dynamic comparative advantage.

Organization of the book

The rest of the book is organized in five parts comprising 11 chapters. Part One, "Industrialization and Growth," provides the economy-wide context for industrialization. The aim is to distil the scholarly work on economic growth, structural change, and the role of industrialization. Chapter 1 surveys what we know about the drivers of, and the interplay between, growth and structural change, and what it would take to make growth sustained and broadly shared. Chapter 2 explains what is meant by industrialization, why it is important, and the various ways to measure the breadth and depth of industrial development.

Part Two, "Theories of Industrialization," explicates the various theories and models of industrialization. Chapter 3 explores the special features of successive catchup industrializations in the twentieth century by latecomers with few knowledge assets. Chapter 4 extends this discussion with a focus on how the new globalization has opened novel possibilities and new constraints for Africa.

Part Three, "Waves of Globalization and Industrialization," examines in detail the pathways for integrating the design, production, and marketing dimensions of manufacturing across activities and the global space. Chapter 5 looks at the pre-1990 modalities of industrialization while Chapter 6 reviews emerging pathways since then. Our aim here is to extract the most instructive lessons for very-latecomers like Africa on both sides of the Sahara.

Part Four, "Africa's Postcolonial Industrial Experience," reviews Africa's own experiences with industrial development since independence. I identify the sources of African growth, the enduring legacies of colonial structural relations, and the constraints on industrial deepening. Chapter 7 surveys the recently available data on Africa's informal and formal industrial activities and also characterizes the African state. Chapter 8 presents case studies of six resource-based industrializers while Chapter 9 takes up the cases of six other labor-based industrializers.

Part Five, "Rethinking Industrial Strategy," distils the relevant lessons from an exhaustive and critical survey of recent debates on nimble industrial policies. Chapter 10 examines the debate on the instruments and objectives of industrial policies in search of smart industrial policies that will help to telescope an African industrial take-off. Chapter 11 concludes by offering final thoughts on Africa's industrial prospects.

The intended readership of the book includes advanced undergraduates and graduate students, scholars, and policymakers looking for a rigorous but non-technical survey of late industrialization. Each chapter begins with a synopsis of the major ideas covered. A glossary and several boxes of key (and often confusing) economic ideas and terms are provided to help the general reader. The key words show up in **bold** the first time they appear. Those wishing to dig deeper may benefit from the appendix on the primary sources of recently available cross-country data on disaggregated branches of manufacturing.

Notes

1 Karl Polanyi (1944) dubbed the triumph of the modern market economy, within which the industrial one is encased, 'the great transformation.'
2 UNECA (2017: 20) puts the challenge this way: "African cities face low productivity, tepid job creation, huge infrastructural and service gaps, weak linkages with rural areas, high levels of informality, increasing inequalities, growing environmental damage, and vulnerability . . . Unless resolved, these impediments will undermine Africa's urban potential for structural transformation."
3 See www.dailymail.co.uk/news/article-3824617/Trump-factory-jobs-sent-China-never-come-back.html#ixzz4UNTm6sIy.
4 See www.marketwatch.com/story/china-inc-moves-factory-floor-to-africa-2014-05-14-20485725.

References

Adelman, I., and C. Morris. (1988). *Comparative Patterns of Economic Development, 1850–1914*. Baltimore: The John-Hopkins University Press.
Africa Economic Outlook (AEO-AFR). (2015). *Africa 2015*. Abidjan: AfDB, OECD, UNDP.
African Development Bank (AfDB). (2011). *The Middle of the Pyramid: Dynamics of the Middle Class in Africa*. [online] Abidjan: AfDB. Available at: www.afdb.org/fileadmin/uploads/afdb/Documents/Publications/The%20Middle%20of%20the%20Pyramid_The%20Middle%20of%20the%20Pyramid.pdf.
African Development Bank (AfDB), Organisation for Economic Co-operation and Development (OECD), and the United Nations Development Organization (UNIDO). (2014). *Global Value Chains and Africa's Industrialization*. Abidjan: AfDB, OECD, UNIDO.
Amsden, A. (2001). *The Rise of 'The Rest': Challenges to the West From Late Industrializing Economies*. New York: Oxford University Press.
Baldwin, R. (2016). *The Great Convergence: Information Technology and the New Globalization*. Cambridge: Belknap Press of Harvard University Press.
Cimoli, M., G. Dosi, and J. Stiglitz. (2009). *Industrial Policy and Development: The Political Economy of Capabilities Accumulation*. Oxford: Oxford University Press.
Clark, G. (2007). *A Farewell to Alms: A Brief Economic History of the World*. Princeton: Princeton University Press.

12 Introduction

de Vries, J. (1994). The Industrial Revolution and the Industrious Revolution. *Journal of Economic History*, 54(2), pp. 249–270.

Findlay, R., and K. O'Rourke. (2009). *Power and Plenty: Trade, War, and the World*. Princeton: Princeton University Press.

Hallward-Driemmeir, M. and G. Nayyar (2017). *Trouble in the Making? The Future of Manufacturing-led Development*. Washington, DC: World Bank Group.

Haraguchi, N., C. Cheng, and E. Smeets. (2017). The Importance of Manufacturing in Economic Development: Has This Changed? *World Development*, 93(May), pp. 293–315.

Heath, R., and M. Mobarak. (2015). Manufacturing Growth and the Lives of Bangladeshi Women. *Journal of Development Economics*, 115, pp. 1–15.

Khan, M. (2013) Political Settlements and the Design of Technology Policy. In: J. Stiglitz, J.Y Lin, and E. Patel, eds., *The Industrial Policy Revolution II: Africa in the 21st Century*. New York: Palgrave Macmillan, 243–280.

Liedholm, C. (1992). Small-scale Industries in Africa: Dynamic Issues and the Role of Policy. In: F. Stewart, ed., *Alternative Development Strategies in Sub-Saharan Africa*. London: Macmillan.

Liedholm, C. (2001). Small Firm Dynamics: Evidence from Africa and Latin America. *Small Business Economics*, 18 (Winter), pp. 227–242.

Mazumdar, D. and A. Mazaheri. (2003). *The African Manufacturing Firm*. New York: Routledge.

Morris, C. and I. Adelman. (1988). *Comparative Patterns of Economic Development, 1850–1914*. Baltimore: The John-Hopkins University Press.

Newman, C., J. Page, J. Rand, A. Shimeles, M. Soderbom, and F. Tarp. (2016). *Made in Africa: Learning to Compete in Industry*. Washington, DC: Brookings Institution Press.

Polanyi, K. (1944). *The Great Transformation: The Political and Economic Origins of Our Time*. New York: Farrar & Rinehart.

Stein, H., ed. (1995). *Asian Industrialization and Africa*. New York, St. Martin's.

Summers, C. (2016). Inside a Trump Chinese Shoe Factory. [online] *Mailonline* and AFP, October 6, 2016. Available at: www.dailymail.co.uk/news/article-3824617/Trump-factory-jobs-sent-China-never-come-back.html#ixzz4UNTm6sIy.

Sutcliffe, R. (1984). Industry and Underdevelopment Reconsidered. *Journal of Development Studies*, 21(1), pp. 121–133.

Tribe, M. (2000). Industrial Development and Policy in Africa: Issues of de-industrialization and development strategy. In: H. Jalilian, M. Tribe and J. Weiss, eds., *Industrial Development and Policy in Africa: Issues of Deindustrialization and Development Strategy* Cheltenham, UK: Edward Elgar.

United Nations Economic Commission for Africa (UNECA). (2017). *Urbanization and Industrialization for Africa's Transformation*. Addis Ababa: UNECA.

Williamson, J. (2011). *Trade and Poverty: When the Third World Fell Behind*. Cambridge: MIT Press.

Wonacott, P. (2014). China Inc. Moves Factory Floor to Africa. [online] *Market Watch*, May 14, 2014. Available at: www.marketwatch.com/story/china-inc-moves-factory-floor-to-africa-2014-05-14-20485725.

World Bank (2018). *The World Development Report 2018: Learning to Realize Education's Promise*. Washington, DC: World Bank Group.

PART I
Industrialization and growth

1

GROWTH, STRUCTURAL TRANSFORMATION, AND INDUSTRIALIZATION

We begin with a bird's-eye view of the core ideas of development economics and development politics with a focus on modern economic growth and the associated structural changes in production, consumption, and income distribution. This overview of theory and empirics is intended to provide the requisite backdrop for a detailed exploration of arguably the most defining form of **structural transformation** – robust industrialization.

Development

As Amartya Sen (2000) rightly notes, development is ultimately about human capability and agency – freedom from material want as well as freedom from political tyranny and social exclusion. Economic development is also a drawn-out and multifaceted process that couples the twin pillars of sustained economic growth and structural change. It entails the transformation of the fundamental human propensities to save and invest, procreate and nurture children, submit to resist the powerful, stay put or migrate, and engage in predation or wealth creation.

Construed broadly, development is about the transition from exclusionary and redistributive political and economic **institutions** to inclusionary and productive ones (Acemoglu and Robinson, 2012). The economic empowerment of ordinary citizens, often labeled the "middling class" or the "middle class," sustains an inclusionary social contract, fosters societal stability, and formalizes economic relations.

The first of the two pillars of economic development, economic growth, is all about increasing the size of the economic pie. The mechanism includes most or all the following: reallocating factors of production from less productive uses to more productive uses, investing in the accumulation of factors of production, enhancing their productivity (through imitation, adaptation, or invention, improving the

16 Industrialization and growth

incentive environment for business), and prudently opening-up to international trade and investment.

Increasing the national pie is a necessary, if not a sufficient, condition for improving the economic well-being of randomly picked members of a given society. Though growth is not everything, it almost is. Substantial poverty reduction cannot be effected without a substantially bigger pie. The reigniting of rapid growth lifted one billion people out of poverty in China and India alone during 1990–2015.

The second dimension of development, structural **economic transformation** (ET), involves significant reallocation of human and non-human resources from low-productivity activities to high-productivity activities within sectors or between sectors. ET is essential for ensuring that economic growth creates well-paying jobs in wide-ranging activities and that growth is resilient and environmentally sustainable.

Economic growth

Economic growth, driven by investment in factors of production or investment in new ideas, is too complex a process to be amenable to full capture by simple models. Complexity implies, for example, that innovation-driven growth is a non-deterministic product of experimentation with new ideas or the discovery of new markets in a world of high risk – political, financial, and technological.

Understanding economic growth also requires understanding the mechanisms by which political institutions and economic institutions interact. This is why the most useful models of growth and structural change are those that are context-sensitive, besides providing testable predictions (Rodrik, 2015).

Let us begin our exposition with ten notable stylized facts (or empirical regularities) of post-World War II economic growth that theory seeks to explain (Jones and Vollrath, 2013; UNIDO, 2009, 2015; Weil, 2012; Bourguignon, 2015; Milanovic, 2016):[1]

1 Differences in real per capita income *levels* increased dramatically across countries between 1800 and 2000 – especially between Europe and its offshoots, and the rest of the world (minus Northeast Asia).
2 Rates of economic *growth* vary substantially across countries, within countries, and over time. Rich countries are much more alike in terms of both income levels and growth patterns than are poor countries.
3 However, a specific country's relative position in the world distribution of real per capita income is *not* immutable. Many economies caught up with leaders while others continue to stumble or even to regress.
4 Growth is easier to *initiate* than to *sustain* for decades through gains in **total factor productivity**.
5 There is a strong positive correlation between investment *levels* and output *levels* across countries. However, the rate of income growth is much less persistent over time than the rate of capital formation.

6 Growth may be constrained by the relative scarcity of any of the complementary factors of production – land, labor, skills, capital, or entrepreneurship.
7 Growth is conditioned by the quality of institutions which provide the requisite incentives to gainfully work, invest, rent, or innovate.
8 Growth in output and growth in the volume of international trade are highly correlated.
9 Income inequality generally rises, peaks around $10,000 per head, and then falls. As real per capita income steadily rises, inter-household consumption of necessities converges first, followed by access to public services and, finally, by earned incomes – the drivers being skill formation, access to finance, initial capital, and the density of social networks.
10 Growth is geographically uneven: initially favoring clusters around cities, mining, plantations, or seaports. As development deepens, location matters less for families than for firms.

The stylized facts enumerated above capture important aspects of African growth, too. I will examine Africa's patterns of growth in detail, but it will suffice to note here, as Figures 1.1 and 1.2 show, that African growth has not been impressive. Its per capita income fell from about half to one-fourth of the global average during 1950–2010. The result is that, while Africa accounts for some 16% of the world's population, Africans claim only 3% of global income.

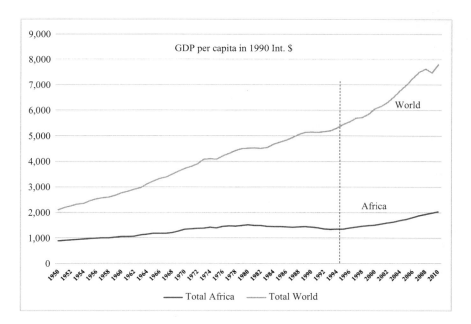

FIGURE 1.1 Real per capita income: Africa versus the world, 1950–2010

Source: Maddison Project Database: www.ggdc.net/maddison/maddison-project/data.htm.

18 Industrialization and growth

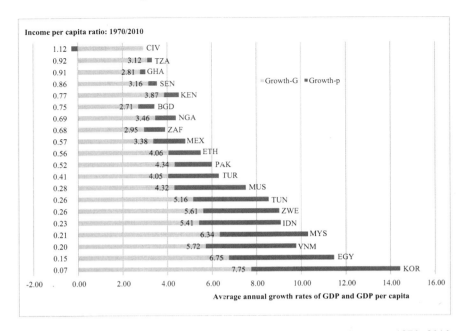

FIGURE 1.2 Convergence rates to "revealed" steady-state per capita incomes, 1970–2010

Sources and notes: Penn World Table 8.1.
Growth-G = annual growth of GDP
Growth-p = annual growth rate of real per capita income
Revealed steady-state per capita income = the highest per capita income (in 2010, except in the case CIV – Cote d'Ivoire) relative to the initial level (in 1970). South Korea, Egypt, and Malaysia recorded the highest realization rates while Cote d'Ivoire, Tanzania, and Ghana reported the lowest

Interestingly, it was not always this way. Africa as a whole had an average per capita income comparable to those of China and India during 1880–1980, after which it was overtaken rather dramatically especially by China (Maddison, 2001). Africa grew robustly in the 1950s and the 1960s, stagnated in the 1970s and the 1980s, and resumed growth in the 1990s and the 2000s. It, however, continued to experience divergence in real per capita income with almost all other world regions – an outcome that was alternatively blamed on market failure, government failure, or both (Aryeetey et al., 2012).

Drivers of economic growth

Economic historians note that a large gap in average living standards emerged between the global core and the global Periphery during 1800–1950. Two factors that favored the Center were responsible for this economic polarization: better institutional fundamentals, and more favorable (and less volatile) terms-of-trade between industrial products and primary products. Williamson (2011) shows that the relative importance of the two changed over time with terms-of-trade accounting for two-thirds of the gap until 1950 and economic fundamentals since then. Economic diversification

Growth, transformation, industrialization **19**

and independence allowed some in the European Periphery to catch up while most suffered income divergence. Some countries in the non-European Periphery have managed to catchup after 1950. This reversal of fortune, as we will see later, is dubbed the **Great Convergence** (Williamson, 2011 Fogel, 1999; Spence, 2011; Radelet, 2015). Economic growth is, therefore, full of surprises as leaders become followers and a handful of followers sprint to become leaders.

We do not yet have a unified theory of growth that provides a common framework for understanding Classical, Neoclassical, and endogenous growth models by integrating the supply and the demand sides of the process (Galor, 2011). Nor do we have a unified theory of development that fully explains the workings of the linkages between the mechanics of growth (such as physical capital, human capital, and technology) and the fundamental determinants of potential growth (such as luck, geography, institutions, and culture) (Solow, 2005; Acemoglu, 2009).

The Commission on Growth and Development (COGD) has, for example, identified five drivers of growth based on the experiences of a selected number of developing countries that achieved remarkably shared growth and economic diversification (COGD, 2008; Spence, 2011). They are: (1) openness to the world economy and access to bigger markets, bigger sources of finance, and rapid transfer technology from leaders; (2) macroeconomic stability in the form of low inflation and manageable budget and trade deficits; (3) future orientation as expressed by high savings and high investment; (4) market-directed reallocation of scarce resources from less productive uses to more productive uses; and (5) good leadership and governance as expressed by capable administration and credible commitments to growth and inclusion.[2]

Growth models, exogenous as well as endogenous, offer various cause-effect relationships. Exogenous growth models incorporate the impact of technological change, but technological progress itself is not explained within the model. Endogenous growth models, on the other hand, show how growth begets growth by explaining within the model the scale or spillover effects of incentivized investment in research and development, education, and public infrastructure (Jones and Vollrath, 2013).

The building blocks of a typical exogenous growth model of factor accumulation comprise the best available technology (production function), the mode of financing of capital formation (investment and saving), the process of labor and skill accumulation (wages and labor force growth), and the trajectory of exogenously given technological progress. By melding the four ideas together, one determines the steady state where growth in income per capita ceases. This is because factor accumulation is constrained by diminishing returns and the natural ceiling on the proportion of income that can be saved or the limits on foreign savings that can be tapped. Although growth is all about creative destruction, conventional growth theory makes things tractable by focusing on short-term growth.

Technological progress is handled better by a new generation of models known as endogenous growth models. These models invoke externalities arising from purposeful investment in the accumulation of new knowledge, investment in human capital, or investment in public infrastructure as sources of ongoing productivity growth which complement growth from factor accumulation, also known as **extensive growth**. However, their mechanistic and steady-state cast is hardly

20 Industrialization and growth

adequate to capture the disruptive nature of Schumpeterian entrepreneurial (and intrapreneurial) innovations that drive growth in dynamic economies (Galor, 2011).

Growth analytics provides a multidimensional framework for integrating these drivers of economic growth. We will take a brief look at three useful ideas in the empirics of growth: growth accounting, development accounting, and growth regressions. These ideas will be invoked at various points in the book.

We begin with two kinds of cross-country comparisons to make sense of the stylized facts of growth. One identifies the primary sources of growth over time, and it is known as *growth accounting*. The other compares income levels at a given point in time, and it is known as *development accounting*.

Growth Accounting: Growth accounting decomposes the contributions of the various sources of growth for a given country (or a sector of the economy) over time. The growth drivers are usually grouped into two: factor accumulation and gains in total factor productivity. Where data are not available to estimate total factor productivity from the production function, an indirect method is employed under the assumption that competitive markets prevail.

Consider, for example, a Cobb-Douglas production of the form

$$Y_t = A_t [K_t^a (hL)_t^b]^\gamma \tag{1.1}$$

where A is multifactor or total factor productivity (TFP) which indexes the efficiency with which factors of production are jointly utilized, K is physical capital including natural resources, L is low-skilled person-years or person-days in the labor force, h is a skill index such as the average number school years per labor unit, "hL" is the quality-adjusted labor input, γ is a measure of returns to scale, a is the elasticity of output (Y) with respect to physical capital (generally falling in the range, 0.35–0.4.00), and b is the elasticity of output with respect to the skill-adjusted labor input. A in level terms is then equal to $Y/[K_t^a(hL)_t^b]^\gamma$.

Since the Cobb-Douglas depicts a constant-returns-to-scale technology, the contributions of factor inputs which, under competitive conditions, receive the value of their marginal products, can be calculated as a product of the partial output elasticities and the scale elasticity (in this case, $\gamma = 1$). Taking the log of both sides and differentiating with respect to time (time subscripts are omitted to avoid clutter), we convert (1.1) into a growth format

$$Y^\wedge = A^\wedge + [aK^\wedge + bL^\wedge] \tag{1.2}$$

where ($\wedge$) denotes percentage change per unit of time for each variable. Since data on multi-vintage K is hard to find, one can use the perpetual inventory method to estimate it. An alternative method is to manipulate $K^\wedge$ (from the definition of $K^\wedge = dK/K = I/K$) to replace $aK^\wedge$ by $r(I/Y)$ where r is the user cost of capital. Data on investment rates (I/Y) are much more plentiful and reliable.

Equation 1.2 decomposes the growth rate of GDP ($Y^\wedge$) into two components: the growth of TFP ($A^\wedge$) and factor accumulation (the share-weighted average of $K^\wedge$ and $L^\wedge$). The growth of TFP is usually calculated as a (Solow) residual. It captures

Growth, transformation, industrialization **21**

the effects of a whole host of omitted variables such as natural resources, institutional quality, political stability, technological progress, and the like.

The illustrative results of such an exercise for the 12 African case-study countries, relative to comparators, are shown in Table 1.1. One discernible pattern from the table is that, contrary to theoretical expectations, growth during 1990–2014 was

TABLE 1.1 Decomposition of the sources of growth, 1990–2014

Country	Annual average GDP growth	Annual average TFP growth	Share of TFP in GDP growth: %
Germany	1.49	0.88	58.7
Ireland	4.33	0.91	21.0
Spain	2.13	−0.58	−27.3
Sweden	1.96	0.20	10.4
Turkey	4.01	−1.20	−29.9
Canada	2.26	−0.27	−12.0
United States	2.38	0.57	23.9
Australia	3.03	−0.12	−4.1
Hungary	0.84	−0.61	−72.7
Romania	0.91	1.32	144.4
Bangladesh	5.35	−0.50	−9.4
Cambodia	6.94	2.31	33.2
China	6.91	0.22	3.2
India	6.33	1.27	20.1
Indonesia	4.95	0.49	9.9
Japan	1.07	0.35	33.0
South Korea	5.11	1.98	38.7
Thailand	4.43	0.26	5.8
Brazil	2.50	−0.32	−12.6
Chile	5.02	−0.16	−3.1
Colombia	3.61	−0.58	−16.1
Venezuela	2.49	−0.22	−8.8
Côte d'Ivoire	1.93	0.08	4.0
Egypt	4.34	0.49	11.3
Ethiopia	5.29	1.30	24.5
Ghana	5.39	3.21	59.5
Kenya	3.36	−0.37	−11.1
Nigeria	5.20	1.01	19.3
Senegal	3.46	−3.13	−90.5
South Africa	2.45	−1.07	−43.7
Tanzania	5.46	2.07	37.9
Tunisia	4.15	1.27	30.6
Zimbabwe	2.28	0.40	17.4

Source: Calculated from The Conference Board, Total Economy Database, September 2015 edition. www.conference-board.org/data/economydatabase/.

22 Industrialization and growth

predominantly driven by factor accumulation. This was the case not just for low-income economies but also for middle-income and some high-income ones. TFP growth accounted for at least a third of growth for Germany, Romania, Cambodia, Japan. South Korea, Tanzania, and Ghana. A productivity collapse is evident in Turkey, South Africa, Senegal, and post-socialist Hungary. For most, growth was earned the old-fashioned way – more by brawn than by brain.

Development Accounting: What if one is interested in explaining differences in income "levels" rather than in income "growth"? Development accounting is a good first-pass exercise for appraising the sources of income differences across countries at a given point in time. By answering the question of how much of the cross-country income variance can be attributed to observed differences in the rate of "factor accumulation" and how much to differences in the growth of "productivity," it does for the cross-section analysis what growth accounting does for the time series analysis.

For the decomposition, rewrite equation (1.1) in per capita terms

$$y = Ak^{\alpha}h^{1-\alpha} = AF \qquad (1.3)$$

where k is the capital/labor ratio (k = K/L), h is human capital per person, A = TFP and F = factor inputs per capita (= $k^{\alpha}h^{1-\alpha}$). Using data on y, k, h, α, we can estimate how much of the variation in y can be explained by the variations in A, k, and h.

To appreciate the usefulness of development accounting, consider per capita income ratios of two distinct sub-regions. Region 1 is a richer North Africa and region 2 is a poorer Sub-Saharan Africa. The relative per capita incomes can be expressed as a product of the TFP ratio and the Factors ratio

$$y_1/y_2 = (A_1/A_2)\,(F_1/F_2) \qquad (1.4)$$

Caselli et al. (1996), for example, derive two alternative measures for a baseline test of how much of the variations in factor inputs (F) can explain the current distribution of per capita income if all countries had the same level of efficiency (A). The first measure, the variance decomposition, is calculated from (1.4)

$$\mathrm{var}[\log(y)] = \mathrm{var}[\log(A)] + \mathrm{var}[\log(F)] + 2\mathrm{cov}[\log(A), \log(F)] \qquad (1.5)$$

where $\mathrm{var}[\log(A)] = \mathrm{cov}[\log(A), \log(F)] = 0$ if all countries have the same level of TFP. Caselli et al. (1996:8) find that the fraction of the variance of income explained by observed factor utilization, $\mathrm{var}[\log(F)]/\mathrm{var}[\log(y)]$, is equal to 0.50/1.30 or 39%.

The second measure, less prone to the undue influence of outliers, is the inter-percentile differential. This measure compares what the 90th-to-10th percentile ratio would be in the counterfactual world of all countries using a common technology and enjoying comparable efficiency levels. They estimated the share of factor accumulation at 34%.

The baseline measures (without corrections for the heterogeneity of capital and skill stocks as well as differences between private capital and public capital) attribute a little above one-third of the inter-country variation in per capita income to variations in factor intensity. The remaining two-thirds reflect inter-country differences in efficiency or productivity.

These results are broadly consistent with the stage-based view that differences in productivity are higher than differences in factor intensity between low-income economies and high-income economies (Weil, 2014). All said, of the two major sources of growth – addition of new capital and improved productivity – the first remains the primary driver. The capital stock/GDP ratio, for example, rose from 2 to 4 for Japan, from 1.2 to 2.7 for South Korea, and from 1.7 to 2.7 for China during 1970–2012 (Kroeber, 2016: Figure 12.1).

The African pattern is, however, not so clear-cut. While North Africa has a higher level of productivity (along with South Africa), the differences in per capita income within Africa are equally likely to be attributable to differences in factor accumulation as well as in efficiency levels.

Growth Regressions: Growth regressions, cross-section or time series, bring theory to data in a more nuanced way. They provide us with measures of the direction and magnitude of the relationships between economic growth (or income level) and the various (mostly supply-side) determinants of growth. The typical cross-country growth regression takes the form

$$g_{it} = \alpha \log y_{i0} + Z_{it}\beta + \gamma_i + \eta_t + \varepsilon_{it} \tag{1.6}$$

where g_{it} is the growth rate of per capita income for country i for the period between time t and $t\text{-}1$ (or averaged over, say, five-year sub-periods), y_0 is the initial per capita income, Z is a vector of exogenous control variables that are presumed to also drive growth, γ is the set of country fixed effects that capture other determinants (such as different technological parameters) of a country's growth path, η is a set of time dummies capturing global shocks, and ε is the stochastic term capturing all omitted variables. Equation 1.6 is sometimes reformulated in "level" form with "$\log y_t$" replacing g_{it}.

The goal of the regression exercise is to obtain statistically significant estimates of α, the convergence parameter ($\alpha < 0$ implies conditional convergence in per capita income at the rate or speed reflected by the value of the coefficient) and β, the causal effects of the various salient explanatory variables (such as investment rates, degree of openness, various policies, institutional quality, and human capital). Regression models are useful only for capturing the effects of proximate causes of growth such as investment, productivity, and institutional quality.[3]

Since this exercise involves the interplay among growth theory, available data, and econometrics, obtaining robust results has been bedeviled by several problems. Durlauf et al. (2005) and Easterly (2005) provide very useful critical surveys of the vast empirical growth literature. One challenge they identify is the endemic problem of _endogeneity_ (reverse causality), that is, growth and the presumed independent

24 Industrialization and growth

explanatory variables are themselves jointly determined, putting into doubt the causal inferences from the growth regressions. Growth, for example, is enhanced by investment and vice versa.

Another is model *uncertainty*, that is, there is no a priori theoretical basis for identifying the appropriate set of explanatory variables without resorting to an ad hoc reliance on a growth model. A third problem is *exchangeability*, that is, the heterogeneity of countries cannot be reduced to differences in the values of the right-hand-side variables since different countries do not represent random draws from a common growth model.[4]

For our purposes here, at least two findings are notable from the empirical literature (distilled in Acemoglu, 2009). First, there is no tendency for the poorer nations to grow faster than the richer nations (no unconditional convergence) at least for the 1960–2000 period. Second, income gaps between countries with broadly similar characteristics appear to diminish over time (conditional convergence). But the literature has not yet pinned down the ultimate underlying drivers of these outcomes over a horizon of 25 plus years. This prompted Solow (2005: 6) to quip that "detailed analysis of institutions is probably a better method than cross-country regressions" to do justice to the growth histories of non-OECD countries in terms of speed, resilience, and similarity.[5]

Broadly speaking, economic growth may assume two forms. Economic growth may take the form of short-term *capacity utilization* by boosting static efficiency by fully mobilizing underutilized productive resources. If business cycles were, by some magic, eliminated, the typical market economy would likely benefit from a one-off gain of about 5% by closing the gap between actual GDP and potential GDP (Baumol, 2002).

While capacity utilization, the preoccupation of economic policy in the rich countries, is important, it is not nearly as important as policies aimed at *capacity stretching* or expanding potential GDP. The power of compounding is such that raising the trend growth rate of Africa's GDP from 0.0% to 5% annually, in the face of a 2% population growth rate, would result in a doubling of national income every 14 years and per capita income every generation.

This increase in overall (total) productivity and per capita income, often called **intensive growth**, is often attributed to investments that enhance the quality of inputs or promote entrepreneurial innovations – organizational or technological. As Spence (2011: 65) succinctly puts it, "Incomes and wealth are determined by absolute (not relative) productivity levels. Trade, on the other hand, is determined by relative productivity levels across sectors. The goal of a poor country is, through investment and knowledge absorption, to increase absolute productivity, and hence, incomes."

Under the right environment, the cumulative effects of prolonged accumulation-driven growth may generate a threshold of development capability (a cadre of entrepreneurs, a growth-friendly ruling class, and a leading industry or two) to produce a sustained takeoff into the regime of productivity-driven growth (Rostow, 1956; Kuznets, 1966). Productivity growth is, in turn, sustained by the accumulation of knowledge-based assets or technology.

William Baumol (2002: 13), in fact, considers productivity-driven growth as the hallmark of capitalist achievement:

> [T]he main achievement of the capitalist economy is, in fact, its spectacular and unrivaled growth performance, and not its rather questionable static efficiency. . . . Only the productive surpluses that innovation began to make possible, first in agriculture and mining and then in manufacturing, made feasible the enormous increases in investment in inanimate and in human capital that are widely judged to have contributed significantly to economic growth.

Developing economies are dominated by two kinds of entrepreneurs (Baumol, 2002; Baumol and Litan, 2007). Among the productive group, replicative entrepreneurs (those who add more output using known technology or discover new markets for existing products) dominate over innovative entrepreneurs (those who commercialize new products, new processes, or both). The unproductive group comprises rent seekers who deploy their political influences to legally benefit from the enactment redistributive policies pursued by the government. Depending on the incentive environment, the non-innovation rent may be squandered or productively invested. The other members of this group are those who employ illegal means to engage in the redistribution of wealth from producers to rent seekers which is generally a growth killer.

Aggregate convergence and divergence

Economic growth is inherently unbalanced leading first to concentration (sector-wise, spatially, and income-wise) and later to dispersion. Changes in the composition of economic activity are shaped not just by the differential growth of products or sectors. They are also affected by the level of development already achieved, the nature and intensity of domestic and international competition, the synchronization of firm capabilities and market opportunities, the availability of long-term finance, and the availability of a supportive business environment that includes adequate public services.

The various competing perspectives on growth and development revolve around claims for convergence camp or non-convergence (Ray, 1998, 2008). We now take a brief look at the instructive insights from each.

The *convergence* perspective embraces the idea that if the less-developed economies share economically significant parameters and institutions amongst themselves and with the developed economies, then market-driven resource allocation will ensure that per capita incomes will converge across economies. Countries farther away from the common steady-state per capita income will grow faster than those closer to it. The reasoning is that countries with a low capital/labor ratio will have a high rate of return to capital. What is needed then is to achieve conditional convergence is getting market-supporting institutions and policies to conform to those of the developed countries.

26 Industrialization and growth

The convergence perspective comes in two flavors. Sigma-convergence refers to the reduction in the dispersion of per capita income *levels* across countries, which implies differential catchup growth rates. Beta-convergence, on the other hand, refers to catchup growth rates being higher for laggards that share the same steady-state per capita income with their successful peers.

Convergence of per capita income across countries (or regions within countries) is therefore inevitable unless frustrated by institutional or policy failure. The success stories from a growing number of emerging economies and the recent decline in poverty levels, even in the poorest countries, are viewed as evidence of an economic transformation underway in the tropics (Spence, 2011; Deaton, 2013; Radelet, 2015).

The evidence rarely supports these bold predictions for various reasons. Since total factor productivity makes ever-larger contributions to output as per capita income rises, divergence in technological capabilities matters greatly. This is so even when transnationals are willing to share technologies with subcontractors of international production networks under regimented conditions. The crafting of institutions that would provide adequate incentives to innovate is also frustrated by persistent political failure (North and Weingast, 1989; Mokyr, 1990; Lin, 2012).

The distribution of the rates of convergence for selected countries during 1946–2006 is shown in Table 1.2 (Szirmai et al., 2013). The data make it clear

TABLE 1.2 Patterns and speeds of catchup growth since 1946

Country	Period	Growth of GDP	Growth of GDP per capita	Rate of catchup[b]
China	1978–2006	8.1	6.9	3.6
West Germany	1950–1973	6.0	5.0	2.7
India	1994–2006	6.7	5.1	2.4
Indonesia	1967–1997	6.8	4.8	2.4
Ireland	1995–2006	6.2	6.2	2.8
Japan	1946–1973	9.3	8.0	3.6
Korea	1952–1997	8.2	6.3	3.0
Malaysia	1968–1997	7.5	5.1	2.6
Russia	1998–2005	7.2	7.2	3.9
Singapore	1960–1973	10.0	7.6	2.5
Taiwan	1962–1973	11.4	8.7	2.8
Thailand	1973–1996	7.6	5.8	3.2
Vietnam	1992–2005	7.6	6.1	2.9

Sources and notes: Adapted and abridged from Szirmai et al. (2013), Table 1.1.

a The periods have been chosen to maximize sustained high growth rates over an extended period.

b Ratio of growth of GDP per capita compared to growth in the lead economy in the corresponding period. The U.S.A. is the reference economy.

that the rate of income convergence for successful latecomers was higher than in the pre-World War I period – especially for China, Japan, and Russia. The rapid paces of globalization, state capability, and technological diffusion are the leading explanatory variables.

Figure 1.2 also provides a snapshot of the sources of the inter-country differential growth rates of per capita income during 1970–2010. If we take the highest point attained during the six decades as the "revealed" steady-state per capita income, the countries that did well at realizing their potentials are South Korea, Egypt, and Malaysia. The greatest underperformers were Cote d'Ivoire, Tanzania, and Ghana.

Barro (2012) revisits the empirical evidence for the reduction in the inter-country dispersion in GDP per workers (Sigma convergence) as well as for higher speed of growth for countries with lower initial per capita income (Beta convergence). He takes the estimates of a Beta convergence rate of 2%, and a Sigma convergence rate of zero as an "iron-law."[6]

The *non-convergence* perspective argues that there is no compelling reason for convergence in living standards across the world. Countries with varying initial incomes can grow in lockstep thereby allowing absolute living standards to rise across the board while the gaps between leaders and followers remain constant. Divergence in income is also possible, and real, as leaders grow faster than laggards conditional on continual technological progress. In other words, fundamentals shared by two African countries at the onset of modern economic growth may produce convergence with leaders for one and divergence for the other because of luck, historical accidents, or policy lock-ins. Given the endogeneity of institutions and technological progress, economies may diverge by transcending different growth paths.

More specifically, the non-convergence or multiple-equilibria view is based on two notable claims (Ray, 2008). First, stagnation can be a product of a self-fulfilling failure of expectations or a failure of coordination of critical investments. Coordination failures abound on the supply and the demand sides of the market because "externality" is ubiquitous, and the economy is a web of complementarities.

Second, underdevelopment may also be a product of unfavorable initial conditions or historical legacies such as parasitic post-colonial states. Since economic development entails several path-dependent or self-reinforcing mechanisms, what appear to be rather "small events" may cumulate and interact perversely with initial conditions (geography, institutions, and history) to lock-in inferior and long-lasting political settlements as in the case of the Democratic Republic of the Congo (Bates, 2008, 2009).

The possibility of multiple equilibria[7] is at the same time hopeful and distressing since one can just as easily be derailed or soon regain footing. Positive shocks facilitate escape from such traps and may require a balanced big-push (Rosenstein-Rodan, 1943), an unbalanced reliance on leading sectors (Hirschman, 1958), or the cumulative effects of small but steady improvements.

Africa's record on growth

Post-colonial Africa has experimented with a gamut of development strategies encompassing state-led development and market-led development. These efforts were underwritten by commodity booms and aid-funded public spending which moderated the massive net outflow of Africa's own savings.

The growth patterns reflect this extraverted process. Figure 1.3 provides the growth record for real per capita income for Africa, relative to East Asia, for the past 50 years. Africa on average saw its real per capita income grow 1.5% per annum relative to 6.5% for East Asia and the Pacific during 1966–2014. The data also show that the two regions diverged in the growth of average living standards in 1975–1995 – a period when East Asia took off – and again during 2005–2014 with East Asia showing greater resiliency to the global financial crisis because of a diversified economy. Despite the doubling of GDP growth to 4.6% in the 2000s relative to the previous decade, a robust domestic economic growth engine remains elusive for all but a handful of African countries.

Africa's growth momentum is not just a story of natural resources. Only one-third of the economic growth since 2000 is attributable to booming commodity prices. Much of the remaining two-thirds came from market-friendly reforms. The provision of more and better public services made up for the remainder. About three-quarters of Africa's growth came from an expanding workforce, which comprises some 40% of Africa's population.

Domestic factors have also mattered for growth on the demand side. Africa is urbanizing fast[8] (projected at 50% by 2030 – comparable to today's China and India) and thereby stands to benefit from industrial and knowledge clusters.

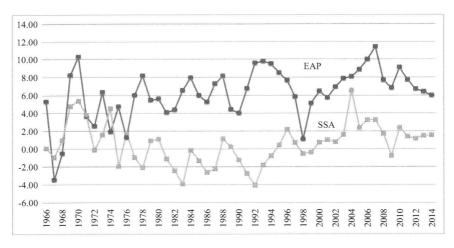

FIGURE 1.3 Growth of GDP per capita in Sub-Saharan Africa, 1966–2014

Sources and notes: World Development Indicators 2015. www.wdi.worldbank.org.
SSA = Sub-Saharan Africa
EAP = East Asia and Pacific

Africa's lackluster economic performance is commonly attributed to persistently weak and exclusionary political institutions that are presumed to emanate from such factors as high ethnic fractionalization (Easterly and Levine, 1997) or the legacies of colonial state formation (Acemoglu and Robinson, 2010). This line of reasoning raises the important question of why different world regions developed economic and political institutions with radically different long-term economic consequences.

Whatever the reasons, African economies were stuck in a world of anemic growth and a treadmill of reforms during 1975–1995. Sub-Saharan Africa (SSA) was, in fact, routinely identified as an "outlier" in cross-country regressions. The implied poverty traps have been labeled – but rarely explained – as those emanating from civil strife, malaria, resource curse, bad geography, tribal parochialism, or misgovernance (CFA, 2005; Collier and Gunning, 1999).

One interesting attempt to provide a context-specific and a period-specific account of growth performance divides SSA into three opportunity or endowment groups (Ndulu, 2007; Ndulu et al., 2008). They are: coastal but resource-scarce (35% of the population versus 88% elsewhere in the world), landlocked and resource-poor (35% of the population versus 1% elsewhere), and resource-rich (30% of the population versus 11% elsewhere).

Combining these endowment groups and the political economy they presumably give rise to, the researchers identified five growth syndromes. They are: *Syndrome Free* (converging) which include small fast growers (Botswana, Gambia, Lesotho, Malawi, and Swaziland); *Regulator* (non-converging) dominated by neopatrimonial regimes seeking and distributing rent to maintain power through state patronage; *Redistributor I* (diverging) which are dominated by state elites engaged in ethno-regional resource transfers; *Redistributor II* (diverging) which engage primarily in inter-temporal transfers from future generations to the present; and *Wrecker* (trapped) which are failed states – accounting for one-fifth of Africans and losing 2% of the annual potential growth.

Official statistics show that Africa's average GDP growth doubled after 1995 to over 5% compared with the previous two decades. This may very well be a significant underestimation. Alwyn Young (2012) argues, based on real consumption-based rather than real income-based measures (such as the ownership of durable goods, the quality of housing, the health and mortality of children, the education of youths, and the allocation of female time in the household), that SSA may have grown at the rate of 3.4–3.7% per year during 1990–2010.

We still lack satisfactory explanations for the growth spurts and crashes that resulted from the interactions between internal and external growth drivers. Jerven (2015), for example, provides a trenchant critique of the extant literature on African growth especially in the realm of methodology. Cross-country regressions, by being ahistorical and averages, lead to a false trap thesis by masking breaks and growth episodes, which tend to be externally driven. Bad institutions and bad policies are hard to pin down and often endogenous.

This significant uptick in African growth has not been sustained enough and inclusive enough to absorb the **demographic dividend** from the youth bulge and

30 Industrialization and growth

to accelerate the formalization of economic activity. According to a recent World Bank report (Beagle et al., 2015), the share of Africans who are poor fell from 56% (280 million) in 1990 to 43% (330 million) in 2012. This was, however, accompanied by an increase in the absolute number of the poor. Poverty reduction has been slowest in fragile countries; rural areas remain much poorer; and the urban-rural gap in poverty rates has narrowed.

Pinkoviskiy and Sala-i-Martin (2014), on the other hand, show rather convincingly that the post-1990 robust growth in much of Africa has lifted all boats. Using survey and national accounts data, they argue that poverty rates, and, to a lesser extent, income inequality fell markedly irrespective of country size, distance from the ocean, historical legacies, or resource endowments.

What are the implications for growth policy? The Commission for Africa (CFA, 2005) and Collier (2000), for example, make the case for higher-quality development aid (especially if multilateral and investment-oriented) and increased trade (market access with threshold of export capacity), better governance (accountable budgets and appropriate regulations), the rule of law, and collective peace-building to break the destabilizing effects of perennial extractive contests.

The policy recommendations for Africa from The Growth Report (COGD, 2008) are wide-ranging, too. They include increasing the productivity and output of agriculture, reducing the cost of doing business through the simplification of administrative procedures, continuing the marked progress toward universal primary education from the current 40%, ensuring the implementation of Millennium Development Goals (MDGs) and post-MDG development agenda, encouraging regional integration which is key to the success of small as well as landlocked countries, giving enterprising citizens secure channels for saving and credit, adopting best practices in the management of revenues from sustainable exploitation of natural resources, and ensuring macroeconomic stability through responsible fiscal policy. It also calls for industrialized economies to grant African countries policy space and time-bound trade preferences for manufactured exports to help them overcome the disadvantages of being late starters, and help in the financing of the expansion of Africa's tertiary education to make up for Africa's brain drain.

Developing countries differ in myriad ways, including in initial technological capabilities, production structures, and institutional environments. A developing economy is, in fact, a classic mongrel economy with many contradictory co-existing economic systems. It combines the Keynesian demand-constrained capitalist economy with the Kaleckian supply-constrained socialist economy (Kornai, 1982). The relative importance of the two constraints informs, in part, the debate on the direction of causality between structural change and economic growth.

The importance of the growth-structure nexus in development thinking has been invoked variously in the preceding discussion. We now turn to the structural side of the coin for a brief review. A slight reformulation of the dramatic opening sentence in Tolstoy's Anna Karenina (Tolstoy, 2014) captures the spirit rather well: "All rich countries (families) are all alike; each poor country (family) is poor in its own way."

Structural transformation

Definitions of structure are influenced more by the focus of analysis than by the desire to provide universal meaning. Kuznets (1966), for example, defines economic development as a process that melds growth and structural transformation. Acemoglu (2009), on the other hand, takes a different tack in the light of the different theoretical traditions which address growth (how balanced growth is attained in a mature market economy) and structural change (various empirical models focused on specific facets of developing economies.[9] Acemoglu interestingly defines development as structural change in low-income economies on their way to structural transformation and uses growth to refer to the way high-income economies with all the requisite institutions in place get bigger. In this circumscribed and rather counter-intuitive sense, Acemoglu seems to flip the two implying that a poor country structurally transforms before growing steadily.

We use "structural transformation" of the economy to refer to non-marginal changes in organizational, production, and technological capabilities. Technological change typically takes place at the firm level or disaggregated industry level thereby producing differential patterns of sectors productivity growth. At the same time, changes in demand and international trade may cascade into structural change whereby production factors such as capital, labor, and intermediate inputs steadily shift across locations and economic activities. Productivity-driven growth, in turn, induces deeper structural change to facilitate further growth.

Several studies of empirical development economics (Chenery, 1960; Chenery and Taylor, 1968; Chenery and Syrquin, 1975; Chenery et al. 1986; Ballance et al., 1982) suggest strongly that the interplay of demand and supply at the microeconomic level produces certain "standard" patterns of structural change as per capita income rises. As an economy escapes all sorts of traps (political, population, or technological) and reaches middle-income status, it will have undergone all or most of the following structural shifts (Abegaz, 2002; Hausmann et al., 2007; Imbs and Wacziarg, 2003; Rodrik, 2013):

1 The share of agricultural employment in economy-wide employment declines from some 70% to 20% or less.
2 The share of agriculture in GDP declines from some 60% to 15% or less.
3 The share of household income spent on food declines (aka Engel's Law) with increases in income.
4 The growth rate of total factor productivity rises in most, if not in all, sectors of the economy.
5 The domestic saving rate rises from about 5% to more than 15% of GDP.
6 The growth rate of population declines from about 3% to less than 2% (aka the Demographic Transition).
7 Inequality of income, which rises along with real per capita income, peaks around $10,000 per head and declines subsequently.
8 Early industrial development takes place in the context of a transition from subsistence agriculture and low-productivity services to the light industry

32 Industrialization and growth

while subsequent industrial deepening entails a structural shift toward skill- and technology-intensive manufacturing. Furthermore, diversified production and export baskets foster higher per capita income levels and growth.

9   There are substantial variations in labor productivity among sectors and firms within the same sector of industrializing economies. However, over time, labor productivity within manufacturing tends to converge unconditionally.
10 Real wage remains low and stable despite rapid growth in industrial output and formal employment, at least until after the labor reservoir is exhausted and productivity-driven growth becomes the norm.

All things considered, economists agree that a characteristic feature of the development process is that prolonged economic growth produces significant structural changes on the supply side (firm mix, employment mix, and spatial distribution) as well as on the demand side (the composition of domestic trade, technological choice, and international trade). Structural change is therefore not just about the direction of compositional shifts within and among sectors. It is also about speed that is largely driven by the rate of technological learning (Alcorta et al., 2013).[10]

Political economy considerations

We lack a coherent theory of the political economy of development although politics matters greatly for successful industrialization drive. We need an interdisciplinary approach to make sense of how economic classes and political elites jointly shape development institutions and policies.

In political terms, development entails changes in the structure of power – away from big owners of natural resources and monopolizers of the instruments of violence and toward economic entrepreneurs, the intelligentsia, and labor. As various regions and classes become progressively integrated into national and international webs of economic intercourse, parochial and primordial identities give way to class-based and citizen-based forms of solidarity (Fukuyama, 2011, 2014).

One can glean from the literature how the exercise of central authority co-evolved with economic development. Here are some of the most discernible patterns in the evolution of political institutions (Fukuyama, 2011, 2014; Huntington, 2006; Bates, 2009; Levy, 2014; Kohli, 2004; Adelman and Morris, 1988):

1   The three elements of **political order** (the state, the rule of law, and accountability to the ruled) vary widely regarding timing and sequencing. All three come together only in modern democratic societies.
2   The patrimonial state emerged, as the critical political institution, in communal polities where self-limiting kinship and reciprocal altruism long reigned.
3   Political power generates economic resources, especially where sensible policies and public investments are significant, which, in turn, buttresses political power.
4   The emergence of the modern state coincided with the industrial revolution, which ushered in continuous *intensive* economic growth to support ever-rising

average living standards and a competent bureaucracy. Where a minimum of economic performance cannot be achieved (because of induced population growth, dissipation of revenues on unproductive patronage, or poor incentive for producers), wars of predation frustrate the emergence of effective states.

5　The interplay between shared economic growth and formal and enforceable rule of law undergirds the emergence of powerful constituencies (an industrialist class and a working class) for popular forms of political governance.

6　Different political institutions, by shaping economic institutions and policies in ways that disproportionately benefit power-holders, generate different steady-state levels of and distributions of income. The distribution of political power is, in turn, shaped by the allocation of control rights over resources.

Where capitalism has not yet developed firm roots, extractive political institutions predominate and tend to be inimical to shared growth for its potential political threat. New beneficiaries of growth may indeed accumulate sufficient economic power to successfully resist the emergence of an organized citizenry that would impose restraints on power-holders (Weingast, 2007). The political transition to broad-based accountability was a protracted process in some countries (the United Kingdom, Scandinavia, Germany, and Japan) and radical in others (France, the United States, Russia, and China).

As incomes and average years of schooling rise, women and previously excluded groups join the modern labor force. When an industrial class emerges, landed, interests are likely to resist the new balance of economic and political power, which is why industrialization is almost always accompanied by civil strife, a see-saw between authoritarianism and populism, or even a revolution. Economic growth, when sustained and broad-based, eventually unleashes a virtuous spiral where entrepreneurial citizens overcome coordination failure to engage in concerted public action to tame violence and to stem predation. Given an auspicious conjuncture, a vicious politico-economic equilibrium may then turn into an irreversible virtuous spiral (Olson, 1993; Bates, 2009; Acemoglu and Robinson, 2012).

Drivers of structural transformation

As Michael Spence (2011: 67) puts it, "Sustained growth and structural change go hand in hand. The structural change driven by shifting prices and market forces is the crucial input to productivity and income growth." Today, development economists study more than economic growth and structural changes in production, trade, and consumption. They also address issues of poverty, inequality, vulnerability, the interplay between political power and economic power, sustainability of livelihoods and the environment, and the quality of life, all of which are intertwined (Deaton, 2013).

Factors identified as drivers of the economic structure include competitive innovation (Schumpeter), inter-sectoral reallocation of factors (Lewis), production and consumption linkages (Hirschman), and patterns of engagement in international

34 Industrialization and growth

production and trade (Chenery and Syrquin, 1987; Baldwin, 2016). Industrialization, as the defining feature of structural transformation, brings changes in the type of goods produced (diversification), where they are produced (vertical integration and spatial agglomeration), and where they are sold (exports across national regions, components, tasks, and products).

The supply-side drivers of structural change underscore the importance of input-output linkages, the quality and quantity of factor inputs, and the pace of innovation. However, there remains a great need to incorporate the demand side (regarding both level and composition) to which we will return.

Structural convergence and divergence

Diversification may indeed serve as the third, and self-reinforcing, source of growth. Differential growth alters the output, employment, and trade mix while structure, in turn, shapes growth prospects. The simple reason is that a highly diversified economy is likely to have various growth centers to better absorb shocks and to ensure a predictably stable pattern of economic development.

Long-term growth *induces* structural change through myriad channels, including deepening industrialization, accelerated urbanization, greater openness to international production and trade, changes in the composition of the consumption basket of the average household, changes in inequality of income and wealth, and changes in demographics. Structural change, in turn, *affects* growth through many channels, including the beneficial impact of diversification on innovation, vulnerability, investment, increased inclusiveness and horizontal equality among demographic groups, enhancement of global competitiveness, and the emergence of a middle class boosting the home market and citizen engagement in the policy-making process.

The narrower interplay between economic structure and economic growth was pioneered by Clark (1940), Lewis (1954), and especially Kuznets (1966, 1973). Kuznets' work on modern economic growth, based on a new framework of national income accounting, generated three major insights which have stood the test of time. He showed that (1) there is a remarkable uniformity across otherwise diverse societies in the experience of modern economic growth; (2) this is largely a product of the rising similarity in globally available modern technologies and tastes, and (3) structural transformation and sustained economic growth are not only interdependent but they also induce major changes in pre-existing political institutions.

As suggested by the stylized facts listed above, the seemingly anachronistic Clark-Kuznets thesis still provides a first-pass analytical framework. Economies generally start out being predominantly agricultural (A), become significantly industrial (I), and then service-based (S) economies.

What is interesting here is that the A-I-S mode of structural transformation does not just apply to the mixes of value added and employment as conceived by the icons of development economics. It also applies to changes in the composition of consumption and exports of mainly whole products.

We also see in the statistics that many low-income economies do not follow the A-I-S sequence. They instead develop a large urban-based, low-productivity informal service sector (S') prematurely before entering the industrial phase in earnest. This modified path, when they manage to industrialize successfully, takes the form: A-S'-I-S.

A modern attempt to bridge the two pathways of structural transformation is the Lewis (1954) model of "economic development with unlimited supplies of labor." W. Arthur Lewis starts out by maintaining the assumption, based on the norm in the early stage of industrialization, that real wages remain rigid just above the subsistence level even in the face of rising demand for industrial labor. Once modern industry gets a firm footing, industrial capital can enjoy high profits at a low and stable unit labor cost until the reservoir of cheap labor is exhausted.

If demand for industrial goods is buoyant and industrialists have all the incentives to remain fully invested, output and employment will grow steadily through this process of labor reallocation. When wages begin to rise, the economy is then able to switch to a productivity-driven growth where high skills, high wages, and ongoing technological improvements become the norm.

The role of export diversification, product mix as well as market destination, in boosting growth has received considerable attention in the literature pioneered by Prebisch (1962) and Singer (1950). Export instability often entails substantial costs to merit a strategy of promoting export levels and diversification. Recent research has also underscored the importance of self-discovery of new products (Hausmann and Rodrik, 2003).

Hausmann and Klinger (2007), for example, consider a robust stylized fact that changes in the revealed comparative advantage of economies are linked to the pattern of product relatedness. Product spaces that are dense and more amenable to export diversification are high in countries with manufacturing capability and sparse in those that are not.

Within manufacturing itself, at the two- or three-digit ISIC levels, there is a discernible shift from labor-intensive and resource-intensive branches to capital-intensive ones and, finally, to technology-intensive activities (Abegaz, 2002, 2008). This shift reflects the acceleration of skill formation and technological upgrading on the supply side and the income-driven changes in the structure of demand.

More generally, inter-industry linkages appear to generate a U-shaped pattern with specialization in low-tech products at low income and high-tech products at high income with the middle-income countries boasting the most diverse industrial base (Imbs and Wacziarg, 2003). Developing economies diversify into a world of rich interlinkages as they grow into the middle-income status and then specialize at higher income levels.

The upshot is that, despite cross-country diversity, successful latecomers experience discernible "structural homogeneity," if not full convergence, with industrial leaders not just in per capita income but also in the composition of production and trade in manufactures (Abegaz, 2002, 2008; Ballance et al., 1982; Kirkpatrick et al., 1984; Bradford and Branson, 1987; Syrquin, 1988; Pack, 1988; Adelman and Morris,

36 Industrialization and growth

1988). In the most recent inflection of globalization, as we will explain in Chapter 6, international production networks of manufacturing have changed the mode of access to technology to accentuate specialization.

Africa's record on structural change

Reflecting its peculiar endowments and circumstances, structural change in Africa has not followed the classic agriculture-industry-service model of economic diversification. Tables 1.3–1.5 provide snapshots of Africa's economic structure regarding production, productivity, and demand. In the 35 years from 1975 to 2010, the share of agricultural value added fell to 22%. During the same period, agriculture's employment share fell by a third to 41%. Furthermore, MVA fell by a third to 10% while its employment share stood at 9% of the labor force.

Overall, the capital-intensive sector has the highest labor productivity (and manufacturing the lowest), but it employed just 1% of the workforce in 2010. Interestingly, the MVA share had increased from 9.2% to 14.7% during 1960–1990 before falling to 10.1% in 2010. The Lewis process of intersectoral reallocation of surplus labor seems to have ended prematurely for industry with the service sector taking up the slack. Premature deindustrialization after 1990 was accompanied by an uptick in GDP growth that is not driven by an industrial engine (Page, 2013; Rodrik, 2015).

Despite its great potential (half of the world's arable land not yet in full use is in Africa), agricultural development in much of Africa has failed to ensure food security and to underwrite the development of agro-processing industries (de Janvry and Sadoulet, 2010). Too many countries appear to have fallen into a vicious circle where predominantly agrarian communities engage in age-old but increasingly myopic responses to population pressure that tend to undermine their long-term livelihoods. The premature explosion of urbanization, reflecting rural-push migration and survival-oriented activities in the informal sector, is fueled by public-sector spending. Until very recently (when mega farms by multinationals began sprouting), only the rich mining endowments of the continent have attracted FDI allied with local elites intent on leveraging political power to convert public assets into private riches.

An even more striking feature of African development is the rather poor legacy of proto- industrious activity. Manufacturing still accounts for just 11% of Africa's GDP today which prompted Justin Lin (2013: 17) to observe that "the failure to develop and upgrade their industrial structure and to diversify is a particularly disturbing stylized fact of African economies."

Many of the empirical puzzles, such as those related to the low impact of episodes of rapid economic growth in gainful employment and poverty reduction, reflect the fact that African growth has not been driven or accompanied by structural transformation. This is so because the basic requirements for transformation (decent institutions, good skill supplies, adequate infrastructure, a sensible business climate, and an appropriate industrial policy) are not yet in place.

TABLE 1.3 The structure of production of African economies

Country	GDP$ billions		Agriculture % of GDP		Industry % of GDP		Manufacturing % of GDP		Services % of GDP	
	2000	2014	2000	2014	2000	2014	2000	2014	2000	2014
Cote d'Ivoire	11	34	25	22	22	21	17	13	54	57
Egypt	100	287	17	14	33	40	9	16	50	46
Ethiopia	8	56	48	42	12	15	6	4	40	43
Ghana	5	39	39	22	28	28	10	5	32	50
Kenya	13	61	32	30	17	19	12	11	51	50
Mauritius	5	13	7	3	31	23	23	16	62	74
Nigeria	46	569	26	20	52	24	4	10	22	56
Senegal	5	16	19	16	23	24	15	13	58	61
South Africa	136	350	3	2	32	29	19	13	65	68
Tanzania	10	48	33	31	19	25	9	6	47	44
Tunisia	22	49	11	9	30	29	18	17	58	62
Zimbabwe	7	14	18	14	24	29	16	12	57	57
World	**33,292**	**77,845**	**4**	**3**	**29**	**26**	**19**	**16**	**67**	**71**
Low income	**111**	**399**	**35**	**32**	**20**	**22**	**11**	**9**	**45**	**47**
Middle income	5,168	24,662	13	10	36	35	25	22	51	56
High income	28,012	52,813	2	2	28	25	18	15	70	74
E. Asia and Pacific	1,734	12,610	15	10	44	42	37	32	41	48
Latin America	1,671	4,775	6	5	31	30	18	14	64	65
M. East and N. Africa	449	1,541	12	11	39	37	15	14	49	52
South Asia	629	2,589	23	18	26	29	15	17	51	53
Sub-Saharan Africa	**361**	**1,729**	**17**	**15**	**34**	**27**	**13**	**11**	**49**	**58**

Source: Based on World Bank, World Development Indicators 2015, Table 4.2.

TABLE 1.4 The structure of demand of African economies

Country	Household consumption % of GDP		General government consumption % of GDP		Gross capital formation % of GDP		Exports of goods and services % of GDP		Imports of goods and services % of GDP		Gross savings % of GDP	
	2000	2014	2000	2014	2000	2014	2000	2014	2000	2014	2000	2014
Cote d'Ivoire	68	66	14	13	10	17	41	43	34	39	5	16
Egypt	76	83	11	12	20	14	16	15	23	24	18	12
Ethiopia	..	70	..	9	0	38	..	12	..	29	..	31
Ghana	84	64	10	18	24	27	49	40	67	49	15	16
Kenya	78	82	15	14	17	21	22	16	32	34	14	10
Mauritius	60	74	14	15	26	23	61	52	62	63	26	10
Nigeria	53	71	8	7	7	16	52	18	20	13	29	33
Senegal	76	77	13	16	20	26	28	27	37	46	14	..
South Africa	62	61	18	20	16	20	27	31	24	33	16	15
Tanzania	78	66	12	14	17	31	13	19	20	30	13	18
Tunisia	61	70	17	19	26	22	40	45	43	55	22	12
Zimbabwe	60	88	24	24	14	13	38	27	36	52	..	..
World	**60**	**60**	**16**	**18**	**24**	**22**	**25**	**30**	**25**	**30**	**24**	**23**
Low income	**80**	**76**	**12**	**13**	**17**	**28**	**20**	**24**	**31**	**43**	**..**	**16**
Middle income	59	56	14	14	25	31	26	27	25	28	26	31
High income	60	61	17	18	24	20	25	30	25	30	24	21
E. Asia and Pacific	50	42	14	13	32	42	31	29	28	26	35	45
M. East and N. Africa	57	59	14	15	26	30	30	29	27	36	28	..
South Asia	66	63	12	11	23	30	14	22	15	25	25	31
Sub-Saharan Africa	**63**	**67**	**16**	**16**	**16**	**22**	**34**	**28**	**29**	**32**	**19**	**16**

Source: Based on World Bank, World Development Indicators 2015, Table 4.8.

Growth, transformation, industrialization **39**

TABLE 1.5 African GDP, employment, and relative sectoral productivity, 1975–2010

Variables:	VAD			EMPL			PROD		
Sectors:	1975	1990	2010	1975	1990	2010	1975	1990	2010
Agriculture	**29.2**	**24.9**	**22.4**	**66.0**	**61.6**	**40.8**	**0.4**	**0.4**	**0.4**
Industry	**30.0**	**32.6**	**27.8**	**13.1**	**14.3**	**13.4**	**3.7**	**3.5**	**2.6**
Mining	*6.2*	*11.2*	*8.9*	*1.5*	*1.5*	*0.9*	*22.4*	*23.3*	*19.5*
Manufacturing	*14.7*	*14.0*	*10.1*	*7.8*	*8.9*	*8.3*	*2.8*	*2.4*	*1.6*
Other industry	*9.2*	*7.3*	*8.9*	*3.8*	*3.9*	*4.2*	*5.8*	*5.3*	*2.9*
Services	**40.7**	**42.6**	**49.8**	**20.9**	**24.1**	**36.8**	**2.5**	**2.4**	**1.6**
Market services	*25.5*	*28.1*	*34.0*	*10.3*	*12.9*	*23.5*	*3.4*	*3.0*	*1.8*
Non-mkt services	*15.2*	*14.4*	*15.8*	*10.6*	*11.2*	*13.3*	*1.7*	*1.8*	*1.3*
Total economy: %	**100**	**100**	**100**	**100**	**100**	**100**	**1.0**	**1.0**	**1.0**

Source and notes: Abridged from de Vries, Timmer, and de Vries (2013), Table 2.
Calculations based on the Africa 10-Sector Database; unweighted averages for 11 countries.
VAD = value added
EMPL = employment
PROD = average labor productivity of a sector relative to economy-wide labor productivity

Linkages: growth, structural transformation, and industrialization

As noted earlier, an economic system consists of a web of economic institutions and organizations that define and enforce property rights. Resources (reproducible and natural) and the efficiency with which they are utilized (technology, broadly construed) are the proximate determinants of economic development while the institutions that define the incentive structure (the market, the state, and the family) are considered fundamental determinants of economic performance. An important driver of development, therefore, is to whom the allocation decisions over scarce resources are entrusted. The competitors for this right of control typically are state elites and the small cadre of private entrepreneurs.

One useful way of framing the development process would then be to meld its economic and political dimensions to identify stages and the possible paths of transition between them. For a sobering thought exercise, consider an industrializing economy as one whose per capita income circa 2010 (in **purchasing power parity** dollars) lies between $1,000 (Ethiopia or Guinea) and $20,000 (Turkey or Russia). Above this threshold, we have Central Europe, Taiwan, and S. Korea in the $30,000 range and much of Scandinavia and Western Europe in the $40,000 range. In between, we can use reasonable cut-off points at $5,000 (India or Pakistan), $10,000 (China or South Africa), and $15,000 (Thailand or Brazil).

On the face of it, Africa is comparatively disadvantaged in industrial development because of its rich resource base, weak but improving infrastructure, colonial patterns of integration into the world economy, the emergence of formidable

40 Industrialization and growth

competitors in Asia and Latin America for products in which Africa might be able to develop new domains of comparative advantage, and the paucity of nationalist elites. High transaction costs, low technological capability, and misguided policies have all conspired to render Africa not just a low-wage but also a low-productivity region (Collier, 2000; Page, 2013; Newman et al., 2016; Oqubay, 2015). In SSA, only Botswana, Lesotho, Mauritius, South Africa, and Zimbabwe have a significant domestic capacity for export penetration in light manufactures (Tribe, 2000). In North Africa, Egypt, Tunisia, and Morocco have managed to go beyond the initial phase of industrialization.

As shown in Table 1.6, economies evince distinctive structural profiles at each income level. Around $10,000, the share of industrial value added in GDP and gross capital formation in GDP both peak at 45%. The share of manufacturing exports in total merchandise exports and the rate of urbanization both rise significantly before

TABLE 1.6 Growth and structural change at four income levels

Per capita income, 2010–12	$1,000 ppp [Ethiopia]	$5,000 ppp [India]	$10,000 ppp [China]	$18,000 ppp [Turkey]
Average annual growth rate, 1980–2010:	%	%	%	%
GDP	5.4	6.3	9.8	4.2
GDP per capita	2.3	4.4	8.8	2.5
FDI/GDP, net inflows	1.9	0.8	3.1	0.9
Economic structure, circa 2010:				
Industry/GDP, output	10.2	38.9	46.2	26.7
Industry/GDP, employ	6.6	24.7	28.7	26.0
Trade turnover	46.1	55.0	49.3	57.8
XM/X	8.6	62.2	93.6	77.7
GCF/GDP	31.6	38.9	47.3	20.1
Gini index	33.2	33.9	42.1	40.2
% Urban	17.3	31.3	49.2	71.8
Welfare indicators, circa 2010:				
Literacy rate, adult	39.0	69.3	95.1	94.9
Life expectancy at birth, years	61.5	66.0	74.9	74.9
Poverty gap @$3.10	26.5	18.5	na	0.6

Sources and notes: World Development Indicators 2015.
http://databank.worldbank.org/data/reports.aspx?source=world-development-indicators.
PPP = purchasing power parity dollars
X = merchandize exports
XM = exports of manufactures
GDP = gross domestic product
Trade turnover = (imports + exports)/GDP
Poverty gap = mean shortfall of income from poverty line at $3.10/day, as % this poverty line.

leveling off, as do life expectancy at birth and adult literacy rates. On the other hand, income inequality continues to rise in the $1,000–$10,000 range while poverty rates fall to insignificance.

These snapshots provide a suggestive framework for conceptualizing inter-stage economic transitions whose drivers (and binding structural constraints) are likely to vary widely. There are four distinct transitions: between $1,000 and $5,000 (Ethiopia to Vietnam), between $5,000 and $10,000 (Nigeria to Indonesia), between $10,000 and $15,000 (Egypt to Mexico), and between $15,000 and $20,000 (Iran to Russia). The first two transitions are most likely to be frustrated by Malthusian dynamics and exclusionary institutions.[11] The last two transitions, on the other hand, are likely to confront both political (anti-growth rent seeking) and technological (the so-called middle-income trap) constraints.

Recent empirical research shows that, at US$10,000, there is a reduction in the share of labor-intensive manufacturing. Furthermore, the per capita income level of US$23,000 is the threshold for a well-established technology-led and skill-intensive manufacturing (Alcorta et al., 2013).

From a very long-term perspective, Clark (2008) argues in this vein that the first turning point in the West (the transition between the agricultural revolution and Malthusian stagnation) was largely a result of mortality-induced changes among the emergent middle class in the pace and structure of population growth. A second turning point, the first industrial revolution of 1750–1850 (which took place in England, Holland, and Switzerland), was a result of the discovery of new sources of energy (coal and the steam engine) as well as institutional innovations which provided incentives for entrepreneurship in search of economic profits.

The role of institutions and policies in facilitating or impeding industrial development matters even more where the state has supplanted the market. The famous "Soviet industrialization debates" of the late 1920s, for example, provided the backdrop for the post-WWII debates on the question of how to electrify the countryside and how best to finance an urban-based industrialization drive (Dobb, 2014).[12] In the U.S.S.R. (1928–1933) and Maoist China (1959–1962), the idea of forcibly extracting peasant surplus to feed the cities and the factories won out, with the agricultural collectivization drive imposing great famines and social dislocation. Ethiopia and Tanzania flirted with such "socialist primitive accumulation" with similarly disastrous results. We are now ready to explore the various dimensions of early and late industrialization.

Notes

1 It will be useful to note here that there are two approaches to an economic inquiry: intriguing hypotheses in search of confirmation or real-world puzzles in search of theoretical explanations. The first approach, favored by theorists, is to construct an appropriately specified economic model and then subject its implications to good data using econometrics and case studies. This, in effect, asks: does what works in theory also work in practice? The more common approach is to take economic puzzles suggested by the data, and then construct mathematical models to make sense of them. This, in effect, asks:

42 Industrialization and growth

does what works in practice also work in theory? In both cases theory and evidence are the two faces of the same coin – theory informs the design and interpretation of empirical work while the evidence provides a test for the explanations generated by the model.

2 This still does not tell us how to produce good leaders or forge good institutions, but it pins down the correlates of high growth performance. We should note here, however, that while blueprints are useful in identifying fruitful areas of policy focus, the dynamic nature of the development process and the heterogeneity of time and space preclude enduring laws of development. The policy environment, along with factor endowments, shapes factor accumulation and allocation as well as the prospects for innovation. The quality of growth and the feedback effects of institutional change close the loop of transmission across the givens, the proximate causes, and the outcomes. Economic growth itself tends to disrupt the balance of power in society thereby generating subsequent modifications in the institutional and policy environment for further growth.

3 The objective here is to generate robust stylized facts of growth to motivate more compelling explanations of the persistent and significantly heterogeneous growth performances of countries at a given period or significant variations in a country's growth rates over time.

4 Aside from poor quality and limited availability for low-income countries, additional econometric concerns include collinearity among the explanatory variables, omitted variables, parameter heterogeneity, outliers (a favorable label for Africa), and measurement errors. All these suggest that growth regressions provide useful insights about the mechanics of growth but they cannot yet support strong claims about its long-term determinants.

5 As noted by Bourguignon (2004), there is an interesting triangular interdependence among poverty, growth, and inequality – the so-called PGI Triangle. The basic idea is that aggregate growth and changes in income distribution are interdependent. Growth affects poverty levels and reduction rates through the filter of initial inequality (of human capital, wealth, and networks) and the relative rewards for various activities. Growth is, therefore, necessary but not sufficient for significant reduction in absolute poverty in the presence of significant inequality. The elasticity of growth and distribution of poverty are dependent on initial income level and the growth rate of mean income, and the distribution of incomes – initial as well as subsequent changes. Wealth inequality, however, seems to matter even more for demand-driven growth (Milanovic, 2016).

6 Acemoglu and Robinson (2015: 3) are rightly skeptical about general laws of capitalism since such formulations ignore the way an economy normally functions, that is, "the endogenous evolution of technology and of the institutions and the political equilibrium that influence not only technology but also how markets function and how the gains from various economic arrangements are distributed."

7 Acemoglu (2009: 116) makes a useful distinction between models of "multiple equilibria" (in which superior equilibria can be reached only if individuals or firms can adjust their mutual expectations) and models of "multiple steady states" (in which path-dependence precludes a switch to a superior steady-state income level or growth path). The latter (which reflects the role of institutions, policies, and the Givens) is more promising for explaining persistent income gaps than invoking luck or being blessed with visionary founding leaders.

8 Rapidly urbanizing Africa has also seen the emergence of a middling class but not as much as would have been the case if the growth was manufacturing-driven with its high intensity in good-wage intensity. The African Development Bank (2011) estimates that the number of African households with an annual disposable income of $3,650–$7,300 – above which they start spending roughly half of it on nonfood items – was about 11% of the population in 2010. Those with incomes more than $7,300 (or $20 per day) added another 19% in 2010. The annual inflow of FDI from diverse sources (mainly from the emerging economies) increased from $16 billion in 2002 to $42 billion in 2012 – relative to GDP, almost as large as the flow into China.

9 The so-called developing countries are too heterogeneous in terms of average living standards, economic inequality, geography, and culture to warrant such labels. Many such

countries have experienced a remarkable economic performance during 1950–2010 to move to middle-income status (say, $5,000–$15,000 per head). We somewhat arbitrarily apply the label developing to refer to countries with per capita income of less than $15,000 in international dollars.

10 Another striking historical fact is the high correlation between rising per capita income and radical breaks in the technology of production, transportation, and communication. The growth of the world's population between 2000 BCE and 2000 CE has the shape of a reverse-L with a radical break around 1800 after which a bewildering series of positive technology shocks propelled the world economy forward (Fogel, 1999). Following two distinct waves of the industrial revolution in the West, China and India lost their prominence in the world economy for two centuries (Maddison, 2001; Spence, 2011).

11 The historical evidence shows that something remarkable happened as early as 1500 that jolted the world from a longstanding per capita income level of $400 (in 1990 prices). The break from a Malthusian growth trap was a product of the convergence of several factors, including better hygiene, new ways of harnessing wind and water, new energy sources such as hydrocarbons, and advances in agricultural technology (such as irrigation, improved seeds, and multiple cropping).

12 Lenin, in fact, sensibly for the time equated industrialization with electrification (Dobb, 2014).

References

Abegaz, B. (2002). Structural Convergence in Manufacturing Industries Between Leaders and Latecomers. *Journal of Development Studies*, 38(4), pp. 69–99.

Abegaz, B. (2008). Determinants of Structural Convergence in the Manufacturing Industries of Newly Industrializing Economies. *South African Journal of Economics*, 76(2), pp. 89–109.

Acemoglu, D. (2009). *Introduction to Modern Economic Growth*. Princeton: Princeton University Press.

Acemoglu, D., and J. Robinson. (2010). Why Is Africa Poor? *Economic History of Developing Regions*, 25(1), pp. 21–50.

Acemoglu, D., and J. Robinson. (2012). *Why Nations Fail*. New York: Crown Business.

Acemoglu, D. and J. A. Robinson. (2015). The Rise and Decline of General Laws of Capitalism. *Journal of Economic Perspectives*, 29(1), pp. 3–28.

Adelman, I., and C. Morris. (1988). *Comparative Patterns of Economic Development, 1850–1914*. Baltimore: The John-Hopkins University Press.

African Development Bank (AfDB). (2011). *The Middle of the Pyramid: Dynamics of the Middle Class in Africa*. [online] Abidjan: AfDB. Available at: www.afdb.org/fileadmin/uploads/afdb/Documents/Publications/The%20Middle%20of%20the%20Pyramid_The%20Middle%20of%20the%20Pyramid.pdf.

Alcorta, L., et al. (2013). Industrial Structural Change, Growth Patterns, and Industry. In: J. Stiglitz, J.Y. Lin, and E. Patel, eds., *The Industrial Policy Revolution II: Africa in the 21st Century*, 1st ed. New York: Palgrave Macmillan, pp. 457–491.

Aryeetey, E., et al. (2012). Overview. In: E. Aryeetey, et al., eds., *The Oxford Companion to the Economics of Africa*. Oxford: Oxford University Press, pp. 1–21.

Baldwin, R. (2016). *The Great Convergence: Information Technology and the New Globalization*. Cambridge: Belknap Press of Harvard University Press.

Ballance, R., et al. (1982). *The International Economy and Industrial Development: Trade and Investment in the Third World*. Brighton: Wheatsheaf.

Barro, R. (2012). Convergence and Modernization Revisited. *NBER Working Paper No. 18295*. Cambridge: MA, NBER.

44 Industrialization and growth

Bates, R.H. (2008). *When Things Fell Apart: State Failure in Late-Century Africa.* Cambridge, UK: Cambridge University Press.

Bates, R.H. (2009). *Prosperity and Violence: The Political Economy of Development.* New York: W. W. Norton.

Baumol, W. (2002). *The Free Market Innovative Machine: Analyzing the Growth Miracle of Capitalism.* Princeton: Princeton University Press.

Baumol, W., and R. Litan. (2007). *Good Capitalism, Bad Capitalism.* New Haven: Yale University Press.

Beagle, K.G., et al. (2015). *Poverty in a Rising Africa: Overview.* Washington, DC: World Bank Group.

Bourguignon, F. (2004). *The Poverty-Growth-Inequality Triangle.* [online] Washington, DC: World Bank. Available at: http://siteresources.worldbank.org/INTPGI/Resources/342674-1206111890151/15185_ICRIER_paper-final.pdf.

Bourguignon, F. (2015). *The Globalization of Inequality.* Princeton: Princeton University Press.

Bradford, C.I., and W.H. Branson, eds. (1987). *Trade and Structural Change in Pacific Asia.* Chicago: University of Chicago Press.

Caselli, F., et al. (1996). Reopening the Convergence Debate: A New Look at Cross-Country Growth Empirics. *Journal of Economic Growth*, 1, pp. 363–389.

Chenery, H. (1960). Patterns of Industrial Growth. *American Economic Review*, 50(4), pp. 624–654.

Chenery, H., and M. Syrquin. (1975). *Patterns of Development, 1950–1970.* London: Oxford University Press.

Chenery, H., and M. Syrquin. (1987). Typical Patterns of Transformation. In: H. Chenery, et al., eds., *Industrialization and Growth: A Comparative Study.* Oxford: Oxford University Press, pp. 37–83.

Chenery, H., and L. Taylor. (1968). Development Patterns: Among Countries and Over Time. *Review of Economics and Statistics*, 50(4), pp. 391–416.

Chenery, H., et al. (1986). *Industrialization and Growth: A Comparative Study.* Washington, DC: World Bank.

Clark, C. (1940). *Conditions of Economic Progress.* London: Macmillan.

Clark, G. (2008). *A Farewell to Alms: A Brief Economic History of the World.* Princeton: Princeton University Press.

Collier, P. (2000). Africa's Comparative Advantage. In: H. Jalilian, M. Tribe, and J. Weiss, eds., *Industrial Development and Policy in Africa: Issues of Deindustrialization and Development Strategy.* Cheltenham, UK: Edward Elgar, pp. 11–21.

Collier, P., and J.W. Gunning. (1999). Explaining African Economic Performance. *Journal of Economic Literature*, 37(1), pp. 64–111.

Commission for Africa (CFA). (2005). *Our Common Interest: Report of the Commission for Africa.* London: Commission for Africa.

Commission on Growth and Development (COGD). (2008). *The Growth Report: Strategies for Sustained Growth and Development.* Washington, DC: World Bank.

Deaton, A. (2013). *The Great Escape: Health, Wealth, and the Origins of Inequality.* Princeton: Princeton University Press.

de Janvry, A., and E. Sadoulet. (2010). Agriculture for Development in Africa: Business-As-Usual or New Departures? *Journal of African Economies*, 19(AERC Supplement 2), pp. ii7–ii39.

de Vries, G., et al. (2013). *Structural Transformation in Africa: Static Gains, Dynamic Losses.* GGDC Research Memorandum 136. Groningen, Netherlands: Groningen Growth and Development Centre, University of Groningen.

Dobb, M. (2014). *Russian Economic Development Since the Revolution*. New York: Routledge.

Durlauf, S., et al. (2005). Growth Econometrics. In: P. Aghion and S. Durlauf, eds., *Handbook of Economic Growth*, vol. 1. Amsterdam: Elsevier, pp. 555–677.

Easterly, W. (2005). National Policies and Economic Growth: A Reappraisal. In: P. Aghion and S. Durlauf, eds., *Handbook of Economic Growth*, vol. 1A. Amsterdam: Elsevier, pp. 1015–1059.

Easterly, W., and R. Levine. (1997). Africa's Growth Tragedy: Policies and Ethnic Divisions. *Quarterly Journal of Economics*, 112(4), pp. 1203–1250.

Fogel, R. (1999). Catching Up With the Economy. *American Economic Review*, 89(1), pp. 1–21.

Fukuyama, F. (2011). *The Origins of Political Order*. London: Profile Books.

Fukuyama, F. (2014). *Political Order and Political Decay*. London: Profile Books.

Galor, O. (2011). Inequality, Human Capital Foundation, and the Process of Development. *NBER Working Paper 17058*. [online] Cambridge: NBER. Available at: www.nber.org/papers/w17058.pdf.

Hausmann, R., and B. Klinger. (2007). The Structure of the Product Space and the Evolution of Comparative Advantage. *CID Working Paper No. 146*. Cambridge, MA: Kennedy School, Harvard.

Hausmann, R., J. Hwang, and D. Rodrik. (2007). What You Export Matters. *Journal of Economics Growth*, 12, pp. 1–25.

Hausmann, R., and D. Rodrik. (2003). Economic Development as Self-Discovery. *Journal of Development Economics*, 72(2), pp. 704–723.

Hirschman, A.O. (1958). *The Strategy of Economic Development*. New Haven, CT: Yale University Press.

Huntington, S. (2006). *Political Order in Changing Societies*. New Haven, CT: Yale University Press.

Imbs, J., and R. Wacziarg. (2003). Stages of Diversification. *American Economic Review*, 93(1), pp. 63–86.

Jerven, M. (2015). *Africa: Why Economists Get It Wrong*. London: Zed Press.

Jones, B.F. (2014). The Knowledge Trap: Human Capital and Development Reconsidered. *NBER*. [online] Cambridge: NBER. Available at: www.kellogg.northwestern.edu/faculty/jones-ben/htm/Knowledge%20Trap.pdf.

Jones, C., and D. Vollrath. (2013). A Simple Model of Growth and Development. *Introduction to Economic Growth*. New York: Norton, Chapter 6, pp. 140–156.

Kirkpatrick, C., F.I. Nixson, and N. Lee. (1984). *Industrial Structure and Policy in Less Developed Countries*. London: Allen & Unwin.

Kohli, A. (2004). *State-Directed Development: Political Power and Industrialization in the Global Periphery*. Cambridge: Cambridge University Press.

Kornai, J. (1982). *Growth, Shortage, and Efficiency*. Berkeley: University of California Press.

Kroeber, A. (2016). *China's Economy: What Everyone Needs to Know*. New York: Oxford University Press.

Kuznets, S. (1966). *Modern Economic Growth: Rate, Structure, and Spread*. New Haven, CT: Yale University Press.

Kuznets, S. (1973). Modern Economic Growth: Findings and Reflections, Nobel Memorial Lecture, December 11, 1971. *American Economic Review*, 63(3), pp. 247–258.

Levy, B. (2014). *Working With the Grain: Integrating Governance and Growth in Development Strategies*. New York: Oxford University Press.

Lewis, W.A. (1954). Economic Development With Unlimited Supplies of Labour. *The Manchester School*, 22(2), pp. 139–191.

Lin, J.Y. (2012). *New Structural Economics: A Framework for Rethinking Development Policy*. Washington, DC: World Bank.

46 Industrialization and growth

Lin, J.Y. (2013). From Flying Geese to Leading Dragons: New Opportunities and Strategies for Structural Transformation in Developing Countries. In: J. Stiglitz, J.Y. Lin, and E. Patel, eds., *The Industrial Policy Revolution II: Africa in the 21st Century*. New York: Palgrave Macmillan, pp. 50–72.

Maddison, A. (2001). *The World Economy: A Millennial Perspective*. Paris: OECD.

Milanovic, B. (2016). *Global Inequality: A New Approach for the Age of Globalization*. Cambridge, MA: Belknap Press.

Mokyr, J. (1990). *The Lever of Riches: Technological Creativity and Economic Progress*. New York: Oxford University Press.

Ndulu, B. (2007). *Challenges of African Growth*. Washington, DC: World Bank.

Ndulu, B., et al., eds. (2008). *The Political Economy of Economic Growth in Africa, 1960–2000*. Cambridge: Cambridge University Press.

Newman, C., J. Page, J. Rand, A. Shimeles, M. Soderbom, and F. Tarp. (2016). *Made in Africa: Learning to Compete in Industry*. Washington, DC: Brookings Institution Press.

North, D., and B. Weingast. (1989). Constitutions and Commitment: The Evolution of Institutions Governing Public Choice in Seventeenth-Century England. *Journal of Economic History*, 49(4), pp. 803–832.

Olson, M. (1993). Dictatorship, Democracy, and Development. *The American Political Science Review*, 87(3), pp. 567–576.

Oqubay, A. (2015). *Made in Africa: Industrial Policy in Ethiopia*. Oxford: Oxford University Press.

Pack, H. (1988). Industrialization and Trade. In: H. Chenery and T.N. Srinivasan, eds., *Handbook of Development Economics*, vol. 1. Amsterdam: North-Holland, pp. 334–380.

Page, J. (2013). Should Africa Industrialize? In: A. Szirmai, W. Naude, and L. Alcorta, eds., *Pathways to Industrialization in the Twenty-First Century*. New York: Oxford University Press, pp. 244–268.

Pinkoviskiy, M., and X. Sala-i-Martin. (2014). Africa Is on Time. *Journal of Economic Growth*, 19, pp. 311–338.

Prebisch, R. (1962). The Economic Development of Latin America and Its Principal Problems. *Economic Bulletin for Latin America*, 7(1), pp. 1–22.

Radelet, S. (2015). *The Great Surge: The Ascent of the Developing World*. New York: Simon and Schuster.

Ray, D. (1998). *Development Economics*. Princeton: Princeton University Press.

Ray, D. (2008). Development Economics. In: L. Blume and S. Durlauf, eds., *The New Palgrave Dictionary of Economics*, 2nd ed. [online] London: Palgrave McMillan. Available at: www.dictionaryofeconomics.com/article?id=pde2008_D000105.

Rodrik, D. (2013). Unconditional Convergence in Manufacturing. *Quarterly Journal of Economics*, 128(1), pp. 165–204.

Rodrik, D. (2015). Premature Deindustrialization. *NBER Working Paper 20935*. Cambridge, MA: NBER.

Rosenstein-Rodan, P. (1943). Problems of Industrialization of Eastern and South-Eastern Europe. *Economic Journal*, 53(210/211), pp. 202–211.

Rostow, W. (1956). *The Stages of Growth: A Non-Communist Manifesto*. New York: Cambridge University Press.

Sen, A. (2000). *Development as Freedom*. New York: Oxford University Press.

Singer, H.W. (1950). The Distribution of Trade Between Investing and Borrowing Countries. *American Economic Review*, 40, pp. 531–548.

Solow, R. (2005). Reflections on Growth Theory. In: P. Aghion and S. Durlauf, eds., *Handbook of Economic Growth*, vol. 1, part 1. Amsterdam: Elsevier, pp. 4–10.

Spence, M. (2011). *The Next Convergence: The Future of Economic Growth in a Multispeed World.* New York: Farrar, Straus, and Giroux.

Syrquin, M. (1988). Patterns of Structural Change. In: H. Chenery and T.N. Srinivasan, eds., *Handbook of Development Economics*, vol. 1, 1st ed. Amsterdam: Elsevier, pp. 203–277.

Szirmai, A., W. Naude, and L. Alcorta. (2013). Introduction and Overview: The Past, Present, and Future of Industrialization. In: A. Szirmai, W. Naude, and L. Alcorta, eds., *Pathways to Industrialization in the Twenty-First Century.* Oxford: Oxford University Press, pp. 3–52.

Tolstoy, L. (2014). *Anna Karenina.* New York: Oxford University Press.

Tribe, M. (2000). The Concept of 'Infant Industry' in a Sub-Saharan Context. In: H. Jallian, et al., eds., *Industrial Development and Policy in Africa: Issues of Deindustrialization and Development Strategy.* Cheltenham: Edward Elgar.

United Nations Industrial Development Organization (UNIDO). (2009). *Industrial Development Report 2009: Breaking in and Moving UP – New Industrial Challenges for the Bottom Billion and the Middle-Income Countries.* Oxford: Oxford University Press.

United Nations Industrial Development Organization (UNIDO). (2015). *Industrial Development Report 2016: The Role of Technology and Innovation in Inclusive and Sustainable Industrial Development.* Geneva: UNIDO.

Weil, D.N. (2012). *Economic Growth*, 3rd ed. New York: Routledge.

Weil, D.N. (2014). *The Fissured Workplace: Why Work Became So Bad for So Many and What Can Be Done to Improve It.* Cambridge: Harvard University Press.

Weingast, B. (2007). Capitalism and Economic Liberty: The Political Foundations of Economic Growth. In: E. Sheshinski, R. Storm, and W. Baumol, eds., *Entrepreneurship, Innovation, and the Growth Mechanism of the Free-Enterprise Economies.* Princeton: Princeton University Press, pp. 48–72.

Williamson, J. (2011). *Trade and Poverty: When the Third World Fell Behind.* Cambridge: MIT Press.

World Bank. (2008). *World Development Report 2009: Reshaping Economic Geography.* New York: Oxford University Press.

Young, C. (2012). *The Postcolonial State in Africa: Fifty Years of Independence, 1960–2010.* Madison: University of Wisconsin Press.

2

INDUSTRIALIZATION

Why and how?

This chapter defines what is meant by "industrial" and explores the various justifications for adopting industrialization as the core of a transformative development strategy. It also presents various measures of the depth and quality of industrial development.

What is meant by industrialization

An "industrial activity" may be usefully defined as an energy-intensive and knowledge-intensive mechanical or chemical transformation of primary materials, substances, or components into substantively new products. Although the above definition fits manufacturing activity nicely, the industrial sector is broader. It includes **non-manufacturing industries** such as the capital-intensive segments of mining, construction, and public utilities (gas, water, and electricity). Manufacturing fits well the notion of the "art and science of transforming materials to make new products and meet new needs" (Marsh, 2012: 247).

Industrialization is a set of historically variable and complex economic, social, and political processes, the core of which is the conscious application of sophisticated technologies and machinery to enhance labor productivity or product quality. Industrialization, especially in later stages, becomes "lumpier." Economic activities (output, employment, trade, consumption, capital, and knowledge accumulation) are increasingly concentrated in urban- and factory-centered industrial complexes.

These **economies of agglomeration** and scope are perhaps why industrialization is implicated in the huge income gap, the Great Divergence, that became evident especially after 1900 between the greater West (North) and the tropics (South). The former, until very recently, typically produced and exported manufactures while most of the latter continue to rely on exports of primary goods and

Industrialization: why and how? **49**

handicrafts (Williamson, 2011).[1] Africa's share in global manufacturing value added and exports are negligible.

Why industrialization matters

The experience with industrialization over the past two centuries suggests strongly that a country needs to industrialize unless it is richly endowed with natural resources such as agro-ecology or minerals, or it is a great location for tourism and entrepot. Some of the richest countries today, for sure, are rentier states, although few have managed to tame the curse of endemic **rent seeking** by developing resource-processing manufactures (much as the U.S.A., Canada, and Australia did previously). The fact remains, however, that hardly any major economy today has reached a high stage of economic, political, and social development in the absence of a significant technologically advanced industrial sector.[2]

While we do not have reliable data on the regional distribution of manufacturing value added (with appropriate corrections for differences in inflation rates and exchange rates), we do have good data for employment distribution. Table 2.1 presents the regional breakdowns, as a share of the regional economy or as a share of the global economy. They are based on the one-digit ISIC (international system of industrial classification) level for a group of countries which together account for well over three-quarters of global manufacturing production and employment.

Globally, industrial employment today accounts for more than 500 million jobs – about a fifth of the world's workforce (UNIDO, 2013). Manufacturing accounted for 14.3% of global employment with Asia reporting the highest dependence on manufacturing jobs at 15% of total employment in 2009 (up from 10% in 1971). Europe lost nearly half and the U.S.A. lost just over 40% in the global employment share of manufacturing during the same period. Overall, in 2009, Asia accounted for 78% of global manufacturing employment while Europe and North America jointly claimed about 10% – down from a third of the global total in 1971.

Counting heads is, of course, misleading since the jobs retained in Europe and the U.S.A. are high paying (some 65 million jobs in the latter case), and the global share of the developed countries should be much higher given the large productivity advantage they enjoy because of their technological superiority.

Manufacturing employment continues to rise steadily in developing countries. The least developed are entering the world market in labor-intensive parts production and assembly (such as food processing, beverages, textiles, and garments) while the middle-income countries are penetrating the metal, plastics, and machinery industries. With better planning and greener technologies, industrial development is also beginning to hold out the prospects for cleaner cities and a higher quality of life (UNIDO, 2015).

Industrial development also has a proven record of rapidly reducing poverty. Most recently, China (and more broadly East Asia) has emerged as the manufacturing workshop of the world with India beginning to follow suit. In China, more than 150 million farmers and crafts-persons left the rural sector to work in factories

TABLE 2.1 National and regional distribution of persons engaged by sector, 1971–2009

Region	AGRI	AGRI	IND	IND	MAN	MAN	BUSR	BUSR	GCSR	GCSR	Nat.	Nat.
	1971	2009	1971	2009	1971	2009	1971	2009	1971	2009	1971	2009
National distribution:	%	%	%	%	%	%	%	%	%	%	%	%
Asia	70.5	41.5	3.1	8.2	10.1	15.9	9.1	19.1	7.2	15.4	100	100
Europe	12.5	3.2	11.2	8.4	27.3	13.5	27.8	41.1	21.3	33.8	100	100
L. America	41.8	15.3	7.2	8.9	15.5	13.3	19.8	35.3	15.6	27.2	100	100
N. Africa	52.4	25.6	4.8	13.3	13.4	12.1	11.6	25.5	17.8	23.5	100	100
N. America	3.2	1.4	6.8	6.2	21.3	8.9	36.8	46.4	31.9	37.1	100	100
SS Africa	70.1	59.4	3.4	3.4	5.8	6.5	12.1	19.7	8.6	11.0	100	100
Total	57.4	35.7	4.4	7.8	12.8	14.3	14.1	23.6	11.3	18.6	100	100
Global distribution:	%	%	%	%	%	%	%	%	%	%	%	%
Asia	84.8	82.0	47.9	73.8	54.9	78.4	44.7	57.1	43.7	58.4	69.1	70.6
Europe	2.0	0.5	23.1	5.8	19.5	5.1	18.1	9.3	17.2	9.7	9.1	5.4
L. America	4.3	3.4	9.6	9.0	7.1	7.4	8.2	11.8	8.1	11.5	5.8	7.9
N. Africa	1.0	1.1	1.2	2.6	1.1	1.3	0.9	1.6	1.7	1.9	1.1	1.5
N. America	0.5	0.3	13.5	5.5	14.6	4.3	22.9	13.7	24.6	13.9	8.7	7.0
SS Africa	7.4	12.8	4.7	3.3	2.7	3.5	5.2	6.4	4.6	4.5	6.1	7.7
% global	100	100	100	100	100	100	100	100	100	100	100	100

Sources and notes: GGDC 10-Sector Database, www.rug.nl/research/ggdc/data/10-sector-database

1. Regions and countries represented:
   SS Africa: Botswana, Ethiopia, Ghana, Kenya, Malawi, Mauritius, Nigeria, Senegal, South Africa, Tanzania, and Zambia
   N. Africa: Egypt and Morocco
   Asia: China, India, Indonesia, Japan, Philippines, Singapore, Taiwan, and Thailand
   L. America: Argentina, Bolivia, Brazil, Costa Rica, and Mexico
   N. America: United States of America
   Europe: Denmark, Spain, France, United Kingdom, Italy, Netherlands, and Sweden.
2. Sector reclassification from 10-sector to 5-sector:
   AGRI [agriculture] = Sector 1 (AtB)
   IND [industry *other than* manufacturing] = Sectors 2 (C) + 4 (D) + 5 (F)
   MAN [manufacturing] = Sector 3 (D)
   BUSR [business services] = Sectors 6 (GtH) + 7 (I) + 8 (JtK)
   GCSR [government and community services] = Sectors 9 (LtN) + 10 (OtP).

Industrialization: why and how? **51**

(Cai and Wang, 2008). The consensus forecast is that between them, China and India will occupy a vast industrial space in the coming decades – thereby adding to their spectacular record of lifting one billion people out of crippling poverty in just one generation.

Industrialization is, therefore, the most remarkable form of structural transformation of a developing economy. Industrialization is the *sine qua non* of compositional shifts on the demand side for at least three reasons.

First, manufacturing is a highly income-elastic activity. It is not tightly constrained by the gifts of nature (land, climate, minerals) or even by the narrowness of the domestic market. It can continue to respond to changes in taste, often by introducing synthetic substitutes for organic inputs, and new products. For most manufacturing, there is a lack of an upper bound that can otherwise be imposed by resource scarcity or market saturation. The advantage of a manufacturing-driven development also lies in the ability to diversify export baskets in response to changes in technologies, prices, or consumer preferences. This matters greatly for the stability of foreign exchange earnings, entry into production chains, and the productive use of resource rents.

Second, manufacturing is highly receptive to productivity-enhancing new technologies on the supply side. It thereby stimulates its own demand by reducing unit costs and by generating by-products. This is because manufacturing is technology- and skill-intensive; it has great room for **economies of scale** and scope; it has great scope for linkage-rich and spillover-rich economies of agglomeration; and it is highly tradable with great potentials for the diffusion of knowledge (UNIDO, 2009, 2013).

Third, manufacturing activity, by widening the market, also affects income inequality, first by expanding access to low-wage jobs until surplus labor is fully absorbed (Islam and Yokota, 2008) and later by skill-driven wage gaps and investment-driven income inequality (Clark, 2007).

Third, industrialization has a spatial dimension. The over-arching concept of central-place theory states that the economic activity mixes in urban centers reveals where agglomeration externalities are strongest. This clustering reflects the distribution of demand and occupational mix. Specialization, market provision, and concentration of demand also mean that firm size increases to the critical minimum level to capture economies of scale. The number and size of cities grow with economic development as the high-income elasticity of demand for manufactures shifts demands toward more specialized goods and services that are provided mainly in urban centers (Henderson, 1997; Fafchamps and Shilpi, 2005).

These claims have long been codified as Kaldor's Laws (Kaldor, 1967) which interestingly provided the motivation for the Solow model of aggregate growth (Solow, 2005). Law 1 asserts that the faster the growth of MVA, the faster the growth of GDP. Law 2 states that there is a strong and positive correlation between the growth of MVA and the growth of manufacturing productivity (also known as Verdoorn's Law). Finally, Law 3 makes the claim of economy-wide dynamism: the faster manufacturing output grows, the faster the productivity gains by other connected sectors.

52 Industrialization and growth

The historical experiences on which Kaldor based his strong arguments and more recent source-of-growth analyses and growth regressions both underpin some regular patterns – most relevant for the pre-1990 era of globalization:

1 The North-South distribution of manufacturing production and employment, as well as global demand, have been progressively skewed against the developed countries and in favor of a minority of recently or newly industrialized countries.
2 Skill- and knowledge-intensive manufacturing, mining, agricultural, and business-service activities have become more closely intertwined in the advanced industrial economies even as these economies continue to suffer erosion in labor- and resource-intensive manufacturing.
3 Within manufacturing, late industrializers have become progressively more similar in terms of the mix of output or employment across labor-intensive, resource-intensive, skill-intensive, and technology-intensive branches.
4 The location of manufacturing activity has become geographically concentrated within developing countries much as it was for the developed economies. Latin America is deindustrializing, Africa and parts of South Asia are industrializing slowly, and East Asia (including China) is claiming substantial share gains in their global MVA.
5 Light manufacturing continues to diffuse to the least developed countries and increasingly as integral parts of global value chains.
6 Although the economic significance of manufacturing globally remains the same, some very-late developers (including some in Africa) are deindustrializing prematurely. Among the very-latecomers, the share of manufacturing value added in GDP and manufacturing employment in economy-wide employment are peaking at a much lower per capita income (U.S.$2,000–$3,000) relative to the experiences of late industrializing countries (U.S.$8,000–$10,000).[3]

Based on these trends, we can safely draw the following conclusions, which will be explored further in chapters 5 and 6. First, facts 1–3 suggest that a largely market-driven and efficient reallocation of manufacturing activity has prevailed among industrializing economies with international production broadly conforming with inter-country endowments. Within countries, rich countries have been specializing in advanced resource-intensive and high-tech activities, middle-income countries in skill-intensive and some resource-intensive activities, and low-income countries in resource-intensive and labor-intensive activities.

A small but growing body of empirical evidence reaffirms the longstanding belief that manufacturing is an important engine of shared growth. Szirmai and Verspagen (2011), in a well-designed study, show that the engine of growth hypothesis implied by Kaldor's Law 1 holds, especially in the early stages of industrialization. The cross-country and within-country regressions also provide support for the engine-of-growth argument at least for recent decades.[4] This claim is conditional on a latecomer satisfying the threshold of human capital accumulation.

Within manufacturing, catchup and learning effects implied by Law 2 are strong only where the requisite domestic capabilities are in place (Rodrik, 2013).

Furthermore, manufacturing boosts productivity in other sectors, as suggested by Law 3, but it is no longer unique in doing this. Modern services can be, and indeed are in some emerging economies, an engine of growth (Dasgupta and Singh, 2006; McKinsey, 2012).

Facts 4–6 underscore the point that the new international division of labor is unequally benefitting those developing countries with the high domestic capability (in terms of skills, infrastructure, and industrial policy) by attracting FDI-intensive manufacturing and thereby accelerating technological diffusion. The remainder gets little more than wage-saving assembly plants for low-tech or bulky manufactures.

Third, all six facts together suggest that manufacturing (which accounts for some 80% R & D investment and 70% exports in the leading nations) remains, despite the growing skepticism, a potent engine of growth (Felipe et al., 2014). It generates output and employment directly and indirectly for many mature and recently industrialized economies while doing less for those at the post-industrial end of the development spectrum.

As noted in Chapter 1, the empirical evidence on structural change suggests that countries with more diversified production, employment, and export structures are those with high per capita incomes (Imbs and Wacziarg, 2003; Abegaz, 2002). Furthermore, the inverted-U relationship between production diversification and per capita income also holds for export diversification. This means production, productivity, and international competitiveness are intertwined capabilities (Klinger and Lederman, 2004; Sutton, 2012; Hausmann et al., 2007; UNIDO, 2009; Cadot et al., 2011). Countries which promote exports of diverse and more sophisticated goods grow faster.

Industrial diversification certainly tends to enhance export diversification, which, in turn, leads to further diversification or specialization (Melitz, 2002). This is a joint product of two interrelated forces: *self-selection* which means that latecomer firms build up industrial competence in new activities and then export, and *self-discovery* which means that a broadened industrial base enhances dominance by high productivity firms through the market filter of entry and exit.

There are, therefore, strong theoretical and compelling empirical arguments in favor of the manufacturing-as-an-engine-of-growth thesis (Szirmai et al., 2013; Baldwin and Venables, 2015). Because industrial activities involve the processing of primary resources, they involve **external economies**, inter-industry as well as intra-industry. Intra-industry **linkages** are inter-branch relationships of input supply and output use in both production and consumption. Production linkages are often complementarities. The advantages of increasing returns to scale are internal to the firm. Marshallian decreases in input costs and technological spillovers are external to the firm but internal to the industry.

The dual inter-sectoral density and long international reach of industrialization provide a broad scope for organizational innovations, too. The corporate model, pioneered by the railroads (Chandler, 1990), allowed for specialization under

54 Industrialization and growth

centralized coordination, which, among other things, permits the acquisition of productivity-enhancing specialized skills. The key to product sophistication, useful knowledge, is itself a product of massive investment with long gestation lags. Large and multi-product firms, which also create dynamic imperfect competition, are compelled to deploy economic rent to boost productivity through additional investment in research and development. With falling communication and transportation costs, vertical integration has recently been giving way to vertical disintegration – within countries as well as across borders.

It should be noted here that manufacturing involves a breaking-in problem since there are "thresholds of competitiveness" to be surmounted. Due to economies of scale, agglomeration, and network externalities, unit costs of production and distribution decline dramatically to generate "explosive growth" on the supply side once industrial thresholds are crossed. For the least developed, the threshold problem is one of entering low-tech manufacturing. For the middle-income economies, it is one of entering high-tech manufacturing. Timing, of course, is necessary. Breaking in at the bottom has become difficult in the presence of China and India but can be done, as we will see in the chapters that follow.

As we will see in the next chapter, import substitution must be accompanied by "export-adequate" growth. Export substitution (readily altering the mix of exports) leads to an export-led growth depending on opportunities. Lastly, import substitution in industry is followed by the exportation of the product with a lag of 5–20 years (Shapiro and Taylor, 1990; Linder, 1967).

There is also evidence for rapid, unconditional convergence of productivity at the level of individual product groups (Hwang, 2006; Rodrik, 2013). Diversification of production acts as a convergence machine: it enables countries to get onto the lower rungs of taller ladders. But getting these new industries off the ground in the first place is hardly automatic. It requires building up productive capabilities (more on this in Chapter 5).

Although path-dependence leads to cumulative advantages for first-movers, **structural convergence** in manufacturing between leaders and followers is a result of imitative product and process innovation. Firms with the greatest opportunities to benefit from technological externalities (arising from increasing returns, learning by doing, spillovers, and networks), informational externalities, thick or dense markets, and urban clusters help to close the technology gap the fastest.[5]

With this said, countries tend to gravitate toward a steady growth rate for each industry which is determined by the expansion rates of the world technological frontier and product demand. Latecomers start the catching up process by closing the technology gap in sectors where the gap is small, the skill requirements are low, and they can build on previous capability. The process of technological learning often entails short-term inefficiency as the price for long-term allocational and technical efficiency. Acute competition from followers for market share and enhanced domestic skills allow early-comer countries to move to industries that are closer to the frontier and have higher price and income elasticities of demand (Abegaz, 2008).

Manufacturing, while still an engine of economic growth and employment generation, may nonetheless become a weaker engine than in the past. It is not the only engine especially with increasing traceability of services. It is instructive that India's IT services industry, which generates 4 million jobs engaged in routine and back-office tasks, is being undermined by the new waves of disruptive technologies that now favor re-shoring (machine learning, the Cloud, big-data analytics, etc.). The implication for telescoping the process for very-late industrializers, such as Sub-Saharan Africa and South Asia, is that the ever-changing areas of opportunities to industrialize can be realized only by mustering the requisite productive capabilities to flexibly shift from an exclusive focus on low-labor-cost advantages to value-adding activities.

Industrialization also carries many potential liabilities that should not be ignored. They include social dislocation, labor dis-protection, and environmental degradation and stress. Enclave-type production of luxuries or export processing zones that generate few linkages with the hinterland (and are attracted by excessive giveaways to foreign investors) create few jobs and little diffusion of new technology.

Finally, industrialization is a deeply political process that ultimately empowers owners of industrial and commercial capital over owners of land, and progressively improves the political clout of the working class, the upper segment of which is the middle class. Economic fundamentals are necessary but not sufficient for an exclusionary industrial transformation.

Metrics for industrial breadth and depth

Monitoring progress often requires sensible measurement. How do we measure the quantitative dimension (relative sectoral significance) and qualitative dimension (technological sophistication) of industrial development? An index of the depth of industrial development captures only a snapshot of the economy at a given point in time. A time series of indexes provides a sharper glimpse of the industrialization process as shown in the form of Venn diagrams of Figure 2.1.

Recently available data on employment, production, and trade structures do provide a rough-and-ready way of dichotomizing the "industrialized" from the "non-industrialized." Following Sutcliffe (1971, 1984), let us define three basic structural features of industrial development: IVA/GDP above 25% (as a broad measure of industrial depth), MVA/IVA above 50% (to capture the prominence of manufacturing within industry), and L_I/L of above 10% (to capture the significance of industry in employment).

Illustrative data from rapidly industrializing countries are presented in Table 2.2. All eight countries (Bangladesh, Brazil, China, India, S. Africa, S. Korea, Thailand, and Tunisia) met the three thresholds by 2010. However, Bangladesh, India, and Tunisia did not fare so well after 1980.

This means that such indicators, partial though they may be, also provide important clues about the pace of industrial deepening and even **deindustrialization** (see Figure 2.1 for a graphic illustration).[6] In the three decades since 1980, for

56 Industrialization and growth

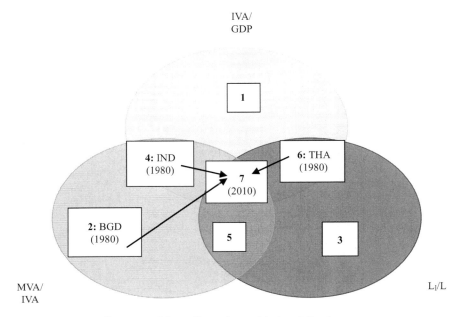

FIGURE 2.1 Venn diagrams of three dimensions of industrialization

Sources and notes: Author.
GDP = gross domestic product
MVA = manufacturing value added
IVA = industrial value added
L_I = industrial employment
L = total economy-wide employment
BGD = Bangladesh
IDN = India
THA = Thailand
1 = processing of primary goods
2 = manufacturing-intensive export or re-export platforms
3 = (probably a null set)
4 = skill- and technology-intensive activities
5 = Low-skill-intensive, assembly-type activities
6 = Non-manufacturing-dominated industrial sector
7 = Broad-based or mature industrial sector

example, Bangladesh, South Korea, and Thailand advanced their industrial development rapidly while Brazil, China, and India showed mixed signs of stumbling or even deindustrializing (Brazil).

Another measure of industrial development is the composite index of Competitive Industrial Performance (CIP) developed by UNIDO (2005). The CIP, a performance index, is based on normalized scores (0 to 1) of selected indicators of industrial capability which are then aggregated through the geometric mean. Each dimension has two sets of elements (each receiving a weight of 1/6). The first dimension captures the capacity to produce and to export (as measured by MVA per capita and manufacturing exports per capita). The second dimension measures

Industrialization: why and how? **57**

TABLE 2.2 Measures of industrial development for selected latecomers, 1980–2010

Country	Measure	1980	1990	2010	1980–1990	1990–2010	1980–2010
Bangladesh	IVA/GDP	20.6	20.7	26.1	0.1	5.4	**5.5**
Bangladesh	LI/L	. .	. .	17.7	. .	. .	**. .**
Bangladesh	MVA/GDP	13.8	12.6	16.9	−1.2	4.3	**3.1**
Bangladesh	MVA/IVA	67.0	61.0	64.6	−6.0	3.6	**−2.4**
Brazil	IVA/GDP	43.8	38.7	27.4	−5.1	−11.3	**−16.5**
Brazil	LI/L	. .	22.7	24.1	. .	1.4	**. .**
Brazil	MVA/GDP	33.5	. .	15.0	. .	. .	**−18.5**
Brazil	MVA/IVA	76.4	. .	54.7	. .	. .	**−21.7**
China	IVA/GDP	47.9	40.9	46.2	−7.0	5.3	**−1.7**
China	LI/L	. .	19.0	44.3	. .	25.3	**. .**
China	MVA/GDP	43.8	36.4	39.7	−7.3	3.3	**−4.0**
China	MVA/IVA	91.3	. .	86.0	. .	. .	**−5.3**
India	IVA/GDP	24.3	26.5	27.2	2.2	0.7	**2.9**
India	LI/L	. .	. .	22.4	. .	. .	**. .**
India	MVA/GDP	16.2	16.2	14.8	0.0	−1.4	**−1.4**
India	MVA/IVA	66.6	. .	54.5	. .	. .	**−12.1**
S. Africa	IVA/GDP	48.4	40.1	30.2	−8.3	−9.9	**−18.2**
S. Africa	LI/L	. .	. .	24.5	. .	. .	**. .**
S. Africa	MVA/GDP	21.6	23.6	14.4	2.0	−9.3	**−7.3**
S. Africa	MVA/IVA	44.7	. .	47.7	. .	. .	**3.0**
S. Korea	IVA/GDP	34.2	38.2	38.3	4.0	0.1	**4.1**
S. Korea	LI/L	29.0	35.4	24.9	6.4	−10.5	**−4.1**
S. Korea	MVA/GDP	22.8	25.0	30.7	2.2	5.7	**7.9**
S. Korea	MVA/IVA	66.9	. .	80.3	. .	. .	**13.4**
Thailand	IVA/GDP	28.7	37.2	40.0	8.5	2.8	**11.4**
Thailand	LI/L	10.3	13.6	20.6	3.3	7.0	**10.3**
Thailand	MVA/GDP	21.5	27.2	31.1	5.7	3.9	**9.6**
Thailand	MVA/IVA	75.0	. .	77.7	. .	. .	**2.6**
Tunisia	IVA/GDP	35.9	33.6	31.5	−2.3	−2.1	**−4.4**
Tunisia	LI/L	33.4	. .	32.7	. .	. .	**−0.7**
Tunisia	MVA/GDP	13.6	19.1	18.0	5.4	−1.1	**4.4**
Tunisia	MVA/IVA	37.9	. .	57.0	. .	. .	**19.2**

Sources and notes: Word Development Indicators (February 2016).
LI/L = industrial employment as a % of economy-wide employment
IVA/GDP = industrial value added as a % of GDP
MVA/GDP = manufacturing value added as a % of GDP
MVA/IVA = manufacturing value added as a % of industrial value added

technological capability (as measured by MVA/GDP and the share of medium- and high-technology manufactures in total MVA). The third dimension is a country's impact on global manufacturing (as measured by the country's share in world MVA and world manufacturing exports).

58 Industrialization and growth

The aggregate CIP indexes for 1990–2012 reveal interesting patterns (Upadhyaya and Yeganeh, 2014). The industrialized countries (Germany, Japan, USA, S. Korea, and Switzerland) have the top five CIP scores. High-industrial countries (40% < MVA/Y < 25%) boast capital- or technology-intensive activities that enjoy scale economies or flexible specializations. Post-industrial economies (MVA/Y < 15%), on the other hand, report a large service sector (business, financial, distribution, social, personal) exceeding 60% of GDP. The middle CIP scorers include China, Mexico, Poland, Thailand, and Turkey. The Northeast Asian late industrializers (Singapore, Taiwan, South Korea, and Hong Kong) reported the highest CIP in 1990 and continued to hold the same position in 2012.

Interestingly, Baldwin (2016) makes a case for a Great Convergence ushered in by the recent prominence of international production networks and know-how readily crossing borders. The major high performers include Hong Kong, Singapore, Taiwan, S. Korea, China, India, Indonesia, Thailand, Poland, Mexico, Brazil, and Turkey (discussed in detail in Chapter 6). Using the measures of "net domestic value added," exports of components account for more than half of net MVA for China (85%), South Korea (75%), Taiwan (70%), Poland (65%), Mexico (60%), and India (55%) (Baldwin, 2016: Figure 28).

Three-digit ISIC sectors can also be classified by production and export intensities as indicators of industrial sophistication (UNIDO, 2009; Rodrik, 2008). These indicators of industrial dynamism and product sophistication (diversification) relative to a country's per capita income are defined by a backward-looking identification of **revealed comparative advantage**. The use of "sector" as the basic unit of analysis, of course, implies that firms within an industry rise or fall together.

The reasoning is as follows. If higher-income countries intensively produce or export a certain manufacture, then that product is classified as sophisticated. Production intensity, the weighted average of the per capita GDP of all countries producing in the sector, indicates whether a country's production in a sector is more concentrated or less concentrated than the world average. The weight is the ratio of the value-added share of the sector in a country's total manufacturing value added relative to the sector's value-added share in world manufacturing value added.

Export sophistication is similarly defined with the weights being the per capita GDP of all countries exporting in that sector. Using a cutoff index value, ISIC 333, 342, 381, 382, 383, 384, and 385 are the most sophisticated while 311, 313, 321, 323, 324, and 355 are the least sophisticated. More generally, branches can be grouped as resource based (ISIC 311, 331, 341, 353, 354, 355, 362, 369), low technology (ISIC 312, 332, 361, 381, 390), medium technology (342, 351, 352, 356, 37, 382–51), or high technology (352, 382, 383, 384, 385).

Notes

1 According to the World Bank's *World Development Indicators* database (as updated in February 2016), industry accounted for about a quarter (or US$20 trillion) of the global GDP of US$76 trillion in 2013 at current prices. The share of manufacturing value added was 16%

Industrialization: why and how? **59**

(or US$12 trillion). Its share of global employment was 14%, 70% of global trade (standing at US$12 trillion in 2013), and 80% of global R & D.

2 Robert Gordon (2016: 1), in his magnus opus, boldly argues that

> The century of revolution in the United States after the Civil War was economic, not political, freeing households from an unremitting daily grind of painful manual labor, household drudgery, darkness, isolation, and early death. . . . The economic revolution of 1870 to 1970 was unique in human history, unrepeatable because so many of its achievements could happen only once.

3 Historically, MVA/GDP peaked around a third of GDP and at a per capita income of $10,000 in 1990 international dollars (McKinsey, 2012). These levels fell subsequently because two forces were at work: offshored FDI directed to certain emerging economies and productivity improvements in mature economies. The share-shift data on MVA can mask a lot of economic process at work since MVA = P*Q. Productivity gains by producers can be shared with buyers in the form of a fall in the price (P) of manufactures. MVA can, therefore, fall even when manufacturing output (Q) remains constant or even increasing.

4 The regression line indicates the cross-section 'average' level of manufacturing production sophistication associated with a given level of development. By the nature of its construction, the country measure of sophistication shows a high positive correlation with aggregate per capita income levels. OECD countries cluster around the regression line in the upper right of each graph. The African economies in the sample are concentrated in the lower left corner of each figure. Because the indices of production sophistication are measured in current US$, it is not possible to compare sophistication levels from year to year directly, since they are affected by price changes. The relevant comparison in the figures is the distance from the predicted relationship. Countries substantially above or below the regression line are of considerable interest. Positive outliers produce goods more typical of countries at higher levels of income. Countries below the regression line produce goods that are less sophisticated than would be predicted by their levels of income.

5 Rapidly growing countries inevitably tend to be those with large manufacturing sectors (40% < MVA/Y < 10%). Growth accelerations are associated with structural changes in the direction of manufacturing and trade. Large variations in average branch growth rates are explained by transition dynamics – initially behind countries grow faster than initially ahead countries.

6 Single measures (such as the Global Competitiveness Index of the World Economic Forum, or the Doing Business Index of the World Bank) are gross simplifications whose results are sensitive to the selection of indicators, the weights put on each, and the methods of normalization and aggregation. Nonetheless, they do provide useful overall measures of economic performance especially for benchmarking and cross-country comparisons (Upadhyaya and Yeganeh, 2014).

References

Abegaz, B. (2002). Structural Convergence in Manufacturing Industries Between Leaders and Latecomers. *Journal of Development Studies*, 38(4), pp. 69–99.

Abegaz, B. (2008). Determinants of Structural Convergence in the Manufacturing Industries of Newly Industrializing Economies. *South African Journal of Economics*, 76(2), pp. 89–109.

Baldwin, R. (2016). *The Great Convergence: Information Technology and the New Globalization*. Cambridge: Belknap-Harvard University Press.

Baldwin, R., and A. Venables. (2015). Trade Policy and Industrialisation When Backward and Forward Linkages Matter. *Research in Economics*, 69(2), pp. 123–131.

60 Industrialization and growth

Cadot, O., et al. (2011). Export Diversification: What's Behind the Hump? *Review of Economics and Statistics*, 93(2), pp. 590–605.

Cai, F. and M. Wang. (2008). A Counterfactual Analysis on Unlimited Surplus Labor in Rural China. *China and World Economy*, 16(1), pp. 51–65.

Chandler, A. (1990). *Scale and Scope: The Dynamics of Industrial Capitalism*. Cambridge: Harvard University Press.

Clark, G. (2007). *A Farewell to Alms: A Brief Economic History of the World*. Princeton: Princeton University Press.

Dasgupta, S., and A. Singh. (2006). *Manufacturing, Services and Premature Deindustrialization in Developing Countries*. [online] Helsinki: UNUWIDER. Available at: www.wider.unu.edu/sites/default/files/rp2006-49.pdf.

Fafchamps, M., and F. Shilpi. (2005). Cities and Specialisation: Evidence From South Asia. *Economic Journal*, 115(503), pp. 477–504.

Felipe, J., A. Mehta, and C. Rhee. (2014). Manufacturing Matters . . . But It's the Jobs that Count. *Asian Development Banking Working Paper No. 420*. Manila: Asian Development Bank.

Gordon, R. (2016). *The Rise and Fall of American Growth*. Princeton: Princeton University Press.

Hausmann, R., J. Hwang, and D. Rodrik. (2007). What You Export Matters. *Journal of Economics Growth*, 12, pp. 1–25.

Henderson, J. (1997). Externalities and Industrial Development. *Journal of Urban Economics*, 42(3), pp. 449–470.

Hwang, J. (2006). *Introduction of New Goods, Convergence, and Growth*. Mimeograph. Cambridge, MA: Harvard University Press.

Imbs, J., and R. Wacziarg. (2003). Stages of Diversification. *American Economic Review*, 93(1), pp. 63–86.

Islam, N., and K. Yokota. (2008). Lewis Growth Model and China's Industrialization. *Asian Economic Journal*, 22(4), pp. 359–396.

Kaldor, N. (1967). *Strategic Factors in Economic Development*. Ithaca: Cornell University Press.

Klinger, B., and D. Lederman. (2004). *Discovery and Development: An Empirical Exploration of "New" Products*. Washington, DC: World Bank.

Linder, S. (1967). *Trade and Trade Policy for Development*. New York: Praeger.

Marsh, P. (2012). *The New Industrial Revolution*. New Haven: Yale University Press.

McKinsey Global Institute. (2012). *Manufacturing the Future: The Next Era of Global Growth and Innovation*. New York: McKinsey & Company.

Melitz, M. (2002). The Impact of Trade on Intra-Industry Reallocations and Aggregate Industry Productivity. *NBER Working Paper # 8881*. Cambridge, MA: NBER.

Rodrik, D. (2008). Industrial Development: Some Stylized Facts and Policy Directions. In: D. O'Connor and M. Kjollerstrom, eds., *Industrial Development for the 21st Century*. London: Zed Press.

Rodrik, D. (2013). Unconditional Convergence in Manufacturing. *Quarterly Journal of Economics*, 128(1), pp. 165–204.

Shapiro, H., and L. Taylor. (1990). The State and Industrial Strategy. *World Development*, 18(6), pp. 861–878.

Solow, R. (2005). Reflections on Growth Theory. In: P. Aghion and S. Durlauf, eds., *Handbook of Economic Growth*, vol. 1, part 1. Amsterdam: Elsevier, pp. 4–10.

Sutcliffe, R. (1971). *Industry and Underdevelopment*. Reading, MA: Addison-Wesley.

Sutcliffe, R. (1984). Industry and Underdevelopment Reconsidered. *Journal of Development Studies*, 21(1), pp. 121–133.

Sutton, J. (2012). *Competing in Capabilities: The Globalization Process*. Oxford: Oxford University Press.

Szirmai, A., W. Naude, and L. Alcorta. (2013). Introduction and Overview: The Past, Present, and Future of Industrialization. In: A. Szirmai, W. Naude, and L. Alcorta, eds., *Pathways to Industrialization in the Twenty-First Century*. Oxford: Oxford University Press, pp. 3–52.

Szirmai, A., and B. Verspagen. (2011). Manufacturing and Economic Growth in Developing Countries, 1950–2005. *Structural Change and Economic Dynamics*, 34, pp. 46–59.

United Nations Industrial Development Organization (UNIDO). (2005). *Industrial Development Report 2005: Capability Building for Catching-up*. Oxford: Oxford University Press.

United Nations Industrial Development Organization (UNIDO). (2009). *Industrial Development Report 2009: Breaking in and Moving UP – New Industrial Challenges for the Bottom Billion and the Middle-Income Countries*. Oxford: Oxford University Press.

United Nations Industrial Development Organization (UNIDO). (2013). *Industrial Development Report 2013. Sustaining Employment Growth: The Role of Manufacturing and Structural Change*. Oxford: Oxford University Press.

United Nations Industrial Development Organization (UNIDO). (2015). *Inclusive and Sustainable Industrial Development*. [online] Geneva: UNIDO. Available at: www.unido. org/fileadmin/user_media_upgrade/Who_we_are/Structure/Director-General/DG_ Brochure_February_2015_Web.pdf.

Upadhyaya, S., and S.M. Yeganeh. (2014). Competitive Industrial Performance Report 2014. *Working Paper 12/2014*. Geneva: UNIDO.

Williamson, J. (2011). *Trade and Poverty: When the Third World Fell Behind*. Cambridge: MIT Press.

PART II
Theories of industrialization

3

THEORIES OF INDUSTRIALIZATION

This chapter provides characterizations of the early, late, and very-late waves of industrialization. It also offers a critical survey of the various models and theories that have been advanced to explain why the industrial revolution engulfed some regions and not others.

Three industrial revolutions in three global centuries

Economic historians tell us that industrialization has shaped, and in turn has been shaped by, the concomitant waves of economic globalization. Though there is no agreement on stagization, typologies abound in the literature. A brief look at the major waves of industrialization and globalization in the past 250 years nonetheless provides a useful backdrop for the scrutiny of the theories and models of **late industrialization**.

The first two phases of the industrial revolution that engulfed Europe and its offshoots (the North) coincided with what is dubbed by Williamson (2011) as the First Global Century (1820–1913). This century was characterized not only by the globalizing effects of industrialization that was triggered by new energy sources and Pax Britannica. A divergence in per capita emerged between industrializers and non- or de-industrializers along with absolute income gains for all in the orbit of the global market economy. Trade was mutually beneficial for those with political autonomy. The mobility of labor and capital matched or exceeded that of goods. This period ended in a retreat from globalization between the two world wars.

The shorter, Second Global Century (1950–1990), saw the industrial takeoff of East Asia and parts of Latin America (the South), aided by Pax Americana, financial integration, and the emergence of global governance institutions. This postwar period saw a golden age of rapid and widespread economic growth between 1950 and 1970 when the international mobility of goods and capital exploded due to the

66 Theories of industrialization

lowering of trade barriers relative to labor migration barriers. The period between 1970 and 1990 was characterized by commodity price shocks, financial globalization, and the end of the socialist system. Trade and technology jointly drove growth recovery which was accompanied by unprecedented increases in economic inequality within and between countries (Milanovic, 2016).

Richard Baldwin (2016) lumps the two global centuries into what he calls Old Globalization when the North industrialized while the South deindustrialized as global trade boomed, and growth took off sooner and faster in the North than in the South. Agglomeration and urbanization created shared growth in the North while producing a great income divergence with the South. While capital and knowledge clustered in the urban regions of the North, openness and falling energy and transportation costs facilitated the decoupling of the country of production of whole "goods" from the country of consumption of whole goods (i.e., the made-here-sold-there form of inter-industry trade). While agglomeration remained subnational, land attracted migrant labor in this phase of globalization reflecting large differences in productivity (wages) and resource costs – the focus of Ricardian and Neoclassical theories of trade.

Williamson's Third Global Century and Baldwin's New Globalization commenced around 1990. In its effects, the early phase of this more deeply globalized industrialization is a historical inflection that promises to be revolutionary in another generation or two. The ICT (information and communications technology) revolution has facilitated the emergence of global production networks and mass customization. A significant outsourcing and cross-border "unbundling" is fast becoming the norm. Capital is decoupled from knowledge, and the country of production of components (parts) or assembly is decoupled from the country of design and marketing. The prominence of the made-there-sold-here form of intra-industry trade, Baldwin (2016) and Taglioni and Winkler (2016) argue, is driven by a regionalized agglomeration of production chains matching labor (wage gaps) with capital (gaps in technological and managerial capabilities).

The fall in the cost of coordination and the embedding of technologies in specific components enabled a high-tech/low-wage combination highly profitable. An example illustrates the point. Apple, which owns only proto-type factories, is a "factory-less goods producer." As a virtual manufacturer, it outsources all fabrication or assembly activities, arranges for all inputs to make its products, controls the production process, and owns and sells the final products (Marsh, 2012). One consequence is a dramatic delineation of headquarters economies from factory economies.

Nested within these three phases of globalization and driven by technological engines, three distinct industrial revolutions (IRs) can be identified (see Tables 3.1 and 3.2). IR1 roughly spanned 1770–1870, IR2 covered 1870–1990, and IR3 has been underway from 1990 on.

During IR1, the pioneering countries introduced such path-breaking organizational **innovations** as the limited-liability company and the factory system to supplant the putting-out system. The concurrent transport and communication

TABLE 3.1 Three industrial revolutions, 1770–2016

Industrial revolution (IR)	Identifying characteristics
IR #1 (1770–1870) Phase 1: 1770–1820 Phase 2: 1820–1870	• First Global Century (1820–1913) • The steam engine and associated innovations • High TFP growth • Western Europe and its offshoots industrialize
IR #2 (1870–1990) Phase 1: 1870–1920 Phase 2: 1920–1970 Phase 3: 1970–1990	• First Global Century (1820–1913) • Second Global Century (1950–1990) • Electricity, the internal combustion engine, and associated innovations • Highest TFP growth • East and Central Europe, Russia, Latin America, East Asia
IR #3 (1990–) Phase 1: 1990–2016	• Third Global Century (1990–) • ICT-facilitated spatial unbundling of production and containerization • Fine-grained and speedy redefinition of the international division of labor • Tight staging of financing, marketing, and production networks • Pan-regional rather than pan-global value and supply chains coordinated by multinational firms

Sources and notes: Culled from various sources discussed in the text, including Clark (2007), Williamson (2011), Mokyr (1990), Baldwin (2016), and Gordon (2016).

innovations propelled IR1 especially with the introduction of the steam-powered railways, steel-hulled ships, and telegraph cables. The momentous divergence in inter-regional living standards that emerged in the nineteenth century is, therefore, best understood as a product of three overlapping revolutions – the industrial revolution, the technological revolution, and intensified economic globalization.

As noted earlier, IR1 was presaged by the proto-industrial activities or crafts along with a variety of seafaring vessels. Economic historians have offered a variety of explanations for the success of such pioneers and early movers in Continental Europe and the European offshoots. They stress the importance of one or more complementary factors. North and Thomas (1973), for example, emphasize the decisive role of institutional quality. Landes (1999, 2003) and Clark (2007) make a case for growth-friendly European cultural values and an early demographic transition. Mokyr (1990), Rosenberg and Birdzell (1986), and Gordon (2016) stress the crucial role of technological and organizational innovations. Others, such as Acemoglu and Robinson (2012), focus on the complementarity between inclusive political and economic institutions.

The grand puzzle of the early waves of the industrial revolution is why a handful of pre-industrial societies managed to embrace modern markets and to initiate a permanent escape from the **Malthusian trap**. We do not have good

68 Theories of industrialization

TABLE 3.2 A stylized characterization of early and late industrializations

	Pioneers	Early-comers
	(1770–1870)	*(1870–1950)*
Age	IR1: Leaders	IR2: Early-comers
Core countries	U.K, China, U.S.A.	Europe, Russia, and Japan
Key economic idea	Smithian	Schumpeterian
Revolution:	Transport (1840–1890)	Science (1860–1930)
• *Knowledge*	Process	Novel products
• *Discipline*	Market-based	Creative destruction
• *Hero*	Entrepreneur	Corporate manager
• *Organization*	Cottage firms	Multidivisional
	Factory system	Mass production
Accent on	Scale economies	Scale and scope
Competition	Create CA via	Exploit CA via
	Innovation rents	Low ULC: high wage with high productivity
Industrial capital	Powerful	Very powerful
Finance capital	Autonomous	Fused
Labor relations	Paternalistic	Institutionalized
Sequencing of stages	Loose	Tightening
Industrial strategy	Market-creating: "first-mover advantage"	Market-shaping: "innovative monopolies"

Sources and notes: Perez (2009), Amsden (2001), Baldwin (2016), Marsh (2012), and Williamson (2011).
CA = comparative advantage; ICT = information and communication technologies
ULC = unit labor cost
FDI = foreign direct investment

theories that identify the conditions under which a cumulative or a sudden break in economic activity, such as the industrial revolution, becomes possible or even inevitable.

Clark (2007) identifies three competing theories. *Exogenous growth theories* argue that countries like England with institutions which were somehow predisposed toward open access (the rule of law, and respect for civil and property rights) elicit long-term investment and innovation (North and Thomas, 1973; North, 1994; Mokyr, 1990). *Endogenous growth theories* suggest that those preindustrial economies incentivized innovative activities and, when coupled with a large population, managed to scale up to produce high and sustained industry-led growth (Kremer, 1993; Galore, 2011). Lastly, *multiple-equilibrium theories* argue that the gradual evolution of latent forces, unleashed by exogenous shocks, produced a transition from "bad" equilibrium that benefits the few at the cost of the many to "good" equilibrium where the scope for shared gain is much wider (Acemoglu and Robinson, 2012). As Clark puts it (2007: 272), "The Industrial Revolution was driven by the expansion of knowledge. Stunningly, unskilled labor has reaped more gains than any other group."

The engine of industrialization, early or late, is the production and diffusion especially of general-purpose technologies (GPTs). GPT innovations, which take decades to permeate the economy, have played a disruptive role in manufacturing to keep some leaders at the head of the pack or to help some laggards leapfrog to leadership (Lipsey et al., 2005; Marsh, 2012). They took various forms, including organizational innovations (such as the factory system, mass production, and **lean production**), process innovations (such as mass-produced steel, chemical synthesis, biotechnology, and nanotechnology), or product innovations (such as the steam engine, railway, internal combustion, electricity, motor vehicle, aircraft, computer, semiconductor, laser, and Internet). The sources of **competitive advantage** for pioneering firms put a high premium on the enhancement of value added from better design, lower cost of processing and assembly, or improved servicing.

Williamson (2011) similarly offers five reasons why industrial development is associated with high productivity and a diffusion S-curve. Urban clusters foster agglomeration economies, and denser urban product markets ensure efficient markets. Furthermore, a denser urban-industrial complex tends to generate a more extensive productivity-enhancing knowledge transfer between firms and industrial firms are more able to draw on the technological best practice used by world leaders.

Some specialization patterns are more conducive to promoting industrial upgrading than others. Developing general-purpose assets that can be deployed in a variety of industries provides a better platform onto new activities. Manufacturing with its denser metaphorical forests, and linkage and agglomeration economies, is best suited to generating such technologies (Krugman and Venables, 1995; UNIDO, 2009). The designs of the new products are freely available to all manufacturers throughout the world, but technological transfers are often characterized by tacitness and high fixed costs of adaptation. Under IR1 and IR2, technological transfers occurred because individuals in an economy learned to use more advanced capital goods, and technologies with increasing returns to scale as well as scope.

Clark (2007) interestingly points out that the first two industrial revolutions were led by innovations that benefitted users where price elasticity of demand was sufficiently high. Innovators were as much motivated by profits as by the novelty of new things. Latecomers had access to the same technology but had to contend with higher efficiency in utilizing it. It benefitted capital where imperfect competition prevailed. Otherwise, the benefits of innovation went disproportionately to users and free riders. Landowners did not benefit as much given the low income-elasticity for agricultural goods, secular declines in farm prices and increasing reliance on inorganic energy.

Gordon (2016), among others, argues that the great inventions of the long century between 1870 and 1990 (i.e., IR2) gave the world economy the greatest boost for productivity-driven growth. Electricity, the internal combustion engine,

70 Theories of industrialization

commercial air transportation, and the computer are the more notable innovations that are unlikely to find parallels in the ongoing digital revolution in terms of economic impact. Using TFP growth rates as the summary index of economic impact, Gordon (2016: chapter 17) points out that TFP grew annually at the rates of 1.80% in 1920–1970, 0.57% in 1970–1994, and 1.03% in 1994–2014.

IR2 was a continental phenomenon especially after 1890. By 1913, it ushered in a momentous bipolar division of the world between a rich North and a poor South (Maddison, 2001; Bairoch, 1995; Clark, 2007). The third phase of IR2 gave us the integrated circuit, the computer, and related innovations in telephony and the Internet.

Inspired by the spectacular economic achievements of the pioneering early movers such as Germany, others in Western Europe imitated and innovated in their own ways. They benefitted from high price elasticity of demand for manufactures, imperfect competition at home for early mover firms, provision of coal-powered electricity, and a capable state ensuring social peace, technical training, and protection of national champions. The science revolution of 1860–1930 fueled the catchup process by producing the steam turbine and cheap steel, the electric motor, and the internal combustion engine. This is the reason IR2 is associated with a good supply of electricity, cheap metals, the internal combustion engines, chemicals, and pharmaceuticals.

The "standard model" of catchup industrialization under IR2 had four key economic attributes (Allen, 2011): a unified national market, universal primary education, development banking, and activist industrial policy. This conventional model of latecomer industrialization, focused as it was on railways, banks, education, and tariffs, had to be modified after 1950. The reasons include quantum leaps in capital intensity and economies of scale of industrial production, and the advantages of early-movers by facing less competition in steadily expanding markets for manufactures. This includes the colonies (such as India and China) which had forcibly opened their markets to less costly imports and thereby had to de-industrialize.

The solution adopted by politically independent latecomers (Japan, USSR, Brazil, Mexico, Argentina, South Korea, and Taiwan) was "**big push**" industrialization. This state-led or state-supported strategy revolved around planning for interdependent investments, openness to export markets and **foreign direct investment** (FDI), and cultivation of new areas of comparative advantage (Gerschenkron, 1962; Lin and Monga, 2011).

Williamson (2011) also has identified the specific features of industrial catchup with the rich industrial core (UK, USA, and Germany) by the poor Periphery (Southeast Europe, Latin America, and Asia) during 1870–1975. Wages rose in the Center but fell in the Periphery. Falling primary-good prices relative to manufactures made domestic manufactures in the Periphery sufficiently profitable. Industrial policy (in the form of protection, real exchange rates, and subsidy) favored the home industry. Falling world transport costs reduced the barriers to industrial growth in countries with limited endowments of intermediate inputs (food, fiber, and mining) and fuels. The speed of industrial catching up surged after 1950 regarding industrial deepening (*intensive* industrialization) and in terms of spread to regional followers (*extensive* industrialization).

He further notes that persistence was not a strong feature of industrial catchup around the poor Periphery over the century since the second industrial revolution. Markets and industrial policies seem to matter more than culture, geography, and political institutions. Finally, the MVA growth rate of followers relative to leaders was not correlated with GDP per capita. What drove MVA growth instead was profitability and competitiveness.

Such late movers had to put a high premium on learning efficiency in an age of lean production, automation, and outsourcing primarily through global offshoring. The most significant technological introductions include computers, aircraft, electric motors, and new (synthetic) materials. During this half-century, the industrialized countries saw their share of global manufacturing jobs decline much faster than the share of output due to their edge in productivity – even in the face of declining prices.[1]

The latest incarnation of the international division of labor has taken the unusual form of privileging "offshorability" and network economies of production over skill or education for international competitiveness. This is because the ICT revolution has made it profitable for firms to spatially unbundle not just the production and sale of "whole products" but also to unbundle production itself. More than ever, firms can locate myriad micro links in the myriad tasks that are involved in the production of both finished goods and complex intermediate goods in several countries. The key driver here is the productivity-adjusted wage gap in the production of each task or component – a subject we take up at several points in subsequent chapters.

IR3, currently underway, is characterized by ICT-based innovations and the associated global value chains (GVCs) as well as global supply chains (GSCs). Prognostications of a mega trend from a couple of decades should be taken with a grain of salt since a deepening of the digitization is likely to have a muted effect – simply replacing paperwork while also opening new possibilities in big-data-related innovations, in biotechnology, nano-technology, and business services. IR3 is, therefore, likely to benefit from disrupting innovations in biotechnology, artificial intelligence, nanotechnology, and the 3-D printer (see Table 3.3).

Baldwin (2013, 2016), in fact, considers the essence of globalization to be the unbundling of things. He calls the developments in the first and second global centuries the "first great unbundling." The trends in the third global century underway, which constitute a radically new paradigm, he dubs the "second great unbundling." Tradability now means little more than offshorability. It is in this global environment of new challenges and opportunities (UNIDO, 2009; World Bank, 2016) that the very-late industrializers of Africa, South America, and Southwestern Asia are trying to mount the latest wave of industrialization. We will take up IR3 in detail in Chapter 6.

72 Theories of industrialization

TABLE 3.3 A stylized characterization of late and very-late industrializations

	Latecomers	*Very-latecomers*
	(1950–1990)	*(1990 –)*
Age	IR2: Multinationals	IR3: Transnationals
Core countries	E. Asia, Mexico, Brazil	China, India, SE Asia, C. America
Key economic idea	Gerschenkronian	Baldwinian
Revolution:	Modern transportation	Global value/supply chains
• *Knowledge*	Diffusionist, catchup	Digital and ICT
• *Discipline*	Competition and contest	Headquarter or policy coordination
• *Hero*	State and private tycoon	Lead transnationals and the State
• *Organization*	Diversified business groups	Offshoring partners
	Flexible specialization	Resource processing
• *Accent on*	Agglomeration	Specialized agglomeration
Competition	Exploit or create CA	Enhance productive capabilities:
	via Low ULC:	industry-specific, component specific
	low wage with	or task-specific
	moderate productivity	
Industrial capital	Fusion with financial	Development banking; FDI-intensive
Labor relations	Repressive	Repressive; mobilizing
Sequencing of stages	Tightly staged (product)	Tightly staged (components and tasks)
Industrial strategy	Market-augmenting:	Market-augmenting:
	"policy activism"	"productivity-capability building"

Sources and notes: Perez (2009), Amsden (2001), Baldwin (2016), Marsh (2012), Taglioni and Winkler (2016), and World Bank (2016).
CA = comparative advantage
ICT = information and communication technologies
ULC = unit labor cost
FDI = foreign direct investment

Laws of industrialization

Four empirical regularities have assumed the status of "laws" of industrialization. They provide us with a good point of departure for exploring the competing theories.

The first is the *Clark-Lewis-Kuznet thesis*, which states that the share of industrial output (employment) rises with per capita income and then falls as the modern service sector dominates at high per capita income (Clark, 1940; Kuznets, 1966; Lewis, 1954). And yet, the largely informal service sector in the poorest economies continues to bloom prematurely. This development is driven by supply-push forces emanating from livelihoods crises in the rural economy rather than by demand-pull forces from an insurgent urban industrial economy.

The second, specific to manufacturing production, is the so-called *Hoffmann's Law* (Hoffmann, 1958). Hoffmann posits that the evolution of the ratio of the MVA

Theories of industrialization **73**

of the consumer-good branches to that of the capital-good branches is U-shaped. Labor-intensive light industry gives way to capital-intensive heavy industry before knowledge-intensive consumer and producer goods eventually gain prominence at the highest per capita income levels.

The third, the *diversify-and-then-specialize thesis*, holds that industrializers diversify their manufacturing activities in the early stages and then proceed to specialize in the most profitable branches where breaking-in problems are important or high thresholds of competitiveness matter. This argument is based on discernible empirical patterns in manufacturing production and exports we addressed in Chapter 3.

The fourth, *Kaldor's Laws* (Kaldor, 1967), was referred to in Chapter 1. The First Law says that there exists a strong positive correlation between the growth of MVA and the growth of GDP. The Second Law states that there exists a strong positive correlation between the growth of manufacturing output and the growth of productivity in manufacturing. The Third Law states that there exists a strong positive relationship between the growth of manufacturing output and the growth of productivity in the non-manufacturing sectors.

The four "laws" of industrialization point to the inescapable conclusion that the proximate driver of industrial development is the volume and quality of capital accumulation. It is capital accumulation that underwrites capital deepening by funding fixed investment, human capital formation, public infrastructure, equipment and structures, R & D, and working capital. Regarding mechanics, scale, scope, agglomeration, and network economies all induce declines in the unit costs of production and distribution. These result in the rapid output and employment growth coupled with higher overall economic stability (or lower risk) that comes with robust, productive diversification (UNIDO, 2009, 2015).

These insights do not, however, constitute a coherent theory of industrialization that tightly integrates the demand and supply sides of the process in an open-economy setting. The ongoing debate on the genesis and dynamics of the much-studied British industrial revolution provides a stark reminder of this reality (Clark, 2007).

One potentially fruitful approach is to borrow generalized concepts from endogenous growth models which invoke the principle of cumulative causation – the notion that ideas induce new ideas in a virtuous spiral. The problem, however, is that despite the growing evidence that manufacturing growth drives GDP growth, aggregate growth models tend to be devoid of structural content (UNIDO, 2009; Ranis, 1981).

Nonetheless, Acemoglu suggests that it is still possible to embed structural transformation within the extended Solow model (Acemoglu, 2009: 217). To see this possibility, consider a continuous-time economy with real per capita income given by

$$y(t) = f[k(t), x(t)] \tag{3.1}$$

where $k(t)$ is the capital-labor ratio, and $x(t)$ is a variable that represents the structural features of the economy where f is assumed to be differentiable, increasing in k and x, and strictly concave in k.

74 Theories of industrialization

Structural change can be represented by the differential equation

$$\dot{x}(t) = g\,[k(t), x(t)] \tag{3.2}$$

where g is twice differentiable and increasing in both k and x.

Finally, capital accumulation in the absence of **technological change** takes the form

$$\dot{k}(t) = sf\,[k(t), x(t)] - (\delta + n)k(t) \tag{3.3}$$

where δ is the depreciation rate, and n is the labor force growth rate.

Using capital deepening as a proxy for income growth in the early stages of development and assuming that $\dot{k}(t) = 0$ is steeper than $\dot{x}(t) = 0$, it can be shown that capital accumulation and structural transformation can be self-reinforcing until a unique steady state is reached.

Informal mental models of industrialization, on the other hand, can draw on the big ideas of high development theory. These ideas include Rostow's stagization of a quasi-automatic industrialization based on the experiences of the West, Gerschenkron's (1962) recognition that latecomers must contend with the huge capital and managerial requirements of catchup industrialization, Rosenstein-Rodan's (1943) ideas about the need to coordinate lumpy and myriad complementary investments where markets often fail to accomplish it, Hirschman's (1958) theory of industrial dynamics through forward and backward linkages (which calls for the need to undertake interlocking investments often ahead of demand), and Akamatsu's (1962) trade-based **flying geese** metaphor that underscores the need for sequential learning from leaders.[2] These supply-oriented ideas must be complemented by attention to ensuring adequate demand for home-produced manufactures.

We can group these mental models, not entirely neatly, into three synthetic classes. The first group is the *production-oriented models* which focus on domestic industrial capability. The second group is the *trade-oriented models* with specific implications for production and employment structure. The third group, dubbed here *fusion models*, obliterates the distinction between domestic production and international trade. We now take a snapshot of each.

Production-oriented theories

The production-based group consists of the old structuralist (dualistic) models and the neostructuralist models. One may also add to this list the Linder thesis (Linder, 1967), which emphasizes the need to build up a large home market as an essential springboard for export penetration. The production-oriented theories emphasize the hysteresis effects of initial conditions (market segmentation or historical legacies) that, in the absence of judicious industrial policy, are likely to frustrate an industrial takeoff.

Production-oriented theories posit that economic diversification is driven primarily by the interplay of domestic demand and domestic industrial capacity, on the one hand, and the interplay between agriculture (rural) and industry (urban) sectors, on the other. The inevitable question then is what should finance and spearhead industrialization: rural development, urban development, or both? How do critical imports and exports fit in this picture?

Theories of **dualism** invoke the inter-sectoral immobility of labor or technology to explain the constraints on rapid industrial growth. An important implication of this line of thinking is that capital accumulation in the industrial sector is the engine of growth. However, the pace of capital accumulation is limited by the ability of the economy to produce surplus food and fiber.

More specifically, production-based theories explicitly seek to incorporate the peculiar features of less-industrial economies and the opportunities for **very-late industrializers**. The Lewis model (Lewis, 1954; Ranis and Fei, 1961; Ranis, 2012; Gong, 2015) and its various extensions provide a simple but seminal framework for imagining how a predominantly agrarian economy with unskilled surplus labor can progressively transform itself into an industrial one through a transfer of surplus labor, food, and fiber to the modern sector.

The labor surplus model is based on the central idea that, provided an adequate supply of food is assured, a low (i.e., lower than is justified by labor productivity) and stable institutional wage can be maintained in a dualistic economy. This would be so until the dynamic reallocation of labor from the non-capitalist sector ceases with the dominance of the modern industrial economy. In this way, the traditional sector finances the industrial sector through implicit **economic rent** appropriation,[3] thereby enabling industrial widening and deepening. With the exhaustion of the surplus at the point of full commercialization, gains in productivity in both sectors and access to external markets will ensure deeper industrialization.

In general, the size of the *marketable* surplus depends on such factors as access to land and other inputs, clarity and security of property rights, social peace, and the availability of incentive goods. *Marketed* surplus, on the other hand, depends on such factors as relative prices, transaction cost (especially transportation, storage, and easily enforceable contracts), information about regional markets, taxes and fees, the availability of incentive goods, and the size of urban markets. Equalizing the two is the proper role of sensible industrial and macro policy.

The simple two-sector model is instructive in other respects. First, input suppliers – farmers or miners – react to unfavorable terms of trade with manufacturing in many ways. These rational responses of primary producers might include going on a strike by willfully producing less, vertically integrating by processing their raw materials themselves, or by exporting raw materials directly. Each of these reactions goes against the interests of the urban-based industrial class.

An important set of considerations for production-based models is the idea that lock-ins abound in laggard economies in the face of hard-to-change factors such as geography, the legacy of colonial specialization, and political deadlocks. This is of great concern to policymakers since income convergence across countries is driven by what a country produces, where it produces (important for local externalities), and with whom it trades (important for global externalities).

The transition from a "low-order" comparative advantage, that is price- or rent-driven, to a "high-order" comparative advantage regime, that is profit- or productivity-driven, inevitably entails two things. One is the need for a political triumph of profit seekers over rent seekers to undergird either state-led industrialization (socialist) or capitalist-led industrialization. The other is the need for appropriate industrial policy (tax, rent, subsidy, public goods, quality, and regional integration) to build up domestic capability in the light of the high "admission fee" for latecomers into higher-productivity activities.

Trade-oriented theories

The trade-based group melds insights from theories of **comparative advantage** and models of international diffusion of technology. These theories emphasize the importance of market-directed allocation of resources and the diffusion of technologies from leaders to followers in the context of an open economy.

The relationship between resource endowments and trade (in final or intermediate products) is complex but may be usefully simplified. In general, countries which are doubly rich in natural resources and labor supply tend to be dominated by smallholder agriculture and thereby experience delayed industrialization. At the other end of the spectrum, countries where both factors are scarce tend to specialize in tertiary activities such as tourism or offshore banking as in the cases of Jamaica and Panama. Where abundant resources are complemented with scarce labor, rentier economies tend to dominate as in the oil-rich Middle East. It is when abundant labor confronts scarce natural resources that the imperative to industrialize is the strongest as in East Asia (Williamson, 2011).

The historical evidence, however, suggests a more nuanced picture. Improvements in terms of trade for agricultural economies can, for example, be growth-reducing if the gains lead to deindustrialization. Furthermore, migration is equalizing only if wages rise in the sending country and fall in the receiving country which was true for Europe but not so for Asia (Williamson, 2011; Clark, 2007).

Traditional theories of comparative advantage, whether Heckscher-Ohlin-Samuelson (based on differences in endowments), Ricardian (based on differences in productivity), or Krugmanian (based on imperfect competition emanating from differences in returns to scale and agglomeration economies), are less theories of production structure than theories of trade structure. These theories are based on the premise that a country's existing endowments (of physical and human capital, labor, natural resources, or institutions) determine relative costs, and hence the patterns of specialization in products and services that are most profitable.

Under certain fanciful assumptions (high divisibility of production, full and costless information, and absence of externality), conventional theories of trade suggest that firms (or countries) would produce and sell goods in conformity with their existing comparative advantage. The Neoclassical view is that only changes in factor intensity should lead to changes in the mix of production or trade. Specific products, such as industrial goods, have no intrinsic economic significance beyond the current market demand for them. Honoring the principles of comparative advantage is both necessary and sufficient since industrial activities that are not directed by the competitive market (where it is in place) would harm income and employment prospects.

The new theories of trade suggest, however, that more realistic assumptions (such as increasing returns, incomplete and costly information, and significant agglomeration externalities) produce different implications for efficient allocation. If changes in technological intensity exceed changes in factor intensity, these models predict that initial conditions and capabilities drive the pattern of production or trade.

There are, however, several interrelated questions that arise in considering dynamic rather than static comparative advantage in manufacturing trade. Is there a systematic relationship between changes in the production structure of manufacturing and changes in the compositions of imports and exports of manufactures? If so, can these changes be identified as a series of connected stages in a ladder of changing comparative advantage?

Two notable considerations are salient here. The first is that specialization patterns are not always pinned down by factor endowments (Hausmann et al., 2007). The second is that growth accelerations are associated with structural changes in the direction of manufacturing (Prasad et al., 2006).

The implications for **dynamic comparative advantage** are especially interesting. If knowledge diffusion and positive externalities generate national (rather than firm) economies of scale, the diffusion of technology downstream may counteract the initial advantages of (Northern) incumbents.

The empirical evidence on the relationship between economic diversification and income level underscores three notable non-monotonic paths of evolution. Just like there is a non-monotonic path of production and employment as functions of per capita incomes, there is also a non-monotonic path of exports as a function of per capita income – diversification triggered by cost discovery is followed by re-concentration (Klinger and Lederman, 2004, 2006). Then there is a non-monotonic path of exports as a function of per capita incomes – diversification along the extensive margin (new products) is followed by diversifications along both intensive and extensive margins up to $20–22k (in PPP terms) before re-concentration sets in along the intensive margin (Cadot et al., 2011).

A platform-oriented conceptualization of dynamic comparative advantage would enable us to posit the following regarding the directionality and the chain of factor content of industrial development. For whole products, a latecomer can begin with catering for the domestic market often with shoddy manufactures, then move to exporting improved light manufactures to other developing-country markets, upgrade to capital-intensive **intermediates** and final goods for the home markets and finally, enter the global market with the threshold capability thus attained. The rub, of course, is that one needs to characterize each of these distinctive stages and explain the factors that drive the transition between stages.

The upshot is that countries which promote exports of more sophisticated goods grow faster. As the productivity frontier is reached, convergence at the product level becomes a reality, and with successful product diversification, laggard countries eventually converge to the level of income implied by their exports. That is, *you become what you export*. The available empirical evidence also suggests that North-South trade is indeed intra-sectoral, while South-South trade has been inter-sectoral, that is, in differentiated capital- and skill-intensive products.

Fusion theories

These patterns are changing markedly under IR3 with the full industrialization of much of East Asia and the prominence of GVCs. The division between production and trade is, therefore, somewhat artificial but useful in helping us appreciate the emerging structural break in the way industrial activity is globalized. Until 1980 or so, countries integrated intermediates (some imported) and final goods to serve both domestic and export markets. With the reduction in the cost of transmission as well as transportation, post-1980 globalization increasingly disintegrated intermediates from final goods. However, the successful late-industrializers tend to have a broad spectrum of both types of production, which enables them to flexibly choose the most profitable and employment-intensive activities.

The growing prominence of FDI-based international production networks of manufacturing has rendered moot the nationwide distinction between producing and exporting. This means (Baldwin, 2016; Taglioni and Winkler, 2016):

- Latecomers no longer need to develop expansive national supply and value chains to launch an industrialization drive. As participants in various nodes of GVCs, they will have automatic (borrowing) access to know-how (design), marketing, and financing to be able to export components or to assemble imported ones.
- As previously intra-factor flows become less lumpy (in geographic space, product space, or time space) than in the past, national borders matter less economically.

This, of course, does not mean that the "instant-industry" mode of industrializing by stages is any easier than the "infant-industry" pathway of industrializing by mastering all stages to produce whole products. It simply poses different challenges and different opportunities. In the final analysis, as Baldwin (2016: 271) rightly concedes: "Development means getting more value added from a country's productive factors. This requires improvements in labor skills and technological capabilities as well as fixing domestic market failures and knitting social cohesion to ensure a consensus stays in favor of economic progress."

Modes of production

For the sake of completeness, we now take a brief look at heterodox thinking on post-colonial industrialization which offers some useful insights. Neo-Marxian theories, which also seek to integrate the production side and the trade side, focus

Theories of industrialization **79**

on historical and structural factors that constrain a self-fueling industrialization process in the capitalist Periphery. Postcolonial latecomers are said to be locked into inherently unequal and marginalizing relationships with multinationals which can only be broken by a nationalistic industrial policy.

Addressing how metropolitan capitalism transformed non-industrial modes of production, Rey (1979) outlines an interesting formulation of a sequential process of economic integration of the Periphery with the Center. In stage one (say, in the early days of the colonial era), the relationship between capitalism and pre-capitalism was one of an arm's-length commercial exchange or trade. This often led to the preservation and even the strengthening of some pre-capitalist classes and institutions. In stage two, insurgent capitalism engaged in selective penetration of the production sphere in the form of the introduction of regimented wage relations in manufacturing, mines, and plantations. The third and final stage, which anticipates GVCs, is the integration of capitalist production and trade in the formal sectors of the Periphery and the survival of some non-capitalist relations in the **informal sector**.[4]

This inexorable process of capitalist expansion is, therefore, characterized by contradictory forces of conservation and dissolution. It can stimulate "dependent" industrialization without free labor markets – all forms of labor repression from indenture to apartheid may be used. Bill Warren (1980) follows Polanyi (1944) in noting that the process of uneven capitalist development is not actually unique to the Periphery. This was, in fact, how capitalism gained ascendancy in the Center itself.

Notes

1 Some 277 million manufacturing jobs were created in developing economies – half of them in China and a fifth of them in India.
2 Matthews (2005: 446) concludes: "The developing countries today have an intellectual treasure trove of the latecomer development ideas of Gerschenkron, in the latecomer industrial dynamics ideas of Akamatsu and followers, in the circular and cumulative causation idea that stemmed from Allyn Young and the recognition of the centrality of increasing returns and its deployment by early development theorists such as Rosenstein-Rodan, Prebisch, Myrdal, Lewis and Hirschman. . . . The fact that East Asia produced a developmental model that works means that the strategic underpinnings of this model needed to be teased out and applied again now, in the very different conditions of the early years of the 21st century." The flying geese process begins with import substitution of simple products, moves to industrial upgrading toward capital- and skill-intensive industries, and then graduation to the highest rungs of the technology and marketing ladder.
3 *Economic Rent* is the difference between what a resource is paid and how much it would fetch in a competitive market to remain in its current use. There are three distinct types of legally generated economic rent. *Innovation rent* refers to the above-normal returns from innovation (which calls for high development costs or scarce talent), which is socially beneficial and will be competed away in due course from imitators or other innovators. *Market-power rent* refers to temporary monopoly arising from natural monopoly (usually in natural-resource industries with government monopolies or with high fixed costs), from being a first-mover or from government-created rights and quotas. *Political rent* refers to supporting and exploiting government rules or regulations to obtain economic gains that are largely inimical to the generation of new wealth.

80 Theories of industrialization

4 The dependency version of this thesis, though lacking a firm empirical grounding, does provide a powerful critique of the traditional-versus-modern sectoral dichotomy of dualistic themes. It decries the mechanistic counter-posing of a progressive capitalist sector with a laggard non-capitalist sector. Instead, it views both as parts of a contradictory whole. Neo-Marxist theories, by recognizing the need to conduct analyses at the interface between the international and the national levels, have also drawn attention to the importance of hyper-globalized politics and economics in the course of industrialization.

References

Acemoglu, D. (2009). *Introduction to Modern Economic Growth*. Princeton: Princeton University Press.

Acemoglu, D., and J. Robinson. (2012). *Why Nations Fail*. New York: Crown Business.

Akamatsu, K. (1962). A Historical Pattern of Economic Growth in Developing Countries. *The Developing Economies*, 1, pp. 3–25.

Allen, R. (2011). *Global Economic History: A Very Short Introduction*. New York: Oxford University Press.

Amsden, A. (2001). *The Rise of 'The Rest': Challenges to the West From Late Industrializing Economies*. New York: Oxford University Press.

Bairoch, P. (1995). *Economics and World History: Myths and Paradoxes*. Chicago: University of Chicago.

Baldwin, R. (2013). Trade and Industrialization After Globalization's Second Unbundling: How Building and Joining a Supply Chain Are Different and Why It Matters. In: R. Feenstra and A. Taylor, eds., *Globalization in an Age of Crisis: Multilateral Economic Cooperation in the Twenty-First Century*. Chicago: University of Chicago Press.

Baldwin, R. (2016). *The Great Convergence: Information Technology and the New Globalization*. Cambridge: Belknap-Harvard Press.

Cadot, O., et al. (2011). Export Diversification: What's Behind the Hump? *Review of Economics and Statistics*, 93(2), pp. 590–605.

Clark, C. (1940). *Conditions of Economic Progress*. London: Macmillan.

Clark, G. (2007). *A Farewell to Alms: A Brief Economic History of the World*. Princeton: Princeton University Press.

Galore. O. (2011). *Unified Growth Theory*. Princeton: Princeton University Press.

Gerschenkron, A. (1962). *Economic Backwardness in Historical Perspective*. Cambridge, MA: Belknap Press of Harvard University Press.

Gong, X. (2015). African Economic Structural Transformation: A Diagnostic Analysis. *Journal of African Transformation*, 1(1), pp. 1–22.

Gordon, R. (2016). *The Rise and Fall of American Growth*. Princeton: Princeton University Press.

Hausmann, R., J. Hwang, and D. Rodrik. (2007). What You Export Matters. *Journal of Economics Growth*, 12, pp. 1–25.

Hirschman, A.O. (1958). *The Strategy of Economic Development*. New Haven, CT: Yale University Press.

Hoffmann, W. (1958). *Growth of Industrial Economies*. Manchester: University of Manchester Press.

Kaldor, N. (1967). *Strategic Factors in Economic Development*. Ithaca: Cornell University Press.

Klinger, B., and D. Lederman. (2004). Discovery and Development: An Empirical Exploration of 'New' Products. *Policy Research Working Paper Series 3450*. Washington, DC: World Bank.

Klinger, B., and D. Lederman. (2006). Innovation and Export Portfolios. *Policy Research Working Paper Series 3983*. Washington, DC: World Bank.

Kremer, M. (1993). Population Growth and Technological Change: One Million B.C. to 1990. *Quarterly Journal of Economics*, 108(3), pp. 681–716.

Krugman, P., and A. Venables. (1995). Globalization and the Inequality of Nations. *Quarterly Journal of Economics*, 110(4), pp. 857–880.

Kuznets, S. (1966). *Modern Economic Growth: Rate, Structure, and Spread.* New Haven, CT: Yale University Press.

Landes, D. (1999). *The Wealth and Poverty of Nations: Why Some Are So Rich and Some So Poor.* New York: W. W. Norton.

Landes, D. (2003). *The Unbound Prometheus: Technological Change and Industrial Development in Western Europe From 1750 to the Present.* Cambridge: Cambridge University Press.

Lewis, W.A. (1954). Economic Development With Unlimited Supplies of Labour. *The Manchester School*, 22(2), pp. 139–191.

Lin, J.Y., and C. Monga. (2011). Growth Identification and Facilitation: The Role of the State in the Dynamics of Structural Change. *Development Policy Review*, 29(3), pp. 264–290.

Linder, S. (1967). *Trade and Trade Policy for Development.* New York: Praeger.

Lipsey, R., K. Carlaw, and R. Lipsey. (2005). *Economic Transformations: General Purpose Technologies and Long Term Economic Growth.* Oxford: Oxford University Press.

Maddison, A. (2001). *The World Economy: A Millennial Perspective.* Paris: OECD.

Marsh, P. (2012). *The New Industrial Revolution.* New Haven: Yale University Press.

Matthews, J. (2005). The Intellectual Roots of Latecomer Industrial Development. *International Journal of Technology and Globalization*, 3(4), pp. 433–450.

Milanovic, B. (2016). *Global Inequality: A New Approach for the Age of Globalization.* Cambridge, MA: Belknap Press.

Mokyr, J. (1990). *The Lever of Riches: Technological Creativity and Economic Progress.* New York: Oxford University Press.

North, D. (1994). Economic Performance Through Time. *American Economic Review*, 84(3), pp. 359–368.

North, D., and R. Thomas. (1973). *The Rise of the Western World: A New Economic History.* New York: Cambridge University Press.

Perez, C. (2009). Technological Revolutions and Techno-Economic Paradigms. *Working Papers in Technology Governance and Economic Dynamics 20.* Tallinn: Tallinn University of Technology.

Polanyi, K. (1944). *The Great Transformation: The Political and Economic Origins of Our Time.* New York: Farrar & Rinehart.

Prasad, E., et al. (2006). How Do Trade and Financial Integration Affect the Relationship Between Growth and Volatility? *Journal of International Economics*, 69(1), pp. 176–202.

Ranis, G. (2012). *Labor Surplus Revisited.* [online] New Haven: Yale Economic Growth Center. Available at: www.econ.yale.edu/growth_pdf/cdp1016.pdf.

Ranis, G., and J. Fei. (1961). A Theory of Economic Development. *The American Economic Review*, 51(4), pp. 533–565.

Rey, P.P. (1979). Class Contradiction in the Lineage Mode of Production. *Critique of Anthropology*, 13(14), pp. 41–61.

Rosenberg, N., and L.E. Birdzell. (1986). *How the West Grew Rich: The Economic Transformation of the Industrial World.* New York: Basic Books, Inc.

Rosenstein-Rodan, P. (1943). Problems of Industrialization of Eastern and South-Eastern Europe. *Economic Journal*, 53(210/211), pp. 202–211.

Taglioni, D., and D. Winkler. (2016). *Making Global Chins Work for Development.* Washington, DC: World Bank Group.

United Nations Industrial Development Organization (UNIDO). (2009). *Industrial Development Report 2009: Breaking in and Moving UP – New Industrial Challenges for the Bottom Billion and the Middle-Income Countries.* Oxford: Oxford University Press.

82 Theories of industrialization

United Nations Industrial Development Organization (UNIDO). (2015). *Industrial Development Report 2016: The Role of Technology and Innovation in Inclusive and Sustainable Industrial Development*. Geneva: UNIDO.

Warren, B. (1980). *Imperialism: Pioneer of Capitalism*. London: Verso.

Williamson, J. (2011). *Trade and Poverty: When the Third World Fell Behind*. Cambridge: MIT Press.

World Bank. (2016). *World Development Report 2016: Digital Dividends*. Washington, DC: World Bank Group.

4

THEORIES OF LATE AND VERY-LATE INDUSTRIALIZATION

In this chapter, we focus on the special challenges faced by industrializers in the post-1950 age of **containerization** and the digital revolution. We address the critical questions of proper sectoral prioritization and effective ways of building productive industrial capability.

Industrialization: late versus very late

Although it also applies to the European Periphery and Japan (see Table 3.2), "late" industrialization will be used here to refer to the industrialization of some post-colonial countries – what Alice Amsden (2001) calls "the Rest." We use the label "very-late" industrializers to refer to the post-1990 industrializers under the ongoing IR3 – what Amsden inaptly dubbed "the Remainder."

During 1870–1913, many countries or sub-regions managed to catch up, including Brazil, Mexico, Japan, Shanghai, Catalonia, Northern Italy, and Russia. By 1950, another cohort had entered the era of catchup industrialization, including Argentina, Colombia, Peru, Greece, Italy, Turkey, India, Korea, Manchuria, the Philippines, S. Africa, and Taiwan (Williamson, 2011). This period was characterized by the emergence of the large managerial firm employing capital-intensive and mass production techniques. Public education and migration (internal and international) provided the semi-skilled labor force needed. Public education was supplemented by intensive on-the-job training.

The second half of the twentieth century witnessed a remarkably successful industrialization drive by a number of Asian countries (most notably, South Korea, China, Taiwan, Hong Kong, Singapore, India, Thailand, Turkey, and Malaysia) and the bigger Latin American countries (most notably, Brazil, Mexico, and Argentina). Energy supply was boosted during this period by cheap electricity (oil and nuclear energy) while the automobile provided a new mode of efficient land

84 Theories of industrialization

transportation. Industrial firms became increasingly transnational in ownership and market horizon, multidivisional, and grouped in loose alliances or tightly knit business groups.

Leading students of the post-1950 waves of industrialization have identified a few key features of successful catchup industrializers. Latecomers generally boast an unlimited supply of semi-skilled labor at low wages; they suffer poor or missing domestic markets which stand to benefit from sensible industrial policy and organizational innovation; they have managed to produce an abundance of competent, salaried managers; and they rely heavily on imported technologies.

Alice Amsden, one of the most astute students of late industrialization, has pinned down the critical features of the remarkable telescoping of the process by a handful of countries. As she puts it (Amsden, 2001: 2):

> The rise of "the rest" was one of the phenomenal changes in the last half of the twentieth century. For the first time in history, backward countries industrialized *without proprietary innovations*. They caught up in industries requiring large amounts of **technological capabilities** without initially having advanced technological capabilities of their own.

The very-late industrializers have few of these attributes of a successful catching up. This is in part because IR3 has been characterized by multiple mega trends. Since 1990, late industrializers have doubled their share of global manufacturing value added (GMVA stood at US$10.5 trillion in 2010 at current prices) to 36%. Just as importantly, this share gain is highly concentrated in a handful of emerging industrial economies, located mainly in East Asia (see Table 4.1).

TABLE 4.1 Distribution of GMVA by development group and region, 1990–2014

Group or region	1990(%)	2000(%)	2014(%)
World:	100	100	100
• Industrialized	82	78	64
• Industrializing	18	22	36
Development:	100	100	100
• Emerging industrial	84	88	90
• Least developed	2	2	2
• Other	14	11	8
Region:	100	100	100
• Africa	9	7	4
• Asia and Pacific	37	54	71
• Latin America	36	28	15

Sources and notes: UNIDO, *Industrial Development Report 2016* (Geneva, 2015), Table 1.
GMVA = global manufacturing value added

Late and very-late industrialization **85**

TABLE 4.2 Profile of globalized manufacturing under IR3, circa 2010

Manufacturing clusters [% GMVA]	Three-digit ISIC industries	R & D intensity	Labor intensity	Capital intensity	Energy intensity
Global innovation for local markets [34%]	• Chemicals • Motor vehicles • Other transport • Electrical machinery • Other machinery	H	L	L	H
Regional processing [28%]	• Rubber and plastic • Fabricated metals • Food-beverage-tobacco • Printing publishing	H	M	M	L
Energy- or resource-intensive [22%]	• Wood • Refined petroleum • Paper • Mineral-based products • Basic metals	M	H	H	M
Global technologies/ innovators [9%]	• Computers, electronics • Semi-conductors, office machinery • Medical, precision, optical	H	M	H	H
Labor-intensive innovators [7%]	• Textile, apparel, leather • Furniture, jewelry, toys	L	H	L	H

Source and notes: Adapted from McKinsey (2012), Exhibit E3.
H = high
M = medium
L = low
GMVA = global manufacturing value added

When we look at the clusters of ISIC3 manufacturing industries by factor intensity, many striking trends stand out. As shown in Table 4.2, the two internationalized clusters (global and regional processing) make up two-thirds of GMVA and half of global employment in manufacturing. The last two clusters, which are polar opposites in productivity, are nonetheless highly tradable and mobile (in production or distribution) with the technology innovators concentrated in the Center and the labor intensives in the Periphery. Finally, and just as notably, manufacturing and service are being blended as manufacturers demand travel, transportation, and telecom services to run their global networks. Some 37% of manufacturing jobs are service type in the U.S.A. and 19% of inputs are purchased from the service sector (McKinsey, 2012).

The debates on latecomer industrialization are understandably centered on issues pertaining to industrial organization and technology (Gerschenkron, 1962; Sutcliffe, 1984; Amsden, 2001; Morris and Adelman, 1988; Baldwin, 2016). Six concerns stand out.

86 Theories of industrialization

The first set is about *sectoral priority* for the generation of savings, the allocation of investment, and the scope for technological absorption – issues which hark back to the German and the Soviet industrialization debates. These concerns include the reaction of proto-industrial households to incentives created by expanding market connectivity which may take the form of diversification into non-agricultural activities, greater specialization within agriculture, or exiting from the market system itself.

The second set pertains to the lumpiness of investment and the high risk of coordination failure involving complementary investments. These concerns emanate from narrow and fragmented domestic markets and the imperative of exploiting economies of scale to penetrate a global market dominated by well-established producers (Gerschenkron, 1962; Hirschman, 1958).

The third factor is the high threshold latecomers must clear to *break in*. Productivity- and quality-based competition favors the industrialized countries since incumbents enjoy many formidable technological advantages including those related to the tacitness of knowledge itself. In this context, productivity-driven growth has two features: the way production and distribution are managed (managerial skills) and the way inputs are transformed into output (technical skills). These two go in parallel with the well-known attributes of commercializable ideas, that is, they are very expensive to produce but very cheap to diffuse.

Incumbents historically enjoyed significant market advantages arising from politico-military holdup (protectionism at home and imperialism abroad), extensive production and distribution networks, and hard-earned brand loyalty. This would explain why industrial leaders, having attained global competitiveness, favor free trade while late-starters, being less competitive, do not (Chang, 2002).

The fourth factor underscores the related fact that late industrialization, which inevitably begins as low-wage industrialization, requires building up a *capability for efficient learning* to ensure rapid ascent up the technology ladder. Learning is a collective, costly, and risky effort.

The fifth factor is that meeting the twin challenges of market failure and government failure ironically requires greater and riskier *state activism* than was the case with early industrializers. Development-friendly state activism can supplement market-based competition. Good policy often involves policy-induced contests for state support, the right mix of foreign debt and FDI financing of major investments, and an appropriate sequencing of **import substitution** and export promotion.

A sixth, and related, consideration is the oft-neglected *balance of political forces* in favor of or against industrial development as the politically weak industrial class (or pro-industrial state elite) and powerful agricultural or mining interests contest the burden of import substitution (Whitfield et al., 2015). High-priced projects have been known to breed both inefficiency and corruption (Ades and di Tella, 1997).

Given the alternative pathways for latecomer industrialization, it is understandable that development economists and international development organizations have had ambivalent attitudes toward the subject. Through the 1960s, industrialization strategies based on import substitution were taken for granted. However, the intellectual climate on industrialization strategies changed in the 1970s. The limits of backward-looking import substitution became evident. A few countries in East Asia (South Korea, Taiwan, Hong Kong, and Singapore) rose to prominence. Their industrialization experiences underscored the fact that late industrialization was not only possible but can also be a spectacular success in an environment of "governed market" (Wade, 2003).

The World Bank, on the other hand, focused on the need to provide appropriate incentives for export-oriented industrialization. A low premium was put on the need for a coherent industrial strategy that includes building up domestic capacity as well as forging transparent and accountable institutions (Meier and Steel, 1989; World Bank, 1993, 1997, 2000). The rationale is that, while judicious bureaucrats did accelerate industrial catchup in East Asia, the requisite discipline for handling such a blunt instrument (political autonomy of technocrats, result-oriented state subsidy, organized contests for public support, high investment rates, and willingness to respect market fundamentals) could not be replicated in Africa or the rest of Asia. We will revisit this issue in detail in Chapter 10.

A quarter of a century later, the global and the technological contexts are quite different for an African industrial takeoff. Very-lateness poses seemingly insurmountable disadvantages, including formidable born-global or micro-multinational competitors from China, India, and Northeast Asia. On the other hand, wages are rising faster than productivity in East Asia thereby raising the unit cost of manufactures quite rapidly; intermediate-good intensive GVCs have proved footloose; and Africa's huge potential in mineral reserves (a third of the global total) and agriculture (half of the under-cultivated land) means that the prospects for rapid catchup are conditioned only on good policies (Dinh et al., 2012).

Table 4.3 provides a synoptic view of various perspectives on dynamic comparative advantage and industrial dynamics. Static comparative advantage reflects initial endowments of factor supplies, organizational capability, and technological capability. To avoid fossilization, the business plans of firms and the policies enacted in support of them must then aim to upgrade industrial structures by building on what has been in place already, and supplying appropriate public capital and services.

For Neoclassical economists, economic structure is endogenous to the regular interplay of the demand and supply sides of the market. So, the role of policy is to remove distortions rather than to guide functioning markets (Pack, 2000; Noland and Pack, 2003). The neoliberal or market-fundamentalist prescription for late industrializers is to opt for market-led growth with the state playing a secondary, supporting role (World Bank, 1993).

This approach favors borrowing universally relevant market institutions, dubbed institutional mono-cropping by Mkandawire (2012), which informed donor advice on policy reforms in the 1980s and 1990s. That structural-adjustment failed to boost growth or to prevent deindustrialization is often rationalized as a product of the incompleteness of the reforms rather than their inappropriateness.[1]

Structuralist approaches focus on building both market institutions and government institutions wherever they exist in incomplete or weak forms. According

TABLE 4.3 Competing perspectives on dynamic comparative advantage

Perspective	Economic structure	Government behavior	Market mechanism	Stance on industrial strategy and policy
1. Neoclassical	Market-determined	Exogenous	Exogenous	CA-conforming: • remove market distortions
2. Classical structuralist Reallocating-diversification [Lewis; Hirschman; Chenery; Kuznets]	Market-guided and policy-supported	[minimalist] Exogenous [activist]	Endogenous	CA-molding: • supply missing public services • promote winners • state disengages progressively
3. Neo-structuralist 1: Capability-identifying [Lin; Monga; Pack]	Market-guided	Exogenous [policy failure]	Exogenous [market failure]	CA-discovery: • growth facilitation • pragmatic emulation • Flying geese • Product life cycle
4. Neo-structuralist 2: Capability-building [Stiglitz; Rodrik; Lall; Chang; Wade; Gasherbrum; Hausmann; Sabel]	Market- and policy-guided	Endogenous [experimentalist: politics maters]	Endogenous [policy failure interacts with market failure]	CA-defying by need: • self-discovery • learning efficiency • risk-sharing • discipline: reciprocity, contests, market competition

Sources and notes: Culled from various sources discussed in the text.

CA = comparative advantage

to so-called old structural economics, structural differences reflect both politically rigged markets and underdeveloped markets.

The structuralist prescription tends to accentuate the consequences of market failure over those of government failure. It criticizes the Washington Consensus for its obliviousness to the peculiarities of very-late development and the very basis of state power in Africa.[2]

Neo-structuralist variants of this mode of thinking differ from their forbearers in their assumption that a functional market exists even in poor market economies. Neo-structuralists acknowledge the seriousness of market failure as well as government failure but assume that the latter (driven perhaps by a Gresham's Law of ideas plus interest group politics) is more pervasive and damaging (Lin, 2013). Neo-structuralist thinking redefines the role of the government more as a facilitator than as a leader in industrial upgrading.

We now turn to two vexed policy challenges. One deals with the issue of how to build industrial capability and the other with sectoral priority.

Industrial capability

The idea of melding pre-given resource endowments with cultivable knowledge about how best to use them to manage complexity is encapsulated by the supply-side notion of "productive capabilities." Global competitiveness in domestic-oriented "whole products" as well as in trade-oriented "parts or tasks" also requires attention to the demand side. GVCs meld the two sides well.

It would be useful to define terms at the outset. *Competency* is understood here as the ability to design, produce, and market progressively sophisticated intermediate goods and final goods (see Box 4.1). *Capability*, on the other hand, refers to a set of distinctive competencies that are rooted in firm-specific know-how (such as product and process technologies) and in specialized human assets.[3] These capabilities enable firms to gain positional advantages in local, regional, or global markets to maximize profits or to increase market share (Sutton, 2012).

The three dimensions of firm-specific strategic capability (productivity, quality, and variety) and industry-wide effects (spillovers, economies scale, and economies of scope) have refashioned inter-industry trade (endowment driven) or intra-industry trade (technology driven). Firm-level capabilities may then decline cluster-level, regional-level, or national-level capabilities that capture a mix of private and public investment. Industrial clusters generally share the common features of geographical proximity to exploit agglomeration economies, sectoral similarity to maximize knock-on effects or spillovers, or the complementarity of subcontracting among industrial enterprises (Schmitz and Nadvi, 1999; Rodriguez-Clare, 2007).

Industrial capability then is the set of skills, capital, management, and technology that a country's resident firms have mastered to be able to design, develop, produce, market, and service a broad array of manufacturing products. The strategic investments by firms and the public sector for capabilities-based competitiveness are also shaped by the level and quality of investments in infrastructure.

90 Theories of industrialization

BOX 4.1 PRODUCTIVE INDUSTRIAL CAPABILITIES

Capacity is about what one has done at a given point in time while capability is what one can do as necessary. At the microeconomic level, *capability* refers to the ability of a decision-making unit (such as a firm or a government agency) to utilize its resources (technology, know-how, working practices, and human assets that are specific to it) to gain positional advantages in an activity or industry by acquiring distinctive competencies whose totality defines capability in each activity.

These competencies generate a *competitive advantage* that may come in the form of advantages upstream in the value chain in terms of intermediate outputs (cost-reducing and productivity enhancing process innovation, quality- and variety-enhancing product innovation) or downstream in net value-creating final outputs (profitability and market share). Firm-specific strategic capability in three key areas (productivity, quality, and variety) and industry-wide effects (spillovers and economies scale) shape the scope and profitability of inter-industry trade (endowment driven) as well as intra-industry trade (technology driven).

Industrial capability then is the set of skills, capital, management, and technology needed to design, develop, produce, market, and service a variety of manufacturing products. The weighted average of these capabilities provides an index of the *comparative advantage* of an economy. The strategic investments by firms and the public sector for capabilities-based competence boost the global competitiveness of a country if they focus on support for R & D and physical infrastructure.

ICT technologies have made it economical to globally unbundle the design, sourcing, fabrication, and marketing of manufactures by facilitating the exploitation of scale economies and coordination economies between integrated headquarters economies and factory economies. This development has also made it inevitable that trade, investment, and intellectual property are deeply interlinked. Since the new international division of labor is built around intercountry and interfirm differences in capabilities, it is imperative for policymakers to understand the process of capability formation and exploitation (Baldwin, 2016; Nubler, 2014; Taglioni and Winkler, 2016).

Where whole-product manufacturing of final goods is profitable, industrial capability entails the building up of a national manufacturing base that is deep-veined and broad-based. The aim is to facilitate the replacement of competitive imports in a big-enough home market, and to serve as a platform for exports.

Where "parts manufacturing" is profitable, building industrial capability includes the cultivation of clusters of globally competitive component-supplying local firms that operate as part of global value/supply chains. Production fragmentation and geographic dispersion of manufacturing are fast becoming the new normal. Transnationals, rather than the old multinationals, in *headquarters economies* "lend" just-enough slices of technologies and know-how to component and task supplying micro-transnationals in *factory economies* (Baldwin, 2013, 2016; Taglioni and Winkler, 2016).

Conceptualizing capabilities broadly as a combination of nontradable social capital and firm-specific inputs, Hausmann and Hidalgo (2011) observe that development is a process of accumulating a large variety of capabilities and of expressing them in a wider network of domestic and export products at the microeconomic level. In this perspective, capability-intensive products are rare in the least developing economies precisely because this product space is too complex for them. This would explain why capability-rich countries tend to produce highly diverse products, including the least ubiquitous products that are not accessible to the less capable economies or firms.

Furthermore, the evidence for a high heterogeneity in the distribution of capabilities across countries points to the need for a threshold of capabilities to take full advantage of increasing returns in the product space. However, both capability and diversification are accumulable economic assets. GVCs, by enhancing the tradability of both, enhance the acquisition of new capabilities as well as new product or process innovations throughout a product's value chain. They may speed up the proverbial ascent on the **capability escalator** (Hausmann and Hidalgo, 2011; Hallward-Driemmeir and Nayyar, 2017).

The prospects for becoming a headquarter economy from the status of a follower goose are improved only if one can shorten the GVC by mastering the capabilities of designing, selling, and after-sale servicing. Furthermore, servicization of manufacturing matters greatly for such high-capability and high-connectivity industries as machinery, transport equipment, electronics, and pharmaceuticals.

Although the diffusion of knowledge is the key to productivity-driven growth, most firms in developing economies are unable to make maximal use of the substantial positive externality generated by frontier technologies of the developed countries due to their inability to innovate. Cirera and Maloney (2017), for example, offer three reasons for this presumed "innovation paradox" inadequate investment directed at innovation, the limited range of firm capabilities for managing profitable innovations, and the complementary public infrastructure and services needed to crowd-in private investment. Structural analyses that focus on existing comparative advantage have failed to take seriously a dynamic perspective that links the need for diversification and productive transformation with the need to build up firm and industry capabilities to expand the options for productive engagement with the global market. When they do, economists take two distinct perspectives on how capabilities

92 Theories of industrialization

determine growth and productive transformation which have yet to be coherently integrated (Nubler, 2014):

1   The structuralist perspective on this focuses on the patterns of transformation (diversification, product differentiation, and technological upgrading) and argues that capabilities determine the products and technologies that firms or whole economies can easily develop (Abramowitz, 1986; Hausmann and Klinger, 2007; Hausmann et al., 2007).
2   The process perspective focuses on the dynamics of transformation (pace and sustainability of structural change) and argues that capabilities determine the efficiency of firm performance in coordinating, investing, learning, innovating, and solving problems (Nelson, 2008; Lall, 1992; Sutton, 2012). Countries need to acquire new competencies so that firms can enjoy a greater number of decision options. A bigger strategic choice set would enable firms to identify new opportunities for organizational change, to invest and expand productive capacities in targeted new industries, and to manage rapid and sustained processes of structural and technological transformation.

We now dissect a bit the two dimensions of industrial capability-building by latecomers. One addresses knowledge-based asset accumulation to derive efficiency rents, and the other deals with organizational innovation to overcome ubiquitous market failures.

Knowledge-based capability

The knowledge-based theory, whose leading proponent is Alice Amsden (1989, 2001), is especially influential. It starts out by noting that late and very-late industrializers exhibit some distinctive characteristics. As Amsden (2001: 2) puts it, "Late industrialization was a case of *pure learning*, meaning a total initial dependence on other countries' commercialized technology to establish modern industries. This dependence lent catching up its distinctive forms." To compensate for their skill and technological deficits, laggards must devise various novel mechanisms such as smart subsidies, publicly funded skilling, diversified business groups, and reciprocity pacts between capital and the state.

For pioneers of a new technology, indivisibilities (high fixed cost and sunk cost) often lead to natural monopolies. They do this by creating (1) *economies of scale* – unit cost declines as size increases for a single good or for a composite good with constant factor proportion emanating either changes in factor intensity, or from changes in input price; (2) *economies of scope* – unit cost declines as the output mix varies; or (3) *increasing returns to scale* – keeping output mix and input mix *fixed*, raising the volume of production would increase output by more than the corresponding increase in inputs.

Furthermore, pre-1990 latecomers had to undertake a three-pronged lumpy investment in modern enterprise (Chandler, 1990). The prongs are: *optimal scale* of plants and up-to-date machinery – a large domestic market enhances firm size which is crucial for investment in skills; *managerial hierarchies* and technical skills – railroads and business groups facilitated technological transfers, modern management, and the emergence of salaried managers of predominantly family-owned firms; and *extensive distribution networks* that would integrate marketing, general trading companies, and financing of sales (especially since foreign capital tends to be risk averse).

Manufacturing capabilities reflect the skills, knowledge, and experience that enterprises need to operate imported technology efficiently. A remarkable feature of the East Asian experience is the presence of a "crowding-in effect" whereby greater public expenditure in education and training attracted private investment of an even greater magnitude. This compensated for limited on-the-job training opportunities provided by the fledgling private firms.

The question of who should have control of major industrial and financial firms, nationals or foreigners, was also a pivotal question in the third stage (1950–1990) of industrialization. Alice Amsden (2001: 286) notes: "The later a country industrializes in chronological history, the greater the probability that its major manufacturing firm will be foreign-owned." Amsden identified two alternative paths of late industrializing in the second half of the twentieth century: the *independent* path favored by nationalists, and the *integrationist* path favored by globalists. We will add a hybrid path to the mix.

Figure 4.1 provides a useful typology of the three canonical paths of late-industrialization. The leftmost arrow shows the FDI- and export-dependent industrialization path. It broadly captures the industrialization experiences of Mexico, Brazil, Argentina, Thailand, Malaysia, and perhaps Indonesia. This path produced resilient economies but with few national champions.

The other end of the spectrum is the *hyper-nationalist* industrialization path, depicted by the rightmost arrow. It was adopted by the socialist bloc as well as India, albeit in a milder version. This strategy produced world-class technological progress in selected industries benefiting from a lot of state support, but it was highly inefficient because of lackluster competition.

The third and the most successful strategy is a mongrel strategy that may be called the *nationalist-integrationist* industrialization strategy. This strategy synchronizes domestic capability with international opportunity (for technological transfer through debt financing and exports). South Korea and Turkey managed to produce national champions to successfully navigate the treacherous road of learning to compete internationally by using the domestic market as a springboard. Taiwan and Singapore produced formidable global subcontractors but few national champions.

For countries which chose the independent path under IR2, such as those in Northeast Asia, the focus was on dynamic comparative advantage (see Table 4.4).

94 Theories of industrialization

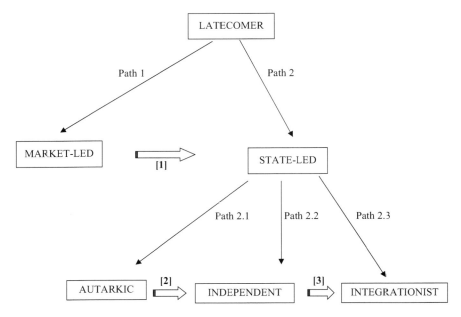

FIGURE 4.1 Pathways of latecomer industrialization

Sources and notes: Author.

Stylized models of industrialization
- Market-led (Hong Kong, Singapore, and Taiwan)
- Autarkic (socialist USSR and pre-1985 China)
- Independent (Japan, South Korea, and India)
- Integrationist (Brazil, Mexico, pre-1985 China, Thailand, and Malaysia)

Transitions (indicated by arrows)
1 Failed Market to Socialist and Quasi-socialist (USSR, China, Vietnam, E. Europe)
2 Failed Socialist (North Korea, Cuba) to global reintegration
3 Nationalist (Chile, South Korea, Russia, Turkey, India) to integrationist

This meant nurturing national project-execution capabilities. Firm composition (in terms of size and ownership) determined the strategic "buy" or "make" decision concerning technology-intensive products. Formerly colonial countries with egalitarian income distribution produced more and bigger national champions that have gone global – South Korea being the prime example in steel, shipbuilding, electronics, and automobiles.

On the other hand, for those that chose the integrationist path, the focus was on attracting FDI, accessing global markets, and mastering the production of goods requiring intermediate skills. This transmogrified later into tightly staged GVCs. Malaysia, Thailand, Brazil, Mexico, and Argentina did not produce as many successful national champions in manufacturing. The Latin American strategy is especially distinguishable by the paucity of technology leaders (save aircraft in Brazil).

Late and very-late industrialization **95**

TABLE 4.4 Notable attributes of leaders and followers in industrialization

Characteristics	Leader	Follower
Technology	Innovation	Assimilation
Locus of decision	Headquarters	Shop-floor
Strategic focus	R & D managers	Engineers
International competition	Intense	Unprecedented
Competitive advantage (firm)	Codification of technology	Licensing and FDI
	Deskilling of craftsman	Upskilling of labor
Comparative advantage	Frontier technologies	Mature technologies
Labor relations	Institutionalized	Repressive
State activism	Followership	Some leadership

Sources and notes: Author.
Synthesized from various sources discussed in the text, mainly Amsden (2001) and Baldwin (2016).

Diversified business groups

While latecomers can "buy" hardware and turnkey plants, taking full advantage of the potential of imported technology presupposes organizational capabilities for "efficient" learning. The latter, in turn, requires investment in skills (disembodied technology), research (adoption and adaptation – itself an innovative activity), managerial innovation aimed at economizing on scarce managerial talent, compensating for thin markets and inadequate infrastructure, and taking full advantage of global networks.

Corporate management and business organization have been revolutionized by radical changes in the technologies of transportation, infrastructure, and communications. During IR2, organizational change was driven by the railroads, the telephone and telegraph, and electricity. The old industrial firm that emerged was the integrated multidivisional firm which did much to solve coordination and monitoring problems. This firm was also based on a social contract among stakeholders (stockholders, labor, and local communities) concerning work rules and surplus sharing to maximize effort and ensure loyalty. Industrial enterprises diversified as needed to economize on scarce managerial talent.

Organizational flexibility to overcome structural constraints in the domestic economy is a form of technological innovation. Two novel forms of organizational innovation by latecomer firms are *group-wise diversification* by business groups in industrializing (as well as marketizing post-socialist) economies, and *network-wise trans-nationalization* by up-and-coming firms in industrialized economies.

Group-wise diversification can be traced to the modes of operation of family-owned conglomerates. Such diversification has two distinguishing features, the first of which is the presence of a cluster of independently registered firms that are controlled by family members or close friends. The second feature is engagement in a variety of, often unrelated, business ventures at home and later abroad.

96 Theories of industrialization

Such family-led groups gave rise to a form of conglomeration known as the diversified business group (DBG). The DBG is essentially a stable network of firms that satisfies three conditions: affiliates are legally independent entities (diversity of membership); affiliates are active in a variety of activities and markets (diversity of assets); and affiliates cede authority to a core manufacturer or a bank that is controlled by an *ultimate owner* (individual, family, or the state).

This cluster of closely held firms, displaying a high degree of coordination and market diversification, has become an important feature of many industries in emerging market economies and many post-socialist economies. The structures and tightness of control of business groups vary greatly. The most salient features of group alliances include varying mixes of director interlocks, cross-equity ownership and debt relationships, trade relationships and personnel exchanges, political ties with the State elites, and social ties among key private-sector players. DBGs control much of the modern economy across the middle-income sphere. Examples include Korea's *chaebol*, Japan's prewar *zaibatsu* and the postwar *keiretsu* to which they gave rise, China's *qiye jituan*, Russia's financial-industrial groups, India's business houses, and Latin America's *grupos economicos* (Abegaz, 2005).

Interestingly, the DBG is viewed widely as an *effective endogenous response* to market failure. The DBG can serve as an effective means of exploiting synergies arising from resource specificity and substituting for missing markets or poor contract enforcement. Long-term relationships in the form of a tight network of assemblers, input suppliers, credit providers, distributors, and investors create an internal market that is far superior to arms-length market contracting. Groups also have a dark side, most notably, rent creation and dissipation, and expropriation of minority investors.

Group-based diversification is, therefore, usefully understood as a response to pervasive market failure as firms search for the right balance between synergy and focus. As emerging economies improved their economic institutions, the market-substitute rationale of DBGs has been giving way to greater specialization in the most profitable areas of core competencies. As with all conglomerates, most DBGs continually balance savings on transaction costs with the organizational costs of coordination (Hoskisson et al., 2005; Abegaz, 2005; Khanna and Yafeh, 2007).

The sequential process of evolution of business organization during industrialization is depicted schematically in Figure 4.2. One interesting view is that in the course of industrial deepening, traditional family groups give rise to modern diversified groups which ultimately turned into publicly traded and centrally controlled multidivisional corporations and holding companies. The argument is that business groups tend to be rent-seeking "parasites" in the early and late stages of industrialization but they are overall "paragons" in the intermediate stage (Khanna and Yafeh, 2007).

The governance systems of trans-nationals are certainly changing fast due to the dynamics of economic globalization and the emergence of powerful international organizations. The perspective of *hierarchy* whereby the industrial firm's managerial concern is focused on decomposing tasks and assembling outputs (supply chains,

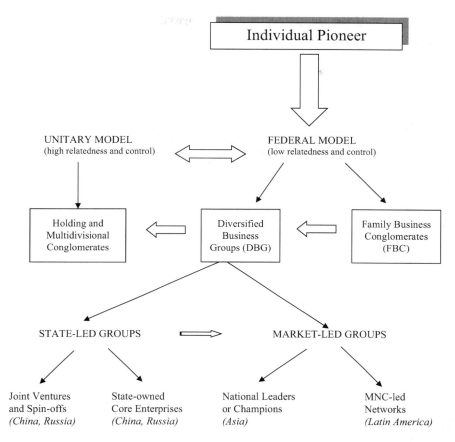

FIGURE 4.2 Pathways of business diversification and control for latecomers

Source: Author.

assembly lines, markets, consumer demand) is fading away. The new *network* perspective views the industrial firm as decentralized and open with managerial concern for constructing optimal search networks (local and global subcontractors, small-batch buyers, and the like) with a premium on collaboration and effective coordination. The trend is to move away from specific-purpose technologies and specific skills to general-purpose technologies and flexible skills.

DBGs and non-DBGs in emerging market economies have also given rise to a new breed of MNCs, dubbed "dragon multinationals" by John Matthews (2002). Compared with incumbents and newcomers in the triad (North America, Europe, and Japan), these firms are "born globals" like the baby gazelles of the Serengeti (since survival calls for avoiding old bureaucratic institutions from the outset), most lack product, process, or marketing innovation, and rely instead on low cost assembly or exclusively on subcontracting (network) opportunities offered by global value chains.

98 Theories of industrialization

They exploit their valuable assets in the form of experience in management as well as experience as parts suppliers and original equipment manufacturers. They do engage in industry-specific strategic innovations to help them "fit" into the existing global network economy, and they are coordinated globally as a part of a truly transnational operation.

One must, however, be very careful not to fall into the trap of "technological determinism," of believing in the easy conversion of a casually employed peasantry into a disciplined and organized industrial proletariat singing the company's anthem. The reality, economic history teaches us, is much more complex.[4]

Sectoral priority

At the core of the ongoing debates on the right industrialization strategy is the choice of sectoral priorities for the allocation of scarce resources. In the early phase of industrialization, the agricultural and industrial (mining and manufacturing) sectors are not only underdeveloped but also poorly "articulated" in the sense that the production and consumption linkages among them are fragile. We will indulge here in the seemingly nebulous thinking of a "development ladder" focused on sectors and subsectors – from agriculture-led to industry-led, and from simple manufactures to advanced manufactures.

The role of agriculture and mining in the industrialization process is multifaceted (Mellor, 1995; Diao et al., 2007). Its market contributions including foodstuffs, raw materials, investable surplus, markets for manufactures, and foreign exchange (earning saving). Inelasticity of agricultural supply (technological stagnation, poor infrastructure, institutions such as land tenure) must be lowered for this contribution to be adequate.

The demand and supply sides of industrial development may be depicted by an ideal-type typology of three sectoral priorities: agriculture-led industrialization (ALI), urban-led industrialization (ULI), or interlocked urban-rural industrialization (URI). Table 4.5 provides a profile of these strategic options on the demand, supply, and policy sides.

Agriculture-led industrialization (ALI)

The postwar debates on whether agriculture or industry is the engine of growth zeroed in on the issue of financing a robust industrialization drive. This, in turn, brought out the related matters of optimal sequencing sector-specific policies. The Lewis-Fei-Ranis view (Lewis, 1954; Fei and Ranis, 1961) was that agriculture served primarily as a supplier of cheap labor, food, and fiber. Hirschman (1958) favored industry for its strong backward and forward linkages, which he thought were rather lacking in agriculture. Later thinking (Adelman, 1984; Vogel, 1994; Torvik, 1997) underscores the role of agriculture as a source of demand for urban goods, as a supplier of labor and materials, and as a relaxer of the frequently binding foreign exchange constraint.

TABLE 4.5 Three stylized strategic sectoral foci for industrialization

Strategy/attributes	Demand for manufactures	Supply of manufactures	Major policy implications
Agriculture-led industrialization (ALI)	• Intra-rural – rising farm income and home market • Exports – labor or secondary demand	• Inputs: mobilization and reallocation of food, fiber, and labor • Integrated ISI	• Key public services • Farmland policy • Research and extension • Seeds and credit • Price and tax policies
Urban-led industrialization (ULI)	• Urban – rising income from services • Exports – dependent on market niche	• Medium- and large-scale industries • Ample skills • Global supply chains • Good infrastructure	• Key public services • Urban land policy • Special zones and parks • Long-term credit • Tax and trade policies
Balanced industrialization (URI)	• Urban • Rural • Exports	• Selectively diversified or specialized	• Focus on synergistic clusters and supply chains

Source and notes: Author.
ALI = agriculture-led industrialization
ULI = urban-led industrialization
URI = urban-rural industrialization (balanced)

Sector-wise thinking (de Janvry and Sadoulet, 2010) stresses the need for complementarity between agriculture and industry since agricultural development can contribute to the creation of comparative advantage in industry. This means agriculture-led industrialization can be two-pronged: via strong demand linkages that allow for a bigger home market for infant industries, and via strong supply linkages that lower domestic prices and raise foreign exchange.

The historic debate on the role of agriculture relative to industry provided the backdrop for modern development economics. It was sometimes cast in the context of trade policy as in the case of the corn-laws debate between Ricardo and Malthus on the role of grain imports in keeping the wages low and stable (Shapiro and Taylor, 1990). In other cases, it focused on intersectoral subsidies as in the case of the Soviet industrialization debates of the 1920s (Sah and Stiglitz, 1984; Dobb, 2014).

Rapid agricultural transformation requires the availability of high-return technologies (especially for rain-fed, smallholder farming) that farmers will adopt when economic incentives to do so are high. Thus, while the availability of appropriate technology, input, and extension packages may matter, these are not sufficient if economic returns cannot be sustained. In a landlocked economy, this requires sufficiently high urban demand and non-agricultural growth to maintain high farm-gate prices (de Janvry and Sadoulet, 2016).

100 Theories of industrialization

One may ask whether it is really in Africa's interest to prioritize its agricultural production in the hope of using it as a leading sector. The "agriculture-first" view presumes that most agricultural products are practically speaking nontradables. Raising agricultural productivity would translate into lower food prices, thereby increasing real incomes and demand for locally produced goods and services, and thus growth outside agriculture. The agriculture-first perspective has a sympathetic view of large-scale farming, which is generally assumed to enjoy strong intersectoral linkages as well as economies of scale in processing, marketing, and transport.

The available econometric evidence suggests that agriculture is significantly more effective than non-agriculture in reducing poverty for the ultra-poor. Historical evidence also shows that the rates of development of agriculture and non-agriculture generally move in tandem (World Bank, 2007). The slow growth in manufacturing and off-farm activities of African economies in the past three decades is not unrelated to the low income growth for some two-thirds of the population engaged in agriculture. The long-term projections of rising costs of energy and intermediate inputs, and a rapidly growing urban population all indicate rising real food costs unless investments are made to boost agricultural productivity.

Economies of scale in cash crop production, marketing, and processing are nonetheless important for the supply of food and fiber for agro-processing. Increasing agricultural productivity is critical to creating a home market to support industrial development provided complementary investments in rural roads, public services, tenure security, credits, and market town development are undertaken. Together, they facilitate a successful transition out of agriculture, not least by the poorer smallholders. Public investments in agricultural research, for example, generate median rates of return of 34% in Africa (World Bank, 2007).

ALI may be demand-driven (via rising rural incomes) or supply-driven (via lower prices of food and fiber) which give it two flavors: agriculture-demand led (ADLI) and agriculture-supply-led (ASLI). We now examine each briefly.

Adelman (1984) provides a definitive articulation of ADLI in making the case for viewing agriculture more as a source of strong demand linkages than as a mere object of surplus extraction. Using simulations based on a computable general equilibrium model of a small, low-income, open, and semi-industrial economy, she concludes that an ADLI strategy supports industrialization just as effectively as an export-led strategy. Moreover, ADLI does this with greater employment generation and, hence, less inequality. For this to occur, the productivity, especially of medium-scale farmers, must be boosted.

Along these lines, using a representative sample of countries at levels of development, Vogel (1994) estimates social-accounting matrix multipliers which show that agriculture does possess strong intermediate demand (production linkages) and final demand components (consumption linkages) to serve as a springboard for a sustained industrialization drive. However, these results are based on the existence of a high elasticity of supply of agricultural and industrial products. One implication is the import substitution of wage goods will have to be undertaken simultaneously with export promotion to sustain agricultural transformation.

A much-noted stylized fact about a mineral-poor African economy is that its growth is constrained by the scarcity of foreign exchange. To get at the role of agriculture from this vantage point, Torvik (1997) estimates a three-sector model (agriculture, exports, nontradables). He concludes that ASLI promotes industrial development by relaxing the foreign exchange constraint on the non-traded segment of the industrial sector and by inducing the depreciation of the real exchange rate as capital flows to agriculture and the export sector. This would be the case only if real wages are flexible, the supply of exports is infinitely elastic, and high commodity prices prevail in the world market.

Urban-led industrialization (ULI)

From the perspective of the widening of the market, as Adam Smith long noted, the magnitude and composition of industrial activity are strongly correlated with the size of the market which is highly concentrated in the urban and peri-urban economy. Aside from the Chinese commune's model of an agro-industrial complex, networks of small manufacturers located in towns and industrial districts have played a pivotal role in serving as the seedbeds of modern manufacturing.

Cities are widely and rightly viewed as geographic centers with the concentration of high skills, modern technology, and modern infrastructure (UNIDO, 2009; UNECA, 2017). There is, however, little work that compares the relative efficacy of ALI and ULI in various economic contexts and stages of development.

Neglect of off-farm as well as urban services as drivers of growth in the policy debate and research stems from the notion that services are merely inputs in goods production, and that they are characterized by low productivity. However, the mid-1990s saw two seemingly separate but related developments. Even though manufacturing continues to be a dominant driver of growth, recent developments suggest that we must include the modern service sector in the debate on the drivers of industrial growth (Glasmeier and Howland, 1993; Mishra et al., 2011).

The proponents of urban dynamism in the early stages of urbanization are much fewer and newer. Where agricultural productivity is low due to poor endowments or where institutions or policies limit technological progress in the sector, the initial impetus for industrial development can and must come from the modern urban economy. The role of urban areas as centers of technological dynamism and higher income means that they provide the requisite demand for agricultural output while supplying key inputs to commercialize agriculture (UNIDO, 2009). In reality, neither rural bias nor urban bias may work well since both sectors need to develop in tandem (Lipton, 1977; Henderson, 1997).

Balanced industrialization

A third alternative perspective, dubbed "agriculture-also" or balanced industrialization, advocates walking on two legs – one being rural, and the other urban. The World Bank's new agricultural assistance strategy (World Bank, 2007, 2010), for example,

102 *Theories of industrialization*

contains a mix of open-market approaches designed to strengthen agriculture via market linkages, dampened price volatility, and improved productivity.

In many ways, the choice between properly conceived ALI and ULI is a false one. A pro-poor development strategy must focus on the needs of the rural population but also mobilize its urban population to spearhead its industrialization drive. In fact, the development trajectory of successful developers in East Asia and India was one of brief rural-led development propelled by the green revolution, followed by a prolonged urban-led development propelled by manufacturing and services. Industrial takeoffs must recognize the dual role of rural productivity growth and expansion of the urban industrial and service sector.

Using a three-sector model (land-specific and labor-intensive agriculture, labor-intensive rural manufacturing, and capital-intensive urban manufacturing) and assuming full intersectoral mobility of labor and capital, Nguyen (2000) shows that a labor-surplus economy can kick-start a successful industrialization drive provided there is an initial technological stimulus for sustained growth of agricultural productivity. A land-augmenting technological progress is shown to raise land values, the marginal productivity of farm workers, and farm employment all of which will boost the demand for manufactures. Higher rural incomes then boost demand for manufactures along with increased capital accumulation. With positive supply responses from agricultural and non-agricultural sectors, the rightward shifts in output demand and supply ensure price stability and rising labor demand (and eventually wages). The resultant resource transfer and demand effects create a virtuous circle of balanced industrial development.

If the two sectors are so intertwined, then two strategic questions arise. Is the development of complementary agricultural and industrial activities sequential or simultaneous? And what is the nature of the complementarities?

In all successful cases, industrialization presupposes tight inter-linkages between the agricultural sector and the emerging industrial sector at the level of the household (diversification of production) or between specialized farmers and specialized manufacturers (Francks, 2005). The input linkages on the supply side and product linkages on the demand side must develop in tandem in order for a well-balanced industrial economy to emerge.

Economic theory suggests a causal mechanism that goes something like this: investment in research, roads and ICT, model factories and farms, vocational training, market infrastructure, and credit all lead to higher incomes for farmers and non-farm producers. Given the underutilization of labor and land in the early stages of development, higher income may be generated by higher employment rather than higher wages to keep the intersectoral terms of trade relatively stable. With coordinated and buoyant demand and supply sides in both the rural and urban economies, a sustained increase in the volume and composition of industrial output will be the long-term outcome.

It turns out that this scenario is most applicable to countries with a threshold of industrial capacity and an agricultural sector where farm productivity and farm-gate prices are both high. Where insufficient urban demand leads to price collapses following good harvests, farmers react by under-producing in the next production cycle. Where the reverse is the case, the terms of trade disfavor the urban user, which reduces the demand for farm products. One must walk on two legs.

Implications for African industrialization

A common sequencing strategy for most of the high performers was to start with labor-intensive exports and to gradually move up to more sophisticated products. This "ladder" approach has been considered for many very-latecomers like China, Bangladesh, Indonesia, and India, which enjoy comparative advantages in both low-tech and mid-tech products. Over two-thirds of global trade in manufactures is today accounted for by mid- and high-technology manufactures. As the physical disintegration of production continues apace by the decoupling of producer and consumer in space and by decoupling the nodes of manufacturing, Africa, with its poor infrastructure, a flimsy enabling environment (clean government, enforcement of rights, good regulations, and consensus with private sector), and slowly accumulating human capital will surely face an uphill struggle to industrialize.

Dani Rodrik (2014), skeptical that Africa can replicate East Asia's export-led industrialization, advises African policymakers to also seek other novel engines of growth miracles such agriculture-led or services-led growth. However, the continent faces monumental hurdles including those related to state capability, an enfeebled private sector, and formidable international competitors.

Manufacturing has increasingly become technology and service intensive. Light manufacturing, however, requires less capital and fewer technical and managerial skills to absorb a good share of the 17 million young Africans who are joining the labor force annually. In light manufacturing, a prerequisite for exporting today is having the capability to fulfill large orders competitively (in terms of price and quality) and quickly. Both require tapping into scale economies associated with labor-intensive, assembly-line production chains – that is, large firm operations. By definition, credit- and skill-constrained smaller firms cannot do this. The striking paucity of medium and large firms explains why Sub-Saharan Africa's light manufacturing has had a hard time charting an export-led growth trajectory (Dinh et al., 2012; Shiferaw, 2007).

In this regard, McMillan and Harttgen (2014) show that a substantive decline of the agricultural labor force has been accompanied by a systematic increase in labor productivity in the recipient industrial and service sectors. These declines are, however, more rapid in countries with good governance and with healthy manufacturing sectors. Where this condition is lacking, premature deindustrialization deprives these economies of opportunities for well-paying factory jobs (McMillan et al., 2014).

An alternative strategy is to accentuate the existing extraction-based development strategy of mobilizing resource rents to diversify the economy. This, of course, carries the well-known vulnerabilities to the volatility of the terms of trade and unproductive rent seeking by local elites and their global allies.

104 Theories of industrialization

An agriculture-led development might be feasible for some if it focuses on boosting smallholder productivity and commercializing agriculture where sensible. The challenge here is that inadequate research on dry lands and tropical climates coupled with the predominance of customary and smallholder landholding have constrained a suitably green revolution in much of Africa.

Global industrial competitiveness for a latecomer is attained by low enough unit costs[5] (UNIDO, 2013; Monga, 2013). These can be achieved either through a low-wage plus low-productivity strategy (which leads only to self-limiting growth) or through the harder but more rewarding high road of competing based on high productivity and high wages. Improving the quality of infrastructure, sensible government regulation and taxation, and trade logistics can also reduce unit costs.

The cost of addressing Africa's infrastructure deficit (especially in the power and road sectors) is estimated by the World Bank at US$75 billion per year in building, operation, and maintenance – thereby leaving a funding gap of US$35 billion per year (Foster, 2008). This and the related challenges facing Africa are summed up by UNIDO (2009: 91) in stark terms: "Weak infrastructure, lack of productive capacities and the inability to meet product specifications and increasingly stringent requirements in terms of quality, safety, health and the environment play strongly against their successful integration into global markets. They lack the capacity to produce goods that can compete in terms of quantity, quality, timely delivery and price in export markets." UNECA (2017) also makes the case for integrating national economic planning with urban and regional planning with a multifaceted industrialization in mind.[6]

As we will argue later in the book, the inescapable conclusion is that a successful African industrialization drive must be premised on tight inter-linkages between the commercializing agricultural sector and the emerging industrial sector at the level of the farm household as well as the firm – especially between commercial farmers and manufacturers. The dense production networks and consumption linkages must develop in tandem for a well-balanced industrial economy to emerge.

Notes

1 Collier and Gunning (1999: 276–277), for example, rationalized it in a rather voluntarist way: "Africa has suffered a growth failure, but this has not been due to fixed effects. It has been determined by policy, which has changed considerably over the past forty years." It is not clear here whether policy is conceptualized as one driven by the vested interests of entrenched elites (structural) or as a product of ignorance (thereby amenable to good advice).

2 State leadership is often decisive in supplying missing ingredients – at least in the initial stages of industrialization. As Lall (2004: 1–2) characterizes them, "The *neoliberal* approach is that the best strategy for all countries and in all situations is to liberalize – and not do much else. Integration into the international economy, with resource allocation driven by free markets, will let them realize their 'natural' comparative advantage. . . . The *structuralist* view puts less faith in free markets as the driver of dynamic competitiveness and more in the ability of Governments to mount interventions effectively. . . . Accepting the mistakes of the past industrial strategies and the need for greater openness, it argues that greater reliance on markets does not preempt a proactive role for the government. Markets are powerful forces but they are not perfect."

Late and very-late industrialization **105**

3 Capability and capacity are also two distinct but related concepts. Capability is all about what can be accomplished, while the latter is about what is in place at a given point. It is essentially the sum of core competencies of firms (or collectively, countries) reflecting the level of productivity, skill, capital, and entrepreneurship. Entrepreneurship is often the scarcest factor whether the entrepreneur is an owner-capitalist, a commercial state enterprise, or a development-friendly political class. Broadly construed, capability is then about norms and institutions that foster openness to new ideas and to pragmatic experimentation. While capability can be nurtured over time, it cannot be purchased. Capacity, on the other hand, is the knowledge and ability that is already in place. Capacity can be purchased and expanded more easily (such as imported turnkey factories) even when capability is limited to fully to internalize the tacit knowledge is embedded in imported equipment (UNIDO, 2005, 2009).

4 In India, for example, urban manufacturers relied on a rural migrant labor force which kept one foot in the mills and the other in the village in order to diversify risk (Chandavarkar, 1994). By the same token, the merchant class of importers of manufactures and exporters of raw materials did not transform themselves into industrialists because they had the capital but not the managerial aptitude for manufacturing. They prudently saw keeping one leg in merchanting and the other in agro-processing as an effective way of mitigating the risk of wildly fluctuating commodity (cotton) prices in the world market. The accidental encounter with fabricating unsellable cotton into textiles opened their eyes to the relative ease and the rewards of entering manufacturing.

5 Monga (2013) rightly notes that competitiveness in attracting jobs which are being released from the emerging industrial economies would depend on *unit cost*. Unit cost, which includes total worker compensation, transaction costs, worker productivity, and exchange rate, is more than just *unit labor cost* (ULC). $UC = [(w+x)/y](e'/e)$ where $w =$ real wage rate per worker, $x =$ real non-wage costs per worker, $y =$ labor productivity, $e' =$ PPP exchange rate, and $e =$ market exchange rate. This means, a purely low-wage-based competitive strategy for Africa is both self-defeating in the long-run (since it perpetuates low wages in the absence of rising productivity) and incomplete (since it ignores cost disadvantages emanating from low-quality infrastructure and poor trade logistics).

6 UNECA (2017: 197) puts the challenges facing African cities this way:

> Africa is the fastest urbanizing region after Asia. . . . But many African cities have excessive primacy . . . big cities face diseconomies of scale and secondary cities are too small or poorly serviced to offer competitive spatial advantages to business and industrial firms.

References

Abegaz, B. (2005). The Diversified Business Group as an Innovative Organizational Model for Large State-Enterprise Reform in China and Vietnam. *International Journal of Entrepreneurship and Innovation Management*, 5(5–6), pp. 379–399.

Abramowitz, M. (1986). Catching Up, Forging Ahead, and Falling Behind. *Journal of Economic History*, 46(2), pp. 385–406.

Adelman, I. (1984). Beyond Export-led Growth. *World Development*, 9, pp. 937–949.

Ades, A., and R. di Tella. (1997). National Champions and Corruption: Some Unpleasant Interventionist Arithmetic. *Economic Journal*, 107(443), pp. 1023–1042.

Amsden, A. (1989). *Asia's Next Giant: South Korea and Late Industrialization*. Oxford: Oxford University Press.

Amsden, A. (2001). *The Rise of 'The Rest': Challenges to the West From Late Industrializing Economies*. New York: Oxford University Press.

Baldwin, R. (2013). Trade and Industrialization After Globalization's Second Unbundling: How Building and Joining a Supply Chain Are Different and Why It Matters. In:

R. Feenstra and A. Taylor, eds., *Globalization in an Age of Crisis: Multilateral Economic Cooperation in the Twenty-First Century*. Chicago: University of Chicago Press.

Baldwin, R. (2016). *The Great Convergence: Information Technology and the New Globalization*. Cambridge: Belknap-Harvard Press.

Chandavarkar, R. (1994). *The Origins of Industrial Capitalism in India. Business Strategies and the Working Classes, in Bombay 1900–1940*. Cambridge: Cambridge University Press.

Chandler, A. (1990). *Scale and Scope: The Dynamics of Industrial Capitalism*. Cambridge: Harvard University Press.

Chang, H.J. (2002). *Kicking Away the Ladder: Development Strategy in Historical Perspective*. London: Anthem Press.

Cirera, X. and W. Maloney (2017). *The Innovation Paradox: Developing-Country Capabilities and the Unrealized Promise of Technological Catch-up*. Washington, DC: World Bank Group.

Collier, P., and J.W. Gunning. (1999). Explaining African Economic Performance. *Journal of Economic Literature*, 37(1), pp. 64–111.

de Janvry, A., and E. Sadoulet. (2010). Agriculture for Development in Africa: Business-as-Usual or New Departures? *Journal of African Economies*, 19(AERC Supplement 2), pp. ii7–ii39.

de Janvry, A., and E. Sadoulet. (2016). *Development Economics*. New York: Routledge.

Diao, X., et al. (2007). *The Role of Agriculture in Development: Implications for Sub-Saharan Africa IFPRI Research Report 153*. Washington, DC: International Food Policy Research Institute.

Dinh, H., et al. (2012). *Light Manufacturing in Africa: Targeted Policies to Enhance Private Investment and Create Jobs*. Washington, DC: World Bank.

Dobb, M. (2014). *Russian Economic Development Since the Revolution*. New York: Routledge.

Fei, J., and G. Ranis. (1961). A Theory of Economic Development. *American Economic Review*, 51(4), pp. 533–565.

Foster, V. (2008). *Overhauling the Engine of Growth: Infrastructure in Africa*. Washington, DC: World Bank.

Francks, P. (2005). Multiple Choices: Rural Household Diversification and Japan's Path to Industrialization. *Journal of Agrarian Change*, 5(4), pp. 451–475.

Gerschenkron, A. (1962). *Economic Backwardness in Historical Perspective*. Cambridge, MA: Belknap Press of Harvard University Press.

Glasmeier, A., and M. Howland. (1993). Service-Led Rural Development: Definitions, Theories, and Empirical Evidence. *International Regional Science Review*, 16(1–2), pp. 197–299.

Hallward-Driemmeir, M. and G. Nayyar (2017). *Trouble in the Making? The Future of Manufacturing-Led Development*. Washington, DC: World Bank Group.

Hausmann, R. and C. Hidalgo (2011). The Network Structure of Economic Output. *Journal of Economic Growth*, 16(4), pp. 309–342.

Hausmann, R., J. Hwang, and D. Rodrik. (2007). What You Export Matters. *Journal of Economics Growth*, 12, pp. 1–25.

Hausmann, R. and B. Klinger. (2007). The Structure of the Product Space and the Evolution of Comparative Advantage, CID *Working Paper No. 146*. Cambridge, MA: Kennedy School, Harvard.

Henderson, J. (1997). Externalities and Industrial Development. *Journal of Urban Economics*, 42(3), pp. 449–470.

Hirschman, A.O. (1958). *The Strategy of Economic Development*. New Haven, CT: Yale University Press.

Hoskisson, R., R. Johnson, L. Tihanyi, and R. White. (2005). Diversified Business Groups and Corporate Refocusing in Emerging Economies. *Journal of Management*, 31(6), pp. 941–965.

Khanna, T., and Y. Yafeh. (2007). Business Groups in Emerging Markets: Paragons or Parasites? *Journal of Economic Literature*, 45(2), pp. 331–372.

Lall, S. (1992). Technological Capabilities and Industrialization. *World Development*, 20(2), pp. 165–186.

Lall, S. (2004). Selective Industrial and Trade Policies in Developing Countries: Theoretical and Empirical Issues. In: C. Soludo, O. Ogbu and H. Chang, eds., *The Politics of Trade and Industrial Policy in Africa*. Trenton: Africa World Press, Inc.

Lewis, W.A. (1954). Economic Development With Unlimited Supplies of Labour. *The Manchester School*, 22(2), pp. 139–191.

Lin, J.Y. (2013). From Flying Geese to Leading Dragons: New Opportunities and Strategies for Structural Transformation in Developing Countries. In: J. Stiglitz, J.Y. Lin, and E. Patel, eds., *The Industrial Policy Revolution II: Africa in the 21st Century*. New York: Palgrave Macmillan, pp. 50–72.

Lipton, M. (1977). *Why Poor People Stay Poor: Urban Bias in World Development*. Aldershot: Avebury.

Matthews, J. (2002). *Dragon Multinational: A New Model of Global Growth*. New York: Oxford University Press.

McKinsey Global Institute. (2012). *Manufacturing the Future: The Next Era of Global Growth and Innovation*. New York: McKinsey & Company.

McMillan, M., and K. Harttgen. (2014). What Is Driving the 'African Growth Miracle'? *NBER Working Paper No. 20077*. Cambridge, MA: NBER.

McMillan, M., et al. (2014). Globalization, Structural Change, and Productivity Growth. *World Development*, 63, pp. 11–32.

Meier, G., and W. Steel, eds. (1989). *Industrial Adjustment in Sub-Saharan Africa*. Washington, DC: World Bank.

Mellor, J.W. (1995). *Agriculture on the Road to Industrialization*. Baltimore: Johns Hopkins University Press.

Mishra, S., et al. (2011). *Sophistication in Service Exports and Economic Growth*. [online] Washington, DC: World Bank. Available at: https://pdfs.semanticscholar.org/4fc9/acfc1054447ffbd83dd44a527be6c0fde199.pdf.

Mkandawire, T. (2012). Institutional Monocropping and Monotasking. In: A. Noman, K. Botchwey, H. Stein, and J. Stiglitz, eds., *Good Growth and Governance in Africa*. Oxford: Oxford University Press, pp. 80–113.

Monga, C. (2013). Winning the Jackpot: Jobs Dividends in a Multipolar World. In: J. Stiglitz, J.Y. Lin, and E. Patel, eds., *The Industrial Policy Revolution II: Africa in the 21st Century*. New York: Palgrave Macmillan, pp. 135–172.

Morris, C., and I. Adelman. (1988). *Comparative Patterns of Economic Development, 1850–1914*. Baltimore: The John-Hopkins University Press.

Nelson, R. (2008). Economic Development From the Perspective of Evolutionary Economic Theory. *Oxford Development Studies*, 36(1), pp. 9–23.

Nguyen, D. (2000). The Plausibility of Agriculture-led Development. *Review of Development Economics*, 4(2), pp. 204–218.

Noland, M., and H. Pack. (2003). *Industrial Policy in an Era of Globalization: Lessons From Asia*. Washington, DC: Institute for International Economics.

Nubler, I. (2014). A Theory of Capabilities for Productive Transformation: Learning to Catch Up. In: J. Salazar-Xirinachs, I. Nübler, and R. Kozul-Wrigh, eds., *Transforming Economies: Making Industrial Policy Work for Growth, Jobs and Development*. Geneva: International Labour Organisation (ILO), pp. 113–149.

Pack, H. (2000). Industrial Policy: Growth Elixir or Poison? *World Bank Research Observer*, 15(1), pp. 47–67.

Rodriguez-Clare, A. (2007). Clusters and Comparative Advantage: Implications for Industrial Policy. *Journal of Development Economics*, 82, pp. 43–57.

108 Theories of industrialization

Rodrik, D. (2014). An African Growth Miracle? *NBER Working Paper No. 20188.* Cambridge, MA: NBER.

Sah, R., and J. Stiglitz. (1984). The Economics of Price Scissors. *American Economic Review,* 74, pp. 125–128.

Schmitz, H., and K. Nadvi. (1999). Clustering and Industrialization: Introduction. *World Development,* 27(9), pp. 1503–1514.

Shapiro, H. and L. Taylor. (1990). The State and Industrial Strategy. *World Development,* 18(6), pp. 861–878.

Shiferaw, A. (2007). Firm Heterogeneity and Market Selection in Sub-Saharan Africa: Does It Spur Industrial Progress. *Economic Development and Cultural Change,* 55(2), pp. 393–423.

Sutcliffe, R. (1984). Industry and Underdevelopment Reconsidered. *Journal of Development Studies,* 21(1), pp. 121–133.

Sutton, J. (2012). *Competing in Capabilities: The Globalization Process.* Oxford: Oxford University Press.

Taglioni, D., and D. Winkler. (2016). *Making Global Value Chains Work for Development.* Washington, DC: World Bank Group.

Torvik, R. (1997). Agricultural Supply-led Industrialization: A Macro Model With Sub-Saharan African Characteristics. *Structural Change and Economic Dynamics,* 8, pp. 351–370.

United Nations Economic Commission for Africa (UNECA). (2017). *Economic Report on Africa 2017.* Addis Ababa: UNECA.

United Nations Industrial Development Organization (UNIDO). (2005). *Industrial Development Report 2005: Capability Building for Catching-up.* Oxford: Oxford University Press.

United Nations Industrial Development Organization (UNIDO). (2009). *Industrial Development Report 2009: Breaking in and Moving UP – New Industrial Challenges for the Bottom Billion and the Middle-Income Countries.* Oxford: Oxford University Press.

United Nations Industrial Development Organization (UNIDO). (2013). *Industrial Development Report 2013: Sustaining Employment Growth – The Role of Manufacturing and Structural Change.* Oxford: Oxford University Press.

United Nations Industrial Development Organization (UNIDO). (2015). *Industrial Development Report 2016: The Role of Technology and Innovation in Inclusive and Sustainable Industrial Development.* Geneva: UNIDO.

Vogel, S. (1994). Structural Changes in Agriculture: Production Linkages and Agricultural Demand-led Industrialization. *Oxford Economic Papers,* 46(1), pp. 136–156.

Wade, R. (2003). *Governing the Market: Economic Theory and the Role of Government in East Asian Industrialization.* Princeton: Princeton University Press.

Whitfield, L., et al. (2015). *The Politics of African Industrial Policy: A Comparative Perspective.* New York: Cambridge University Press

Williamson, J. (2011). *Trade and Poverty: When the Third World Fell Behind.* Cambridge: MIT Press.

World Bank. (1993). *The East Asian Miracle: Economic Growth and Public Policy.* Washington, DC: World Bank.

World Bank. (1997). *World Development Report 1997: The State in a Changing World.* New York: Oxford University Press.

World Bank. (2000). *Can Africa Claim the 21st Century?* Washington, DC: World Bank.

World Bank. (2007). *World Development Report 2008: Agriculture for Development.* New York: Oxford University Press.

World Bank. (2010). *Industrial Clusters and Micro and Small Enterprises in Africa: From Survival to Growth.* Washington, DC: World Bank.

PART III

Waves of globalization and industrialization

5

PRODUCTION AND TRADE UNDER THE FIRST UNBUNDLING

Building on our overview of late industrialization, this chapter explores in some detail the dynamics of domestic manufacturing diversification for "whole products." Using a framework that accommodates various pathways and sequences of production and trade, we examine the complementarities between market-led and policy-led industrial deepening for very-latecomers such as Africa.

Industrial densification and diversification

Richard Baldwin, in a series of papers and now in a magnificently written book (Baldwin, 2016), has proposed a provocative three-cascading-constraints view of the latest phase of globalization. His overarching reading of the historical trend is encapsulated by the observation (Baldwin, 2016: 301):

> Until the late twentieth century, the main driver [of globalization] was a massive cut in the cost of moving goods, which was ultimately triggered by the steam revolution. The main driver switched to phenomenal drops in the cost of moving ideas when the ICT revolution came along. In the future, the main driver may be transformative reductions in the cost of telepresence and telerobotics triggered by the virtual presence revolution.

He argues that the successive fall of three "separation costs" (the mobility of goods, technology, and people) has transformed the geography of production between the industrialized North and the rapidly industrializing sub-regions of the global South. He conceptualizes the dramatic rise in the tradability of previously non-traded goods and services as the three "unbundlings."

The *first unbundling* entailed the decoupling of the country of production of "whole" manufactures from the countries of consumption. This unprecedented

112 Globalization and industrialization

mobility of goods (relative to that of technology or people) was facilitated by a significant fall in transportation costs and the enforcement of a liberal trade regime by the big powers. This mode favored the North (capitalists as well as workers) with its enormous lead in agglomeration economies as well as in the endowments of skill and capital. We will examine this regime in detail in this chapter.

The *second unbundling*, which will be examined in the next chapter, entailed a high mobility of technology, the fractionalization of production of manufactures into components, and the dispersion of the production of whole products across myriad borders. The decoupling of capital from knowledge and the decoupling of the country of production of components (parts) from the country of design or assembly was enabled especially by the ICT revolution. The new mode of competitive advantage for transnationals is driven by differences in firm-specific productive capabilities rather than in pre-given national endowments. It is scale-sensitive assets (such as technology, management, and entrepreneurship), rather than static factor endowments, which have defined the shifting equilibria between the forces of dispersion and agglomeration.

The *third unbundling*, barely perceptible now, entails high international mobility of people (as face-to-face costs decline sufficiently) and business services (as virtual-migration costs decline sufficiently). These currently binding constraints are technological as well as political. The intensification of the tradability of nearly all economic activities threatens to fulfill the Law of One Price by leveling wages and prices across countries. The principle of 'made for us and made with us' will then prevail.

Industrialization, as noted repeatedly, entails significant interlocked changes in the composition of domestic production. More specifically, one discerns distinct phases of evolution between the initiation of industrial development and its maturity (see, for example, the formulation by Ohno and Ohno, 2010). Furthermore, these three stages of production sophistication entail two risk-prone transitions. The first follows the exhaustion of low-tech activities. Countries that successfully effect this transition will face the risk of prolonged stagnation (the so-called **middle-income trap**). They inevitably confront other constraints – competition from low-wage entrants coupled with an inability to boost productivity by assimilating advanced technologies.

Furthermore, comparative advantage may be a given in the short run (which is why it should be affirmed) but it certainly is not in the long run (which is why it should be defied as appropriate). Reshaping comparative advantage is possible and desirable but rather difficult in a world of great uncertainty and unproductive rent seeking. One must then look for high learning opportunities and high demand elasticities while discouraging rent seeking that is unrelated to learning to build new competencies.

If the three formal institutional legs (market, hierarchy, and state) are all weak, as in the cause of much of Africa, the right fix might be for each institution to focus on its comparative advantage in a framework of a mutually supporting (as well as mutually restraining) partnership. However, this dilemma is often couched in terms of exclusionary competition (rather than emulation) between private and public institutions.

Production promotion and import substitution

One paramount concern is whether there is a natural sequence of deepening of industrial production and trade in the course of industrial development. The historical evidence suggests that, outside of export processing zones, production capacity must often be in place to serve the home market before penetrating export markets for manufactures. This, in turn, boosts the exploitation of potential scale and agglomeration economies as well as diversification into more technologically demanding products.

As the experiences of Singapore and Mauritius amply illustrate, even small economies can pursue a viable import substitution (IS) strategy, if only for a brief period, because of their limited domestic markets. For large countries, the scope is wider, but they must still synchronize capability with opportunity in a timely manner. The built-up capability under a hyper-IS regime has undergirded spurts of industrial growth when liberalization is belatedly undertaken, as demonstrated spectacularly by China after 1985.

This, of course, raises the question of which comes first – domestic capability or trade opportunity. The default answer has been that a springboard of built-up capability, with a long gestation lag, is necessary but not sufficient for global competitiveness. Industrial deepening and diversification do take place through a chain of IS and export substitution (ES) phases.[1]

Import substitution, the idea of replacing actual or potential imports by home production, is a deceptively simple concept. IS decisions are driven by many considerations. One is the make-or-buy decisions of firms. Another is the decision by consumers to purchase homemade goods or imports. Yet a third factor is the assessment of policymakers to support certain domestic industries with due regard for positive externalities and spillovers or just for symbolic nationalism. Import substitution, market-induced or policy-induced, is the natural way to initiate industrial development.

Success in import-substituting industrial development is predicated on a number factors, including the degree of income inequality, the size and capability of the industrial class, the stock of human capital of natives and émigrés, the availability of venture capital and long-term finance, the size of the domestic market for noncompetitive industrial imports, and the scope for domestic production linkages and externalities.

The growth-promoting effect of openness has been predicated on the existence of a threshold of industrial capacity to serve as a springboard. This is why mere openness has shown limited payoffs in many, if not most, African economies since industrial capability even in the face of market-access concessions from the North is so limited. Only a well-prepared dry prairie can benefit greatly from drenching rains of full engagement with globalization.

IS can be conceptualized in terms of several dimensions: stages, objectives, time horizon, efficacy, policy stance, or market focus. Consider, for example, the following variants of IS.

One variant is *import reproduction* or the replacement of previously imported manufactures by domestic products with identical characteristics and quality. This reverse engineering of foreign products with little or no adaptation tends to be a feature of turnkey factories or export enclaves. A forward-looking version of IS in this sense is one that preemptively replaces next-generation importable manufactures.

Another conceptualization is *import repression*, which entails the reduction or elimination of certain imported manufactures without a concerted effort to replace them with domestic production. This may be the case either because the goods are considered harmful or luxuries in the face of a severe foreign exchange constraint. Either way, import repression is bound to induce the production of distant substitutes of the repressed imports or importables.

These nuanced notions suggest that it is simplistic to think of the industrial sector, especially the manufacturing sector, as homogenous in terms of demand and technology (UNIDO, 2009, 2015). One can, for example, usefully disaggregate the various branches of manufacturing into distinct sub-groups based on factor intensity or technological sophistication. This is shown in Tables 5.1 and 5.2: IS1 or low technology (ISIC 311–342, 353–354, 361–381), IS2 or medium technology (ISIC 351–352, 355–356, 384, 390), and IS3 or high technology (ISIC 382–385). Latecomers generally begin the process by mastering the "easy" IS or light manufacturing and progressively moving up the ladder of sophistication to traverse all three stages.

IS1, the starting point, involves the development of *low-technology* manufacturing which is labor-intensive, primary-processing or artisanal – mostly textiles and garments under sizeable tariff protection. IS1 may be prone to transitional inefficiencies. The inefficiencies are the inevitable result of inexperienced management and labor, low levels of technological capability, scale diseconomies, distorted financial markets, and corrupt governments. Learning by doing, which takes time, generally overcomes these transitional inefficiencies, but as Amsden (2001) rightly notes, the more backward the learner, the more difficult is effective technological transfer.

IS2 is associated with the development of *mid-technology* industries which rely on imported technology (machinery) under the leadership of pioneering firms. These include light industries such as food processing and beverages, capital-intensive industries such as cement, paper, chemicals, iron, and steel, and semi-skilled activities such as non-metallic products and metal products.

Entry into IS3 presupposes the mastery of *high-technology* activities. Typical industries include pharmaceuticals, industrial chemicals, machinery, advanced automotive equipment, and scientific instruments. A substantial investment is needed here in modern infrastructure as well as vocational and tertiary education. Strategies for speedy technological transfer need to be executed through a combination of franchises, licenses, FDI, management contracts, and reverse engineering.

The impetus for IS may come from one of two economic forces, and usually from both. The first, *market-induced* IS, arises from the profitability of a large enough domestic market, or reduced access to imported manufactures emanating from wars

TABLE 5.1 A stylized demography of manufacturing industries

Attributes	Early industries	Middle industries	Late industries
ISIC3	331, 312, 331, 332, 341, 353, 354	342, 351, 352, 356, 37, 382 355, 361, 362, 369, 381, 390	352, 382, 383, 384, 385
Inputs:			
Supply	Resources and labor	Labor and capital	Capital and skills
Cost	Low	Moderate	High
Production:			
Economy-wide	Agriculture	Industry/Services	Services/Industry
Industry	Construction/Mining	Manufacturing	Manuf./Utilities
Manufacturing	Light/Consumer	Heavy/Intermediate	Capital/Durables
Size dist. firms	Triangular	Bimodal	Bimodal
Geog. distribution	Dispersed	Semi-dispersed	Clustered (urban)
Trade:			
Exports	RL-intensive	RK-intensive	KS-intensive
Imports	C- and K-goods	K goods	K goods
Both	Inter-industry	Inter-industry	Intra-industry
Technology:			
Product	Standardized	Old and redesigned	Differentiated
Process	Mature: imitation	Mature: redesign	Innovation
Economies of scale	Low	Bimodal	High
Externalities	Low	Moderate	High
Productivity	Low	Moderate	High
Unit labor cost	High	Moderate	Low
Capital flows	FD/ODA Debt	FDI Debt	FDI Portfolio

Sources and notes: Adapted from Findlay and O'Rourke (2009: Chapter 6); Amsden (2001).
1. IS Type 1: Upstream (finished) and then move downstream (semi-finished and intermediate).
2. IS Type 2: Downstream (intermediate) and then move upstream (finished goods).
ISIC = international system of industrial classification
FDI = foreign direct investment (inward and outward); KS = capital and skill
RL = resource and labor; C = consumer
RK = resource and capital; ODA = official development assistance

or market collapses (as in the inter-war decades of de-globalization). Although supply-side factors may matter (as in the case where greater access to finance and better and infrastructure that enables small manufactures to upgrade their products), this process is demand-driven.

The second impetus is *policy-induced* IS which arises from direct or indirect state modification of market forces for traversed infant industries. If the government is good at picking winners, this supply-driven IS in risky technology-intensive or

116 Globalization and industrialization

TABLE 5.2 A taxonomy of manufacturing industries by factor and technology intensities

Factor intensity Technology intensity	Labor (unskilled and semi-skilled)	Capital (fixed and working)
	LL: Early industries 1 (US$5,000 or less: Nigeria)	**LK: Early industries 2** (US$5,000–$10,000: Egypt)
Low (standard, mature)	• Tobacco • Apparel • Textiles • Leather • Furniture	• Food and beverages • Printing and publishing • Coke and petroleum • Non-metallic minerals
	HL: Middle industries (US$10,000–$23,000: S. Africa)	**HK: Late industries** (US$23,000+: S. Korea)
High (advanced, novel)	• Paper • Basic metals • Fabricated metals • Precision instruments	• Chemicals • Machinery, electrical • Machinery, non-electrical • Transportation equipment • Rubber and plastic

Sources and notes: Adapted from Alcorta et al. (2013), UNIDO (2009), Rodrik (2013), and McMillan et al. (2014).
Per capita incomes, which are intended to be suggestive, are in 2005 PPP dollars.

scale-intensive activities may go a long way toward supplementing the market-induced IS. If the government is not, because of incompetence or political capture by special interests, then a cascading network of inefficient firms will end up dominating the home market.

Figure 5.1 clarifies the various conceptualizations of IS for a single or a composite product. On the product transformation curve between importables (MM) and domestic production (MD), the intersection with the horizontal axis to the right of MD_4 shows the theoretical maximum of apparent consumption (of home and imported manufactured goods) that can be provided by domestic producers at the point of full self-sufficiency.

If we heroically assume that there are no binding constraints on assimilating imported technology, the effective exchange rate (inclusive of all market-determined and policy-determined returns), p, then provides a good measure of the incentives for domestic firms to home-produce or to import manufactures.

Point B (where $p = 1$) is the point where imports are just as competitive as domestic manufactures. MD_3 will be sourced from domestic production (import-substituted)

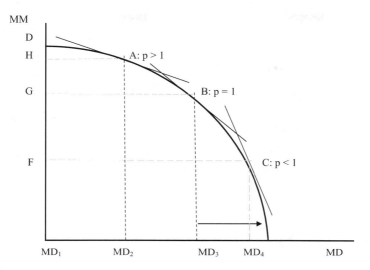

FIGURE 5.1 IS: incentives versus capacity

Source and notes: Author.
p = eP_{MD}/P_{MM} = effective exchange rate of domestic replacements relative to importables
e = nominal exchange rate (US$/domestic currency)
P = price index
MM = importable manufactures
MD = domestic production of importable manufactures (IS)
MD$_4$ = apparent domestic consumption when imports are fully displaced

and G will be imported. To the left of B, such as A, where p > 1, imports become relatively less expensive and will rise to H. The opposite is the case to the right of B, such as C, where p < 1 and imports become more expensive and will fall to F. Domestic supply will then take up the slack by supplying MD$_4$.[2]

Poorly designed import substituting industrialization can be self-limiting for at least two reasons. First, by discouraging the expansion of exports and agriculture, the strategy may not ensure that foreign exchange earnings keep pace with the need for the rapidly rising imports of non-competitive intermediate goods to feed and upgrade the IS industries. This policy also has redistributive effects by sharpening the proclivities for unproductive rent seeking. Second, prolonged high effective protection makes the import-dependent industries inefficient in terms of domestic resource cost or innovativeness unless firms are exposed to external competition in a timely manner.

Supporters and critics alike rarely address market-induced IS explicitly, although non-intervention still entails some IS which may be sub-optimal. Critics take policy-driven IS as too self-limiting or counterproductive. There are, of course, counterfactuals such as those from the forced openness of many colonies (India or Ireland being the prime examples) which deindustrialized them. As we will argue below, marketists focus on the follies of intervention without explaining convincingly how nearly every successful latecomer pursued some form of activist industrial policy.[3]

118 Globalization and industrialization

Another vantage point for appraising inter-stage transition on the production side is market orientation. The exploitation of the existing and the potential domestic market for manufactures may require movements away from crafts with simple technologies to a progressively increasing technological ladder: early manufactures (IS1) to be followed by middle industries (IS2) and, finally, to late industries (IS3).

If there is no alternative to IS to launch an industrialization drive, then what is debatable is how best to sustain it through the right mix of market-led and policy-led substitution. If the mix is flexibly appropriate, intersectoral allocation of factor use will pave the way for a TFP-driven growth, and a virtuous circle would emerge between production upgrading and export upgrading. Mistakes are likely to be made during the inter-stage transitions. Needless to say, there are no easy shortcuts to industrial deepening.

Export promotion and export substitution

IS speaks mainly to the supply side of homemade manufactures. There is a large literature that unhelpfully classifies trade orientation based on the relative real effective exchange rate for importables and exportables. Non-neutrality, measured by the totality of incentives between importable manufactures and exportable manufactures, is used as a convenient way of classifying countries as inward-looking or outward-looking (Liang, 1992). We need to address the demand side, especially of exports.

Let us be a bit more specific here to highlight the role of hard domestic constraints for regions such as Africa. These pertain to the costs of trade logistics, the quality infrastructures, or necessary capital to access global marketing networks. This is illustrated in Figure 5.2 where p' is the relative effective exchange rate of domestic sales relative to export sales of manufactures. Where domestic manufactures can be fully transformed into exports and assuming domestic production capacity just to the right of Y4, p' = 1 suggests that Y3 will be sold at home and E will be exported. If relative prices favor exports, such as p' > 1 at A, then exports rise to J and domestic sales of home-produced manufactures concomitantly fall to Y2. The opposite would be the case, such as p' < 1 at C, which raises domestic sales to Y4 and reduces a fall in exports to D.

But what if there are binding constraints on exporting that limit the market choices of home producers? The bolded line segment DC depicts the binding domestic constraint. At the neutral relative price of p' = 1, this constraint effectively imposes a ceiling of D on exportables, far below E. In other words, the D − K region of the transformation curve, while technologically feasible and incentive compatible, becomes infeasible.

These complications might explain why the relationship between openness and industrial growth is not empirically robust. There is some evidence for the causality going from trade volume to growth (see Rodríguez and Rodrik, 2001, for a skeptic's guide). At the three-digit ISIC level, there is also no conclusive evidence that openness enhances total factor productivity in manufacturing (Abegaz and Basu, 2011).

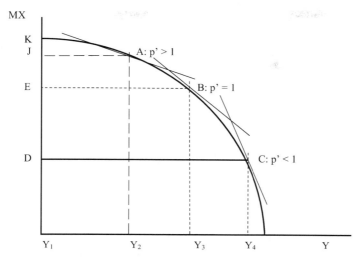

FIGURE 5.2 IS and ES: incentives versus market choice

Source and notes: Author.
p' = eP_{MD}/P_{MX} = effective real exchange rate of domestic sale relative to exporting
e = nominal exchange rate (US$/domestic currency)
P = price index
Y = domestic sales of domestic manufactures
MX = exportable manufactures from domestic sources (exclusive of re-exports)
Y4 = domestic full capacity and self-sufficiency

Let us now turn to the two trade orientations that are unfortunately conflated in the literature. One is a largely market-directed process of diversifying one's export basket in favor of high-income elasticity and tech-intensive products. This we call *export substitution* (ES). The other goes beyond avoiding export biases to include affirmative discrimination in favor of higher and more diversified exports. Export substitution away from less profitable products is labeled here *export promotion* (EP). ES and EP may also be understood as an *ex ante* desire while export replacement (ER) implies an *ex post* outcome.

EP, as a product of encouragement for manufacturing exports, comes in two flavors. The weaker version underscores policy neutrality between exports and imports, that is, the effective exchange rate (p') is the same for both. The mercantilist version resorts to the active promotion of manufacturing exports with the help of myriad schemes that are designed to boost exports and to discourage non-competing industrial imports.

ES, on the other hand, focuses on accelerating the diversification of export baskets in favor of high-quality and high value-added exports of manufactures by resident (native as well as multinational) producers. For whole products, successful ES requires close location to markets, availability of cheap inputs and infrastructural services, and a robust enforcement of property rights. Where ES is task-based, nearness to markets matters less than access to global networks.

120 Globalization and industrialization

ES also has two dimensions, one of which involves changes in the export mix (Xi/X). The other takes the form of changes in export intensity (Xi/Yi) where Yi is the total supply of a manufactured product.

Analogous to our framing of discussion on IS, we will work with three distinct stages of ES: primary, secondary, and tertiary. The *primary stage* is labor-intensive exports (ES1). The *secondary stage* is capital- or resource-intensive exports (ES2). The *tertiary stage* is skill- or technology-intensive exports (ES3). In the global marketplace, latecomers move from a simple processing of primary goods to exporting labor-intensive and resource-intensive manufactures (ES1).

As skills and technological capabilities improve and foreign exchange earnings facilitate importation of more advanced machinery and intermediate goods, the export basket tilts toward such exports (ES2). The final stage entails export capability for high-skill and high-tech manufactures such as machinery (ES3). Let us now take up the challenges of measurement before considering the dynamic of transition across the various phases of IS and ES.

Measuring IS and ES

Employment generation aside, one good measure of IS is the net national value-added of the product, which explains why domestic content requirements abound under FDI-driven industrialization. Sequenced from the least significant to the most significant levels, it takes the forms of the domestic assembly of almost entirely imported components, processing of domestic primary inputs, intensive use of domestic components or tasks, production of the product in its entirety with local inputs and know-how, and production of the entire product using domestically produced equipment and almost all other inputs.

While the three-stage framework is easy enough, measuring the various levels of IS and ES is not so simple. The alternative measurements of IS and ES reflect specific definitions. One approach focuses on sectoral orientation to craft a patterns-based definition: exportables (X), importables (M), and nontradables (N). Another approach uses an activity-based definition by industry-type (ISIC) or end-use (SITC). Time series measures can then be constructed by country, endowment type, income levels, or end uses (capital goods, intermediates, fuels, consumer goods).[4]

Another taxonomy of measures invokes price-based incentives (positive, negative, or neutral): the price index of exports relative to those of nontradables, or the price index of imports relative to those of nontradables. Interestingly, this approach yields many possible mixes, such as export dis-protection with IS (Africa), neutrality on both fronts which amounts to a free trade stance (Hong Kong), and export promotion with import neutrality (East Asia).

The most intuitive measure of import replacement (IR) is "absolute" IR (i.e., changes in the value of imports). The theoretically more meaningful measures, however, are those pertaining to "relative" IR (i.e., changes in import ratios). Using import penetration ratios, one can then develop a series of indices.

For manufacturing imports, we can construct from the readily available data the following industry-specific measures whose usefulness would depend on the purpose of analysis. The first index is the IR rate

$$IR = (D/S) \qquad (5.1)$$

where D = actual domestic sales of home manufactures, and S = importables (actual and potential). Absolute IR can then be calculated as IR x S. One can then use $(IR_t - IR_0)$ to estimate the distance traveled in building up domestic capacity in each branch over time.

A second index is the Import Penetration (IP) rate, which can be constructed as

$$IP = (M/A) \qquad (5.2)$$

where M = imports, and A = apparent consumption which is equal to imports plus domestic sales of home manufactures. The denominator serves as a measure of national purchasing power on the assumption, valid only for short-run analysis, that the consumption basket remains stable as income rises.

A third index captures the degree of national Self-sufficiency (SS)

$$SS = (MVA-X)/A \qquad (5.3)$$

where MVA-X = domestic sales of home manufactures (i.e., domestic production net of exports), and A = apparent consumption. As countries industrialize, the absorption of domestic manufactures by the home market is likely to fall. It does so slowly at first and then rapidly because of both inter-industry exports (middle-income level) and intra-industry exports as product differentiation intensifies at high-income levels.

For exports of manufactures, we have some measures depending again on the purpose of the analysis. One is the Export Expansion (EE) rate

$$EE = (X/MVA) \qquad (5.4)$$

where X = exports of manufactures, and MVA = domestic manufacturing value added.

The Export Diversification (ED) rate can be similarly constructed

$$ED_i = X_i/X \qquad (5.5)$$

where X_i = value added for various types of manufacturing exports (simple consumer goods, consumer durables, intermediate goods, equipment, and the like), and X = total manufacturing exports.

For meso-level analysis, the trade turnover for manufactures is widely used. For inter-industry trade, we can express the Trade Ratio (TR) as trade turnover

$$TR = (X-M)/(X+M) \qquad (5.6)$$

122 Globalization and industrialization

where X-M is net exports of manufactures, and it is expressed as a fraction of the gross trade (imports plus exports) in manufactures.

Finally, we can decompose both IS and ES in several ways, including

$$ES = lag (IS) \tag{5.7}$$

where ES = export substitution and IS = import substitution. Here, we are positing that latecomers must import substitute to export-substitute later. The gestation lags will vary depending on a latecomer's learning efficiency. Krugman (1984) calls this "import protection as export promotion" thereby decrying the simplistic notion of an inevitable trade-off between EP/ES and IR/IS strategies. We now return to the (political) economics behind these production-cum-trade orientations.

Paths of IS and ES for components and whole products

Several questions arise at this point as one tries to make sense of the interconnections between domestic production capacity and international competitiveness. How tightly staged is the evolution of industrial heterogeneity and technological learning? Do such stages of industrial sophistication involve simultaneous patterns or sequenced patterns of IS and ES? What domestic and external factors drive the transition between any pair of distinct IS and ES stages?

Production orientation and trade orientation, as we have seen, are two sides of the same coin. In fact, trade ultimately transforms domestic production into exports, imports into domestic production. That is why the changing composition of trade in manufactures is both a cause and an effect of successful industrialization.

The sequential evolution of IS and ES cautions against interpreting the coefficient on MVA growth in GDP growth regressions as evidence of IS inefficiency for early-stage industrializers given the long gestation lags between the two. One study suggests that IS precedes ES in given branch by the wide range of 5–20 years (Shapiro and Taylor, 1990). Long gestation lags bear the risk of sinking a lot of scarce resources in an industry which may turn out to be the wrong choice at maturity because of changing global conditions. It may, of course, foster the emergence of globally competitive national champions.

Economic theory suggests that transitions between phases of industrial development involve changes in relative sectoral productivity and output cost, trade orientation, and the mixes of output and employment. The policy choices open to firms and governments during these transitions may also be contingent on several factors. Countries with a poor natural-resource base will, for example, find it imperative to diversify faster into skill-intensive activities, while resource-rich countries facing secular declines in relevant commodity prices will have to do the same for resource processing.

As noted earlier, the standard model of trade before 1990 was for the *unbundling of production and sale*. Whole products were manufactured in one country and sold

The first unbundling **123**

throughout the world. The links between ES and IS for whole products, as we suggested earlier, are evident at various levels. It is not fruitful to treat the two as mutually exclusive strategies. On the demand side, market orientation may alternate between emphasis on the domestic or the foreign depending on expected profitability. On the supply side, successful IS makes exports possible while buoyant exports enable full utilization of existing capacity as well as economies of scale, and the financing of advanced IS.

Since domestic production capacity presupposes IS of some sort (except in cases of **export processing zones**, EPZs[5]), it is hard to imagine ES without prior IS. Multinationals and transnationals do not invest heavily in countries without a prior history of industrial development. FDI follows domestic investment in manufacturing the way private investment is crowded-in by demand-driven public investment in infrastructure. This explains why Africa has not been a prime destination of FDI-driven manufacturing – at least until now.

One theoretically plausible sequence through time of IS and ES is the IS-ES path where a latecomer import-substitutes to export-promote and obtain sufficient foreign exchange and technological upgrading to import-substitute more advanced products or components. Latecomers begin with IS1 to facilitate ES1. Next, they shift to ES1 as quickly as possible to fully exhaust IS1 potentials and to finance IS2, which makes ES2 possible. Then, they transition to ES2, which is both feasible and desirable to fully exploit the potentials of IS2 industries and to finance IS3, which in due course makes ES3 possible. Finally, they enter ES3, enhance the assimilation of frontier technologies by resident firms, and begin to push the frontier itself.

This is, in fact, a faithful depiction of the Nipponian Model of industrialization adopted by Japan and South Korea. These two countries became headquarters economies – a triumph of IS and then ES strategy in each branch of manufacturing. Taiwan, Hong Kong, and Thailand also did well by privileging ES over IS but they did remain factory economies. Singapore and Malaysia tried to meld the two to good effect, but one is left to wonder whether they would rival South Korea in producing national champions if the two did not split after independence.

Once a platform of IS1 industries is in place, the next stage of industrial deepening presents two options. The first path involves converting domestic production capability into export success, i.e., IS1 to ES1. This transition may require dismantling or neutralizing those IS policies that discriminate against exports directly (overvalued exchange rates) or indirectly (raising the cost of inputs or lowering their quality due to non-competitive IS industries).

There are, of course, many possible obstacles in switching form the domestic market to the foreign market. Vested interests may prevent switching to ES unless the benefits far exceed the returns from protection. Foreign markets may be closed or monopolized through control over marketing channels. And learning efficiency during the IS period may be too low for acquiring the capabilities for global competitiveness.

The alternative path, IS1-IS2-IS3, is one that favors self-reliance by extending domestic-oriented IS into capital-intensive or skill-intensive industries. This is the

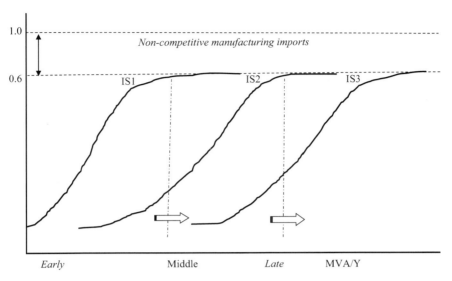

FIGURE 5.3 Evolutionary ladder of an IS-biased industrialization strategy

Sources and notes: Author. The proportions are for illustration only.
A = apparent consumption (homemade plus imported sales in domestic market)
MVA = manufacturing value added (domestic only)
Y = gross domestic product

Soviet Model that was adopted by many statist countries. It is feasible, but rarely efficient, for large countries with a substantial pool of skills and financial capital from resource rents. Figure 5.3 illustrates the stylized characteristics of this inward-looking path by comparing the ceiling on home manufactures (replacing all but non-competitive imports) and the ceiling on the share of manufacturing value added in GDP (about 40%, as in China or South Korea around 2000).

Such countries, therefore, confront two binding constraints. One comes in the form of saturation concerning domestic absorption of domestic manufactures. The other emanates from the need for substantial investment in globally uncompetitive industries and the requisite skills. This inevitably makes reintegration rather protracted and costly – as the wrenching experiences of the former Soviet Republics and Southeastern Europe amply demonstrate.

For countries which choose to export a given IS1 product as soon as they can do so, the next move takes the form of developing IS2 industries. The transition from ES1 to IS2 makes sense for such countries for several reasons. The foreign exchange constraint is less binding given the buoyant foreign exchange earnings, as is the technological assimilation that come with greater exposure to global customers and competitors alike.

There are challenges for the alternating sequence, too. The level and form of protection under IS2 are likely to be higher than before since the requisite technological sophistication is higher. Furthermore, less competent industrialists or agencies may be tempted to use political influence to gain prolonged protection or larger

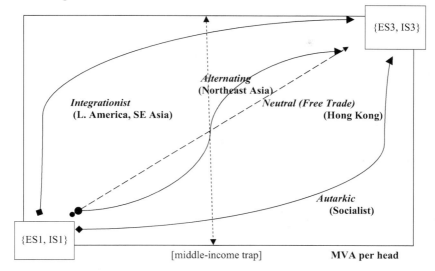

FIGURE 5.4 Alterative paths of catchup industrialization: autarkic, integrationist, neutral, and alternating

Source: Author.

subsidies than is socially necessary. Finally, labor is now better organized to join capital in putting pressure on the State for more protection.

After completing secondary IS (IS2), two possible pathways open (see Figure 5.4). One is the extraverted path whereby countries export intermediate-technology goods, i.e., IS2 to ES2. For those countries which have completed ES1, the experience provides a good platform for penetrating international markets for more advanced manufactures. Vested interests in the importing countries may resist significant market losses. Governments in exporting countries are tempted to repress labor and capital alternately to keep costs down and to encourage competition on behalf of a politically entrenched industrialist class.

Alternatively, a statist path may push ahead onto tertiary IS, i.e., IS2 to IS3. They will likely find the transition from IS2 to ES1 (or from IS3 to ES2) rather difficult. This autarkic strategy rarely succeeds since the requirements of the most technologically sophisticated industries (mostly machinery) are likely to be quite high concerning infrastructure, skills, and investment.

Finally, a hyper-extraverted strategy that is often taken as a free-trade model of industrialization is the ES1 to ES2 to ES3 path often associated with city-states (Hong Kong), regions (Guangdong), or platform economies (Mauritius). In all these cases, an IS1 stage was already in place – built up by industrialist refugees from the mainland in the case of Hong Kong, the socialist hinterland in the case Guangdong, and an IS1 garment sector ready for upgrading in the case of Mauritius. What differentiates such a strategy is what took place after IS1, which is an accelerated transition into exporting under a pro-export environment and with FDI financing.

126 Globalization and industrialization

These are, as we will see in the next chapter, fast becoming the norm rather than the exception that proves the rule. Larger countries continue to need more extensive and deeper import substitutions that must be disciplined by domestic and external competition.

The open-economy path facilitates the transition from ES2 to IS3 for several reasons. The massive investment requirements in human capital and modern technology can only be met with the help of foreign exchange earnings and foreign capital. The early stages of industrial development, as well as the rising demand for agricultural goods and business services, may also have a virtuous cycle of expanding the domestic market for advanced homemade manufactures. Some countries facilitated preferential access to government procurement contracts to help upstart industries (shipbuilders in South Korea or Airbus in Europe come to mind). Regional integration, science parks, and highly targeted subsidies have also proven effective provided they lie within the restrictive parameters of the WTO.

The final stage involves exploiting IS3 capability for mastering the most lucrative and sophisticated industrial export markets, i.e., IS3 to ES3. This transition, even when technically manageable, must contend with the challenge of marketing products as an own-brand manufacturer (OBM). Entering the market with one's own brand requires substantial outlays for marketing research, provision of trade credit to distribution agents, establishing a network of service facilities, and co-financing major retail outlets and dealers. This difficulty explains why Taiwan, Poland, Thailand, Mexico, Bangladesh, and Malaysia are still transitioning away from reliance on component or **original equipment manufacturing** (OEM), that is assembling foreign-designed and branded products.

In this vein, the product cycle model (PCM) addresses the challenges of industrializing without proprietary innovations and with the help of multinational firms (Vernon, 1979; Perez, 2009). PCM is a theory of the development of technological and managerial capability for late-mover firms in developed countries as well as homegrown firms in late industrializing countries. It focuses on product innovation (a market concept that reflects substitution in demand) or process innovation (an industry concept that reflects substitution in production). As such, it speaks largely to one, albeit important, facet of the industrialization process – the mechanics of knowledge diffusion involving whole products in the second machine age.

PCM identifies three distinct stages in an S-shaped development of new intermediate and final industrial products. These relate the degree of maturity of a product and the trajectory of its evolution as it eventually diffuses to latecomer firms and countries (see Table 5.3).

Stage 1 involves the *introduction* of a new product by a pioneering firm in the North by commercially applying general knowledge that may be accessible to all. During this phase of radical innovation, the pioneering firm incurs a high fixed cost in developing the product but a low marginal cost in marketing it.

Stage 2 involves the *expansion* of the market for the new product beyond the initial batches of customized production for pioneer users, to a bigger set of customers. This is when the firm begins to collect significant innovation rent to recoup its high

The first unbundling **127**

TABLE 5.3 Product life cycle and trajectories of technological diffusion to latecomers

Attribute/phase	Introduction/expansion	Mature/saturation
Innovation	Radical innovation	Incremental innovation
	Product then process	Standardized product/process
Competition	Few then entry	M & A, spinoffs
	Customized	Variety, quality, and cost
	Price competition	Non-price competition
Factor use	Skill-intensive R & D	Labor-intensive
	Customized production	Mass production
Location	Central region	Low-cost Periphery
	Export rises and falls	Exports, domestic use
Diffusion to	Licensing and externalities	Licensing, Reverse Eng.
Latecomers	Technical support	FDI, GVCs

Sources and notes: Vernon (1979), Perez (2009), and OECD (2011).
R & D = research and development
M & A = mergers and acquisitions
FDI = foreign direct investment

investment in new technology and perhaps more. The first two stages take place in the home country of the pioneering firm thus benefiting the domestic cluster that includes itself, its suppliers and users, and the local government.

Stage 3 is the *saturation* stage where the domestic market for the new product is big enough to warrant standardization and mass production at a low cost. It is at this stage that the mature design and production technology of the new product becomes accessible to follower firms in the home market and abroad. Developing countries, via multinational investment or their own resources, gain an opportunity to join in the division of the rapidly dissipating rent. Laggard firms enter the industry to engage in cost-based competition usually based on cheap labor. The last phase of this stage involves the decline in the share of the mature product as demand is exhausted and pioneer firms have shifted to developing new products.

Competing on the basis of high productivity rather than on low wages means that latecomers cannot industrialize simply by specializing in a low-technology industry. Industrial development, in this case, entails moving from processed primary products and labor-intensive whole-product manufactures to products reflecting advanced managerial and technological skills (Balassa, 1979).

A related idea, the productivity-driven and design-driven *competitive advantage* of firms, was offered by Michael Porter (1990). Porter argues that traditional sources of comparative advantage (land, location, natural resources, labor, or population size) are structural factors (or the givens) and, therefore, do not generate dynamic comparative advantage. Instead, competitive advantage in the contemporary global economy derives from clusters – groups of interconnected firms, suppliers, and related

128 Globalization and industrialization

industries – that arise in certain locations. Clusters such as Silicon Valley (computers), Rotterdam (logistics), Bangalore (IT software), Hollywood (movies), and Paris (fashion) provide a new source of comparative advantage by increasing firm productivity, innovation, and business formation (McCormick, 1999; Schmitz and Nadvi, 1999; Sonobe and Otsuka, 2011).

The flying geese model (FGM) of the leader-follower dynamics also underscores the sequential perspective. It is built around three dimensions (Hiley, 2000; Akamatsu, 1962). The *intra-industry* aspect focuses on product development within a particular developing country, with a single industry growing over time in production and exports. The *inter-industry* aspect deals with the sequential appearance and development of whole (or parts of) industries. The third, the *global* aspect, focuses on the relocation of industries from leaders to followers because of significant changes in relative costs and productivities.

The FGM metaphor, therefore, captures the changing patterns of industrial followership across countries that display a diversity of initial conditions and endowments as they climb the technological ladder at different paces. However, FGM is too general a formulation to provide specific guidance about how to create a context-specific incentive environment for such an imitative process or about the mechanism that has allowed some followers to leapfrog leaders. The flying-geese/product-cycle (FG-PC) composite model also supports the import-replace-export sequence of learning, especially for the age of "whole-product" manufacturing. This means there is a leader-follower relationship that is pervasive among firms, among sectors, and among countries.

One way to gauge how well "countries become what they produce and export" is to compare the productivity levels embedded in the baskets of rich-country products (exports) with those of poor-country products (exports). The process of upgrading the quality of poor-country product baskets is one that involves market or cost discovery by risk-taking entrepreneurs who should be subsidized for the positive externalities they generate (Hausmann and Rodrik, 2003; Hausmann et al., 2007). This way, barriers to entrepreneurship (low appropriability due to informational externalities, credit constraints, institutional weakness, and limited entry and exit) can be minimized or removed to allow for outcomes that would have been generated by a dynamically efficient market.

The choice of industries to promote would, then, depend on many factors. One consideration is elasticity on both the demand side and the supply side. This yields four possible product groups. The two extreme cases are the profit-seekers paradise where high elasticities prevail on both sides (consumer durables and machinery), and the rent seeker's paradise where low elasticities prevail on both sides (such as copper, uranium, and pharmaceuticals). The two mixed cases are also noteworthy – high supply-elasticity but low demand-elasticity would mean that the incentive to innovate is rather weak (such as in the cases of garments and electronics), and low supply-elasticity but high demand-elasticity would imply that sellers are vulnerable to price fluctuations (such as diamond and some high-tech products).

The first unbundling **129**

Ready-made garment (RMG) exports have historically provided initial access for those in the early phase of an industrialization drive.[6] Subcontracted sales of unbranded apparel to local or foreign distributors may lead to upgrading to OEM sales to foreign buyers under the latter's own brand name. Only the more advanced developing countries such as South Korea have been able not only to diversify participation in more networks and to enter higher rungs in the GVC ladder, but also to market their own brands of high value-added manufactures globally.[7] This feat was a joint product of capacity building at home and synchronizing this capacity with global opportunities – a subject we will explore in Chapter 10.[8]

The bottom line is that successful industrialization is transformational not only in economic terms but also in political and social terms. There are short-term losers and long-term gainers and vice versa. Landlords tend to lose out in the long run while peasants-turned-factory-workers as well as the industrialist class are big winners in the long run. Overvalued exchange rates tax cash crop exporters while shoddy domestically produced manufactures tax consumers and domestic users.

Conflicts between the nationalist industrial bourgeoisie and the comprador bourgeoisie allied with transnationals are legendary. What this means is that industrialization requires a political mechanism by which distributional conflicts are settled in a manner that is supportive of industrial deepening and shared growth. For many latecomers, it may take the form of an authoritarian but developmental regime as in East Asia and in parts of Latin America. In other cases, it could take the form of repressive and exclusionary regimes as in the case of Apartheid South Africa.

Notes

1 ES is confusingly labeled in the literature as "export promotion," which conflates outcomes (substitution or diversification) and policies (promotion).
2 Constraints on domestic capacity-building (such as access to foreign exchange or public infrastructure services) may, of course, frustrate the full realization of IS possibilities. Even where capacity expansion is feasible, over-protection or misguided policies may, and often do, prevent optimal capacity utilization, which is a big problem in many African countries.
3 One common misconception treats IS as equivalent to an inward-looking (or even autarkic) strategy. The other misconception is that expected profitability alone provides adequate incentive to automatically elicit the requisite capacity to supply the market. Hong Kong hardly provides a generalizable counterfactual.
4 ISIC = International system of industrial classification. SITC = Standard international trade classification.
5 The transition, regarding pace and success, among the three ES stages, each of which has *distributional consequences*. The policy-induced process entails several forms: (1) export processing zones (EPZs) producing for export manufactures ranging from those with high domestic content to re-exports with minimal domestic value added; (2) industrial parks which are often designed for upstream manufactures with the help of publicly provided infrastructure, direct subsidies, and generous tax holidays; and (3) targeted products for niche export markets that are produced by firms in the hinterland.
6 Bangladesh provides a fascinating case study of a very-latecomer leapfrogging into the global RMG sector as the second largest exporter in the world. Privatization of clothing factories and liberalization of the economy in the second half of the 1970s gave rise to export processing zones and expanded domestic sales. FDI and worker training by Daewoo

130 Globalization and industrialization

and other Korean firms, under a cloud of export quotas for each country under the Multi-Fiber Arrangement during 1974–2004, provided the springboard for international competitiveness since 1980 primarily in woven but also in knit garments. Aided by supportive industrial policy and the low wages, Bangladesh's 5 million garment workers (some nine out ten are female) in its 4,000 factories today contribute over 80% of the country's export earnings. It also seems to have empowered young women workers by incentivizing investment in education and providing financial independence (Hassan, 2014).

7 Value-chain deepening begins with original-equipment assembly or original-equipment manufacturing before a late-mover develops the capability to engage in original-design or even original-brand manufacturing.

8 Suffice it to quote Carl Dahlman (2008: 48) here:

> The challenge for developing countries is, therefore, to determine how best to be open to international competition while at the same time nurturing the development of their own production capabilities. If they liberalize too early, they run the risk of having their domestic industries wiped out by well-established and stronger foreign competitors.

References

Abegaz, B., and A.K. Basu. (2011). The Elusive Productivity Effect of Trade Liberalization in the Manufacturing Industries of Emerging Economies. *Emerging Markets Finance and Trade*, 47, pp. 23–45.

Akamatsu, K. (1962). A Historical Pattern of Economic Growth in Developing Countries. *The Developing Economies*, 1, pp. 3–25.

Alcorta, L., N. Haraguchi, and G. Rezonja. (2013). Industrial Structural Change, Growth Patterns, and Industry. In: J. Stiglitz, J.Y. Lin, and E. Patel, eds., *The Industrial Policy Revolution II: Africa in the 21st Century*, 1st ed. New York: Palgrave Macmillan, pp. 457–491.

Amsden, A. (2001). *The Rise of 'The Rest': Challenges to the West From Late Industrializing Economies*. New York: Oxford University Press.

Balassa, B. (1979). A 'Stages Approach' to Comparative Advantage. In: I. Adelman, ed., *Economic Growth and Resources*. New York: Macmillan, pp. 121–156.

Baldwin, R. (2016). *The Great Convergence: Information Technology and the New Globalization*. Cambridge: Belknap-Harvard Press.

Dahlman, C. (2008). Technology, Globalization, and International Competitiveness: Challenges for Developing Countries. In: D. O'Connor and M. Kjollerstrom, eds., *Industrial Development for the 21st Century*. London: Zed Press, pp. 29–83.

Findlay, R. and K. O'Rourke. (2009). *Power and Plenty: Trade, War, and the World*. Princeton: Princeton University Press.

Hassan, F. (2014). RMG Industry of Bangladesh: Past, Present and Future. *Dhaka Tribune*, September 19.

Hausmann, R., J. Hwang, and D. Rodrik. (2007). What You Export Matters. *Journal of Economics Growth*, 12, pp. 1–25.

Hausmann, R., and D. Rodrik. (2003). Economic Development as Self-Discovery. *Journal of Development Economics*, 72(2), pp. 704–723.

Hiley, M. (2000). Lessons for Sub-Saharan Africa From the Experiences of East Asia: SADC and ASEAN Compared. In: H. Jallian, M. Tribe, and J. Weiss, eds., *Industrial Development and Policy in Africa: Issues of Deindustrialization and Development Strategy*. Cheltenham: Edward Elgar.

Krugman, P. (1984). Import Protection as Export Promotion: International Competition in the Presence of Oligopoly and Economies of Scale. In: H. Keirzkowski, ed., *Monopolistic Competition and International Trade*. Oxford: Oxford University Press.

Liang, L. (1992). Beyond Import Substitution and Export Promotion: A New Typology of Trade Strategies. *Journal of Development Studies*, 28(3), pp. 447–472.

McCormick, D. (1999). African Enterprises Clusters and Industrialization: Theory and Reality. *World Development*, 27(9), pp. 1531–1551.

McMillan, M., D. Rodrik, and I. Verduzco-Gallo. (2014). Globalization, Structural Change, and Productivity Growth. *World Development*, 63, pp. 11–32.

Ohno, K., and I. Ohno. (2010). Dynamic Capacity Development: What Africa Can Learn From Industrial Policy Foundation in East Asia. Paper Presented to *Initiative for Policy Dialogue, African Task Force Meeting*. Addis Ababa, July 2008.

Organisation for Economic Co-operation and Development (OECD). (2011). *Globalisation, Comparative Advantage and the Changing Dynamics of Trade*. Paris: OECD.

Perez, C. (2009). Technological Revolutions and Techno-Economic Paradigms. *Working Papers in Technology Governance and Economic Dynamics 20*. Tallinn: Tallinn University of Technology.

Porter, M. (1990). *The Competitive Advantage of Nations*. Cambridge, MA: Harvard University Press.

Rodríguez, F., and D. Rodrik. (2001). Trade Policy and Economic Growth: A Skeptic's Guide to the Cross-National Evidence. *NBER Macroeconomics Annual 2000*, 15(1), pp. 261–338.

Rodrik, D. (2013). Unconditional Convergence in Manufacturing. *Quarterly Journal of Economics*, 128(1), pp. 165–204.

Schmitz, H., and K. Nadvi. (1999). Clustering and Industrialization: Introduction. *World Development*, 27(9), pp. 1503–1514.

Shapiro, H., and L. Taylor. (1990). The State and Industrial Strategy. *World Development*, 18(6), pp. 861–878.

Sonobe, T., and K. Otsuka. (2011). *Cluster-Based Industrial Development: A Comparative Analysis of Asia and Africa*. New York: Palgrave Macmillan.

United Nations Industrial Development Organization (UNIDO). (2009). *Industrial Development Report 2009: Breaking in and Moving Up – New Industrial Challenges for the Bottom Billion and the Middle-Income Countries*. Oxford: Oxford University Press.

United Nations Industrial Development Organization (UNIDO). (2015). *Industrial Development Report 2016: The Role of Technology and Innovation in Inclusive and Sustainable Industrial Development*. Geneva: UNIDO.

Vernon, R. (1979). The Product Cycle Hypothesis in the New International Environment. *Oxford Bulletin of Economics and Statistics*, 4(4), pp. 255–267.

6

PRODUCTION AND TRADE UNDER THE SECOND UNBUNDLING

In the current phase of globalization, production itself is being offshored to where it is most profitable. This does not necessarily mean that national value chains will disappear. It simply means that the mastery of a variety of competencies in designing and managing whole products differentiates lead firms from their subcontractors with the former occupying the highest value-added niches in global value chains. We will tease out below the meanings of this mega trend and the implications for very-late industrializers.

Global value chains for tasks and components

New information and communication technologies (ICT) and rapidly falling trade and travel costs – thanks to trade liberalization, containerization, and cheap air travel – have enabled a wide-ranging geographic dispersion of individual segments of a production process while still allowing for sufficient control and coordination. Fragmentation (or the unbundling of production itself) has meant that latecomers can join segments of the industrial bases of other countries into coherent global value chains (Baldwin, 2016; Baldwin and Venables, 2015; Hallward-Driemmeir and Nayyar, 2017).

The global environment for industrial production and trade has changed markedly since about the end of the 1980s. Trade in tasks or components has now eclipsed trade in whole manufactures because firms located in different countries can jointly manufacture a whole product, with each firm doing a piece of the overall work. The share of the G-7 countries in manufacturing has consequently fallen below one-third of global industrial trade. The multinationals of the first unbundling have become the transnationals of the second unbundling. These transnational corporations, based in the West and Japan, conduct about three-quarters of world

The second unbundling **133**

trade, with some 40% of this trade taking place within corporate systems rather than in open markets especially with respect to the most technology-intensive activities (UNIDO, 2015).

For much of the twentieth century, the combination of mass production pioneered by Henry Ford and mass consumption became the norm. The post-1970 decades saw, as a response to a large global middle class and intense global competition, a de-emphasis on mass production and renewed emphasis on customization in high-income markets. Fordism gave way to Toyota's flexible specialization with expanded product variety and shop-floor control. This process has intensified since 1990 with the progressive inclusion of high-end products in globalized chains.

Table 6.1 provides a synoptic view of the globalization of manufacturing production and sales in the last one-and-half centuries. The interplay between production and sales generates four business models, each typifying a distinct phase of industrialization (Marsh, 2012). The industrialization of early-comers under IR1 can be usefully interpreted as a case of no mass production and no customization. The emphasis then was on producers of small-batch production using standardized technologies and interchangeable parts.

To cast the latest trend in a broader historical context, two criteria are worth considering. One is the importance of *mass production* of standardized products or components. When it is the right profit-maximizing strategy, firms scale up the

TABLE 6.1 The changing nature of manufacturing production and sales

Mass production customization	*Yes*	*No*
Yes	**1970–2000** Flexible specialization; GVC via global FDI: integrated then disintegrated. (Toyota)	**2000–** Flexible personalization; GVC: disintegrated and demand-seeking in Emerging. (Sailor)
No	**1900–1970** Inflexible standardization; Outsourcing and demand-seeking FDI in Developed. (Ford)	**1850–1900** Inflexible, low-volume domestic customization; interchangeable parts. (Crafts; Shipyards)

Sources and notes: culled from Marsh (2012) and Gordon (2016). The periodization is purely illustrative.
Essilor = Paris-based world's biggest maker of spectacle lenses
Ford = Fordist assembly line
Toyota = Toyota Production System

production of a limited assortment of products to serve large and cost-sensitive markets. Where mass production is less profitable, firms naturally tend to focus on process innovations such as flexible design for small batches of large assortments to serve niche or high-end customers. The other is the growing importance of *customization*. Where it is important, firms cater to buyers in terms of quality, price, and service. Where customization is not important, quantity and price provide the competitive edge.

Global value chains are pyramid networks of a division of labor among firms located in one region or across the globe, each of which adds value to the creation of a product. They are facilitated by the diffusion of skills and easier communication and transportation resulting in an unprecedented global dispersion of industrial production and distribution (Gereffi, 1999; Gereffi and Fernandez-Stark, 2011; Marsh, 2012). As Marsh (2012: 214–215) puts it,

> The way goods are designed and made will become more complex. Processes such as development, production, and service will be spread across a global "value chain" of operations. Across this value chain, there will be opportunities for businesses based in many countries, both high-cost and low-cost, to play a part. . . . Reflecting this move to homogeneity, companies will increasingly spread their manufacturing between emerging economies and "developed" nations in a "hybridized" style. The new period will be an age of "industrial democracy" in its truest sense.

Figure 6.1 depicts the hybrid manufacturing that has emerged from the processes of unbundling production and consumption. The mix between the organizational and geographical structures of production involving domestic affiliates,

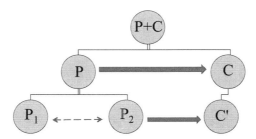

FIGURE 6.1 The twin unbundling of production and consumption

Sources and notes: Author.
P = production (subscripts indicate cross-regional or cross-country offshoring)
C = consumption (sales)
(P+C) = national bundling of both production and consumption (home production in integrated value chains for home market)
(P, C) = national production (integrated domestic value chains) for sale at home or abroad
(P1, P2, C' = C1, C2) = global unbundling of both production (cross-country manufacturing) and sale or consumption (cross-country markets)

The second unbundling **135**

domestic suppliers, foreign affiliates, and foreign suppliers yields four possible combinations. The case of national autonomy starts with integrated production and sale of manufactures within a national boundary (P + C). FDI firms doing the same in a foreign country still fall within this model of the bundling of production and sale in a country-delimited supply chain and value chain. With the expansion of the world market, headquarters firms keep production at the Center but market less bulky and high value-added manufactures to far-flung markets. In the open-economy case involving complete products, production remains bundled while consumption is unbundled (P → C). This case differs from the case of double unbundling since, in the case of the latter, both production and consumption (sales) are unbundled across countries (P → C').[1]

Consider the following stylized facts about the second unbundling (Baldwin, 2012, 2013, 2016; Taglioni and Winkler, 2016; World Bank, 2016):

1   The North deindustrialized while a small number of developing countries industrialized and saw their growth rates soar.
2   Commodity prices experienced the knock-on effects of a super-cycle benefiting greatly those countries with the richest natural endowments.
3   Back-and-forth trade between North and South intensified because of deeper trade liberalization, and it has been less pan-global than geographic-specific (concentrated in the neighborhoods of dynamic headquarters economies of the U.S.A., Germany, and Japan).
4   The second unbundling impacted national economies (a) with a finer degree of resolution than was the case under the first unbundling, i.e., operating at the level of production-stages and components as well as at the level of occupational skills, (b) in a more sudden way because of the unpredictability of new computer and communications technologies, (c) with a rupture of the close link between national capital and national labor as transnationals pursued higher profits, and (d) by reducing the economic significance of distance, at least in the areas of component production and fabrication. GVC rendered competitiveness less national and more firm-specific, and endowment-based comparative advantage much less attractive than **capability**-based competitive advantage.

Tasks are identifiable nodes (outputs) in a chain that requires distinct skills, uses labor or capital in different proportions, requires distinct inputs or has distinct consequences for the local environment. Each task or stage in the integrated production and distribution process may also involve economies of scale. Location matters for task-based specialization as firms balance the benefits from space-bound specialization with the costs of transportation, communication and effective coordination across space and business cultures. Production and trade in tasks also involve two distinct chains – **supply chains** and **value chains**.

We need to distinguish between the two chains which are often used interchangeably (see Box 6.1). A *supply chain* is the logistical system of organizations,

136 Globalization and industrialization

people, technology, activities, information, and resources that are involved in moving a product or service from the supplier to the customer. Supply–chain activities transform natural resources, raw materials, and components into a finished product with a focus on cost efficiency (by enhancing productivity and sourcing inputs from low-price suppliers) rather than on product innovation per se. This means some components or tasks may profitably be offshored.

When profitability arises from product innovation (higher quality product design, for example) to meet existing or anticipated demand, *value chain* management becomes the primary source of firm competency. Both supply chain and value chain activities enhance profit and can be national, regional, or global in scope, but the emphases are different – the demand side for value chains and the supply side for supply chains.

BOX 6.1 VALUE CHAINS AND SUPPLY CHAINS

From a perspective of business organization, firms compete along many dimensions. These include, as Porter (1990) argued, support activities mainly on the supply side (input sourcing, assembly, and distribution) and primary activities mainly on the demand side (marketing, sales, and servicing). By synchronizing the two sides, businesses minimize unit cost, enhance quality and reliability, boost productivity, and ensure customer loyalty. In this sense, value chains and supply chains are two sides of the same coin.

A *value chain* (VC) comprises the full range of interconnected value-adding activities that firms undertake to bring a product or service from its design through production and end use by final consumers or users. At each step in the chain, a revenue-boosting value is added in the forms of quality, product mix, customized specification, and after-sales service. This type of firm capability is demand-shifting at every price, and it is focused on raising "unit value" (Sutton, 2012).

A *supply chain* (SC) consists of a shorter range of supply-side activities that firms undertake to bring a product from production to retail and servicing points. It differs from value chain in its focus on "unit cost" – delivering a given quality and assortment at the lowest cost possible. That is, the emphasis of SC is on shifting the supply curve at all price levels by economizing on input cost or by raising productivity. Organizational forms ranging from just-in-case to just-in-time inventory are employed in supply-chain management.

Profits and market shares are enhanced by demand-driven, quality-based competition emphasized by value chains as well as by supply-driven, price-based competition emphasized by supply chains. Defined this way, supply chains may be easier to offshore to developing economies than value chains since the managerial and technological capability required by the latter is much higher. In much of the literature, the two concepts tend to be conflated (see, for example, Baldwin, 2013; Taglioni and Winkler, 2016).

National value chains (NVCs) tend to cater largely to the domestic market while *global value chains (GVCs)* employ networks that coordinate design, production, and marketing globally. Various tasks along the production chain can now be disintegrated (unbundled) and carried out in distant locations, depending on the respective comparative advantages of different regions within a country or across countries. Each stage carries, to varying degrees, opportunities for new local activities, jobs, and corporate profits, as well as the associated new skills, technology, know-how, and public revenues in the form of taxes. Successful integration into a value chain potentially allows a country to seize a bigger share of those benefits (Gereffi and Fernandez-Stark, 2011; OECD, 2015).

The densities of GVCs depend primarily on customization to meet buyer needs, the cost of coordinating geographically far-flung activities from headquarters economies, and the global environment that governs the degree of mobility of economic resources across borders. Distance has become progressively less significant nationally and internationally as the costs of packaging, shipping, information, and communication plummet. Network economies are also increasingly trans-nationalized as clusters of production, research and development, and dense product markets appear in almost every sub-region of the world.

The acceleration of the process of offshoring of production and even R & D is not well understood, if only because of rapidly changing technologies and the associated institutional transformations. Baldwin (2016:196–7) provides a fruitful way of conceptualizing the process when he says:

> The economics of offshoring is best looked at by decomposing it into two phenomena: fractionalization and dispersion. Fractionalization concerns the unbundling of production processes into finer stages of production. Dispersion concerns the geographic unbundling of stages. The two are linked insofar as the organization of stages may be crafted with dispersion (offshoring) in mind.

The new international division of labor is driven by inter-country, inter-industry, and inter-firm differences in "productive capabilities" which are partly shaped by static endowments of factors and largely by long-term investments in capabilities. Productive capabilities are personal and collective skills, productive knowledge embedded in organizations that firms need to perform different productive tasks in-house or in coordinating outsourcing in the home economy as well as across national boundaries. The determinants, enablers, precursors, and outcomes comprise the diagnostics needed for identifying the different trajectories of productive capabilities for designing sensibly selective industrial policies (Andreoni, 2011).

Human-capital-intensive tasks are generally kept in the "headquarters economies" located in the mature industrialized countries while unskilled-labor-intensive tasks are exported to those "factory economies" in developing countries with the lowest **unit labor cost**. The capability-rich headquarters firm provides the design, financing, assembling, and marketing support while factory firms located in far-flung places (mainly in East Asia and Latin America) carry out the production and final assembly. Lead firms with strategic assets do not have to be large entities.

Regional and global chains under the coordination of global investment and operations involving intricate divisions of labor are eclipsing national chains for widely traded manufactures. The integrator firms are the primary beneficiaries since they assume the risk of and the responsibility for product design and development. They oversee the entire global network by coordinating product and process development, input procurement, and output marketing across spatially mobile and immobile factors (natural resources and labor) in host economies. Lead firms located in headquarters economies ensure the proper exploitation of rapid, efficient, and competitively priced communication as well as logistics and skills-task matches.

As in the cases of previous waves of economic globalization, the benefits of this the new globalization are unequal for both countries and firms (OECD, 2015). Task-based production and trade may allow even the poorest countries to enter at a low rung of production ladders of sophisticated manufactures and even offices in the service sector. This benefits groups of workers with high-demand skills in developing countries while rendering uncompetitive the low-skill segment of the workforce in the rust belts of developed countries. Given the ubiquitous role of the world market in setting prices for most products and the unpredictability of the intersectoral and inter-spatial reallocation of resources, protecting and educating individual workers (rather than protecting jobs, firms, or sectors) for maximum agility should be the primary concern of industrial policy.

The most dramatic example is the emergence of China as the hub of globalized manufacturing, which initially focused on the assembly of low-tech and medium-tech products. This stage was followed by a policy-driven effort to upgrade to high-tech manufacturing while exporting low-value added production via outward FDI. This was enabled by the acquired know-how and the big war chest of foreign exchange earnings. The biggest participants have so far been those countries located in the dynamic "neighborhoods" of Germany, Japan, and the U.S.A. – Hong Kong, Singapore, Taiwan, S. Korea, China, India, Indonesia, Thailand, Poland, Mexico, Brazil, and Turkey (Baldwin, 2016).

Southeast Asia, the region with the most comprehensive and deepest regional integration, has the highest average share of intra-regional GVC participation (58% of GVC output in total regional GDP in 2011). In Eastern and Southern Africa, this

The second unbundling **139**

share was 16% in 2011. The Middle East and North Africa, Western and Central Africa, and South Asia lag with intra-regional GVC participation below 10% in 2011 because they lack dynamic leaders located in the neighborhood (AfDB et al., 2014; OECD, 2015).

In this new Center-Periphery division of labor, "mother plants" in North America, Europe, or Japan take care of R & D, product design, marketing, processes, and administration (see Figure 6.1). Under the spatial separation of production across countries (P1, P2) and sales (C1, C2), "child plants" in the Periphery (China, Mexico, Brazil, Thailand, Malaysia, or Taiwan) are then allotted less sophisticated activities such as assembling labor- and skill-intensive products using a combination of imported and domestically sourced components to specification. Nike, Cisco, and Apple are examples of factory-less or fabrication-less designers which contract manufacturers in East Asia to produce stuff cheaply and efficiently (Marsh, 2012; Baldwin, 2012).

Country-specific characteristics tend to be strong determinants of participation rate differences in GVCs. The size and geographical location of countries and their manufacturing share in GDP appear to explain most of the variation in participation rates between countries. Entrepreneurship is also crucial to full integration on mutually beneficial terms, especially in terms of boosting productivity.[2]

Switching from the capability to the opportunity side of the coin, it would be fair to say that three major forces have driven the explosion in global trade in manufactured goods and the subsequent boost to economic growth. They are spatial concentration of production, the emergence of extensive global supply chains, and lock-ins by first-movers. The last was possible because of factors like reductions in transport cost, greater input availability in the developing economies, and the virtuous cycles created by economies of scale and agglomeration.[3]

Externalities often arise from localized (same industry) and region-wide (diversified) industrial clusters and may be exploited whenever leading transnationals are provided the right incentive to locate in **special economic zones** (SEZs). SEZs may or may not include industrial parks (zones, estates), export processing zones (EPZs), or free trade zones (FTZs). Coordination externalities may also be facilitated by free ports and specialized **industrial districts**, the latter consisting of networked medium-size manufacturers benefiting from targeted public services and agglomeration economies – the prime example being the industrial districts of Northern Italy (see Box 6.2).

Africa has so far captured only a small share of global trade in value-added terms, but a good part of it is the sale of unprocessed commodities. In terms of gains from global value chains, export and productivity growth have been easier to achieve than employment growth (AEO – AFR, 2014; Gong, 2015).

With wages rising rapidly in China, labor-intensive and low-tech segments of these GVCs/GSCs are migrating elsewhere within China, in the Indo-China region, and globally. Some estimates suggest that 85 million manufacturing jobs will migrate from coastal China over the next 20 years (Lin, 2012). Sub-Saharan

140 Globalization and industrialization

BOX 6.2 SPECIAL ECONOMIC ZONES, INDUSTRIAL PARKS, AND INDUSTRIAL DISTRICTS

Industrial Cluster, a generic concept, is a spatial concentration of resources within a specific product group in **industrial parks** that are rich in upstream and downstream linkages. The Silicon Valley built around San Francisco and two world-class universities (U. Cal-Berkeley and Stanford) is the quintessential example.

A *Special Economic Zone* is a segregated region within a country in which lax business, labor, and trade laws and regulations are enacted to attract FDI with some restrictions about the destination of the output – usually for exports. Incentives include modern infrastructure, lower taxes, and the right of investors to run the businesses as they wish. The best-known example is the southeastern coastal provinces and cities of China, which benefitted from increasingly liberal terms since 1980 and served as the country's industrial growth engine in the 1990s.

An *Industrial Park* (zone, estate) is an economically concentrated geographical area with the requisite infrastructures and business support services, streamlined customs and regulations procedures. An *Export Processing Zone* refers to airports, seaports, or any other designated areas for duty-free imports of intermediate goods intended mainly for re-export. If well cesigned, such agglomerations foster multiplier effects and knowledge-spillover externalities that enable fledgling young industrial firms to obtain a solid footing.

An *Industrial District* is a localized cluster of specialized firms relying on network externalities emanating from knowledge-sharing and production linkages while maintaining organizational autonomy. As in Northern Italy, regional governments provide the requisite public services. It is Marshallian localization, taking advantage of territorially defined networks and developing them into a larger agglomeration. These networks of SMEs can benefit from targeted public infrastructure and coordination support services while accentuating positive network externalities. The external economies thus derived can be as potent as the internal scale economies that large firms enjoy.

China is known for relying on large special economic zones, more focused industrial zones and specialized industrial clusters (specialty cities). Replicating them in Africa requires greater political stability, provision of key skills and input suppliers, and integration of the domestic private sector into the planning and execution of such clusters.

Africa is expected to be a beneficiary much like Cambodia and Bangladesh (AfDB, 2014).

The different regional economic communities in Africa have made progress in reducing barriers to trade, although intra-regional trade still suffers from similarities in economic structures and capabilities, relatively high tariffs, incompatible rules of origin across the different trading blocs, and implementation issues. Benefits are most likely to emerge from trade facilitation efforts, both in terms of soft and hard infrastructure, since the African regions have the highest trade costs of all regions (both in terms of intra- and inter-regional trade).

Regional value chains in Africa remain significantly underdeveloped. Apparel represents the one exception, where regional trade has developed significantly in recent years. In assessing the factors that appear to matter most for competitiveness in the production of GVC intermediates – logistics capabilities, strong institutions, human capital, financial capital, and proximity to markets – South Africa's basket of capabilities compares reasonably well with Southeast Asian industrializers (Farole, 2016).

South Africa already operates as the trade and transport gateway for the region, much as China did in the 1990s for East Asian economies. Internationally, South Africa struggles to attract transnational headquarters, with increasing competition from offshore locations (such as Dubai and Mauritius). Farole (2016) cautions that being in a value chain today is no guarantee of being in one tomorrow, or of getting much value out of it.

Table 6.2 presents comparable data for the indexes of what Hallward-Driemmeir and Nayyar (2017) call the three C's: connectedness, capabilities, and competitiveness. Conceptualized rather narrowly but operationally, connectedness deals with market connectivity, capability with technological know-how, and competitiveness with the business environment. For the Capability and Connectedness indexes, countries are ranked based on their z-scores. For the Competitive index, countries are ranked by partitioning the data into terciles and aggregating over the relevant dimensions. Compared with the reference economies, the Africa-12 do poorly on capability; they are slightly below average on connectedness; and they are on par on competitiveness.

Mauritius, Tunisia, South Africa, and Kenya compare favorably with middle-income countries across the three dimensions. Generally high competitiveness and high connectedness characterize the ubiquitous products of textiles, garments, and leather products. High capability branches include rubber and plastics, and fabricated metals. On the other hand, high competitiveness branches of manufacturing comprise food processing, chemicals, and coke and refined petroleum.

Industrial deepening under the two unbundlings

One useful way of framing industrial deepening along the technology ladder is to endogenize the process of productivity-enhancing learning. In a model of diffusion of technology from leaders to followers, under the assumption that all countries share the same technology, the rate of diffusion of technology relative to the level of total factor productivity is captured by the ratio, h/A. This ratio approaches 1.0 as a laggard economy reaches the steady-state level (Jones and Vollrath, 2013: chapter 6). In other words, the degree of **h** indexes mastery of use over the range of

TABLE 6.2 The three C's for African and selected comparator economies

Code	Connectedness	Capabilities	Competitiveness						
	Logistics performance	Total trade restrictiveness	Service trade restrictiveness	Fixed broadband	Tertiary enrollment	IPR payment and receipt	Doing business	Rule of law	Transactions by mobile
	Index	Index	Index	Subscription	(% gross)	(% trade)	Index	Index	(% age 15+)
CIV	2.6	25.4	68.0	0.5	8.8	0.0	52.3	-0.6	-0.3
EGY	3.2	31.6	81.5	3.8	32.7	0.4	56.6	-0.5	-0.7
ETH	2.4	12.4	84.0	0.4	8.1	0.0	47.3	-0.4	-0.9
GHA	2.7	9.1	44.0	0.3	15.3	..	58.8	0.1	-0.2
KEN	3.3	6.4	73.0	0.2	4.0	0.4	61.2	-0.5	1.4
MUS	2.5	4.5	42.0	14.5	38.4	0.2	72.3	0.9	-0.6
NGA	2.6	30.1	36.0	0.0	9.8	..	44.6	1.0	-0.2
SEN	2.3	41.8	36.5	0.7	10.2	0.1	50.7	-0.2	-0.7
TUN	2.5	..	79.0	4.5	34.4	0.1	64.9	-0.1	-0.7
TZA	3.0	55.0	51.5	0.2	3.8	0.0	54.5	0.4	-0.2
ZAF	3.8	4.7	62.0	3.0	19.3	0.9	65.2	0.1	1.2
ZWE	2.1	..	60.0	1.0	6.7	0.2	47.1	-1.4	-0.3
Reference:									
BGD	2.7	..	35.0	2.0	13.4	0.0	40.8	-0.7	-0.7
IND	3.4	13.1	87.5	1.3	24.6	0.5	55.3	-0.1	-0.5
KOR	3.7	4.5	66.0	39.0	97.3	1.2	84.1	1.0	3.0
MEX	3.1	13.8	42.5	10.6	29.2	0.2	72.8	-0.4	-0.9
VNM	3.0	..	31.5	6.7	28.1	..	63.8	-0.3	-0.6

Source: Hallward-Driemmeir and Nayyar (2017), Table A.1.

Reference countries are: Bangladesh, India, S. Korea, Mexico, and Vietnam. For the Capability and Connectedness indexes, countries are ranked based on their z-scores which are aggregated across the three dimensions. For the Competitive index, countries are ranked by partitioning the data into terciles and aggregating over the relevant dimensions. Compared with the reference economies, the Africa-12 do poorly on capability; they are slightly below average on connectedness; they are on par on competitiveness.

intermediate goods ranked by sophistication. **A** is an index of the world technology frontier.

Baldwin (2013) and Sutton (2012) provide a complementary framework. This framework is recast here to relate it directly to our exploration in the previous chapter of the interlinked import substitution and export substitution industrializations.

We make the following assumptions regarding the production of final (whole) products: (1) the marginal cost (MC) curve is downward-sloping because of external economies from higher and broader industrial competencies; (2) the MC for cottage/craft manufacturing is not subject to scale economies; and (3) the net export price for manufactures differs from the domestic price because of natural and man-made barriers (transport costs, quotas, exchange-rate misalignments, and the like).

The two price lines partition the horizontal axis of Figure 6.2 (a) three ways: segment A where competencies are so low that cottage industries preempt the establishment of modern factories, segment B where **infant industries** outcompete craft industries but the small size of the domestic market and over-protection keep domestic firms globally uncompetitive, and segment C where global competitiveness is achieved on the basis of NVC/NVS platforms on the supply side and access to the large world market on the demand side (see Table 6.3).

TABLE 6.3 Flexible industrialization under NVC and GVC

Competing perspectives	National value chains (NVCs) (pre-1990: whole products)	Global value chains (GVCs) (post-1990: tasks)
CA-conforming: — Production and trade (Lin/Monga; Baldwin)	• Brief IS1,2,3 → ES1,2,3	• ES of TB with brief IS → • TB1 (low-value parts) → TB2 (high-value parts)
CA-defying: Production and trade (Stiglitz and Lall)	• IS1 → ES1 → IS2 → ES2 → IS3 → ES3 • IS1 → IS2 → ES1,2 → IS3 → ES3	• IS1,2 → ES1,2,3 (whole or TB)
Shared by both perspectives	• Developmental state • Technological learning • Captive domestic market before exporting • Long-term finance: development banks	• Developmental state • Technological learning • High value-value adding activities and nodes • Long-term finance: domestic plus FDI

Sources and notes: Author.
CA = comparative advantage
IS = import substitutes
ES = export substitutes
TB = task-based products or components
FDI = foreign direct investment
NVC = national value chain
GVC = global value chain

144 Globalization and industrialization

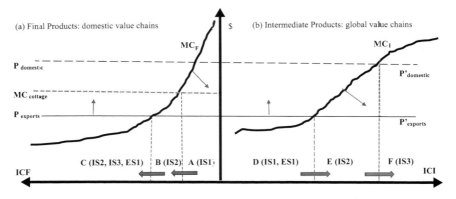

FIGURE 6.2 Industrial capability and catchup under two regimes

The hard task is to model the transition from A to B and again from B to C. Obviously, both entail three big-push effects: investment in competencies on the supply side being ahead of the requisite demand (demand-constrained case), latent demand eliciting capacity expansion (supply-constrained case), or a coordinated appearance of the two sides. The location of the MC curve for final goods would then depend on the level of wages (fixed until the reservoir of labor is exhausted), the size of the domestic market, and the efficiency with which imported machinery can be profitably deployed.

The dynamics are such that productivity gains shift the MC downward while quality gains shift the net price of exports upward, thereby facilitating the transition to higher industrial capability. On the downside are commodity booms, big exchange-rate revaluations, and aid-funded social support programs that may raise wages independently of productivity gains thereby making manufacturing less profitable. These outcomes may lead to industrial stagnation or even deindustrialization.

For intermediate-goods production under the new globalization, we can make the following reasonable assumptions: (1) the production of the final good requires intermediate inputs (parts, components, or tasks) which range from the technologically simple to the complex; (2) just as importantly, the MC is upward-sloping because the domestic production of increasingly sophisticated intermediates requires ever-higher competencies whose mastery cost rises with the sophistication of the product. For given levels of upstream production and intermediate-good production, countries with broader ranges of competencies enjoy lower MC. Similarly, countries with a wide range of competencies produce a greater variety, ranked in terms of complexity, of downstream products.

As shown in Figure 6.2 (b), for a given net export price, the economy produces all parts up to a threshold of sophistication (D to E), and it imports the rest (F). If the MC is above any possible domestic prices, then everything is imported. The two price lines (P' for domestic sales and for export sales) partition the horizontal axis three ways: domestic firms have the competencies to profitably sell at home and abroad around the lower nodes of the global value chains (region D); local firms move up the domestic value chains by producing high-cost IS2 products for the domestic market (often rendering domestic final-good producers less competitive globally) but they are not yet globally competitive given the lower net price for exports (region E); and domestic firms lack the requisite competencies to replace the imports of the most sophisticated capital or consumer goods (region F) (Taglioni and Winkler, 2016).[4]

There are several possibilities for expanding from D to E and from E into F. For a given level of human resources, infrastructure, and business climate, multinationals provide the requisite capital, lend the relevant slices of technology, and share the necessary managerial know-how to enable a latecomer to join the global value supply chain that is commensurate with its comparative advantage.

The latecomer, in this case, does not need to worry about demand since headquarters firms also provide global market access (D). Moving up the global value chain from D to E requires a broader range of capabilities that are necessary for shifting the MC downward to expand the scope for both domestic sales and export sales. This means laggards can leapfrog into global manufacturing without "building" higher industrial capability, but the gains in income or high-wage employment from joining GVCs would depend highly on the capacity of the country to master components with high national value added (Baldwin, 2013).

As we noted repeatedly, very-late industrializers face three sets of challenges. They are: market failures that are ubiquitous and often serious; government failures that are equally ubiquitous and often serious; and an ever-changing global environment reflecting appreciative changes affecting the prospects for the cross-country diffusion of technology, falling costs of doing business abroad, and significant changes in the distribution of income within and among countries (Lall, 2004; Greenwald and Stiglitz, 2006, 2013).[5]

Greening industrialization

One major way of building on the advantage of low wages for the international competitiveness of African manufacturing is to reduce **unit cost** further by reducing the cost of transportation and energy. Given the lack of a rich legacy of a carbon-intensive industrial base and the concentration of oil and gas in a handful of countries (Angola, Nigeria, and Algeria), much of Africa is starting out from an almost clean slate for a workable strategy of **green industrialization**.

Africa has a large reservoir of clean energy – hydropower in central, southern, and northeast Africa; solar energy almost everywhere; wind energy in the highlands and coastal areas; and geothermal energy and bio-energy in selected regions (Sampath and Oyelaran-Oyeyinka, 2015). These energy sources require massive investments in roads, power generation, and power transmission.

This is not an easy task since the massive investments in renewable energy should be tethered to corresponding investments in industrial activity. This way, the supply-driven energy sources will be in sync with the demand for them by business and households alike and make it financially viable. If done right, a climate-resilient

146 Globalization and industrialization

African industrialization, being path-dependent, is likely to benefit from a virtuous cycle of global competitiveness and environmental sustainability (UNECA, 2016; Altenburg and Lutkenhorst, 2015).

Implications for Africa

What then are the implications of the new globalization for Africa's industrial prospects? The next few decades are likely to solidify a radically new international division of labor, especially in the way manufactures and services are designed, produced, and marketed domestically and globally. Before that, production was decoupled spatially from markets for final products whereas now production itself is being unbundled across national borders.

In reality, latecomers are producing whole manufactures with predominantly domestic-sourced as well as imported components while also participating in global production networks as component fabricators or as assemblers of final products. In other words, the first two unbundlings can and do coexist with varying mixes and interconnections.

One can, for example, think of two distinct pathways in which whole products and tasks can merge. Where manufacturing capability for whole products (say, automobiles made in Korea) is already in place, it opens up opportunities for emerging industrial firms to serve either as headquarters firms or as senior partners of headquarters firms. Where this capability is in place, dynamic subcontractor firms may successfully climb the technology ladder to eventually master the entire value chain or switch to deep-veined ones.

Under the first unbundling, latecomers diversified the production of upstream components and tasks to maximize net value added in the production of whole manufactures. This required a big push, especially for capital-intensive activities. Having mastered the production of a variety of whole-product manufacturing, the most successful countries then specialized in components or technologically advanced whole products depending on the dictates of the global market. Japan and South Korea are the most glaring examples of this pathway to being headquarters economies.

Under the second unbundling, it becomes possible to reverse this sequence. Malaysia or China, for example, started out as assemblers or component suppliers as participants in FDI-driven international production networks. With the help of small nudges or a big push (depending on the activity in question), they are upgrading the productivity of their domestic firms to diversify not just into the production of more components but also selectively into whole manufactures. Taiwan is the counter-example here in that it has done well by producing components or assembling high-end manufactures in the era of both unbundlings.

Baldwin (2016) therefore seems to overplay his hand in emphasizing the radical break effected by global chains and in dichotomizing big-pushes and small-nudges as belonging to two distinct eras of industrialization. It may be more prudent to think of the two as complementary rather than as mutually exclusive strategies. For

Africa, the central lesson is that there are multiple and fraught roadways to a modern industrial economy.

Notes

1 The whole-product pathway for a large open-economy industrializer with integrated VC of production at home and disintegrated sales across countries may take the form: IS1 → ES1 → IS2 → ES2 → IS3 → ES3. The production and trade orientation under GVC (with disintegrated VC and consumption) might take this pathway for a large open-economy industrializer: IS1 → {ES1, ES2} → IS2 → {ES1, ES2, ES3} → IS3 → {ES1, ES2, ES3}.
2 In this regard, Rodrik (2013) finds unconditional convergence in productivity at the industry level, that is, the farther a country is behind the technological frontier in a manufacturing industry, the faster the growth of that industry's labor productivity will be. McMillan and Rodrik (2011) also suggest that productivity differences within manufacturing are indicative of inefficiencies which can be remedied with more efficient factor reallocations. A recent econometric study using manufacturing survey data from 52 developing countries also shows that closing the productivity gap among firms within manufacturing, attributable to misallocation of capital and labor, would increase manufacturing productivity by an average of 62%, but closing the productivity gap with the frontier countries would have a much bigger gain (Inklaar et al., 2016).
3 Industrial clusters comprise firms in the same industry (with access to industry-specific knowledge including spillovers, skills, material inputs, and services) or closely related industries. Agglomeration economies, which may assume the form of *scale economies* or *scope economies,* involve the same process but different products and different firms. In this regard, UNIDO (2009: 35) notes that "globally, a firm operating in a city of 10 million people has unit costs some 40 percent lower than if it operated in a city of only 100,000 people." Most benefits come from co-location of similar activities.
4 Taglioni and Winkler (2016: 2–3) explain the contrasting options this way: "In the past, for a country to become an apparel exporter, for example, it would need design capabilities and textile mills; to export in automotive, it would need to produce engines and all the subcomponents, and be able to produce on the scale necessary to compete with foreign producers. Under the new trade dynamics, a country can specialize in certain activities . . . and import the balance of manufacturing needs. Although such a situation does not guarantee significant value capture and upgrading from inception, it does provide a vital first step toward producing world-class, high-quality goods and services."
5 Market failures take several forms: involving self-discovery externalities since private value often falls short of social value, and coordination externalities or increasing returns attributable to the simultaneity and lumpiness of many new investments, or missing public inputs due to the complementarity of the two (soft and hard infrastructure). Government failures might take the form of over-emphasis on short-term revenue or employment maximization, poorly developed firm hierarchies, political capture by special interests or bureaucratic rigidity, and limited state capability to identify and rectify market failures.

References

Africa Economic Outlook (AEO-AFR). (2015). *Africa 2015.* Abidjan: AfDB, OECD, UNDP.
African Development Bank (AfDB), Organisation for Economic Co-operation and Development (OECD), and the United Nations Development Organization (UNIDO). (2014). *Global Value Chains and Africa's Industrialization.* Abidjan: AfDB, OECD, UNIDO.
Altenburg, T., and W. Lutkenhorst. (2015). *Industrial Policy in Developing Countries: Failing Markets, Weak States.* Cheltenham: Edward Elgar.

148 Globalization and industrialization

Andreoni, A. (2011). Productive Capabilities Indicators for Industrial Policy Design. *Working Paper No. 17/2011*. United Nations Industrial Organization (UNIDO).

Baldwin, R. (2012). *Global Supply Chains: Why they Emerged, Why they Matter, and Where they Are Going*. Geneva: Centre for Trade and Economic Integration.

Baldwin, R. (2013). Trade and Industrialization After Globalization's Second Unbundling: How Building and Joining a Supply Chain Are Different and Why It Matters. In: R. Feenstra and A. Taylor, eds., *Globalization in an Age of Crisis: Multilateral Economic Cooperation in the Twenty-First Century*. Chicago: University of Chicago Press.

Baldwin, R. and A. Venables. (2015). Trade Policy and Industrialisation when Backward and Forward Linkages Matter. *Research in Economics*, 69(2), pp. 123-131.

Baldwin, R. (2016). *The Great Convergence: Information Technology and the New Globalization*. Cambridge: Belknap Press of Harvard University Press.

Farole, T. (2016). *Factory Southern Africa?: SACU in Global Value Chains – Summary Report*. Washington, DC: World Bank Group.

Gereffi, G. (1999). International Trade and Industrial Upgrading in the Apparel Commodity Chain. *Journal of International Economics*, 48(1), pp. 37–70.

Gereffi, G., and K. Fernandez-Stark. (2011). *Global Value Chain Analysis: A Primer*. [online] Durham, NC: Center on Globalization, Governance & Competitiveness, Duke University. Available at: www.cggc.duke.edu/pdfs/2011-05-31_GVC_analysis_a_primer.pdf.

Gong, X. (2015). African Economic Structural Transformation: A Diagnostic Analysis. *Journal of African Transformation*, 1(1), pp. 1–22.

Gordon, R. (2016). *The Rise and Fall of American Growth*. Princeton: Princeton University Press.

Greenwald, B., and J. Stiglitz. (2006). Helping Infant Economies Grow: Foundations of Trade Policies for Developing Countries. *American Economic Review*, 96(2), pp. 141–146.

Greenwald, B., and J. Stiglitz. (2013). Learning and Industrial Policy: Implications for Africa. In: J. Stiglitz, J.Y. Lin, and E. Patel, eds., *The Industrial Policy Revolution II: Africa in the 21st Century*. New York: Palgrave Macmillan, pp. 1–24.

Hallward-Driemmeir, M., and G. Nayyar. (2017). *Trouble in the Making? The Future of Manufacturing-Led Development*. Washington, DC: World Bank Group.

Inklaar, R., et al. (2016). The Role of Resource Misallocation in Cross-Country Differences in Manufacturing Productivity. [online] *Macroeconomics Dynamics*, 20(1), pp. 1–24. Available at: http://dx.doi.org/10.1017/S1365100515000668.

Jones, C., and D. Vollrath. (2013). A Simple Model of Growth and Development. In: *Introduction to Economic Growth*. New York: Norton, Chapter 6, pp. 140–156.

Lall, S. (2004). Selective Industrial and Trade Policies in Developing Countries: Theoretical and Empirical Issues. In: C. Soludo, O. Ogbu, and H. Chang, eds., *The Politics of Trade and Industrial Policy in Africa*. Trenton: Africa World Press, Inc.

Lin, J.Y. (2012). *New Structural Economics: A Framework for Rethinking Development Policy*. Washington, DC: World Bank.

Marsh, P. (2012). *The New Industrial Revolution*. New Haven: Yale University Press.

McMillan, M. and D. Rodrik. (2011). Globalization, Structural Change and Productivity Growth. *NBER Working Paper No. 17143*, Cambridge, MA: NBER.

OECD, WTO, and WBG. (2014). *Global Value Chains: Challenges, Opportunities, and Implications for Policy*. Sydney: G20 Trade Ministers Meeting.

Organisation for Economic Co-operation and Development (OECD). (2015). The Participation of Developing Countries in Global Value Chains: Implications for Trade and Trade Related Policies. *OECD Trade Policy Paper No. 179*. Paris: OECD.

Porter, M. (1990). *The Competitive Advantage of Nations*. Cambridge, MA: Harvard University Press.

Rodrik, D. (2013). Unconditional Convergence in Manufacturing. *Quarterly Journal of Economics*, 128(1), pp. 165–204.

Sampath, P., and B. Oyelaran-Oyeyinka, eds. (2015). *Sustainable Industrialization in Africa: Toward a New Development Agenda*. London: Palgrave Macmillan.

Sutton, J. (2012). *Competing in Capabilities: The Globalization Process*. Oxford: Oxford University Press.

Taglioni, D., and D. Winkler. (2016). *Making Global Value Chains Work for Development*. Washington, DC: World Bank Group.

United Nations Economic Commission for Africa (UNECA). (2016). *Economic Report on Africa 2016: Greening Africa's Industrialization*. Addis Ababa: UNECA.

United Nations Industrial Development Organization (UNIDO). (2009). *Industrial Development Report 2009: Breaking in and Moving UP – New Industrial Challenges for the Bottom Billion and the Middle-Income Countries*. Oxford: Oxford University Press.

United Nations Industrial Development Organization (UNIDO). (2015). *Inclusive and Sustainable Industrial Development*. [online] Geneva: UNIDO. Available at: www.unido.org/fileadmin/user_media_upgrade/Who_we_are/Structure/Director-General/DG_Brochure_February_2015_Web.pdf.

World Bank. (2016). *World Development Report 2016: Digital Dividends*. Washington, DC: World Bank.

PART IV
Africa's postcolonial industrial experience

7

AFRICAN INDUSTRIAL DEVELOPMENT

We are now ready to explore the diversity of African economies and their record on industrial development. African industrial activity is significantly informal with few robust channels of transition to formality. In this and the two chapters that follow, we take stock of the available evidence from the country case studies and cross-country regressions to identify the major challenges and opportunities facing one of "the last frontiers" of industrialization in the twenty-first century.

One continent, many Africas

Although there is an economic continuum between Africa and the sub-regions of the two neighboring continents (Mediterranean Europe and Western Asia) and certainly within the continent itself, international organizations tend to slice Africa in myriad ways. It is quite common to see Africa divided north-south by the Sahara Desert as if this provides a clear demarcation by race (Arab versus Black), religion (Muslim versus Christian), or historical experiences (colonized versus non-colonized). Africa-centered organizations such as the Economic Commission for Africa and the African Development Bank pragmatically prefer finer and more economically sensible groupings: North Africa, West Africa, Northeast Africa, East Africa, Central Africa, and Southern Africa.

Samir Amin (1972) provides a useful sorting of the regions of this variegated continent. His heroic attempt to meld geography, culture, economy, and history yields three Sub-Saharan macro-regions of agro-climatic and mineral zones. They are: (1) the *Africa of the colonial trade economy* which covers coastal western Africa (warm semi-arid and tropical savanna) and its hinterlands where smallholder agricultural surplus was taxed heavily by both the colonial and the postcolonial state, (2) the *Africa of the concession-owning companies*, especially in the Congo River Basin (equatorial and monsoon), where brutal means of primitive accumulation were

154 *Africa's postcolonial experience*

deployed by unusually avaricious colonial companies to extract forest products and minerals, and (3) the *Africa of the labor reserves* covering eastern and southern Africa (tropical and sub-tropical savanna) where extensive land dispossession and forced labor were employed to benefit the otherwise unprofitable plantations and mines.

By extension, two sub-regions remain. They are (4) *North (Maghreb) Africa* with Mediterranean-coastal and Arabized Berber populations dominated alternately by Asian and European empires and (5) *The Remainder* – an array of historical exceptions such as Ethiopia, Somalia, Madagascar, and Mauritius.

All five sub-regions are well-represented in our analyses. The next two chapters will tunnel down these macro-regions to country and industry levels. From the standpoint of industrial development, much of Africa is an industrial wasteland except for macro-region #3. While we should be careful not to overgeneralize, the balance between homogeneity and heterogeneity for our purposes surprisingly favors the former.

So, what are the notable stylized facts of African economic development? The most frequently cited generalizations are that the continent (UNECA, 2016, 2017; AfDB, OECD, and UNIDO; 2017; de Janvry and Sadoulet, 2010; Young, 2012; Newman et al., 2016):

1 has factor endowments which comprise ample arable land, semi-skilled and unskilled labor, mineral resources, and major rivers;
2 suffers poor market connectivity because of landlockedness, inadequate infrastructure, and highly fractionalized and fragmented polities;
3 has a predominantly subsistence agriculture with an ever-changing mix of pastoralism, staples, and cash crops;
4 has small domestic markets due to its low and unequally distributed income;
5 lacks strong inter-regional complementarities largely because of poor infrastructural (and market) connectivity and limited product differentiation;
6 has a low income-growth elasticity of poverty and the lowest responsiveness of poverty rates to changes in income distribution;
7 boasts relatively poor craft culture and cottage industries, compared with Asia, to serve as a springboard for modern industry;
8 over-relies on revenues from commodity exports as well as FDI flows that are concentrated until very recently in the extraction of precious metals and scarce fuels;
9 has a colonial legacy of a weak and extractive state whose capture has been the object of competition among rent-seeking political entrepreneurs, and
10 has nurtured a low-productivity traditional service sector that is prematurely becoming a significant provider of employment for the urban economy.

As we noted in Chapter 1, the Africa "rising" and then "falling" narrative reflects simple extrapolations from recent trends which betray the superficiality of our understanding of external and internal structural constraints and opportunities faced by the continent. The so-called African growth tragedy has unfortunately

African industrial development **155**

triggered several clever meta explanations that confuse cause and effect (UNECA, 2016, provides a critical synthesis). These explanations blame tropical climate, bad neighborhood, ethnic fractionalization, colonialism, or a culture of religiosity and communalism.[1] The central problems of Africa's industrial failure may be better understood as a reflection of the failure of political and market institutions.

An overview of African industry

Structural transformation in Africa's economies remains a big challenge as well as a high priority. The latest UNECA report (UNECA, 2016), notes, for example, that achieving the African Union's Agenda-2063 and fulfilling the United Nations' Sustainable Development Goals (SDGs) calls for a re-design of growth and industrialization strategies to better reflect Africa's endowments, the global imperatives of sustainability, and mutually beneficial regional integration.

As we noted in Part One, there are plenty of reasons for Africans to make a serious attempt to industrialize. Africa persistently faces fluctuations in its terms of trade (between manufactures and resources or between manufactures and cash crops). Since wages are generally productivity-driven, skilling the workforce and expanding high-productivity industries is the best way to boost high wages. If this is not enough, a broad-based and industry-based economy is one of the best ways to mitigate risk by making income flows reasonably predictable in a resilient economy.

As in other regions of the world, there is a strong correlation between MVA per capita and GDP per capita. This is, of course, confounded by large inter-African variations in resource endowments. Resource-dependent African economies, for example, account for 60% of the continent's GDP (UNECA, 2016). However, Nigeria and South Africa alone account for half of this endowment, albeit with a large difference in MVA per head.

Most African countries flirted with the then prevailing IS strategy between independence and the second oil shock of the late 1970s. The data show that initial spurts of growth in output and productivity were followed by stagnation as existing potentials are exhausted. Africa switched to export promotion in the 1980s under pressure from donor countries and institutions. The results, however, produced only marginal improvements since the other side of export success – a threshold industrial base – was not in place. Africa was no China or India where openness alone was the missing link.[2]

More specifically, African industrial development went through three broad phases since independence. The first phase, which began in the 1960s and ended in the late 1970s, is the import substitution industrialization phase led by state enterprises. The second phase, which represents the structural adjustment programs era, began in the early 1980s and ended in the late 1990s. The third phase, still underway, is the era of donor-driven investment-climate reform and poverty-reduction strategy which has prioritized social spending (Ayittey, 2012; Newman et al., 2016).

Despite these externally driven policy experiments, or perhaps because of them, African industrialization has shown a remarkable lack of resiliency. According to

156 *Africa's postcolonial experience*

the most recent reviews of African industrial development (UNIDO and UNCTAD, 2011; UNECA, 2016; AfDB, OECD, and UNIDO, 2017), African manufacturing industry continues to lose ground to better-prepared Asian economies in the export markets as well as in the home market itself for labor-intensive manufactures. The continent remains heavily dependent on small native-owned enterprises where the prospects are poor for graduating to mid-size status (by capturing bigger market share and upgrading technological capability), and inter-firm relations continue to be idiosyncratically informal (Shiferaw, 2007).

African firms produce mainly light consumer goods to satisfy the rising domestic intermediate and final demands of a relatively small urban population. Such industries, however, have failed to establish strong forward or backward linkages within the industrial sector and with other sectors of the economy, most notably with the agricultural sector. The continent was littered with un-competitive import-substituting industries that are heavily dependent on external sources for raw materials and other factor inputs.

Egypt, Morocco, and Cote d'Ivoire were notable in switching to export-oriented strategies. The export-oriented strategy that accompanied import substitution was mainly agriculture-led, although the processing of basic metals was also promoted. Few plowed back foreign exchange earnings into downstream processing activities. Some export-oriented industries were also heavily protected by tariff and non-tariff measures as well as subsidies. Major problems such as an inadequate supply of industrial skills, the lack of technological capability, and the inability to exploit and process Africa's immense agricultural, mineral, and energy resources all contributed to the downturn of industrial production from 1980–2000.

In this vein, there is consensus on at least two preconditions for a successful global integration of Africa. First, agricultural productivity should be high enough to keep the price of food and fiber down. Second, manufacturing productivity must also be high enough to make industrial goods affordable to low-income households in the rural economy as well as internationally competitive.

African countries, nearly all with per capita incomes of less than $10,000 in purchasing power parity dollars, are often characterized by a low index of human assets and a high index of economic vulnerability. They are poor ultimately because they are low-productivity economies. Industrialization of the right kind, therefore, holds much promise in most of these countries for boosting equitable growth.

These considerations raise a fundamental question: can high-risk but resource-rich Africa nurture a comparative advantage in manufactures? In theory, high resource endowments lead to high wages that render manufacturing non-competitive. Some, therefore, argue that being better endowed in land and natural resources, Africa would be better off deepening its specialization in exporting primary goods (Wood and Mayer, 2001). Others suggest that acquiring a comparative advantage in manufactures is possible but only with significant physical and human investment under higher quality institutions and policies (Collier, 2000; Page, 2013). Although African industrial firms, being furthest behind from the frontier, do have the greatest *potential* to appropriate the large stock of globally available technological knowledge,

African industrial development **157**

they also have a limited but cultivable capability for exploiting such profitable opportunities.

African industrial firms are constrained by many factors on the demand and the supply sides. The most binding is scarcity of credit, for working capital and long-term investment. Second in importance is limited demand because of macroeconomic instability, misaligned or rigid exchange rate regimes, draconian economic controls on capital outflows, and shallow markets. Third in importance is inadequate public services (power, roads, rails, and telephone), including poor regulations (corruption and contract enforcement).

Regarding opportunity (incentives) to break in, the limited size of the domestic market for manufactures and the enormous first-mover advantages enjoyed by firms in rich or emerging economies means that fledgling African firms must face a traumatic loss of domestic market shares they enjoyed because of natural and policy-induced protection. Since trade liberalization, by inducing changes in the real exchange rate, has a more immediate effect on incentives than on productive capability, the possible becomes the probable only when the severe constraints on the ability of African firms to compete globally are in place (Biggs and Raturi, 1997; World Bank, 2000; Stein, 2012; Bora et al., 1999).

This might help explain why willy-nilly trade liberalizations turned out to be largely disappointing and why a stark reversal of fortune occurred between African and East (and now South) Asia in the postwar decades. The Gerschenkronian (Gerschenkron, 1962) notion of "advantages of backwardness," it turns out, presupposes the existence of a minimum level of domestic industrial capacity to enable late starters to telescope the catching up process. Even if late entrants into the world market face formidable barriers of entry, switching to outward orientation in a timely fashion still holds great potential for enhancing technical efficiency, credit worthiness, and access to better market information.

Firm-level studies on formal manufacturing

Because of limitations of theory and data, SSA economies remain poorly understood. Existing studies of industrial development in SSA fall into two categories. The first is a growing body of largely descriptive literature by economic historians, and analytical case studies based on data from surveys of industry by international organizations and government agencies. The second comprises econometric studies using firm-level data.

The empirical analyses show that African industry is doubly dualistic. One form of dualism exists between micro and small-scale enterprises (MSSE) in the informal sector and medium and large-scale enterprises (MLE) in the formal sector. The other pertains to ownership – between native-owned small-scale enterprises and large-scale firms owned by expatriates or the state.

Empirical studies at the micro level suggest that African manufacturing enterprises display several peculiarities (Bigsten and Soderbom, 2006). A remarkable, and perhaps a hopeful, feature of African industry is its heterogeneity. There is a

158 Africa's postcolonial experience

wide range of performance outcomes across firms within countries as well as across countries with differing investment climates (Tybout, 2000; Tribe, 2000; Mazumdar and Mazaheri, 2003; Van Biesebroeck, 2003; Bigsten and Soderbom, 2006).

The full list of constraints on African manufacturing includes the availability of low-cost and good quality inputs, access to finance, the availability of managerial and technical skills, adequate supply of relevant occupational skills (not just formal education), and access to reliable and efficient infrastructure and trade logistics (Dinh et al., 2012).

To overcome these challenges, Newman et al. (2016), based on eight case studies and econometric evidence from firm-level data, argue that African industrial policy should put special emphasis on competitiveness and on export-oriented industries to take advantage of domestic market growth and the accelerating divestment from labor-intensive manufactures in East Asia.

The second characteristic of African industry is the particularly pernicious role played by extractive political institutions which provide stronger incentives for "costly acts of income redistribution" than for long-term wealth creation. We will revisit this issue later in this chapter.

A third characteristic is that industrial entrepreneurs in Africa face significant investment-retarding uncertainty about price, demand, customer payment, infrastructure, and isolation. Reviewing the research based on two waves of enterprise surveys in the 1990s under the regional program on enterprise development (RPED), Bigsten and Soderbom (2006) offer the following assessment:

- investment in physical capital has remained low primarily because of a high level of uncertainty;
- exports have remained low primarily because of the high costs (regulatory and infrastructural) of entering the export market; and
- exporting leads to efficiency gains for Africa perhaps due to the anti-trade biases of the past and the large scope for learning arising from a substantial technological gap.

The World Bank's RPED provides both perception-based and objective data from a comprehensive set of enterprise surveys. One clear message from the RPED is that there is a considerable variability in economic performance across firms. Bigsten et al. (2000), for example, show that for Cameroon, Ghana, Kenya, and Zimbabwe, one-fourth of the sampled firms are less than half as productive as the median firm, while another fourth of the firms are more than twice as productive as the median firm in the sample, and the variability is even more pronounced in for-profit rates.

The data further suggest that wages, as well as labor productivity, are abysmally low. The net result of international competitiveness in labor-intensive manufactures is that the productivity disadvantage is more than made up for by the wage advantage to yield a lower unit-labor-cost than most competitors in Asia. When non-labor costs are added, the unit cost in Africa is much higher. In terms of job creation, wage employment has increased in absolute terms but did not keep pace with labor force growth of some 17 million annually; the share of the informal sector in total employment has increased rapidly; and African economies with high unemployment rates surprisingly tend to have small informal urban sectors (Liedholm, 1992; Mazumdar and Mazaheri, 2003).

The microeconomic evidence further shows that as industrial development deepens the distribution of firms by size becomes bimodal. Exporting firms tend to have higher technical efficiency and credit worthiness. There is convergence in size as small firms tend to grow faster than large firms. Profitability tends to be positively correlated with the size of the firm since size is positively correlated with efficiency in terms of unit cost (Newman et al., 2016).

Newman et al. (2016) note that inputs are a binding constraint in two of five light manufacturing subsectors (agribusiness and wood products) and an important constraint in the other three (apparel, leather, and metal products). On average, across the five subsectors, inputs (which represent more than 70% of total production costs) are more than 25% more expensive in Africa than in China, a 20% production cost penalty. In most cases, higher input costs wipe out Africa's labor cost advantage.

We also know from several cross-country studies that exporting and higher levels of efficiency (TFP) are positively correlated with the direction of causality going from domestic productivity to international competitiveness. Given the narrowness of the domestic markets, learning by exporting appears to accelerate the initial efficiency advantages of larger firms for pioneering firms. In the long run, a virtuous circle becomes operative: efficient firms are more likely to export (self-selection), and exporting helps those firms learn faster and exploit scale economies – all of which seem to operate in Africa, too (Van Biesebroeck, 2003; Bigsten and Soderbom, 2006; Rankin et al., 2006).

However, the direction of causality is not always clear: do firm's record export success because they are willing to export or do they export because they are simply extending their domestic success to the export market? The latter is more likely the case since firm performance tends to be positively correlated with the quality of infrastructure and trade logistics. As we will see in the country case studies, African firms identify input supply – including availability, quality, and cost – as a leading obstacle to developing competitive light manufacturing.

Sub-Saharan Africa's potential competitiveness in light manufacturing is based on two advantages (Dinh et al., 2012). The first (latent) advantage arises from the fact that Africa has low unit labor cost in some activities. Clarke (2012), however, notes that some branches of manufacturing in Africa are high-wage and high-productivity for reasons related less to innovation than to a business environment that favors politically connected firms. The second advantage is an abundance of natural resources that can supply raw materials for domestic processing such as skins for the footwear industry, hard and soft timber for the furniture industry, and land for the agribusiness industry.

As noted in the previous chapter, the second unbundling has produced momentous challenges and opportunities for Africa (Gong, 2015). As we will see in the next section, Africa has experienced growth acceleration since the mid-1990s

160 Africa's postcolonial experience

linked largely to commodity booms. Unfortunately, the growth acceleration has not been associated with economic transformation thereby rendering it less inclusive and sustainable after the mid-2010s. Agriculture in most countries does not generate a large enough surplus (for processing, domestic consumption, and exports) to finance an industrial drive.

Competition from cheap imports from Asia has now devastated much of the inefficient import-substituting manufacturing in Africa. Even the more industrialized South Africa is having a hard time withstanding the competitive pressure at home and certainly abroad. Only a handful of countries has managed to take advantage of the preferential access to the EU and the U.S.A. markets for manufactures (Wood and Mayer, 2001; Elbadawi et al., 2006; Collier and Venables, 2007).

The twin production-trade dynamics of African manufacturing are obviously interlinked. Productivity-driven growth requires the coupling of production capability and market opportunity, and we need a good performance index that combines the two features of industrialization.

A promising candidate is the African Transformation Index (ATI), developed by the Africa Centre for Economic Transformation (ACET, 2014). ACET defines economic transformation based on five key outcome measures of the economy: diversification, export competitiveness, productivity growth, technology upgrading, and improvements in human economic well-being collectively referred to as DEPTH. ATI is an equal-weighted average of the individual indexes for each of the five variables.

The ATI indexes for 2010 show Mauritius, South Africa, Cote d'Ivoire, Senegal, Uganda, Kenya, and Gabon as the top seven rapidly transforming economies in Africa. The middle seven are Cameroon, Madagascar, Botswana, Mozambique, Tanzania, Zambia, and Malawi. The least transformed are Benin, Ghana, Ethiopia, Rwanda, Nigeria, Burundi, and Burkina Faso.

Africa's manufacturing deficit, the share of MVA standing at half of its peers from low-income Asia, clearly has microeconomic foundations in its firm structure. African manufacturing is dominated by small firms whose low investment rates, productivity, wages, and employment-generating capacity are all positively correlated. Given the large dispersions of such features across firms and branches of manufacturing, policies that break the infrastructural, credit, skill, and competitive constraints are likely to bring large TFP gains as firms scale up (Newman et al., 2016).

African informal manufacturing

The preceding survey of the formal manufacturing sector in Africa suggests a mixed record of promising inroads and structural barriers. Africa's informal manufacturing sector is also important both as a provider of goods and jobs, and as a potential incubator of modern industrial firms.

There is substantial literature on informal enterprises, especially in Latin America, but much less so on informal industrial activity. Distinct from the shadow economy, the informal sector is characterized by heterogeneity, non-legality, non-regulation, little or no presumptive taxation, fragility, and the provision of crisis-induced self-employment.

Benjamin and Mbaye (2012) provide a definition of informality that rightly accentuates the importance of a continuum between formality and informality in Africa. They employ six criteria: size, tax regime, honesty of accounts, registration, fixity of workplace, and access to credit – of which the first three were found particularly significant. A simplification yields four distinct types of firms: small informal, large informal, small formal, and large formal – all four of which are interconnected in a web of sub-contracting on both the supply and marketing sides. In West Africa, large informal firms, which meet all the criteria for formality except one (clean accounts), are comparable in size and productivity to firms in the formal sector.

By all accounts, the informal sector in Africa is large in terms of both value added and employment.[3] The specific nature of African informality includes very low wages, few global linkages, and extremely vulnerable labor. Sub-Saharan Africa, in fact, stands out as the most informalized region of the world, with an informal economy that accounts for as much as 80% of the non-agricultural labor force, and for nearly half of its national output (La Porta and Shleifer, 2011; Meagher, 2013). Schneider et al. (2011) estimate that the informal sector accounts for about 38% of GDP in Sub-Saharan Africa. By comparison, the informal sector accounts for only about 18% in East Asia and the Pacific.

Benjamin and Mbaye (2012: 54–55) find that the informal sector is concentrated in nontradable industries, mainly services, commerce, distribution, construction, or locally sourced food products or raw materials. As such, informality accounts for as high as 90% of employment and over 50% of output in West Africa while the formal sector accounts for less than 10% of jobs – most in the public sector. The size of the informal sector labor force, depending on the definition used, was in the 80%–90% range in Zimbabwe in 2015. Another name for underdevelopment, of course, is pervasive informality.

In terms of firm characteristics, a crucial but little-studied attribute of the informal sector in Africa is the coexistence of large and small informal operators, including differences in the attitude of policymakers between the two. In West Africa, however, large informal firms resemble formal firms. Informality is clearly a continuum, with formal firms regularly engaging in informal activities and practices. The regulatory environment also plays a crucial two-way role in fostering the pervasiveness of the informal sector. Weaknesses in the business climate and regulatory framework induce firms to opt for informal-sector status; and the dominance of the informal sector further undermines compliance with tax rules, regulations, and codes of conduct (Benjamin and Mbaye, 2012).

As we will see in the next two chapters, formal-sector firms ironically and incessantly complain about "unfair competition" from informal firms. This is in large part because a major part of the informal sector revolves around smuggling to evade import barriers which are intended to protect formal-sector manufacturers. Other reasons for this complaint include tax avoidance, corruption to gain access to public

162 Africa's postcolonial experience

services, and use of effective but discriminatory kinship and religious networks to compensate for the lack of formal access to long-term finance and business services.

Informal operators are here to stay. They occupy a prominent place in artisanal manufacturing and light manufacturing such as wood products, metals, and clothing. Liedholm (2001) argues, for example, that three markets (clothing; food products, including alcoholic drinks; and wood products) constitute 75% of the manufacturing activities of small firms in urban areas and 90% in rural areas in Africa.

Formalization generally means greater access to public services conditional on compliance with regulations and regular payment of taxes. Participation in the formal sector engenders both fixed costs such as those related to registration and variable costs such as those related to various taxes. The negative correlation between productivity and informality also reflects a two-way causality: self-selection of informality by low-productivity firms, and reduced access to public services, in turn, perpetuating low productivity.

One reason for the higher productivity of formal-sector manufacturing is that it engages in capital-intensive activities. In this respect, Dinh et al. (2012: chapter 4) find that access to finance and informal sector competition is the most binding constraint for firms in Africa. Given the high degree of informality in manufacturing and the tendency of informal manufacturing to absorb the unemployed disengaged from the formal manufacturing sector, policy should cultivate mutually beneficial linkages between the two sectors.

An interesting question arises at this point concerning how firms transition from smallness to largeness, and from informality to formality. There are, in fact, three important transitions: from small informal to large informal, small informal to small formal, and large informal to large formal. The drivers include the education level of owner, the friendliness of the regulatory environment, the lucrativeness of formal contracts, and the ease of evasion of taxes and fees.

The transition that matters most for African industrialization is the one from small-scale agro-processing to formal and modern manufacturing. With few exceptions that are widely seen as trailblazers, Africa lacks the long and rich tradition of handicraft and cottage activity that was the hallmark of proto-industrialization in Europe, India, China, and Japan which served as a springboard for modern industry (Amsden, 2001; Morris and Adelman, 1988). As in Latin America, colonial urbanization, émigrés (settlers), and extractive activity provided the impetus for modern manufacturing only in a handful of countries (South Africa, Zimbabwe, Cote d'Ivoire). Even when the industrial legacies are rich, as in the latter two countries, they appear to be too vulnerable to state fragility.

Bigsten and Soderbom (2006) note in this respect that many unanswered questions remain concerning the association between enterprise size and growth, the fact of small and relatively productive firms having high exit rates, the drivers of the transition from the informal sector to the formal sector (Kaufmann et al., 2010; Shiferaw, 2007), and the drivers of a reorientation from the domestic market with low value-added products to exports of high value-added products.

These considerations make the policy implications rather clear-cut. To facilitate the transitions and make formalization attractive, it is important to collect reliable data to appreciate the intricate interdependencies across firm statuses. Policies must be designed to accommodate the needs of each node of the formal-informal continuum. The needs of small informal firms to grow may focus on the availability of reasonably priced and reliably supplied inputs from both the formal and the agricultural sectors while those of the large informal firms may focus on reasonable taxation, school-to-work programs, secure property rights, and access to basic public services.

State capacity lies behind these policy preferences and their full implementation since only a capable and legitimate state ensures control of territory and the transformation of society and has a reciprocal fiscal contract with citizens. Unfortunately, the legacies of extractive colonialism and the dominance of external forces have created a peculiar mix of formal and informal institutions. The Achilles Heel of African industrialization may very well be the elusiveness of a capable and accountable State.

The African state: developmentalist or parasitic

Mass politics has historically been a product of industrialization by enabling organized labor to restrain powerholders – business elites and state elites alike (Acemoglu and Robinson, 2012; World Bank, 2017). As Gerschenkron (1962) argued, and the experiences of late industrializers have by and large affirmed, capable and activist states often play a make-or-break role in industrial development. In the case of Africa, the extent of state and business capabilities is limited, and the appropriateness of the degree and nature of state activism is widely questioned.

Seen from the broad sweeps of history, countries went through distinct modern political orders ending up in a functional state, the rule of law, and some form of accountability to citizens (Fukuyama, 2012, 2014; Huntington, 2006). In the post-1750 era, organized political orders sprang from patrimonial states where kin-based reciprocity defined and reproduced personalized political authority. Because of domestic imperial imperatives or external pressure, many political units evolved into neopatrimonial states by superimposing semi-professional bureaucracies on the foundations of age-old patrimonialism. With the advent of industrialization, a quasi-Weberian clientelist state emerged where a strong incentive to capture it rendered the state highly contestable. Mature industrial and post-industrial societies eventually managed to contain destabilizing violence through a combination of credible elite pacts and a progressive instilling of trust in impersonal institutions.

There is a correspondence between specific forms of economic transition and political transition since there appears to be an affinity between exclusionary (inclusive) political institutions and exclusionary (inclusive) economic institutions (Acemoglu and Robinson, 2012). The first development transition is characterized by the presence of a strong state to ensure order and provide basic public services by collecting adequate revenues, enforcing respect for market fundamentals, and a demographic transition induced by the reduction of mass poverty.

The handmaiden of the second development transition is a development-friendly state that combines market fundamentals with active industrial policy. The concomitant emergence of organized interest groups to press the interests of fundamental stakeholders in society gives rise to effective institutional mechanisms for preference aggregation and conflict resolution. The end point is full industrialization, global integration, and a fully accountable state (paternalistic or democratic) under the rule of law.

The institutional forms that meet the needs of market-driven growth need not be uniform across countries (World Bank, 2017). In fact, given the diversity of cultures, income levels, political systems, and growth prospects, institutions (and the policies that emanate from them) cannot be but heterogeneous. A good example is provided by cases where an agro-extractive old elite is tamed to accept a reduction in wealth inequality (such as land reform) to broaden the home market, and domestic consumers are subjected to choices limited largely to shoddy homemade manufactures during the learning period.

The politico-economic system, by resolving distributional conflicts efficiently and imposing discipline on the various economic actors at a low cost, shapes the incentives for budding industrialists to exploit domestic as well as external opportunities. Where political settlements create positive incentives that favor productive activities, the economy generates rapid and shared growth (Khan, 2013). Where they do not, unproductive rent seeking becomes rampant.

Analytical work, of course, is complicated by the feedback effects from policies and outcomes which endogenously influence the quality of the institutions and policies themselves (North, 1994). But in all cases, institutions must be tailored to local circumstances especially in the formative stages. The Chinese experience with unorthodox institutions is one demonstration of this fact (Cai and Wang, 2008).

Many have argued that the most binding constraint on Africa's industrial development is the myopic and parochial nature of its state elites as well as business elites. This is in part because native elites inherited an extractive, contested, and coercive colonial state. Many such African states are steadily disintegrating into kin-based patrimonial reciprocity between tribute payers and their protectors (World Bank, 1997; Moss et al., 2006; Hyden, 2008; Ayittey, 2012; Kelsall, 2013).

African state elites are also sandwiched between international and transnational actors and domestic forces that are challenging their legitimacy to rule. One outcome is that the transition from patronage-based politics to citizenship-based politics has been short-circuited by unearned income from resource rents, siphoning off urban land value from the poor, and geopolitically motivated aid. Another is the hostility of rulers toward an autonomous private sector (and non-state organizations in general) that can serve as a competing power base. Finally, growing diaspora has contradictory effects on this political evolution as an important source of remittances, skills, and an escape valve for dissidents while also shifting the locus of the political opposition abroad.

One organizing concept on offer for analyzing the African political economy is **neopatrimonialism**. Neopatrimonialism is *patrimonial* in the sense that collective goods are parceled out by politicians to constituencies who observe these and related norms concerning the role of authority, and it is *new* in the sense that informal or personalistic relations with supporters are encased in poorly honored formal bureaucratic (or legal-rational) institutions (van de Walle, 2001).[4]

Neopatrimonialism can be fruitfully applied to the process of African postcolonial state (re)formation which reconciles two conflicting objectives: forming an effective coalition for state building and regime maintenance, and developing the bureaucratic capacity to promote long-term economic development. Political control requires effective management of patron-client relations while rapid growth calls for an entrepreneurial and rule-bound bureaucracy partnering with an autonomous native business class operating in a functioning market space.

Examples abound regarding well-designed but failed industrial drives when "politics are not right." Whitfield et al. (2015) and Khan (2013) note, for example, that variations in neopatrimonialism are driven by three conditions that shape the efficacy of industrial policy. One condition is the relative power among the factions within the ruling coalition (contestability). The second is the leverage (over the state elite) enjoyed by the domestic industrialist class in terms of its ability to assimilate advanced technology and to withhold investment (vulnerability). And the third is the technocratic capability (efficiency) and autonomy of the state bureaucracy (trust).

Where this political balance exists, as in South Africa and Mauritius, an institutionalized and constructive contestation emerges between the fundamental interest groups. Where the business class is too weak or too dependent on the state but the state elite is secure, an enlightened regime can undertake growth-friendly policies – a sort of developmental patrimonialism as in the cases of Ethiopia and Rwanda (Kelsall, 2013; Abegaz, 2018). Where both are insecure, a neopatrimonial collusion prevails as in Ghana and Zambia (Handley, 2014).

It would then be fair to conclude that state formation and industrialization in Africa are taking place simultaneously. Seemingly incongruent practices coexist (violent and peaceful, the rule of law and rule by law, formal and informal, unproductive rent seeking and productive rent seeking, and nationalist and comprador).

What we lack, therefore, is something that goes beyond the narrow scope of economic analysis. We need a sound theoretical framework to identify the conditions under which the political processes and the economic processes in an industrializing economy can allow for a viable state to emerge. More narrowly, we need a political-economy framework to help us understand how growth-supporting (capital-accumulative and entrepreneurial) institutions emerge from the varying configurations of growth retarding (predatory, parasitic, extractive, or redistributive) politico-economic contests that all countries had to endure on the eve of industrialization (Chang, 2013; Acemoglu and Robinson, 2012).

The commonly cited agents of economic transformation are a developmental regime, a nucleus of an entrepreneurial business class, and a large enough initial

166 Africa's postcolonial experience

investible surplus (from resource rent, development aid, or trade margins). As Wade (2012: 263) puts it: "The key discriminating institutional features between the catch-up countries and the falling-behind countries are related to the state's capacity to coordinate agents, stabilize their confidence in the state's behavior, and establish national development as an urgent overarching project."

A *Developmental State* (DS) is essentially a state with effective politico-economic institutions that can render the transformative vision of a *developmental regime* (DR) politically feasible and economically desirable (see Box 7.1). The DR, as a particular political settlement among party, military, bureaucratic, and business interests, can be usefully grouped into one of two distinct classes: a *partnership* between a hegemonic ruling elite and a coalition of powerful non-state political and economic elites or a *benevolent dictatorship* which may still harbor paternalistic hostility toward an independent business class.

The marketist DR, in turn, comes in two flavors. The first variant is the quasi-democratic corporate coalition for growth such as India after 1990, Thailand, Indonesia, or Malaysia. Other examples are the party-led and a market-friendly partnership with the private sector as was the case with pre-1980 S. Korea or Taiwan (Amsden, 1989; Wade, 2003). The second variant is what we call vanguardist DR which is hostile to the politically uncaptured business class and prefers, for example, national mobilization for growth by diktat. Examples include post-socialist China and Vietnam as well as the authoritarian-populist regimes of Ethiopia and Rwanda (Abegaz, 2013).

The implications for industrial policy are clear enough. Ansu (2013: 519), for example, prescribes an ideal African industrial policy as being consistent with a marketist DR:

> At the core of the emerging industrial policy approach is a partnership between the state and the private sector; a strategic partnership in which the state, in consultation with the private sector, sets the overall direction for economic transformation, and the private sector, actively supported by the state, leads in implementation.

We will return to this implication in Chapter 10.

The 12 country case studies

We need to tunnel deeper than the bird's-eye view of African industrial development provided in this chapter. In Chapter 8, we present case studies of six "resource-rich" industrializers: Cote d'Ivoire, Ghana, Nigeria, Mauritius, South Africa, and Zimbabwe. In Chapter 9, we present case studies of six "labor-rich" industrializers: Egypt, Ethiopia, Kenya, Senegal, Tanzania, and Tunisia.

BOX 7.1 THE DEVELOPMENTAL STATE

A *Developmental State* (DS) is a neopatrimonial state with effective politico-economic institutions that can render the transformative vision of a *developmental regime* (DR) politically feasible and economically desirable. This working definition implicitly assumes that "developmentalism" is a characteristic feature of a regime rather than of a state. The two are in sync only when a DR succeeds in embedding and infusing developmentalism throughout the state apparatus. Thus defined, it is possible to imagine a DS to be captured by non-DR state elite at a given point in time. It is also possible to have a DR without a capable and inspired DS bureaucracy to faithfully implement its long-term and ambitious development program.

A functioning DS has the following attributes: (1) a regime which seeks popular legitimacy out of enlightened self-interest, i.e., has the *political will* to be pro-growth and pro-poor; (2) a regime which enjoys sufficient *autonomy* from the contending groups especially within business society to be able to effectively monitor and enforce the terms of the reciprocal bargain; (3) a *capable* state machinery with a monopoly over violence to ensure peace and stability, a bureaucracy with the capacity to enforce the rule by law, if not the rule of law; and a politically insulated technocracy that can implement the regime's program; (4) a politico-economic settlement of *partnership* between hegemonic ruling elite and a coalition of powerful non-state political and economic elites or, alternatively, a *benevolent dictatorship* with some hostility toward an independent business class and an ability for self-restraint to render the enforcement of the bargain credible (especially the centralized allocation of sizable economic rent between patronage for regime maintenance and productive investment); and (5) an insecure regime with a narrow political base which has captured a state with an *existential angst* thereby making a regimented development drive a do-or-die proposition.

The first two attributes pertain to hegemony whereby a far-sighted DR seeks to minimize the exercise of violence by socializing the population into the populist ideology of developmentalism. Attributes 2, 3, and 4, on the other hand, speak to the issue of capability – political and technocratic. An effective DR is one that can enforce the primacy of state authority over other competing sources of authority. It enjoys legitimacy at home (with a workable mix of fear and respect) and abroad. It also can manage distributional conflicts effectively and the centralized allocation of investible resources efficiently (through a mix of organized contests for public support, targeted public investments, and result-based distribution of rewards). The failure of attribute 5 inevitably leads to a growth-stunting and unbridled rent seeking.

168 Africa's postcolonial experience

Well-designed country case studies are useful because they consider both the global environment under which industrial takeoff is being mounted as well as the country-specific idiosyncrasies and specificities. This way, we are closer to providing adequate explanations for inter-country variations in economic performance.

To get a better sense of the commonalities as well as the diversity among the case-study countries, we will, first, group them into two (factor-based and resource-based) and, second, take a bird's-eye view of each of the countries. The distinction between the two endowment-based categorizations is not a tight one. Resource-rich industrializers are mineral-rich while factor-rich industrializers are labor-rich. Some in each category are land-rich while others are not. By these criteria, Mauritius and Egypt straddle the two categories, but we have assigned them to different categories to even-out the groupings. Space limitations prevented us from including other industrially interesting countries, especially Lesotho, Cameroon, and Morocco.

As noted in the Introduction, we examine the changing profiles of African manufacturing at two- and three-digit ISIC levels for these countries precisely because they are representative of the various macro-regions of the continent on both sides of the Sahara and the Congo Basin. The 12 countries together represent 50% of Africa's 1.15 billion people, 60% of $1.7 trillion continent-wide markets, and 75% of its $215 billion manufacturing value added in 2014.

Regarding breadth, the 12 case-study countries represent various sizes, mixes of endowments (labor, land, and mining), regions (north, west, east, and south), and history (Anglophone, Francophone, settler colonies, and non-colonies). They encompass a significant portion of Africa's population, economy, and industrial capacity (see Table 7.1).

Regarding overall development patterns, the human development index (HDI) and real per capita income are strongly and positively correlated with the level of industrial development of the case-study countries. Social indicators such as mean years of schooling and life expectancy at birth are much more (negatively) correlated with the Gini coefficient and inclusive policies (positively) than with resource endowment per se (see Table 7.2).

Resource-based industrializers are prone to rampant rent seeking as shown by corruption indexes and the Gini coefficients. They also report better infrastructure. Those countries with a better handle on the ever-present resource curse tend to do well regarding both economic diversification and real per capita income.

Rather simplistically but helpfully, we define the *factor-based countries* as those countries whose industrial strategy are naturally based on labor endowments and *resource-based countries* as those countries relying on natural-resource endowments (land for agro-processing, or minerals and fuels for resource-processing). These classifications suggest two distinct pathways of industrialization as shown in Figure 7.1.

The FB Pathway nurtures manufacturing activity that is initially based on unskilled labor toward one that is based on skilled labor. The RB Pathway nurtures manufacturing activity initially focused on simple processing of agricultural or extractive products toward high value-added processing. The two pathways merge into a knowledge-intensive or technology-intensive manufacturing as the industrial sector matures.

African industrial development **169**

TABLE 7.1 Economic profiles of the case-study countries, 2014

Countries[c]	Popl. in mill.	GDP, bill. mkt$	GDP, bill. PPP$	MVA as % GDP	GCF as % GDP	Income per capita, Atlas $	Income per cap, PPP$	Popul. under $3.10 per day (%)	Adult literacy, %	Infrast. index, 1–8
Resource-based:										
Cote d'Ivoire	22	34	92	13	17	1,450	3,130	19.5	43.1	3
Ghana	27	39	109	5	27	1,590	3,900	60.5	76.6	1
Mauritius	1	5	23	16	23	9,630	18,150	3.0	90.6	5
Nigeria	178	569	1,000	10	16	2,970	5,910	78.5	59.6	..
South Africa	54	350	705	13	20	6,800	12,700	33.3	94.3	4
Zimbabwe	15	14	27	12	13	840	1,650	..	86.5	1
Factor-based:										
Egypt	90	287	943	16	14	3,050	10,260	..	73.8	..
Ethiopia	90	56	145	4	38	550	1,500	76.2	49.1	..
Kenya	45	61	132	11	21	1,290	2,940	45.9	78.0	7
Senegal	15	16	34	13	26	1,050	2,300	65.8	57.7	..
Tanzania	52	48	128	6	31	920	2,510	77.9	70.6	..
Tunisia	11	49	126	17	22	4,230	11,020	13.3	81.8	4
References:										
North Africa	180	704	1,993	14	30	3,917	10,837	..	..	..
Sub-Sahara	973	1,729	3,392	11	22	1,638	3,382	..	..	..
Africa	1,153	2,433	5,385	12	24	2,110	4,536[b]	..	..	..
World	7,261	77,845	1,08,600	16	22	10,787	14,931[a]	..	..	..

Sources and notes: Calculations based on data from World Bank, World Development Indicators 2015: www.wdi.worldbank.org.
MVA = manufacturing value added; GCF = gross capital formation
PPP = purchasing power parity
Infrast. Index = Infrastructure Index (1 lowest, 8 highest)
Global GDP in purchasing power parity dollars was $108,600 trillion in 2014 – some 40% higher than global GDP based on market exchange-rate conversions.
In 2014, Africa's real per capita income was only 20% of the global per capita income using market exchange rates while it is 30% of the global average by the standards of the more realistic PPP exchange rates.

These sweeping characterizations capture rather well the experiences of late industrializers of the twentieth century. We may safely conclude with the insights gleaned from the preceding discussions that the path of industrialization open to Africa is in many ways qualitatively different, in both productive and trade dimensions, from that of the early-comers of Europe or that of East Asia and Latin America.

Africa's catchup industrialization is bound to be rather tortuous. The continent has little to build on by way of proto-industrial legacies. But what is rather intriguing is the possibility of leapfrogging since Africa now has a better-educated and globally

TABLE 7.2 Human development indicators for the case-study countries, 2014

Country (in rank order of HDI)	HDI (value)	Life expectancy (years)	Mean years of schooling (years)	GNI per capita (2011 PPP $)	Gini coefficient (2013, %)
Mauritius (MAU)	0.77	74.4	8.5	$17,470	35.8
Tunisia (TUN)	0.72	74.8	6.8	10,404	36.1
Egypt (EGY)	0.69	71.1	6.6	10,512	30.8
South Africa (ZAF)	0.67	57.4	9.9	12,122	63.1
Ghana (GHA)	0.58	61.4	7.0	3,852	42.8
Kenya (KEN)	0.55	61.6	6.7	2,762	47.7
Tanzania (TZA)	0.52	65.0	5.1	2,411	37.6
Nigeria (NGA)	0.51	52.8	5.9	5,341	48.8
Zimbabwe (ZWE)	0.51	57.5	7.3	1,615	50.1
Senegal (SEN)	0.47	66.5	2.5	2,188	40.3
Cote d'Ivoire (CIV)	0.46	51.5	4.3	3,171	41.5
Ethiopia (ETH)	0.44	64.0	2.4	1,428	33.6
Highest HDI: **Norway**	**0.94**	**81.6**	**12.6**	**64,992**	**25.8**

Sources and notes: UNDP, Human Development Report 2015, Table 1; World Bank, World Development Indicators 2015.
HDI = human development index
GNI = gross national income

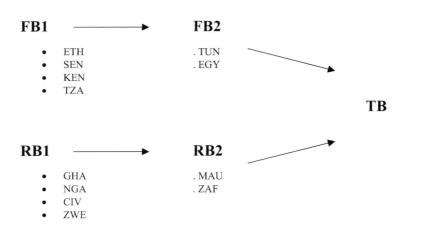

FIGURE 7.1 Two African pathways of industrialization

Sources and notes: Author.
FB = factor-based
RB = resource-based
TB = technology-based

connected youth, and an even better infrastructure than early-comers at the same stage of industrial development. As we will argue below, it also needs to formulate smarter industrial policies to put together all the ingredients of success. It is in this light that I share the enthusiasm of Newman et al. (2016: 59) when they argue:

> Given its late start, can Africa reasonably aspire to break into the global market for industrial goods? . . . We believe the answer is yes, for a number of reasons. First, economic changes are taking place in Asia that create a window of opportunity for late-industrializers elsewhere to gain a toehold in world markets. Second, the nature of manufactured exports themselves is changing. A growing share of global trade in industry is made up of stages of vertical value chains – or tasks – rather than finished products.

Notes

1 These explanations can be easily discounted for their underestimation of Africa's track-record of adaptivity under some of the most difficult economic environments in the world; the readily available counter examples of other tropical regions that have successfully overcome the presumably insurmountable barriers, and the endogeneity of institutions and even culture itself to slow-changing economic environments. Regarding an anti-growth African culture, evoking how Catholicism, Orthodoxy, Islam, and Hinduism were blamed variously for economic failure, UNECA (2016: 10) bluntly makes an important counterpoint: "Bordering on racism, the argument is that Africans possess cultures that are inimical to economic development; they do not work hard, do not plan for the future, and cannot cooperate with each other."

2 Here is how *The Economist* (February 16, 2013) sums up the challenge: "Transport is a perpetual problem in Africa. Potholed roads and missing rail links get in the way of economic growth. Intra-regional trade accounts for just 15% of total commerce, compared with 53% in emerging Asia. Landlocked countries suffer the most. Transport costs can make up 50–75% of the retail price of goods in Malawi, Rwanda and Uganda. Shipping a car from China to Tanzania on the Indian Ocean costs $4,000, but getting it from there to nearby Uganda can cost another $5,000. . . . Subsistence farmers who sell surplus crops typically receive less than 20% of the market price. The rest is eaten up by transport and transaction costs."

3 The International Labour Organization (ILO) has, for example, identified five facts about the informal economy in Africa circa 2014: (1) Nearly eight out of ten employed persons in Sub-Saharan Africa were in vulnerable forms of employment (own-account or unpaid family workers) which is significantly higher than the global average of 45%; (2) Informal, non-agricultural employment accounted for two-thirds of employment; (3) In Sub-Saharan Africa, 74% of women's employment (non-agricultural) is informal, in contrast with 61% for men; (4) Informal employment is the standard condition among most youth in Sub-Saharan Africa where at least eight in ten young workers fall into the category of informal employment; and (5) Self-employment accounts for as much as 53% of non-agricultural employment in Sub-Saharan Africa and 31% in North Africa. www.ilo.org/addisababa/whats-new/WCMS_377286/lang—en/index.htm. In 2015, 83% (or 12.6 million) of eligible workers in Kenya were non-wage workers in the informal sector. www.africaresearchinstitute.org/newsite/publications/kenya-failing-create-decent-jobs/.

4 Neopatrimonial relations are broader and different from clientelistic relations since the latter rely on doling out state assets to individuals rather than groups in exchange for political support such as votes. There is a big literature that critiques the all-encompassing deployment of the concept to explain African political processes and rent seeking as exceptional "pathologies" rather than as particular forms of state formation in Africa. The confusion is attributed variously to misreading of the violent and extractive nature of European state formation, misreading of Weber's theory of patrimonialism in the process of state formation, attributing African processes exclusively to external forces and colonial legacies, implicit rejection of

172 Africa's postcolonial experience

the agency of Africans, and inadequate attention to the empirical evidence which shows a diversity of political and economic outcomes in African countries that are uniformly labeled neopatrimonial (Mkandawire, 2012; Kelsall, 2013; Handley, 2008; Whitfield et al., 2015).

References

Abegaz, B. (2013). Political Parties in Business: Rent-seekers, Developmentalists, or Both? *Journal of Development Studies*, 49(11), pp. 1467–1483.

Abegaz, B. (2018). *A Tributary Model of State Formation.* New York: Springer.

Acemoglu, D., and J. Robinson. (2012). *Why Nations Fail.* New York: Crown Business.

Africa Centre for Economic Transformation (ACET), (2014). *Growth with Depth: 2014 Africa Transformation Report.* Accra: ACET.

African Development Bank (AfDB), Organization of Economic Cooperation and Development (OECD), and United Nations Industrial Organization (UNIDO) (2017). *African Economic Outlook: Entrepreneurship and Industrialisation*, Abidjan.

Amin, S. (1972). Underdevelopment and Dependence in Black Africa: Origins and Contemporary Forms. *Journal of Modern African Studies*, 10(4), pp. 503–524.

Amsden, A. (1989). *Asia's Next Giant: South Korea and Late Industrialization.* Oxford: Oxford University Press.

Amsden, A. (2001). *The Rise of 'The Rest': Challenges to the West From Late Industrializing Economies.* New York: Oxford University Press.

Ansu, Y. (2013). Industrial Policy and Economic Transformation in Africa: Strategies for Development and a Research Agenda. In: J. Stiglitz, J.Y. Lin, and E. Patel, eds., *The Industrial Policy Revolution II: Africa in the 21st Century.* New York: Palgrave Macmillan, pp. 492–528.

Ayittey, G. (2012). *Defeating Dictators: Fighting Tyranny in Africa and Around the World.* New York: St. Martin's Griffin.

Benjamin, N., and A. Mbaye. (2012). *The Informal Sector in Francophone Africa Firm Size, Productivity, and Institutions.* Washington, DC: World Bank.

Biggs, T., and M. Raturi. (1997). *Productivity and Competitiveness of African Manufacturing.* Washington, DC: World Bank.

Bigsten, A., P. Collier, S. Dercon, B. Gauthier, M. Fafchamps, J. W. Gunning, A. Isaksson, A. Oduro, R. Oostendorp, C. Pattillo, M. Söderbom, F. Teal, A. Zeufack and S. Appleton. (2000). Rates of return on physical and human capital in Africa's manufacturing sector. *Economic Development and Cultural Change* 48, pp. 801–827.

Bigsten, A., and M. Soderbom. (2006). What Have We Learned From a Decade of Manufacturing Enterprise Surveys in Africa? *World Bank Research Observer*, 21(2), pp. 241–265.

Bora, B., P. Lloyd, and M. Pangestu. (1999). *Industrial Policy and the WTO.* [online] Geneva: UNCTAD. Available at: http://unctad.org/en/Docs/itcdtab7_en.pdf.

Cai, F., and M. Wang. (2008). A Counterfactual Analysis on Unlimited Surplus Labor in Rural China. *China and World Economy*, 16(1), pp. 51–65.

Chang, H. J. (2013). Industrial Policy: Can Africa Do It? In: J. Stiglitz, J.Y. Lin, and E. Patel, eds., *The Industrial Policy Revolution II: Africa in the 21st Century.* New York: Palgrave Macmillan, pp. 114–134.

Clarke, G. (2012). Manufacturing Firms in Africa. In: H. Dinh and G. Clarke, eds., *Performance of Manufacturing Firms in Africa An Empirical Analysis.* Washington, DC: World Bank, Chapter 3.

Collier, P. (2000). Africa's Comparative Advantage. In: H. Jalilian, M. Tribe, and J. Weiss, eds., *Industrial Development and Policy in Africa: Issues of Deindustrialization and Development Strategy.* Cheltenham, UK: Edward Elgar, pp. 11–21.

Collier, P., and A. J. Venables. (2007). Rethinking Trade Preferences: How Africa Can Diversify Its Exports. *World Economy*, 30(8), pp. 1326–1345.

African industrial development **173**

de Janvry, A., and E. Sadoulet. (2010). Agriculture for Development in Africa: Business-as-Usual or New Departures? *Journal of African Economies*. 19 (AERC supplement 2), pp. ii7–ii39.

Dinh, H., et al. (2012). *Light Manufacturing in Africa: Targeted Policies to Enhance Private Investment and Create Jobs*. Washington, DC: World Bank.

Elbadawi, I., T. Mengistae, and A. Zeurack. (2006). Market Access, Supplier Access, and Africa's Manufactured Exports: A Firm Level Analysis. *Journal of International Trade & Economic Development*, 15(4), pp. 493–523.

Fukuyama, F. (2012). *The Origins of Political Order: From Prehuman Times to the French Revolution*. New York: Farrar, Strauss, and Giroux.

Fukuyama, F. (2014). *Political Order and Political Decay: From the Industrial Revolution to the Globalization of Democracy*. New York: Farrar, Straus, and Giroux.

Gerschenkron, A. (1962). *Economic Backwardness in Historical Perspective*. Cambridge, MA: Belknap Press of Harvard University Press.

Gong, X. (2015). African Economic Structural Transformation: A Diagnostic Analysis. *Journal of African Transformation*, 1(1), pp. 1–22.

Handley, A. (2008). *Business and the State in Africa: Economic Policymaking in the Neo-Liberal Era*. Cambridge: Cambridge University Press.

Handley, A. (2014). Varieties of Capitalists? The Middle Class, the Private Sector and Economic Outcomes in Africa. *WIDER Working Paper 2014/101*. August.

Huntington, S. (2006). *Political Order in Changing Societies*. New Haven: Yale University Press.

Hyden, G. (2008). Institutions, Power, and Policy Dynamics in Africa. *APPP Discussion Paper No. 2*. [online] London: Overseas Development Institute. Available at: www.institutions-africa.org/filestream/20080623-discussion-paper-2-institutions-power-and-policy-outcomes-in-africa-goran-hyden-june-2008.

Kaufmann, D., A. Kraay, and M. Mastruzi. (2010). The Worldwide Governance Indicators: Methodology and Analytical Issues. *Policy Research Working Paper 5430*. Washington, DC: World Bank.

Kelsall, T. (2013). *Business, Politics, and the State in Africa: Challenging the Orthodoxies on Growth and Transformation*. London: Zed Press.

Khan, M. (2013). Political Settlements and the Design of Technology Policy. In: J. Stiglitz, J.Y. Lin, and E. Patel, eds., *The Industrial Policy Revolution II: Africa in the 21st Century*. New York: Palgrave Macmillan, pp. 243–280.

La Porta, R., and A. Shleifer. (2011). The Unofficial Economy in Africa. *NBER Working Paper 16821*. Cambridge, MA: National Bureau of Economic Research.

Liedholm, C. (1992). Small-scale Industries in Africa: Dynamic Issues and the Role of Policy. In: F. Stewart, ed., *Alternative Development Strategies in Sub-Saharan Africa*. London: Macmillan.

Liedholm, C. (2001). Small Firm Dynamics: Evidence from Africa and Latin America. *Small Business Economics* 18 (Winter), pp. 227–242.

Mazumdar, D., and A. Mazaheri. (2003). *The African Manufacturing Firm*. New York: Routledge.

Meagher, K. (2013). *Unlocking the Informal Economy: A Literature Review on Linkages Between Formal and Informal Economies in Developing Countries*. Cambridge, MA: WIEGO. Available at: www.vumelana.org.za/wp-content/uploads/2014/03/Document-49-Meagher_WIEGO_WP27.pdf.

Mkandawire, T. (2012). Institutional Monocropping and Monotasking. In: A. Noman, K. Botchwey, H. Stein, and J. Stiglitz, eds., *Good Growth and Governance in Africa*. Oxford: Oxford University Press, pp. 80–113.

Morris, C., and I. Adelman. (1988). *Comparative Patterns of Economic Development, 1850–1914*. Baltimore: The John-Hopkins University Press.

Moss, T., G. Pettersson, and N. van de Walle. (2006). An Aid-Institutions Paradox? A Review Essay on Aid Dependency and State Building in Sub-Saharan Africa. *Working Paper Number 74*. Washington, DC: Center for Global Development.

Newman, C., J. Page, J. Rand, A. Shimeles, M. Soderbom, and F. Tarp. (2016). *Made in Africa: Learning to Compete in Industry.* Washington, DC: Brookings Institution Press.

North, D. (1994). Economic Performance Through Time. *American Economic Review*, 84(3), pp. 359–368.

Page, J. (2013). Should Africa Industrialize? In: A. Szirmai, W. Naude, and L. Alcorta, eds., *Pathways to Industrialization in the Twenty-First Century.* New York: Oxford University Press, pp. 244–268.

Rankin, N., et al. (2006). Exporting From Manufacturing Firms in Sub-Saharan Africa. *Journal of African Economics*, 15(4), pp. 671–687.

Schneider, F., A. Buehn, and C.E. Montenegro. (2011). Shadow Economies All Over the World: New Estimates for 162 Countries From 1999 to 2007. In: F. Schneider, ed., *Handbook on the Shadow Economy.* Cheltenham, UK: Edward Elgar, pp. 9–77.

Shiferaw, A. (2007). Firm Heterogeneity and Market Selection in Sub-Saharan Africa: Does It Spur Industrial Progress. *Economic Development and Cultural Change*, 55(2), pp. 393–423.

Stein, H. (2012). Africa, Industrial Policy, and Export Processing Zones: Lessons From Asia. In: A. Noman, K. Botchwey, H. Stein, and J. Stiglitz, eds., *Good Growth and Governance in Africa.* Oxford: Oxford University Press, pp. 322–344.

Tribe, M. (2000). Industrial Development and Policy in Africa: Issues of De-industrialization and Development Strategy. In: H. Jalilian, M. Tribe, and J. Weiss, eds., *Industrial Development and Policy in Africa: Issues of Deindustrialization and Development Strategy.* Cheltenham, UK: Edward Elgar.

Tybout, J. (2000). Manufacturing Firms in Developing Countries: How Well Do They Do and Why? *Journal of Economic Literature*, 38, pp. 11–44.

United Nations Economic Commission for Africa (UNECA). (2016). *Transformative Industrial Policy for Africa.* Addis Ababa: UNECA.

United Nations Economic Commission for Africa (UNECA). (2017). *Urbanization and Industrialization for Africa's Transformation.* Addis Ababa: UNECA.

United Nations Industrial Organization (UNIDO) and United Nations Conference on Trade and Development (UNCTAD). (2011). *Africa Report 2011: Fostering Industrial Development in Africa in the New Global Development.* Geneva: UNIDO.

Van Biesebroeck, J. (2003). Exporting Raises Productivity in Sub-Saharan African Manufacturing Firms. *Journal of International Economics*, 67, pp. 373–391.

Van de Walle, N. (2001). *African Economies and the Politics of Permanent Crisis.* Cambridge: Cambridge University Press.

Wade, R. (2003). *Governing the Market: Economic Theory and the Role of Government in East Asian Industrialization.* Princeton: Princeton University Press.

Wade, R. (2012). How Can Low-Income Countries Accelerate their Catch-Up With High-Income Countries? The Case for Open-Economy Industrial Policy. In: A. Noman, K. Botchwey, H. Stein, and J. Stiglitz, eds., *Good Growth and Governance in Africa.* Oxford: Oxford University Press, pp. 243–272.

Whitfield, L., O. Therkildsen, L. Buur, and A.M. Kjær. (2015). *The Politics of African Industrial Policy: A Comparative Perspective.* New York: Cambridge University Press.

Wood, A., and J. Mayer. (2001). Africa's Export Structure in a Comparative Perspective. *Cambridge Journal of Economics*, 25(3), pp. 369–394.

World Bank. (1997). *World Development Report 1997: The State in a Changing World.* New York: Oxford University Press.

World Bank. (2000). *Can Africa Claim the 21st Century?* Washington, DC: World Bank.

World Bank. (2017). *World Development Report 2017: Governance and the Law.* Washington, DC: World Bank.

Young, C. (2012). *The Postcolonial State in Africa: Fifty Years of Independence, 1960–2010.* Madison: University of Wisconsin Press.

8

RESOURCE-BASED INDUSTRIALIZERS

This chapter profiles the six resource-based African industrializers. We will take stock of the available evidence on institutions, business environment, economic diversification, efficiency, employment generation, and international competitiveness.

Resource-based industrialization

Apart from the most precious metals, commodities (such as mineral products and cash crops) and energy products are vulnerable to booms and busts. As shown in Figure 8.1, the real indexes of major commodities display interesting trends. There is a general decline in prices for all groups during the great global moderation of 1980–2000. Energy and precious metal prices are the most stable while agricultural commodities are the least stable. Commodity-based industrialization, therefore, requires political discipline and a long-term policy perspective to manage such fluctuations of revenue, and an institutionalized mechanism to restrain the proclivity of state elites for unproductive rent seeking.

Michael Roemer (1979) provides an early assessment of the state of knowledge on the contributions (to growth, employment creation, equality, and autonomy) of resource-based industrialization. He summarized the special characteristics of resource processing as follows: use of capital-intensive methods to reduce raw material costs, high transport costs of bulky raw metals and petroleum products, economies of scale in resource processing in a world dominated by large multinational firms, high but falling shipping freight rates, substantial effective protection against semi-processed exports from developing countries, and strong forward linkages and external economies.

Roemer concluded that processing natural resources fosters *dependency* – either on export markets or imported technology. Similarly, Dahlman (2008) notes that, because technological diffusion tends to concentrate on related activities,

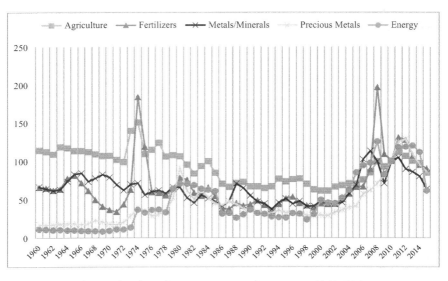

FIGURE 8.1 Real annual indices for major commodity groups, 1960–2015

Sources and notes: World Bank Commodity Price Data (as updated on February 4, 2016). In real 2005$, 2010=100.

linkage-poor resource processing inevitably fosters *dualism*. These are, however, constraints rather than traps.[1] Many countries have, through sensible policies (local content requirements, for example), managed to maximize the benefits of natural resource exploitation which include foreign exchange and employment while minimizing overdependence and self-limiting enclaves.

Resource-based industrialization strategies confront several concerns and opportunities. One reservation is that resource-based industries face the same challenge of managing scarce resources as any other path of industrial development. Policies designed to invest resource rents productively, such as investing in human capital and infrastructure, have enabled many latecomers (Indonesia, Argentina, Malaysia, and Thailand) to diversify their economic bases (Reinhardt, 2000).

Some critics have expressed that many resource-processing activities lack dense linkages and rich positive externalities to escape enclave industrialization (Hirschman, 1958, 1968; Singer, 1950). While this is true of many resource-rich developing countries with parasitic elites, the historical experiences of Scandinavia, North America, and Oceania show that, with the right policies, a dense network of upstream and downstream activities can be developed to serve as an engine of growth.

Another criticism is that many resource-based manufacturing industries, being highly capital intensive, do not directly generate adequate employment opportunities. This argument is challenged by the emerging dynamics of the global division of labor (Kaplinsky and Morris, 2007; McMillan and Harttgen, 2014). Even where direct job creation is low, the income from natural resources can boost employment in other labor-intensive sectors of the economy. Furthermore, declining global unit prices and labor-saving technologies have dented the job-creating capacity of non-resource-based industries.

If the competitiveness of home-grown firms depends on such things as access to cheap raw agricultural and mining materials, assimilable technologies, ample supply of skills, and functioning marketing channels, then they are likely to offer an attractive partnership for lead firms in GVCs. A commodity-based industrialization strategy, therefore, is not unique in the sense that it also requires a development-friendly state to discipline both labor and capital while nurturing the capabilities of both.

African resource-based industrializers, despite their path-dependent extractive political legacies and their reliance on mining or agro-industries, are diverse in terms of investment climate, growth performance, income levels, and economic profiles (see Figures 8.2 and 8.3). South Africa and Mauritius, for example, have the highest per capita incomes and worker productivity (along with Tunisia and Egypt from the factor-based group). These two economies are also the fastest growers in the group – Mauritius after 1980 and South Africa after 1992.

The post-1980 growth record for Mauritius (also the case for Botswana) has been quite remarkable. Its real per capita income overtook stumbling Zimbabwe's after 1985 and South Africa's after 1992. Just as interestingly, Mauritius holds the highest index of industrialization with $1,000 manufacturing value added per capita.

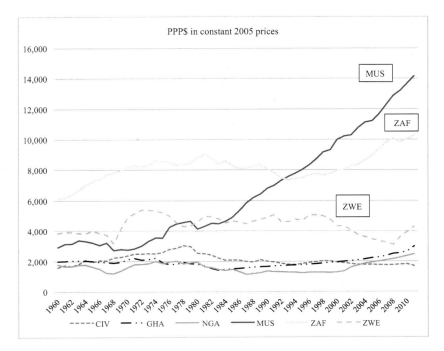

FIGURE 8.2 Real GDP per capita for the resource-based industrializers, 1960–2011
World Bank Commodity Price Data (as updated on February 4, 2016). In real 2005$, 2010=100

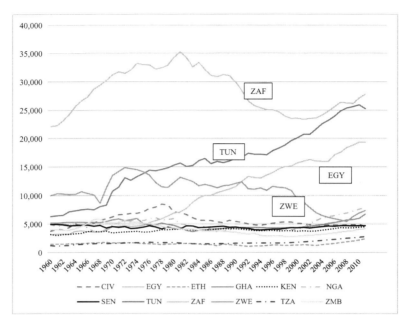

FIGURE 8.3 Real GDP per worker, 1960–2011
Source. PWT 8.1: www.ggdc.net/pwt.

One clue to this pattern of economic performance is provided by the data on investment rates and worker productivity (Figure 8.3, Tables 8.1 and 8.3). Real GDP per worker endured a downward slide in South Africa during 1980–2002, and in Zimbabwe during 1980–2008 (especially after the 1996 political crisis). These setbacks are directly responsible for the drop in gross capital formation from its high levels in 1990 (see Table 8.1.). As growth theory tells us, a high rate of capital formation is necessary but not always sufficient as a driver of worker productivity and economic growth.

Mauritius, South Africa, and Zimbabwe also have the most diversified economies with a significant share of manufacturing and other industrial sectors (mainly mining in the case of the latter two). In each of the three countries, manufacturing value added accounts for at least 15% of GDP and well over half of the merchandise exports (Tables 8.1–8.2).

At the other end of the spectrum are the three remaining countries whose low and unstable growth patterns and investment rates have resulted in low worker productivity and per capita income. Cote d'Ivoire is a case of a fast starter that ran out of steam especially after the 1998 political crisis. Ghana is a case of a stumbler that finally found a firm footing. Nigeria remains a country of great promise and ever disappointing achievement. The trinity also has a very low level of manufacturing intensity, if not industrial development. This is especially the case for Ghana and Nigeria with less than $100 per capita of manufacturing value added.

This differential economic performance across countries over the past quarter century reflects the various indicators of a challenging business climate. While the limited availability of long-term finance at an affordable cost and the unreliability

Resource-based industrializers **179**

TABLE 8.1 Economic profiles of resource-based industrializers, 1990–2014

Country	Series	1990	2000	2014
Cote d'Ivoire	GNI per capita, PPP$	1,780	2,140	3,130
Cote d'Ivoire	GCF (% of GDP)	7	10	17
Cote d'Ivoire	Industry (% of GDP)	26	22	21
Cote d'Ivoire	Population	12,165,909	16,517,948	22,157,107
Cote d'Ivoire	Services (% of GDP)	41	54	57
Ghana	GNI per capita, PPP$	1,220	1,750	3,900
Ghana	GCF (% of GDP)	14	24	27
Ghana	Industry (% of GDP)	17	28	28
Ghana	Population	14,628,260	18,824,994	26,786,598
Ghana	Services (% of GDP)	38	32	50
Mauritius	GNI per capita, PPP$	4,850	8,940	18,150
Mauritius	GCF (% of GDP)	30	26	23
Mauritius	Industry (% of GDP)	33	31	23
Mauritius	Population	1,058,775	1,186,873	1,260,934
Mauritius	Services (% of GDP)	54	62	74
Nigeria	GNI per capita, PPP$	1,770	1,950	5,710
Nigeria	GCF (% of GDP)	14	7	16
Nigeria	Industry (% of GDP)	45	52	24
Nigeria	Population	95,617,345	122,876,723	177,475,986
Nigeria	Services (% of GDP)	23	22	56
South Africa	GNI per capita, PPP$	6,440	7,690	12,700
South Africa	GCF (% of GDP)	18	16	20
South Africa	Industry (% of GDP)	40	32	29
South Africa	Population	35,200,000	44,000,000	54,001,953
South Africa	Services (% of GDP)	55	65	68
Zimbabwe	GNI per capita, PPP$	1,580	1,890	1,650
Zimbabwe	GCF (% of GDP)	17	14	13
Zimbabwe	Industry (% of GDP)	33	. .	29
Zimbabwe	Population	10,484,771	12,499,981	15,245,855
Zimbabwe	Services (% of GDP)	50	. .	57

Sources and notes: World Development Indicators 2015.
GCF = gross capital formation

of electricity are common complaints of firms in all the six countries, formal-sector firms frequently cite informality (that unregistered businesses benefit from low taxes and regulatory costs), corruption, and crime as additional problems. Politically unstable Zimbabwe ranks the lowest in all the three dimensions of the country policy and institutional assessment (CPIA) categories (economic management, public management, and structural policies)[2] as shown in Tables 8.3 and 8.4.

All things considered, South Africa has the best business climate and enterprise characteristics that are most conducive to growth. Ghana, Mauritius, and Nigeria stand out as countries with the least attractive business climates and firm characteristics. Firms shoulder the most losses from power shortages, rely heavily on

TABLE 8.2 Manufacturing in resource-based industrializers, 2014

Country	Profile (MVA in 2005 US$)
Cote d'Ivoire:	
MVA	2,554.4 million
MVA per capita	123
Share of MVA in GDP	11%
Major manufacturing activities	. .
Share of manufactured exports (2012)	51%
Ghana:	
MVA	1,415.7 million
MVA per capita	54
Share of MVA in GDP	7%
Major manufacturing activities	Food and beverages (32%)
Share of manufactured exports (2012)	60%
Mauritius:	
MVA	1,351.8 million
MVA per capita	1,082
Share of MVA in GDP	15%
Major manufacturing activities	Food and beverages (46%)
Share of manufactured exports (2012)	98%
Nigeria:	
MVA	8,235.1 million
MVA per capita	46
Share of MVA in GDP	4%
Major manufacturing activities	. .
Share of manufactured exports (2012)	17%
Zimbabwe:	
MVA	871.4 million
MVA per capita	60
Share of MVA in GDP	14%
Biggest manufacturing activity	. .
Share of manufactured exports (2012)	45%
South Africa:	
MVA	47,371.0 million
MVA per capita	891
Share of MVA in GDP	15%
Biggest manufacturing activity	Food and beverages (22%)
Share of manufactured exports (2012)	74%

Source: UNIDO Industrial Briefs, June 2015. www.unido.org/Data1/IndStatBrief/.

TABLE 8.3 Firm characteristics and business climate in resource-based industrializers

Indicator (survey year)	Cote d'Ivoire (2009)	Ghana (2013)	Mauritius (2009)	Nigeria (2014)	S. Africa (2007)	Zimbabwe (2011)	LMI (2013)
Business climate:							
Incidence of graft index	13.3	29.7	3.6	29.8	4.3	8.0	20.2
Days needed to obtain operating license	14.5	24.5	19.1	14.4	36.2	5.9	28.1
Management time spent dealing with regulations	1.8	4.0	9.4	7.5	5.9	2.5	10.5
Number of visits with tax officials	3.6	2.7	0.5	2.3	0.8	1.8	1.9
Firm characteristics:							
Firm age in years	7.4	14.9	15.5	15.9	15.6	33.4	16.6
% foreign-owned	13.6	14.5	8.3	3.1	8.9	5.1	7.5
% internal financing of investment	88.9	76.0	51.9	52.7	68.5	84.7	72.3
Collateral as % loan	55.9	240.0	59.9	227.7	103.6	261.3	210.1
% sales lost due to power outages	5.0	11.5	22.0	11.2	1.6	6.9	4.0
% of ind. firms importing foreign inputs	27.1	68.5	56.5	30.0	37.8	63.4	57.8
Days it takes to clear industrial imports	31.2	14.8	10.3	8.6	5.2	7.6	11.6
% firms trusting the courts	35.2	44.4	63.6	66.0	59.6	61.0	41.0
% internal quality certificate	4.3	9.2	11.1	7.1	26.4	18.0	15.5
Average number of full-time workers	11.1	23.5	38.2	15.8	48.9	53.7	37.6
% full-time female workers	29.0	24.7	30.1	24.3	29.1	23.4	27.8
Top three obstacles identified by firms	– Finance – Instability – Corruption	– Finance – Electricity – Customs	– Finance – Informality – Electricity	– Finance – Electricity – Corruption	– Crime, theft – Electricity – Finance	– Finance – Instability – Informality	

Sources and notes: Compiled from World Bank, Country Profiles; Enterprise Surveys. www.enterprisesurveys.org/reports LMI = lower middle-income countries

TABLE 8.4 Quality measures of African economic institutions and policies, 2005–2014

	CPIA *cluster average*	2005	2006	2007	2008	2009	2010	2011	2012	2013	2014
Middle income	**Economic management**	**3.69**	**3.71**	**3.70**	**3.67**	**3.66**	**3.63**	**3.57**	**3.53**	**3.50**	**3.42**
Cote d'Ivoire	Economic management	2.00	1.83	2.33	2.50	2.83	2.67	2.83	3.33	3.50	3.67
Ethiopia	Economic management	3.67	3.50	3.50	3.30	3.67	3.67	3.67	3.50	3.50	3.50
Ghana	Economic management	4.17	4.17	4.00	3.70	3.67	3.67	3.83	3.50	3.00	2.50
Kenya	Economic management	4.17	4.17	4.17	4.00	4.17	4.17	4.17	4.50	4.50	4.33
Nigeria	Economic management	3.83	4.00	4.33	4.30	4.33	4.17	4.00	4.33	4.50	4.33
Senegal	Economic management	4.17	4.00	4.17	3.80	4.00	4.00	4.00	4.17	4.17	4.17
Zimbabwe	Economic management	1.00	1.00	1.00	1.00	1.67	1.67	1.83	2.00	2.00	2.33
Tanzania	Economic management	4.50	4.50	4.33	4.30	4.33	4.17	4.17	4.17	4.00	4.00
Middle income	**Public sector management**	**3.21**	**3.18**	**3.20**	**3.23**	**3.24**	**3.24**	**3.23**	**3.24**	**3.22**	**3.19**
Cote d'Ivoire	Public sector management	2.50	2.50	2.40	2.50	2.60	2.40	2.70	2.80	3.00	3.10
Ethiopia	Public sector management	3.10	3.30	3.30	3.30	3.20	3.20	3.30	3.40	3.40	3.50
Ghana	Public sector management	3.70	3.90	3.90	3.90	3.80	3.70	3.70	3.70	3.70	3.40
Kenya	Public sector management	3.30	3.40	3.30	3.30	3.30	3.30	3.30	3.40	3.40	3.40
Nigeria	Public sector management	2.80	2.80	2.90	2.90	2.90	2.90	2.90	2.90	2.80	2.80
Senegal	Public sector management	3.60	3.60	3.50	3.40	3.40	3.50	3.60	3.60	3.60	3.60
Zimbabwe	Public sector management	2.10	1.90	1.80	1.60	2.00	2.10	2.20	2.20	2.20	2.70

Tanzania	Public sector management	3.80	3.80	3.70	3.50	3.50	3.30	3.30	3.30	3.40	3.40
Middle income	**Structural policies**	**3.52**	**3.50**	**3.55**	**3.55**	**3.55**	**3.54**	**3.50**	**3.46**	**3.45**	**3.40**
Cote d'Ivoire	Structural policies	3.17	3.17	3.17	3.30	3.33	3.33	3.33	3.33	3.33	3.33
Ethiopia	Structural policies	3.17	3.17	3.17	3.20	3.17	3.17	3.17	3.17	3.17	3.17
Ghana	Structural policies	3.83	3.83	4.00	4.00	4.00	4.17	4.17	4.00	4.00	3.67
Kenya	Structural policies	3.83	3.83	3.83	3.80	4.00	4.00	4.00	3.83	3.83	3.83
Nigeria	Structural policies	2.83	3.00	3.17	3.30	3.50	3.50	3.50	3.50	3.50	3.50
Senegal	Structural policies	3.83	3.67	3.83	3.80	3.83	3.83	4.00	4.00	4.00	4.00
Zimbabwe	Structural policies	2.17	2.20	2.00	1.50	2.17	2.33	2.33	2.33	2.33	2.50
Tanzania	Structural policies	3.67	3.70	3.67	3.80	3.83	3.83	3.83	3.83	3.83	3.83

Sources and notes: World Development Indicators 2015.

CPIA = Country policy and institutional assessment (World Bank).

Econ Management = Macro, fiscal, and debt policies.

Pub Management = Property rights, revenue mobilization and use, and quality of public admin.

Structural Policies = Trade, financial and business regulation.

184 Africa's postcolonial experience

self-financing and imported intermediates, and do not have much faith in the Courts. The data show that resource-based industrializers have worse business environments and less attractive firm attributes than factor-based industrializers. We now turn to the economic and industrial profiles of each of the six resource-based economies.

Cote d'Ivoire (CIV)

Cote d'Ivoire is a medium-size country with a population of 22 million and a GDP, at market prices, of $34 billion in 2014. By African standards, the GNI per capita of $3,130 stands as middling in PPP terms.

Contrary to expectations, CIV has a low HDI score of 0.46 which reflects the low life expectancy of 51.5 years, a 20% rate of poverty at $3.10 per day, and 4.3 mean years of schooling. Its Gini coefficient of 41.5% also puts it in the middle of the pack.

CIV's economic success during 1960–1980 made it the richest country in West Africa by the end of the period. This remarkable economic record was a product of an outward-looking, agriculture-led, and public-investment-driven growth strategy. Real per capita income was, however, halved during 1980–2010 as commodity prices fell, state enterprises and marketing boards became increasingly burdensome, public investment went to unprofitable projects, and external debt rose to compensate for declining revenues (World Bank, 2012).

The Ivorian labor force is young (a third of the population is in the 16–35 age group), and not well-schooled (with 40% never schooled and about 10% completing secondary school). In its highly segmented labor market, a small urban formal sector coexists with a large informal sector (self-employment or family work) which employs two-thirds of the labor force. The better-paid one-third of the workforce is engaged in wage employment in the private sector earning, on average, five times as much as family workers. The most productive and privileged are employed in the civil service, in the extractive industries, or in finance (World Bank, 2015a).

Overdependence on external financing of investment and global commodity booms (for cocoa, coffee, and cashews) made the Ivorian economy vulnerable to the vicissitudes of the world economy as well as the rains. This glass-house of an economy was further made vulnerable by the narrowly based neopatrimonial political system and the over-reliance on expatriate (mostly French) high-level manpower.

During the period 1993–1999, the country experienced heightened social strife and polarization, emanating from inter-ethnic and inter-regional inequalities, particularly concerning access to agricultural land. Following the coup d'état of 1999, the country was effectively divided along a North-South axis in 2002. The protracted conflict induced a sad period of decline in national output over 2002–2007 as well as the suspension of the country's relations with the international community. This was followed by electoral violence and civil strife in 2010. The socio-political crisis, coupled with economic mismanagement, corruption, and the withdrawal of donor support took a heavy toll on the Ivorian economy (N'guessan, 2012).

The Ivorian GDP grew by an average of 2% during 2004–2011 before managing a robust recovery after a new political settlement was agreed upon (AEO-CIV, 2015). Following a drop in real GDP of 4.7% during the post-election crisis in 2011, the economy recovered to a remarkable annual average growth rate of 9% in 2012–2013 before slowing down to 7.9% in 2014. It grew at an annual average rate of 9.2% during 2012–2015.

Contrary to the experiences of most post-conflict countries, the growth recovery of Cote d'Ivoire was driven more by domestic factors than by external factors. The service sector was also an important source of growth relative to the pre-1980 decades when growth was powered by agriculture, mainly export crops. The rebound in agriculture was driven by increases in cocoa, cashew, cotton, and other food-crop production (rice, plantain, cassava, and corn). Industrial production also increased across the board.

This broad-based growth, urban as well as rural, benefitted from buoyant public and private investments with rapid expansions in the construction, transport, and financial sectors. The revival was highly visible to those who visited Abidjan with its numerous construction cranes, cars, and banks (World Bank, 2015a). However, the much-needed momentum may not be sustainable given the significant and enduring fall in commodity prices that began in 2015.

More hopefully, gross capital formation tripled since 1990 to a still modest level of 17% of GDP in 2014. Although the share of FDI assets in its manufacturing sector fell from about two-thirds in 1975 to one-third in 1990 (Harrison, 1996). Its young firms are among the highest foreign-invested compared with their African peers or with the average for lower middle-income countries. While the business environment is relatively good, firms continue to complain about the scarcity of long-term finance, political uncertainty, and corruption (see Table 8.3).

Internationally comparable economic data on competitiveness is scarcer for Cote d'Ivoire than for its peers. The available internationally comparable data on changes in the structures of Ivorian employment, output, and productivity in manufacturing industries at the three-digit ISIC level are presented in Tables 8.5 and 8.6. Cote d'Ivoire's manufacturing value added rose from some $0.17 billion in 1970 (in 2005 international dollars) to $5.6 billion (garnering some 67,000 jobs) in 1980. However, we lack comparable data to 2010. In other words, while the Ivorian MVA rose by a factor of 40 during 1970–1980, employment only doubled – the implication being that productivity rose by an unlikely factor of 20.

If the manufacturing survey data compiled by UNIDO (2015) are to be believed, there was a precipitous decline in the output shares of the labor-intensive sectors and petroleum products (ISIC 15–18 and 23 in Table 8.6). The decline was a remarkable 50 percentage points from 66% in 1970 to a mere 16% in 1990. The biggest beneficiaries were metal products, chemicals, and machinery which gained 57 percentage points. They collectively rose from 12.8% of GDP to 69.7% of GDP in only one decade.

It is not clear how much of this reflects disruptions in the national value chains of agro-processing industries, in industrial deepening toward skill-intensive manufacturing or a mixture of both. Changes in the shares of employment shown in Table 8.7, however, suggest otherwise: the employment share of the former cluster rose by 10 percentage points in a decade from 47.5% while the latter barely budged. It is hard to believe that such a mismatch can be produced in just ten years even with the introduction of an extremely labor-saving technology by the gainers.

It must be noted here that measures based on gross value added, while useful for gauging the efficiency with which intermediates are transformed into final output,

186 Africa's postcolonial experience

TABLE 8.5 Global competitiveness index for resource-based industrializers

	CIV	GHA	MUS	NGA	ZAF	ZWE
Global competitiveness index (*Best GCI is 5.8, Switzerland*)	**3.9**	**3.6**	**4.4**	**3.5**	**4.4**	**3.5**
A. Basic requirements:	**4.1**	**3.5**	**5.0**	**3.2**	**4.4**	**3.7**
Institutions	4.0	3.9	4.5	3.2	4.4	3.3
Infrastructure	3.6	2.7	4.8	2.1	4.1	2.4
Macroeconomic environ	4.7	2.8	4.7	4.6	4.5	4.2
Health and primary ed	3.9	4.5	6.1	2.9	4.2	4.9
B. Efficiency enhancers:	**3.7**	**3.8**	**4.2**	**3.9**	**4.5**	**3.1**
Higher ed and training	3.4	3.6	4.6	2.8	4.1	3.1
Goods market efficiency	4.3	4.2	4.9	4.1	4.6	3.5
Labor market efficiency	4.2	4.0	4.3	4.5	3.8	3.3
Financial markets	4.0	3.8	4.4	3.8	5.0	3.1
Technological readiness	3.1	3.2	4.1	3.0	4.6	2.8
Market size	3.5	3.7	2.8	5.1	4.9	2.8
C. Innovation and sophistication:	**3.6**	**3.6**	**3.8**	**3.2**	**4.1**	**2.9**
Business sophistication	3.7	3.9	4.4	3.7	4.4	3.2
Innovation	3.4	3.3	3.2	2.8	3.7	2.6

Source: World Economic Forum, the Global Competitiveness Report, 2015–2016.

http://reports.weforum.org/global-competitiveness-report-2015-2016/economies/.

suffer a high correlation between intermediate inputs and fixed capital stock to confound the effects of each on output. On the other hand, efficiency measures based on value added, while good at identifying capital's productivity, tend to inflate the effects of capital and labor on output (Söderbom and Teal, 2002).

CIV has an impressive industrial sector, surpassed in West Africa only by Nigeria. Agriculture and industry account for about 22% of GDP each, and services claimed 56%. Half of the industrial sector was in manufacturing in 2014. The share of manufactured exports, at 51% in 2012, was quite impressive.

As shown in Table 8.8, Cote d'Ivoire had about the average African MVA per capita and an average MVA share in GDP. Its international competitiveness was such that both manufactured exports and processed agricultural exports have more than doubled in value since 2002.

Cote d'Ivoire's international competitiveness has improved on every pillar except for the macroeconomic environment (see Tables 8.3 and 8.5). It posted the biggest gains in areas such as innovation, financial market development, and institutions – all pillars on which the country scores in the top half globally. Despite progress in health and primary and higher education, human capital formation nonetheless remains its weakest area.

The overall picture is that the industrial deepening that began at the close of the twentieth century petered out although some recovery is evident after 2012. While CIV has managed to move steadily toward a broad-based manufacturing sector, the kind of economic transformation achieved by the likes of Mauritius and Tunisia has so far eluded it.

TABLE 8.6 Structural change in manufacturing output for resource-based industrializers

Countries	CIV	CIV	GHA	GHA	NGA	NGA	MAU	MAU	ZAF	ZAF
Value added (%)	1970	1990	1970	1980	1970	1980	1970	2010	1970	2010
Food and beverages	22.0	1.2	24.0	23.8	27.3	17.2	69.8	39.4	13.6	21.9
Tobacco products	5.0	1.2	9.9	13.3	8.7	4.0	4.9	. .	1.1	. .
Textiles	13.4	4.3	12.8	9.1	23.5	9.5	1.7	5.3	6.7	1.0
Wearing apparel, fur	2.3	0.3	3.4	1.7	2.1	1.1	4.2	25.3	6.2	0.2
Leather and leather products	. .	. .	. .	. .	. .	. .	. .	0.4	. .	0.6
Wood products (excl. furniture)	5.7	4.6	9.4	6.6	1.9	3.7	1.2	0.5	2.0	2.3
Paper and paper products	2.7	0.7	2.5	0.3	1.7	1.6	0.0	0.9	3.8	3.0
Printing and publishing	. .	. .	2.3	1.9	2.5	3.1	2.6	5.1	4.2	3.4
Furniture; manufacturing n.e.c.	3.0	0.7	1.1	0.9	1.4	2.9	3.1	3.7	3.9	8.4
Coke and petroleum products	22.7	9.2	3.8	15.2	8.4	3.2	0.0	4.9	2.5	12.9
Rubber and plastics products	. .	0.4	3.3	2.4	5.3	5.1	0.9	8.7	3.5	3.7
Non-metallic mineral products	2.8	19.3	2.7	2.7	3.0	4.6	2.7	. .	6.0	4.6
Basic metals	0.1	0.1	12.8	12.5	0.1	1.5	0.0	0.5	10.0	7.3
Fabricated metal products	3.6	13.4	3.2	2.7	6.4	5.8	1.6	2.5	8.7	5.3
Chemicals and chemical products	6.3	27.0	4.4	4.5	6.2	12.2	2.5	. .	9.9	6.9
Machinery and equipment n.e.c.	0.1	10.0	0.1	0.0	0.2	1.0	2.0	1.0	6.9	6.3
Office and computing machinery	. .	. .	. .	. .	. .	. .	. .	. .	. .	. .
Electrical machinery and apparat	1.0	4.5	1.4	0.7	1.0	1.9	0.8	0.7	4.3	2.3
Communication equipment	. .	. .	. .	. .	. .	. .	. .	. .	. .	0.7
Medical and optical instruments	. .	0.5	0.0	0.5	0.0	0.0	0.0	0.7	0.4	0.5
Motor vehicles and trailers	9.2	2.7	2.9	1.2	0.3	21.7	1.9	0.3	6.2	6.3
Other transport equipment	. .	. .	. .	. .	. .	. .	. .	. .	. .	1.1
D Total manufacturing (mill 2005$)	**172**	**5,571**	**194**	**854**	**553**	**8,984**	**24**	**1,353**	**4,262**	**4,5412**

Source: Based on UNIDO, Indstat 2 database, 2015.

TABLE 8.7 Structural change in manufacturing employment for resource-based industrializers

Countries	CIV	CIV	GHA	GHA	NGA	NGA	MAU	MAU	ZAF	ZAF	ZWE	ZWE
Employment	1970	1980	1970	1980	1970	1980	1970	2010	1970	2010	1970	1990
Food and beverages	21.6	33.3	14.0	20.5	14.0	20.5	14.0	20.5	14.0	20.5	14.0	20.5
Tobacco products	4.9	3.9	1.7	1.6	1.7	1.6	1.7	1.6	1.7	1.6	1.7	1.6
Textiles	17.7	17.5	19.4	20.5	19.4	20.5	19.4	20.5	19.4	20.5	19.4	20.5
Wearing apparel, fur	3.3	2.7	7.8	4.0	7.8	4.0	7.8	4.0	7.8	4.0	7.8	4.0
Leather and leather products	..	..	..	..	..	..	..	..	..	..	..	..
Wood products (excl. Furniture)	21.4	13.5	22.3	19.7	22.3	19.7	22.3	19.7	22.3	19.7	22.3	19.7
Paper and paper products	2.1	2.3	1.3	0.7	1.3	0.7	1.3	0.7	1.3	0.7	1.3	0.7
Printing and publishing	..	..	5.4	6.0	5.4	6.0	5.4	6.0	5.4	6.0	5.4	6.0
Furniture; manufact., n.e.c.	7.5	5.7	3.5	2.2	3.5	2.2	3.5	2.2	3.5	2.2	3.5	2.2
Coke and petroleum products	0.7	1.3	0.7	0.8	0.7	0.8	0.7	0.8	0.7	0.8	0.7	0.8
Rubber and plastics products	..	..	3.0	3.1	3.0	3.1	3.0	3.1	3.0	3.1	3.0	3.1
Non-metallic mineral products	2.6	2.4	3.6	3.1	3.6	3.1	3.6	3.1	3.6	3.1	3.6	3.1
Basic metals	0.1	0.3	4.5	3.5	4.5	3.5	4.5	3.5	4.5	3.5	4.5	3.5
Fabricated metal products	3.9	4.9	4.4	4.3	4.4	4.3	4.4	4.3	4.4	4.3	4.4	4.3
Chemicals and chemical products	9.7	7.5	4.2	5.0	4.2	5.0	4.2	5.0	4.2	5.0	4.2	5.0
Machinery and equipment n.e.c.	0.2	0.2	0.2	0.1	0.2	0.1	0.2	0.1	0.2	0.1	0.2	0.1
Office and computing machinery	..	..	..	..	..	..	..	..	..	..	..	..
Electrical machinery and apparat	..	..	3.4	2.5	3.4	2.5	3.4	2.5	3.4	2.5	3.4	2.5
Communicat. equipment			..	..	..	..	..	..	..	..	..	..
Medical and optical instruments	..	..	0.0	0.8	0.0	0.8	0.0	0.8	0.0	0.8	0.0	0.8
Motor vehicles and trailers	3.3	3.3	0.0	0.8	0.0	0.8	0.0	0.8	0.0	0.8	0.0	0.8
Other transport equipment	..	..	..	..	..	..	..	..	..	..	..	..
D Total manufacturing employment	33,352	67,172	57,674	80,315	127,500	432,210	13,731	79,819	1,076,000	1,187,010	57,674	80,315

Source: Based on UNIDO, Indstat 2 database, 2015.

Resource-based industrializers **189**

TABLE 8.8 Cote d'Ivoire: competitive industrial performance, 1990–2012

Year	MVA per capita	M Exports per capita	MHM in MVA	MHX in MX	MVA in GDP	M Exports in exports	Industrialization intensity index
	$	$	%	%	%	%	
1990	182	65	14	9	17	31	0.74
1991	176	65	13	9	17	31	0.75
1992	174	65	13	9	18	31	0.75
1993	170	65	12	9	18	31	0.76
1994	168	65	14	9	18	31	0.37
1995	181	65	15	'9	19	31	0.38
1996	189	68	16	9	19	29	0.39
1997	220	112	15	17	21	42	0.42
1998	213	117	13	23	20	42	0.39
1999	210	120	13	25	20	45	0.39
2000	215	104	13	10	22	48	0.42
2001	206	98	13	21	21	45	0.41
2002	190	117	13	34	20	40	0.39
2003	168	115	13	40	18	38	0.35
2004	170	188	13	39	19	51	0.35
2005	175	219	13	36	19	54	0.35
2006	159	213	13	31	18	48	0.33
2007	157	203	13	27	17	47	0.32
2008	157	226	13	17	17	44	0.32
2009	165	220	13	25	18	41	0.35
2010	152	188	13	33	16	36	0.31
2011	150	159	13	19	17	29	0.33
2012	160	182	13	16	17	35	0.32

Sources and notes: UNIDO, Competitive Industrial Performance (CIP) database, 2014.
MHM = medium- and high-technology manufacturing production
MHX = medium- and high-technology manufacturing exports
MX = manufacturing exports
MVA = manufacturing (M) value added

The country has an enormous potential as a producer and exporter of agricultural products, including cocoa and tropical fruits. It is Africa's leading cashew-nut producer and a top international exporter.

A mixture of liberalization and selective import substitution attracted foreign skills and significant foreign direct investment in manufacturing (Riddell, 1990). It is also a strategically located coastal country and can enhance its considerable expertise in port logistics to serve the larger West African market. These advantages are becoming evident. Manufactured exports rose, both as the share of output and all exports, from the mid-1960s to the mid-1970s before stabilizing subsequently.

190 Africa's postcolonial experience

There are signs that the composition of output has been adversely affected by the alternating episodes of war and peace. The share of the war-vulnerable manufacturing sector, for example, fell from 20% in 2000 to 16% in 2014. Total factor productivity experienced a -0.8% growth rate per annum during 1980–2010 before recovering at an annual rate of 0.4% subsequently (World Bank, 2015a). Furthermore, as Diagana et al. (2015) rightly note, such post-conflict catchup growth is not automatic, and matters greatly for ensuring a broad-based growth recovery.

Ghana (GHA)

Ghana, with 27 million people, had a GDP at market prices of $39 billion in 2014. Its GNI per capita was, however, $3,900 in PPP terms. Ghana's poverty rate exceeds 60% of the population at $3.10 per day.

Its middling HDI score of 0.58 reflects a mixed bag of economic and social indicators. As shown in Table 7.2, life expectancy in 2014 was 61 years and the mean years of schooling was 7.0. By contrast, the Gini coefficient stood at 42.8%.

The first half of Ghana's 50 years of independence was one of political instability, mixed statist and marketist development paradigms, and policy reversals (Tsikata, 2001). Ghana's regimented economy induced a one-third drop in the country's real per capita income during 1974–1983 (Fosu, 2012). The growth uptick that began in the early 1980s accelerated after 2000 (World Bank, 2013).

From 1983 to 2005, Ghana's political stability paid off in improved growth. As shown in Figures 8.1–8.3, a slowdown in population growth boosted real per capita income. However, GDP per worker remains among the lowest in its peer group.

Market-oriented reforms and the emergence of multi-party democracy undergirded the robust recovery. Growth has since been supported by significant official and private capital inflows and favorable terms of trade generated by the currently slack commodity prices. Expansion of the construction and the energy sectors allowed manufacturing to keep pace with the rest of the industrial sector.

Ghana's economic growth after 2000 was also stimulated by the price booms of its main commodity exports of gold and cocoa, and the commencement of commercial oil production in 2011 (Herrera and Dilek, 2014). The poorly managed volatility of commodity prices as well as the volatility of capital flows clearly hindering robust growth. Overall, the major drivers of growth include political stability (a populist dictatorship giving way to a generation-deep electoral democracy after 1990), improved economic policies, and better terms of trade. The exploitation of commercial oil and gas resources since 2010 has raised expectations for rapid growth for years to come.

Ghana's industrialization experience replicates the path traversed by the other resource-based industrializers. It began with import substitution during 1960–1983, moved to an outward-looking strategy during 1984–2000, and then to a private sector-led value-adding processing of Ghana's natural resource endowments. Import substitution, when combined with protection and public investment, boosted the share of manufacturing in total industrial output from 10% in 1960 to 14% in 1970. It also generated an average 8% growth rate per annum in industrial sector employment.

Ghana's manufacturing sector, while small, is a provider of employment for about 10% of the formal-sector labor force. Its employment share has declined from nearly 20% in 1970 because of a rise in capital intensity. Gross capital formation doubled during 1970–2014 to a respectable 27% of GDP (Table 8.2). The share of manufacturing in the industrial sector in GDP declined significantly in the 1990s, albeit remaining a dominant subsector. Today, the composition of GDP shows a 22% share for agriculture, 28% for industry (only a quarter of which is manufacturing), and 50% for services.

The economic restructuring programs of the 1980s and the 1990s included the revamping of industrial and allied sectors which raised capacity utilization and enhanced industrial support institutions (Republic of Ghana, MOTI, 2011). These policy initiatives complemented a new Ghanaian industrialization strategy that emphasized efficiency, international competitiveness, intersectoral linkages, and the development of appropriate technologies for small-scale manufacturing clusters (Ackah et al., 2016).

According to the internationally comparable data reported in Table 8.9, the 16% drop in employment in agriculture during 1970–2010 was picked up by the service sector rather than by the more productive industrial sector. The output share, as well as the employment share of manufacturing, declined during the period. Output per worker declined, too, with the productivity of manufacturing in 2010 among the lowest of the major sectors of the Ghanaian economy.

Some have suggested that manufacturing underperformed most sectors over the past three decades because of unreliable supplies of electricity and water as well as exchange rate volatility for the highly import-dependent sectors. Furthermore, the uncertainty of revenue flows resulting from volatile commodity prices and climate-sensitive products continues to pose challenges in attracting the substantial long-term investments needed for robust diversification (AEO-GHA, 2015).

Manufacturing firms in Ghana are domestic-market oriented and lag their comparators in Kenya and Vietnam based on selected indicators of export orientation. The business environment in Ghana has been particularly unfavorable for manufacturers in the last few years because of a persistent energy crisis and macroeconomic instability. Manufacturing firms complain about shortages of critical skills in mechanical and electrical engineering, quality control, and information technology (Sutton and Kpentey, 2012; Nti, 2015).

A switch to a policy of industrial deepening, agro-processing, and export promotion, under democratic governments in the 2000s, did induce a quick recovery. The

TABLE 8.9 Ghana: changes in sectoral economic structure, 1970–2010

	1970	1980	1990	2000	2010	Diff: 2010–1970
Employment structure:	%	%	%	%	%	%
Agriculture	57.0	56.5	53.5	53.6	41.6	−15.5
Mining	1.0	0.6	0.9	1.8	1.1	0.1
Manufacturing	12.1	14.4	12.9	10.6	10.8	−1.3
Utilities	0.4	0.4	0.4	0.3	0.4	0.0
Construction	2.4	2.0	1.6	2.9	3.1	0.7
Trade and hotels	13.8	14.4	17.1	17.0	24.3	10.5
Transport-storage-comm.	2.7	2.0	2.7	2.9	3.5	0.8
Finance and business srvcs.	0.3	0.4	0.7	1.4	2.3	2.0
Government services	7.0	7.1	5.8	5.2	6.6	−0.4
Community services	3.2	2.3	4.3	4.1	6.3	3.1
Total employment[a]	3,133	4,687	6,542	7,428	10,243	7,110
Output structure:	%	%	%	%	%	%
Agriculture	37.5	40.2	31.2	32.9	29.5	−8.0
Mining	5.4	2.7	3.0	2.8	2.9	−2.5
Manufacturing	18.9	15.0	12.8	11.1	8.8	−10.1
Utilities	0.7	1.4	2.0	1.8	1.9	1.3
Construction	9.9	9.1	5.8	5.4	8.6	−1.3
Trade and hotels	11.2	8.9	10.6	11.2	11.6	0.4
Transport-storage-comm.	8.4	9.4	15.1	15.4	16.6	8.2
Finance and business srvcs.	1.2	1.9	4.4	5.8	5.9	4.6
Government services	5.6	9.7	10.8	9.4	10.0	4.4
Community services	1.4	1.7	4.3	4.0	4.2	2.8
Gross value added[b]	38,154	46,091	51,099	70,589	155,759	117,605
Productivity structure[c]:	$	$	$	$	$	Ratio: 2010/1970
Agriculture	1,061	808	641	928	1,388	1.31
Mining	8,858	5,477	3,566	2,403	5,212	0.59
Manufacturing	2,522	1,179	1,088	1,579	1,592	0.63
Utilities	2,730	3,832	5,481	7,941	9,688	3.55
Construction	6,655	5,234	3,894	2,792	5,516	0.83
Trade and hotels	1,304	701	685	997	930	0.71
Transport-storage-comm.	4,955	5,188	6192	8,066	9,169	1.85
Finance and business srvcs.	6,642	5,352	6,540	6,110	4,982	0.75
Government services	1,279	1,559	2,021	2,730	2,965	2.32
Community services	687	848	1,103	1,483	1,306	1.90
Economy-wide	1,615	1,134	1,099	1,512	1,957	1.21

Sources and notes: Calculations are based on the 2014 version of the GGDC 10-sector database: www.rug.nl/research/ggdc/data/10-sector-database which is documented in M.P. Timmer, G.J. de Vries, and K. de Vries, "Patterns of Structural Change in Developing Countries," GGDC Research Memorandum 149, Groningen Growth and Development Centre, 2014.

a Economy-wide persons engaged, in thousands.

b Gross value added in millions of 2005 international dollars.

c Gross value added per person engaged in 2005 international dollars.

Resource-based industrializers **193**

share of manufacturing in Ghana's GDP nonetheless decreased from 10.2% in 2006 to 5.8% in 2013 as non-manufacturing industrial production picked up. Ghana also experienced a steady relative decline in manufacturing production, export diversification, and export competitiveness over the 2000s along with a rising dependence on unprocessed mineral exports (notably gold and bauxite).

Ghana's economy has traditionally been dependent on exports of cocoa, timber, and minerals – especially gold, and now oil. Export of cocoa beans accounted for about 55% of total exports during 1957–1997. However, there is evidence of slow but steady diversification. Non-traditional exports grew rapidly, spearheaded by the exports of canned tuna, pineapple, and veneer (Zakari and Boly, 2013). Areas that hold much promise for boosting light manufacturing in Ghana currently include cocoa processing, food and agro-processing, textiles and garments, and pharmaceuticals.

We present a battery of measures of industrial efficiency and international competitiveness for Ghana in Tables 8.3–8.5. The food processing and beverages sectors, which account for about one-third of MVA, are by far the most efficient branches of manufacturing.

Though Ghana ranks well on the World Bank's CPIA ratings on structural policies and public-sector management, the domestic environment for industrial firms is not yet globally competitive. Finance is the most frequently cited binding constraint along with inadequate infrastructural services such as electricity supply. Ghanaian firms must put up high collateral (240% of the loan) which forces three-quarters of the firms to rely on self-finance. Ghana also has a high proportion of foreign-owned manufacturers and more temporary industrial workers than its resource-based peers.

Teal (1996) and others looked at firm-level data to compare manufacturing firm performance in Ghana with other African countries. Industrial firms in Ghana do compare more favorably in productivity than their peers elsewhere (Bogetic, 2007). The food processing sector and well-established companies tend to be more productive and higher paying (Ackah et al., 2016).

The global competitiveness index reported in Table 8.10 ranks Ghana much lower than Mauritius or South Africa. This is attributed to poor infrastructure and relatively low human capital which dent its technological capability. Overall, as shown in Table 8.10, the post-1990 share and composition of manufacturing exports and its overall industrialization index all show little or no discernible trend toward industrial deepening.

Having grown at the relatively moderate annual average rate of 2.3% for ten years, the manufacturing sector slowed down subsequently. Ghanaian manufacturers, like producers all over West Africa, have found themselves grappling with an influx of low-cost imported manufactured goods, particularly from China. A combination of over-valued exchange rates, the high cost of doing business, and crowding out by the extractive sector in the capital market contributed to the outcome (Oxford Business Group, 2012).

194 Africa's postcolonial experience

TABLE 8.10 Ghana: competitive industrial performance, 1990–2012

Year	MVA per capita	M Exports per capita	MHM in MVA	MHX in MX	MVA in GDP	M Exports in exports	Industrialization intensity index
	$	$	%	%	%	%	
1990	67	16	7	7	18	20	0.27
1991	66	16	13	7	17	20	0.29
1992	66	16	13	7	17	20	0.29
1993	36	16	13	7	9	20	0.17
1994	35	16	10	7	9	20	0.19
1995	35	37	10	3	9	26	0.18
1996	35	37	10	3	9	26	0.18
1997	37	21	10	3	9	23	0.18
1998	37	21	10	3	9	34	0.18
1999	38	26	10	11	9	38	0.18
2000	39	25	10	6	9	29	0.19
2001	39	28	10	6	9	32	0.18
2002	40	28	10	6	9	32	0.18
2003	41	23	1	6	9	21	0.12
2004	42	21	10	13	9	18	0.17
2005	43	50	10	8	9	35	0.17
2006	44	43	10	3	8	26	0.17
2007	42	34	10	13	8	22	0.16
2008	43	32	10	18	8	20	0.16
2009	41	31	10	20	7	14	0.16
2010	43	27	10	25	7	12	0.16
2011	48	265	10	6	7	36	0.15
2012	50	91	10	20	7	12	. .

Sources and notes: UNIDO, Competitive Industrial Performance (CIP) database, 2014.
MHM = medium- and high-technology manufacturing production
MHX = medium- and high-technology manufacturing exports
MX = manufacturing exports
MVA = manufacturing (M) value added

The prospects for manufacturing growth, however, look good. The country has an abundant source of feedstock, a rapidly growing economy, a large ECOWAS market, a stable yet open political space, and a progressively improving infrastructure. As we will review in Chapter 10, the government has also launched successive industrial plans to increase industrial competitiveness.

Mauritius (MAU)

Mauritius, a multiethnic island economy of 1.3 million, had a GDP at market prices of $12.6 billion in 2014. An overcrowded island once described in Malthusian terms, it has managed to achieve an enviable GNI per capita of $17,470 today in PPP terms. Along with Botswana, MAU is often cited as Africa's answer to Singapore in terms of development trajectory.

Its high HDI score of 0.77 reflects an impressive set of economic and social indicators. As shown in Table 7.2, life expectancy is an impressive 74 years and the mean years of schooling stands at 8.5, just below South Africa's. Furthermore, Mauritius is an egalitarian society approaching zero population growth. Just 3% earn less than $3.10 per day. A Gini coefficient of 36%, among the lowest in the world, also elicits an easy comparison with the egalitarian and manufacturing-led middle-income East Asian economy.

Mauritius has the region's most efficient market, the best infrastructure, and the best-educated workforce. To move further up the technological ladder, however, it needs to improve the quality of higher education.

Real per capita GDP grew by 4.1% per year during 1970–2003 and continued to accelerate subsequently (see Figure 8.2). The data reported in Table 8.11 also show that, during 1970–2010, the share of agriculture in nationwide employment declined by a remarkable 30 percentage points although much of it was picked up largely by manufacturing and services.

Mauritius did not subscribe to the prevailing development orthodoxy of the 1960s and the 1970s which emphasized inward-oriented and state-led import substitution. Instead, starting in 1970, the country followed a policy of import substitution coupled with incentives for exports through the export-processing zone (EPZ). This two-pronged strategy encouraged resident enterprises to produce for the small home market as well as for the export market.

Mauritius deepened its trade liberalization after 1983. The most distinctive feature of this policy turn is the gradualist approach to reducing import protection and to reforming other aspects of its regimented industrial regime (Wignaraja, 2003). By the mid-1990s, Mauritius had become considerably more open and market friendly. It stands today as one of the most liberal economic regimes in Africa.

Mauritius is certainly an outlier in Africa for its impressive industrial performance. In the past two decades or so, the economy has undergone a remarkable transformation from mono-crop sugar production to become one of the leading exporters of manufactures in all of Africa. Manufacturing value added per head nearly quadrupled between 1980 and 1998 (from US$210 to US$706).

Another distinctive feature of the Mauritian development experience is that sustained industrial competitiveness generated significant new employment opportunities (Table 8.7). Manufacturing employment in the formal sector rose from 13,370 in 1970 to 79,820 in 2010. Manufacturing, in fact, accounted for 19% of

TABLE 8.11 Mauritius: changes in sectoral economic structure, 1970–2010

	1970	1980	1990	2000	2010	Diff: 2010–1970
Employment structure:	%	%	%	%	%	%
Agriculture	37.3	23.7	16.7	11.4	7.2	−30.1
Mining	0.1	0.1	0.2	0.3	0.2	0.1
Manufacturing	10.6	21.3	32.2	28.8	19.1	8.5
Utilities	1.6	1.9	0.9	0.8	1.0	−0.6
Construction	7.8	12.1	10.0	9.4	10.0	2.2
Trade and hotels	7.7	10.3	11.0	17.6	21.5	13.8
Transport-storage-comm.	5.8	5.7	6.1	6.7	8.3	2.5
Finance and business srvcs.	1.1	2.1	2.8	4.6	9.5	8.4
Government services	12.1	9.8	11.8	14.4	16.5	4.4
Community services	15.9	12.9	8.4	6.0	6.8	−9.1
Total employment [a]	192	277	407	466	522	330
Output structure:	%	%	%	%	%	%
Agriculture	13.1	14.9	12.0	7.4	5.2	−7.9
Mining	3.0	2.7	2.2	1.7	0.4	−2.7
Manufacturing	17.5	18.5	25.4	23.7	18.8	1.3
Utilities	1.7	1.4	1.5	2.0	1.9	0.2
Construction	7.9	6.0	5.8	5.7	7.2	−0.8
Trade and hotels	22.7	19.3	20.3	20.0	20.3	−2.4
Transport-storage-comm.	9.9	9.5	9.3	11.3	15.7	5.8
Finance and business srvcs.	5.3	4.0	6.4	10.9	11.7	6.3
Government services	16.5	21.3	15.0	14.1	14.6	−1.9
Community services	2.3	2.4	2.1	3.2	4.3	2.1
Gross value added [b]	16,671	40,010	73,332	130,252	191,553	174,882
Productivity structure [c]:	$	$	$	$	$	Ratio: 2010/1970
Agriculture	30,471	90,853	129,078	180,594	265,679	8.72
Mining	3,629,013	5,904,250	2,479,154	1,643,635	732,880	0.20
Manufacturing	143,085	125,161	142,073	229,933	360,937	2.52
Utilities	91,652	106,331	310,809	683,835	693,851	7.57
Construction	88,609	71,682	104,552	170,565	264,233	2.98
Trade and hotels	256,419	271,619	331,060	317,639	346,076	1.35
Transport-storage-comm.	148,615	241,392	274,334	473,468	698,375	4.70
Finance and business srvcs.	413,877	270,658	408,774	663,569	448,439	1.08
Government services	118,970	312,425	230,104	273,421	325,481	2.74
Community services	12,426	26,460	45,657	149,384	235,111	18.92
Economy-wide	86,976	144,550	180,223	279,733	367,282	4.22

Sources and notes: Calculations are based on the 2014 version of the GGDC 10-sector database: www. rug.nl/research/ggdc/data/10-sector-database which is documented in M.P. Timmer, G.J. de Vries, and K. de Vries, "Patterns of Structural Change in Developing Countries," GGDC Research Memorandum 149, Groningen Growth and Development Centre, 2014.

a Economy-wide persons engaged, in thousands.

b Gross value added in millions of 2005 international dollars.

c Gross value added per person engaged in 2005 international dollars.

both national employment and national output in 2010. It boosted wages in a non-inflationary way since manufacturing increased its productivity by a factor of 2.5 during 1970–2010.

Another interesting aspect of the Mauritian manufacturing sector is its lopsidedness. Some two-thirds of MVA and half of the industrial labor force are concentrated in three branches: food processing, beverages, and apparel (Table 8.6). Furthermore, both gross capital formation and industrial value added declined from 33% each in 1970 to 23% each in 2010. These trends suggest that Mauritius, over 95% of whose exports are manufactures, is specializing along its dynamic comparative advantage within manufacturing.

The Mauritian economic structure resembles that of South Africa with agriculture accounting for a mere 3% of GDP, services a whopping 74%, and industry (two-thirds being MVA) for 23%. As early as 1990, there were telltale signs that Mauritius was reaching the limits of labor-intensive industrial development that had underpinned this success. Poor logistics and high transport and communications costs were becoming more of a handicap for technological upgrading in an ever tightly integrating global economy (World Bank, 2007a). The significant fall in capital formation in industry is also not encouraging especially given the lower industrial innovativeness score (Table 8.5).

Over the past decade, the sugar industry has diversified into specialty sugars, ethanol, and bagasse electricity cogeneration which now supplies nearly a fifth of the country's power demand. The textiles and apparel sectors have upgraded by investing heavily in sophisticated design and fabrication capabilities. Foreign direct investment consequently poured in, which along with rising female labor force participation, increased productivity and global competitiveness.

Detailed data on the relative efficiency of industries is surprisingly hard to find for Mauritius. The available data on global competitiveness (Table 8.5) and competitive industrial performance (Table 8.12) both show that Mauritian performance regarding production and exports per capita has been good. However, firms continue to complain about long-term finance, informality, and the unreliability of electricity.

Thanks to a capable and professional civil service and a government commitment to a partnership with the private sector, Mauritius avoided the extremes of state control but not its intricate web of regulations (World Bank, 2007a). Its political economy is undergirded by a viable democratic order that balances the competing interests of its ethnically diverse society (Vecatachellum, 2012).

As noted earlier, Gerschenkron's classic idea of leapfrogging has recently taken a twist. Latecomer firms with the capability especially for learning can now leverage the efforts of more advanced rivals by linking to global value chains and eventually gaining access to sophisticated technologies. The lack of a broad-based industrial base means that the transition toward skill-intensive and tech-intensive branches is a major source of concern. As an escape valve from a middle-income trap, Mauritius has instead opted to cultivate its dynamic comparative advantage in financial services and tourism. The jury is still out.

198 Africa's postcolonial experience

TABLE 8.12 Mauritius: competitive industrial performance, 1990–2012

Year	MVA per capita	M Exports per capita	MHM in MVA	MHX in MX	MVA in GDP	M Exports in exports	Industrialization intensity index
	$	$	%	%	%	%	
1990	634	1,127	9	7	21	98	0.32
1991	654	1,113	9	7	21	98	0.34
1992	687	1,200	7	7	21	98	0.33
1993	702	1,302	7	6	21	98	0.34
1994	720	1,179	7	7	21	98	0.36
1995	752	1,328	8	8	21	98	0.37
1996	792	1,453	7	4	21	98	0.37
1997	831	1,349	4	5	21	98	0.33
1998	873	1,418	3	6	21	98	0.34
1999	883	1,292	3	5	21	98	0.34
2000	943	1,218	3	5	21	98	0.34
2001	975	1,229	3	5	21	98	0.34
2002	941	1,350	2	8	20	94	0.32
2003	931	1,436	2	9	20	95	0.29
2004	927	1,464	3	9	19	91	0.28
2005	868	1,081	3	4	17	87	0.26
2006	895	1,607	2	22	17	87	0.25
2007	909	1,501	3	11	17	86	0.24
2008	932	1,508	3	12	16	81	0.24
2009	946	1,254	3	9	16	92	0.25
2010	937	1,096	3	3	15	96	0.22
2011	938	1,401	8	4	15	96	0.26
2012	948	1,359	7	4	14	96	0.24

Sources and notes: UNIDO, Competitive Industrial Performance (CIP) database, 2014.
MHM = medium- and high-technology manufacturing production
MHX = medium- and high-technology manufacturing exports
MX = manufacturing exports
MVA = manufacturing (M) value added

Nigeria (NGA)

Nigeria, with a population of some 180 million in 2014, is now Africa's largest economy with a revised GDP of nearly $600 billion at market prices. With a GNI of over $1 trillion in PPP terms, its per capita income stands at the more respectable level of $5,700. Nigeria is one of the most ethnically fractionalized and regionally fragmented countries in the world. The three major ethnic groups (Hausa, Yoruba, and Igbo) are divided across the north-south and east-west geopolitical axes.

Nigeria's low HDI index of 0.51 reflects its poor economic and social achievements since independence in 1960. Over half of its people are in poverty at the poverty line of $2 per day. NGA's life expectancy stood at 52.8 years in 2014. And the mean years of schooling at 6.0 years is average for Africa, and income inequality is very high with a Latin-American type Gini index of 48.8%.

A combination of lackluster growth and rapid population growth produced a drop in real per capita income during 1985–2002. Resumption of a healthy GDP growth produced a sustained increase in real per capita income during 2002–2014 (see Figures 8.1–8.3).

With the end of the oil price boom in 2015, this gain is likely to be reversed rather markedly (Litwack et al., 2015). This is because, since the 1960s, Nigeria's economy has been oil driven. With the oil sector accounting for over 80% of government revenue and over 90% of exports, falling oil prices adversely affected the fiscal and external positions after 2014. Furthermore, lower levels of domestic production have been compounded by oil revenue theft and pipeline vandalism by marginalized local communities (AEO-NGA, 2015). Its prolonged dependence on rent from oil had, however, helped undertake significant infrastructural investments. It also attracted rent-seeking politicians and businesspersons who siphoned off as much as half a trillion USD since independence (Okonjo-Iweala, 2012; World Bank, 2014).

Like many other African countries, post-independence Nigeria's industrial strategy initially relied heavily on import substitution. Oil revenues underwrote rapid growth of urban-based manufacturing which triggered urban-bound migration and the appreciation of the Naira. With the exhaustion of the easy phase of import substitution and windfall revenues generated from oil exports, wages rose rapidly as did unrestrained rent seeking by the political elites and their business allies.

As is the case with many other resource-based economies, Nigeria's agricultural sector was unwisely neglected even as food imports rose dramatically. In 2010, it claimed some 60% of GDP and 38% of employment. The mining sector saw its share decline from a 45% share of GDP in 1990 to just 24% in 2014 (Table 8.1). Industry claimed a quarter of GDP (Table 8.2) and manufacturing for just 35% of GDP (see Table 8.13). By comparison, with a smaller GDP, South Africa produced $47 billion worth of manufactures in 2014 as opposed to $8 billion for Nigeria. Evidence of the **Dutch Disease** is palpable.

The country's gross capital formation is a tepid 16% of GDP. Deindustrialization is evident with respect to manufacturing (see Table 8.13). Nigeria's manufacturing sector was halved from 8.4% of GDP in 1980 to just 4% in 2014. Its MVA per capita of $46 pales in comparison to $890 for South Africa and $1,000 for Mauritius and Mexico. Manufacturing firms tend to be small, invest very little, and have low technology intensity. Nigeria does have several large industrial estates, but they typically do not engage in exports and have a lot of unused capacity averaging 55% (World Bank, 2007b; Chete et al., 2016).

TABLE 8.13 Nigeria: changes in sectoral economic structure, 1970–2010

	1970	1980	1990	2000	2010	Diff: 2010–1970
Employment structure:	%	%	%	%	%	%
Agriculture	64.8	48.3	50.0	63.7	60.7	−4.1
Mining	0.1	0.5	0.4	0.1	0.2	0.1
Manufacturing	7.0	6.6	4.4	3.1	4.2	−2.8
Utilities	0.1	0.5	0.5	0.3	0.2	0.1
Construction	1.0	2.5	1.1	0.7	1.6	0.6
Trade and hotels	15.3	21.2	26.9	18.9	16.9	1.6
Transport-storage-comm.	1.3	3.6	3.2	2.2	3.0	1.7
Finance and business srvcs.	0.3	0.4	0.8	0.6	2.8	2.5
Government services	4.7	5.4	6.3	4.2	4.3	−0.4
Community services	5.3	11.0	6.4	6.3	6.1	0.8
Total employment[a]	22,463	27,973	30,988	39,651	52,073	29,610
Output structure:	%	%	%	%	%	%
Agriculture	35.8	18.0	23.2	27.9	37.7	1.9
Mining	48.1	63.1	55.9	50.9	29.7	−18.4
Manufacturing	1.7	3.5	3.8	3.1	3.5	1.8
Utilities	0.1	0.1	0.1	0.1	0.1	0.1
Construction	1.8	2.8	1.4	1.8	2.2	0.4
Trade and hotels	10.6	9.6	11.5	11.8	20.2	9.5
Transport-storage-comm.	0.6	0.8	0.6	0.7	2.0	1.5
Finance and business srvcs.	0.4	0.7	1.9	1.6	2.2	1.8
Government services	0.5	0.8	1.2	1.2	1.1	0.6
Community services	0.4	0.5	0.4	0.9	1.2	0.7
Gross value added[b]	4,410,683	7,186,748	7,774,383	9,120,822	18,154,189	13,743,507

Productivity structure[c]:	$	$	$	$	$	Ratio: 2010/1970
Agriculture	108,407	95,960	116,197	100,679	216,518	2.00
Mining	64,908,849	30,433,186	35,925,667	164,401,448	44,710,531	0.69
Manufacturing	47,567	136,849	213,009	226,240	295,602	6.21
Utilities	74,079	52,637	69,290	105,012	222,504	3.00
Construction	350,863	285,212	328,869	587,384	468,448	1.34
Trade and hotels	22,946	34,306	13,252	21,837	44,574	1.94
Transport-storage-comm.	82,657	56,971	46,869	75,503	231,268	2.80
Finance and business srvcs.	298,542	487,961	603,207	576,566	282,813	0.95
Government services	21,478	39,857	48,052	66,851	91,091	4.24
Community services	16,602	12,079	15,306	33,778	68,436	4.12
Economy-wide	196,353	256,921	250,880	230,026	348,632	1.78

Sources and notes: Calculations are based on the 2014 version of the GGDC 10-sector database: www.rug.nl/research/ggdc/data/10-sector-database which is documented in M.P. Timmer, G.J. de Vries, and K. de Vries, "Patterns of Structural Change in Developing Countries," GGDC Research Memorandum 149, Groningen Growth and Development Centre, 2014.

a Economy-wide persons engaged, in thousands.

b Gross value added in millions of 2005 international dollars.

c Gross value added per person engaged in 2005 international dollars.

202 Africa's postcolonial experience

During the years from 1975 to 1999, Nigerian per capita exports halved, while those of Botswana and Mauritius doubled. Furthermore, the firm-level data on productivity differentials suggest that the food sector enjoys a high productivity and suffers high capacity utilization while the textile sector ranks relatively low on these counts (Söderbom and Teal, 2002).

Nigerian businesses complain bitterly about three constraints: inadequate finance, unreliable electricity, and rampant corruption (Table 8.3). However, the country does reasonably well in the areas of economic management and structural policies but rather poorly on public-sector management (Table 8.4).

Overall, Nigeria rates rather low on the global competitiveness index (Table 8.5) and the industrial intensity index as well, especially after 2000 (Table 8.14). Poor

TABLE 8.14 Nigeria: competitive industrial performance, 1990–2012

Year	MVA per capita	M Exports per capita	MHM in MVA	MHX in MX	MVA in GDP	M Exports in exports	Industrialization intensity index
	$	$	%	%	%	%	
1990	22	1	17	34	3	1	0.08
1991	24	1	17	34	4	1	0.08
1992	22	1	16	34	3	1	0.08
1993	21	1	14	34	3	1	0.07
1994	20	1	19	34	3	1	0.16
1995	19	1	34	34	3	1	0.26
1996	18	1	33	34	3	1	0.25
1997	18	5	29	65	3	5	0.21
1998	16	1	29	82	2	3	0.21
1999	17	1	29	61	3	1	0.21
2000	17	0	29	61	2	0	0.21
2001	17	0	29	78	3	0	0.20
2002	19	10	29	57	3	7	0.20
2003	19	5	29	75	3	2	0.20
2004	21	5	29	75	3	2	0.20
2005	23	28	29	16	3	7	0.20
2006	24	28	29	16	3	7	0.20
2007	26	8	29	37	3	2	0.20
2008	27	30	29	73	3	6	0.22
2009	29	17	29	35	3	5	0.23
2010	30	114	29	7	3	21	0.22
2011	31	121	29	9	3	16	0.22
2012	33	121	29	11	3	14	0.20

Sources and notes: UNIDO, Competitive Industrial Performance (CIP) database, 2014.
MHM = medium- and high-technology manufacturing production
MHX = medium- and high-technology manufacturing exports
MX = manufacturing exports
MVA = manufacturing (M) value added

infrastructure and poor governance reduce productivity, and hence competitiveness, for at least two reasons. First, they add to firm costs. Second, they dent the discipline needed to ensure innovativeness by firms. An unreliable and costly supply of electricity, for example, impels firms to invest in costly self-generation while creating some monopoly power for those firms with deeper pockets to begin with.

Nigeria has not been making effective use of a relatively large domestic market to help improve firm efficiency and productivity. Domestic markets are segmented, and participants must endure the predatory behavior of public officials or well-connected competitors. Fully integrated national markets and regional markets such as ECOWAS, which will drive competition and help to exploit scale-linked efficiency gains, have yet to emerge fully.

In the past two decades, Nigeria has started to rectify its costly neglect of agriculture and its proclivities for corruption-driven and unsustainable fiscal deficits. The country is, however, a long way off from diversifying into manufacturing. It needs to do so resolutely to reduce its dependence on resource rents which can be turned from a curse into a blessing by raising the quality of institutions and the inclusiveness of policies.

South Africa (ZAF)

South Africa, with a population of 50 million, had a GDP at market prices of some $350 billion in 2014. Most notably, it is Africa's most industrialized and the second largest economy after Nigeria. Despite a GNI per capita of $12,700 in PPP terms, its social indicators are comparatively low.

South Africa's HDI was 0.67 in 2014 (about that of Egypt) reflecting, in part, the rather low life expectancy of 57 years especially when compared to Egypt's 71 years. One-third of the population lives on under $3.10 per day. Its mean years of schooling, at 10.0 years, is, thanks to a high non-White educational attainment, among the highest in Africa. The combination of its history of wide-ranging and deep-seated racial polarization and its middle-income status has made it the most unequal economy in the world. ZAF's Gini coefficient stood at an unenviable level of 63.0% in 2013 (Table 7.2).

A defining feature of South Africa's political economy is encapsulated in one word: gold. Gold, whose price was fixed under the Gold Standard, is very labor-intensive in extraction as are diamonds. The "paradox of scarce labor and low wages" was solved by the English-owned South African mines through the unbelievably repressive internal labor-reserves and regional labor-migratory system. Echoing the violence that preceded the emergence of a doubly "free labor market" in nineteenth-century Europe, entire social systems in the greater southern Africa region were dispossessed of land and seriously disrupted by this regimentation whose effects linger today.

The wanton confiscation of land, which denied native South Africans an alternative means of livelihood while reserving skilled jobs for over-paid Whites under

204 Africa's postcolonial experience

the color bar, ensured mining profitability – especially when gold prices were not high. The regimented and discriminatory labor system was institutionalized and generalized to the entire economy when the Apartheid compact was struck between Afrikaner labor and English capital and lasted for nearly half a century (1948–1994).

South Africa, much like Latin America, started a vigorous program of resource-based industrialization during the interwar period but faced momentous challenges. Until recently, the country, in the words of Feinstein (2005: 135),

> was locked into the constraints of low wages and low productivity, it was preventing most of its population from obtaining training and exercising their skills, it was restricted by the limited size of its home market, and it remained totally dependent on gold mining to pay for its imported materials and capital goods.

South Africa's real per capita income rose by half during 1960–1980, stagnated during 1980–1998, and resumed a slow but steady climb after that (Figures 8.1–8.3). ZAF nonetheless boasts the highest average GDP per worker in Africa.

South Africa's anemic growth performance since 1990, relative to the African average, has meant that the economy has been unable to absorb the underemployed and the unemployed workforce. The unemployment rate, at 25%, remains one of the highest in the world (Bhorat, 1996).

As was the case with a grotesquely racialized Brazil in economic (but not in social) terms, South Africa's elites missed a historic opportunity to strike a "grand economic bargain" in the mid-1990s to reverse the economic legacies of Apartheid while avoiding lasting damages to its modern economic institutions or inducing massive capital flight.[3] In hindsight, Nelson Mandela's vision was overly cautious, and the White elites were too myopic. The new political settlement left many of the structural constraints on Black economic empowerment intact. The various affirmative action and Black empowerment programs benefitted the tiny Black political elite, instead. The results have been a lackluster economic performance and increasingly better educated but politically restless Black youth.

McKinsey (2012) has identified five opportunities to reignite growth in South Africa. They are: (1) building advanced manufacturing on South Africa's extensive industrial experience, skilled labor, and modern infrastructure; (2) enhancing infrastructure productivity by closing gaps in the efficiency and sufficiency of public utilities; (3) building natural gas plants to relax the binding constraint of energy supply; (4) boosting service exports by exploiting its world-class service industries – especially in the financial sector, IT, and tourism; and (5) focusing on processed agricultural exports of high value added products.

The composition of ZAF's GDP, in fact, resembles that of a mature industrial economy. Industry claims 29% (half of which is manufacturing), services 68%, and commercialized agriculture a mere 2% of GDP in 2014. Food and beverages constitute the largest branch of manufacturing with a share in MVA of 22%, followed by rubber and plastics at 13%, and petroleum products at 8% in 2010 (Table 8.6). Interestingly, the output shares of textiles and apparels declined precipitously from 13% in 1970 to just over 1% today although they still account for a quarter of the manufacturing labor force. In fact, South Africa's failure to use manufacturing as an engine of job creation is most evident by the fact that total manufacturing employment rose by just 1 million in 40 years since 1970 to 1.75 million.

The share of employment in agriculture and mining fell by half from one-third of the labor force between 1970 and 2010 while the output share in the two primary sectors fell by two-thirds to just 9% in 2010. This is partly a reflection of the fact that these sectors modernized their labor productivity during the period (Table 8.15). At the three-digit ISIC level, transport equipment, footwear, and beverages were the fastest growers during 1965–2004 (Table 8.16).

Table 8.17 presents several indirect measures of manufacturing performance. Strong backward linkages abound for food processing, tobacco, wood products, chemicals, and transport equipment. The highest wage intensities (wages per dollar of value added) are found in textiles and apparel, printing and publishing, furniture, and electric machinery. Predictably, a strong correlation exists between labor productivity and average pay.

South Africa's manufacturing sector, despite its seemingly good position to compete globally after the lifting of sanctions in the early 1990s nonetheless, failed to face up to the challenges coming from China and India. Manufacturing enterprises faced several constraints, including insufficient domestic demand. The supply side was not buoyant either. Shortages of skilled labor and raw materials are perennial complaints. These constraints are compounded by factors like a history of fractious labor relations, prolonged maintenance downtime, and unreliability of power supply.

Studies show that jobs in such sectors as the automotive products are generated through the extensive backward-linkage effects of manufacturing exports which are nearly 4.5 times greater than the direct employment impact. Indeed, while the minerals sector is credited for the biggest direct job creation due to its dominance in the export basket and relative labor intensity, its weak backward linkages with the domestic economy stifle its overall employment impact. Service sector linkages also matter greatly especially for high-skill jobs through global value-chain integration (World Bank, 2015b).

Second, exporters are highly concentrated. The top 5% of the domestic firms account for more than 90% of the country's exports. Compared with Brazil, Turkey, and Colombia, South Africa's apparel and electronics sectors appear fairly diversified in their export structures.

Third, super-exporters are losing dynamism and competitiveness. And yet, smaller, more dynamic exporters are not yet large enough to drive aggregate exports. The super-exporters' sophisticated, technology-intensive exports play against South Africa's comparative advantage in semi-skilled labor. Unlike many resource-rich

TABLE 8.15 South Africa: changes in sectoral economic structure, 1970–2010

	1970	1980	1990	2000	2010	Diff: 2010–1970
Employment structure:	%	%	%	%	%	%
Agriculture	34.7	26.0	21.5	18.7	15.0	−19.7
Mining	8.8	9.4	8.8	3.5	2.1	−6.7
Manufacturing	13.3	16.5	14.7	13.6	11.9	−1.4
Utilities	0.6	0.9	1.0	0.5	0.6	0.0
Construction	5.8	5.2	5.7	5.0	7.3	1.4
Trade and hotels	13.5	15.4	17.6	20.7	20.0	6.5
Transport-storage-comm.	4.4	4.8	5.0	5.3	5.3	0.9
Finance and business srvcs.	2.5	3.2	4.9	7.6	11.3	8.8
Government services	5.8	9.1	10.7	14.6	15.5	9.7
Community services	10.5	9.4	10.2	10.4	11.0	0.5
Total employment[a]	7,682	8,209	11,210	13,372	14,619	6,937.1
Output structure:	%	%	%	%	%	%
Agriculture	3.5	3.7	3.7	3.3	2.7	−0.7
Mining	23.3	14.6	11.6	9.3	6.5	−16.8
Manufacturing	19.9	23.7	22.3	21.0	18.4	−1.5
Utilities	1.4	2.0	2.6	2.7	2.2	0.8
Construction	4.7	4.4	3.3	2.5	3.8	−1.0
Trade and hotels	13.7	14.0	14.3	15.2	14.7	1.0
Transport-storage-comm.	6.1	7.6	7.2	9.7	10.9	4.8
Finance and business srvcs.	5.3	6.9	8.8	11.4	18.1	12.8
Government services	17.5	18.5	20.6	18.0	16.2	−1.3
Community services	4.6	4.6	5.6	6.9	6.5	2
Gross value added[b]	520,835	726,754	877,426	1,061,442	1,533,166	1,012,332
Productivity structure[c]:	$	$	$	$	$	Ratio: 2010/1970
Agriculture	6,756	12,631	13,460	13,930	1,8983	2.81
Mining	179,112	137,832	103,869	212,787	325,321	1.82
Manufacturing	101,498	127,493	118,842	122,238	162,286	1.60
Utilities	145,985	192,245	197,074	390,044	380,967	2.61
Construction	55,242	74,745	45,336	39,294	54,510	0.99
Trade and hotels	68,858	80,464	63,732	58,267	76,752	1.11
Transport-storage-comm.	94,026	140,084	112,349	143,924	216,128	2.30
Finance and business srvcs.	145,645	189,077	141,092	119,379	167,367	1.15
Government services	204,459	178,936	151,353	97,923	110,000	0.54
Community services	29,606	43,571	42,763	52,747	62,179	2.10
Economy-wide	6,756	12,631	13,460	13,930	18,983	2.81

Sources and notes: Calculations are based on the 2014 version of the GGDC 10-sector database: www.rug.nl/research/ggdc/data/10-sector-database which is documented in M.P. Timmer, G.J. de Vries, and K. de Vries, "Patterns of Structural Change in Developing Countries," GGDC Research Memorandum 149, Groningen Growth and Development Centre, 2014.

a Economy-wide persons engaged, in thousands

b Gross value added in millions of 2005 international dollars.

c Gross value added per person engaged in 2005 international dollars.

TABLE 8.16 South Africa: growth performance of three-digit manufacturing industries, 1965–2004

Industry	ISIC3	Index of production (1995=100)				
		1965	1975	1985	1995	2004
Food products	311	17	47	86	100	107
Beverages	313	102	135	130	100	118
Tobacco	314	47	67	87	100	103
Textiles	321	42	65	87	100	49
Wearing apparel, except footwear	322	29	45	81	100	103
Leather products	323	43	67	74	100	104
Footwear, except rubber or plastic	324	32	61	97	100	139
Wood products, except furniture	331	32	65	94	100	127
Furniture, except metal	332	42	49	73	100	114
Paper and products	341	52	75	87	100	105
Printing and publishing	342	95	89	96	100	118
Other manufactured products	390	41	55	77	100	130
Petroleum refineries	353	30	55	69	100	109
Misc. petroleum and coal	354	32	75	100	100	107
Rubber products	355	58	102	107	100	97
Plastic products	356	29	49	79	100	104
Pottery, china, earthenware	361	13	71	90	100	107
Glass and products	362	25	51	64	. .	. .
Other non-metallic mineral	369	38	74	138	100	104
Iron and steel	371	38	78	94	100	88
Non-ferrous metals	372	22	49	88	100	99
Fabricated metal products	381	28	58	70	100	97
Industrial chemicals	351	60	73	90	100	107
Other chemicals	352	38	53	62	100	177
Machinery, except electrical	382	71	90	107	100	90
Machinery, electric	383	45	72	113	100	. .
Transport equipment	384	66	118	76	100	128
Professional and scientific equipment	385	37	51	74	100	82

Source: Based on UNIDO Indstat database, various years.

countries, South Africa has a strong base in manufacturing that requires a rich technological knowledge.

Fourth, Sub-Saharan Africa has emerged as the dominant market for South Africa's non-mineral exports (Purfield et al., 2014). Sub-Saharan Africa is also the primary destination of ZAF's outward FDI.

After an initial spurt, manufactured exports expanded rapidly, but by the mid-1990s the pace of growth had begun to slow, and this slowdown accelerated in the 2000s. In fact, while the share of manufactured exports rose, there is no strong evidence of a deepening of industrial sophistication (see Table 8.18).

TABLE 8.17 South Africa: efficiency of three-digit manufacturing industries, 1963–2009

Three-digit manufacturing industry	ISIC	(Y-V)/Y	W/V	K/L	V/L	W/L
	Code	%	%	$	$	$
Food products	311	78	45	355	11,963	5,413
Beverages	313	67	24	596	32,984	7,941
Tobacco	314	83	37	18,397	20,475	7,478
Textiles	321	71	66	449	6,267	4,125
Wearing apparel, except footwear	322	64	76	56	4,432	3,377
Leather products	323	72	52	88	5,484	2,865
Footwear, except rubber or plastic	324	67	56	101	6,507	3,671
Wood products, except furniture	331	76	49	1,735	11,262	5,474
Furniture, except metal	332	73	72	86	6,736	4,867
Paper and products	341	72	44	729	19,552	8,590
Printing and publishing	342	41	71	345	12,866	9,134
Other manufactured products	390	61	18	110	33,206	5,917
Petroleum refineries	353	66	39	1,224	40,800	15,804
Misc. petroleum and coal products	354	74	4	485,039	231,076	8,251
Rubber products	355	68	55	528	14,614	8,103
Plastic products	356	67	42	207	15,153	6,319
Pottery, china, earthenware	361	46	. .[a]	. .[a]	1,383	6,756
Glass and products	362	61	48	344	18,001	8,710
Other non-metallic mineral products	369	61	50	557	10,372	5,157
Iron and steel	371	71	51	1,553	21,469	10,955
Non-ferrous metals	372	62	25	497	38,422	9,564
Fabricated metal products	381	66	54	278	12,297	6,585
Industrial chemicals	351	68	71	1,654	23,202	16,520
Other chemicals	352	76	49	179	21,359	10,430
Machinery, except electrical	382	66	62	261	14,316	8,852
Machinery, electric	383	69	76	203	11,375	8,594
Transport equipment	384	80	58	346	15,401	8,888
Professional and scientific equipment	385	64	60	5,572	15,845	9,526
Manufacturing	**300**	**71**	**49**	**801**	**14,732**	**7,182**

Source: Based on UNIDO Industrial Database, various years.

Definitions: Y = gross output, V = value added, K = fixed capital, L = employment, W = total wage bill.

Indexes of Efficiency: Share of Purchased [(Y-V)/Y], Unit Labor Cost (W/V), Productivity of Capital (V/K), Productivity of Labor (V/L), Capital Intensity (K/L), Average Wage (W/L).

a = Ratios set to missing since the numbers are unrealistically odd.

South Africa's exports also exhibit interesting patterns. First, South Africa's 20,000 exporters sell nearly 5,000 different products, covering more than 90% of all possible goods classified for trade. Just a small subset of these, encompassing the fuels, minerals, and metals sectors, make up around half of all exports by value.

TABLE 8.18 South Africa: competitive industrial performance, 1990–2012

Year	MVA per capita	M Exports per capita	MHM in MVA	MHX in MX	MVA in GDP	M Exports in exports	Industrialization intensity index
	$	$	%	%	%	%	
1990	836	213	28	31	18	39	0.35
1991	779	213	30	31	17	39	0.36
1992	735	213	30	31	17	39	0.36
1993	716	287	29	28	17	47	0.37
1994	718	294	29	29	17	48	0.46
1995	749	387	29	32	17	57	0.47
1996	745	396	30	31	17	71	0.46
1997	753	369	29	31	17	70	0.45
1998	740	306	29	36	17	68	0.45
1999	734	369	25	41	16	70	0.41
2000	782	410	26	40	17	70	0.42
2001	796	392	27	43	17	68	0.43
2002	807	388	26	45	17	77	0.41
2003	784	484	25	46	16	71	0.39
2004	812	584	24	48	16	69	0.38
2005	853	679	23	48	16	69	0.38
2006	897	722	23	48	17	66	0.38
2007	934	852	22	49	17	65	0.36
2008	950	1,036	21	51	16	69	0.36
2009	846	733	23	47	15	68	0.36
2010	886	974	24	46	15	68	0.37
2011	912	1,156	26	44	15	63	0.38
2012	926	1,076	26	45	15	63	0.37

Sources and notes: UNIDO, Competitive Industrial Performance (CIP) database, 2014.
MHM = medium- and high-technology manufacturing production
MHX = medium- and high-technology manufacturing exports
MX = manufacturing exports
MVA = manufacturing (M) value added

South Africa also tops the region for the efficiency of its financial markets, a pillar on which it ranks twelfth globally. It also performs reasonably strongly on the pillars of infrastructure and institutions, although corruption and security remain notable concerns. The country also needs to make significant progress on health and education.

Global competitiveness requires much more than export-oriented policies. Capabilities, as we noted earlier, matter at least as much. South Africa needs to devote resource-based revenues to significant investments in technological and other manufacturing capabilities and might boost the skills of the long-neglected Black African labor force through formal schooling and firm-level training. Overall, despite some inroads in the production of motor vehicles, world-class universities, there is only a halting movement toward high-technology sectors.

Zimbabwe (ZWE)

Zimbabwe, with a population of some 15 million, had an economy of $14 billion at market prices in 2014. Its GNI per capita was $1,650 in PPP prices – surprisingly among the lowest in Africa.

Zimbabwe's HDI, at 0.51, matched Nigeria's in 2014 as did its level of inequality with a Gini index of 50.1% – among the highest in the world. Though its mean years of schooling, at 7.3 years, were equal to Ghana's, its life expectancy had shrunk to just 57.5 years (Table 7.2). The headcount poverty rate at the national poverty line exceeded 70% of the population in 2011.

Zimbabwe, at independence in 1980, was a highly promising resource-based settler-economy. Its per capita income then stood around $1,000 at market prices; manufacturing accounted for nearly a quarter GDP; it enjoyed food self-sufficiency; and it had a substantial surplus for export from the White-owned commercial farms which claimed nearly half of the cultivated land (Mlambo, 2012).

Although its natural endowment and economic structure were broadly like that of the neighboring colonial economies of southern Africa, Zimbabwe's post-independence political quagmire triggered a contraction of the economy that began to reverse only after 2009. Among the resource-based industrializers, Zimbabwe still enjoyed the third highest real GDP per capita. Mauritius, for example, matched and exceeded Zimbabwe in real per capita income only after the mid-1980s.

Zimbabwe's GDP growth experienced a great depression in the second half of the 1990s, turned negative between 2001 and 2008, but has managed a bold recovery since then (Figure 8.2). During 1997–2008, GDP declined by 40% and per capita income by two-thirds before recovering to its 1980 level in 2014.

After 1990, the ZANU ruling elite instituted a confiscatory land reform program largely to benefit ruling-party supporters. The terrible price was the undermining of the country's modern White-owned commercial agriculture, and politico-economic crises that ensued.

These confiscatory actions dissipated Zimbabwe's productive agricultural base as well as its import-substituting manufacturing base. The manufacturing sector has always had strong linkages with the agricultural sector, with agriculture purchasing over half of intermediate goods, such as insecticides, stock feeds, and fertilizer. In return, nearly half of agricultural output (food and fiber) was sold to the manufacturing sector. The performances of the two sectors, therefore, remain highly interdependent.

Unsustainable fiscal deficits coupled with the unprecedented hyperinflation caused Zimbabwe to suffer a large-scale emigration of its skilled citizens. This brain drain harmed the modern sector and severely eroded the country's institutional capacity.

The adoption of a multicurrency regime in early 2009 effectively dollarized the economy. This desperate action reestablished price stability and laid the foundation for a sustainable economic recovery. Having dollarized, Zimbabwe obtained a monetary discipline to build on as it recovers economically.

While some agricultural subsectors have since recovered, sectoral value chains remain weak, and irrigation networks are thin. The perceptions of insecure property rights (especially with the renewed initiative for the Zimbabweanization of all firms) continue to discourage foreign direct investment and to fuel capital flight (Herderschee, 2016).

Zimbabwe's economy grew by more than 10% per year during 2010–2012 as prices stabilized and bank credit expanded rapidly. The fragile growth decelerated after 2013, as the initial stabilization effects of dollarization-led growth ran its course. Meanwhile, global commodity prices weakened, and the depreciation of the rand against the dollar eroded the competitiveness of Zimbabwe's traded goods sector.

Burdensome regulations, outdated infrastructure, and weak institutional capacity contributed to declining competitiveness. The manufacturing sector was hit especially hard, and exports of manufactured goods fell to less than half their 2010–2011 levels. As employment opportunities in the formal sector evaporated, informality became increasingly pervasive (Herderschee, 2016).

The Zimbabwean economy is still highly diversified in comparison with other African economies, with a broad-based potential for recovery in all sectors, from mining to agriculture, manufacturing, and services. The mining sector, benefitting from recent Chinese investment, is emerging as the driver of growth in the current phase of the recovery. The agricultural sector also presents an important potential of supply-response to improved conditions, along with the potential recovery of tourism.

Until the late 1990s, Zimbabwe was noted for having one of the most developed manufacturing sectors in Sub-Saharan Africa. Half of Zimbabwe's GDP came from manufacturing, and its manufacturing base consisted of companies producing a wide array of products, from food-stuffs to steel. In 2014, industry accounted for 29% (half of which was manufacturing), services for 56%, and agriculture for just 14% of GDP.

Zimbabwe must still contend with long-run negative trends that were evident before the decade-long crisis: slowdown in the pace of structural change, loss of competitiveness of the manufacturing sector, arrested human development, short-termism in policy mindset, and serious political tensions. Growth in the manufacturing sector is primarily dependent on the internal demand generated by agriculture and mining. Low capacity utilization is the norm which stems not only from lower prices due to important inflows of imports but also from supply-constraints and high costs of doing business across the economy (World Bank, 2014).

We do not have good internationally comparable data for Zimbabwe to assess its competitiveness. The existing data do show that Zimbabwean firms, at an average age of 33 years, are twice as old as those of a typical lower middle-income country or nearby South Africa. Given the onerous level of collateral (261% of the loan), Zimbabwean firms must resort to self-financing 85% for their investment. The highest ranked business constraints identified in surveys were political uncertainty, access to finance, informality, and electricity supply (Table 8.3).

Zimbabwe's CPIA scores are rather low in all the three areas of economic management, public-sector management, and structural policies (Table 8.4). Its overall global competitiveness index is also the lowest among its peers (Table 8.5).

Nonetheless, Zimbabwe's manufactured exports grew to reach US$700 million before the political crisis of 2000 when the Mugabe regime closed off political space for any form of organized opposition. Its above-average schooling and on-the-job

212 Africa's postcolonial experience

training (offered by large, mainly non-African enterprises) have enabled it to do well in garments and engineering products.

Regulatory barriers continue to pose a major obstacle to Zimbabwe's recovery. The 2015 World Bank's *Doing Business* report highlighted insolvency as an important constraint for Zimbabwe's private sector. Moreover, capital costs remained elevated due to external pressures, including a large debt burden. High capital costs were especially damaging to the inherently capital-intensive mining and manufacturing sectors, which had already suffered immensely from an erratic electricity supply and administrative trade barriers.

Notes

1 UNIDO (2009: xiii) observes the remarkable impact of industrial development in even the unlikeliest places:

> Industrialization has been fundamental to economic development. Only in circumstances such as extraordinary abundance of land or resources have countries succeeded in developing without industrializing. Not only is industrialization the normal route to development, but as a result of the globalization of industry, the pace of development can be explosive. Twenty years ago, Qiaotou in China was a village. Today, it produces two-thirds of the world's buttons. . . . This potential for explosive growth is distinctive to manufacturing. As manufacturing activity expands, instead of running up against shortages of land or resources that inevitably constrain the growth of agriculture or the extractive industries, it benefits from economies of scale: unit costs of production fall.

2 We present in Tables 8.3 and 8.4 suggestive evidence concerning the constraints facing the private sector from the World Bank's *Doing Business* surveys. The survey data are, however, criticized as ill-suited for the evaluation of specific country regulatory frameworks (Arrunada, 2007). Looking for evidence of the binding constraints on African growth or industrial development is largely fruitless, according to those in the know (Newman et al., 2016: 207): "First, Doing Business was not designed to be used as a country-level diagnostic tool. It is a 'league table' for cross-country benchmarking exercise, and the indicators were developed to support cross-country comparisons. Second, the indicators all have uniform weight, even if it is clear that not all reforms will have equal impact at the country level."
3 During this historic window of opportunity for crafting an inclusive economic dispensation, a one-off wealth tax (say, 10%) might have been politically palatable to the White oligarchy. The funds could have created quasi-public endowments and non-profit corporations to channel well-managed transitional investments in such areas as secondary and vocational education, housing, and start-up capital for small and medium enterprises. A Zimbabwean-like self-destruction lurks behind the edifice of a liberal post-Apartheid economy with its unprecedented inequality of income and wealth.

References

Ackah, C., C. Adjasi, and F. Turkson. (2016). Industrial Policy in Ghana: Its Evolution and Impact. In: C. Newman et al., eds., *Manufacturing Transformation: Comparative Studies of Industrial Development in Africa and Emerging Asia*. Oxford: Oxford University Press, pp. 50–71.

Africa Economic Outlook (AEO-CIV). (2015). *Cote d'Ivoire 2015*. Abidjan: AfDB, OECD, UNDP.

Africa Economic Outlook (AEO-GHA). (2015). *Ghana 2015*. Abidjan: AfDB, OECD, UNDP.

Arrunada, B. (2007). Pitfalls to Avoid When Measuring Institutions: Is *Doing Business* Damaging Business? *Journal of Comparative Economics*, 35(4), pp. 729–747.

Bhorat, H. (1996). South Africa: An Emerging Market in an Emerging Continent. In: T. Biggs, M. Miller, C. Otto, and G. Tyler, eds., *Africa Can Compete!*. Washington, DC: World Bank.

Bogetic, Z. (2007). *Ghana – Country Economic Memorandum: Meeting the Challenge of Accelerated and Shared Growth: Synthesis*. [online] Washington, DC: World Bank. Available at: http://documents.worldbank.org/curated/en/598481468249681693/Synthesis.

Chete, L., J. Adeoti, F. Adeyinka, and F. Oladapo Ogundele. (2016). Industrial Policy in Nigeria: Opportunities and Challenges in a Resource-rich Country. In: C. Newman, et al., eds., *Manufacturing Transformation: Comparative Studies of Industrial Development in Africa and Emerging Asia*. Oxford: Oxford University Press, pp. 115–135.

Dahlman, C. (2008). Technology, Globalization, and International Competitiveness: Challenges for Developing Countries. In: D. O'Connor and M. Kjollerstrom, eds., *Industrial Development for the 21st Century*. London: Zed Press, pp. 29–83.

Diagana, O., A. Mijiyawa, and E. Riordan. (2015). *Cote d'Ivoire Economic Update: Ivorian Economic Performance Since the End of the Post-Election Crisis*. Washington, DC: World Bank Group.

Feinstein, C. (2005). *An Economic History of South Africa*. Cambridge: Cambridge University Press.

Fosu, A. (2012). Growth of African Economies: Productivity, Policy Syndrome and the Importance of Institutions. *Journal of African Economies*, 22(4), pp. 523–551.

Harrison, A. (1996). Determinants and Effects of Direct Foreign Investment in Cote d'Ivoire, Morocco, and Venezuela. In: M.J. Roberts and J.R. Tybout, eds., *Industrial Evolution in Developing Countries: Micro Patterns of Turnover, Productivity, and Market Structure*. Washington, DC: The World Bank, pp. 163–186.

Herderschee, J. (2016). *Zimbabwe Economic Update – Changing Growth Patterns: Improving Health Outcomes*. Washington, DC: World Bank Group.

Herrera, S., and A. Dilek. (2014). Long-Run Growth in Ghana: Determinants and Prospects. *Policy Research Working Paper No. 7115*. Washington, DC: World Bank.

Hirschman, A.O. (1958). *The Strategy of Economic Development*. New Haven, CT: Yale University Press.

Hirschman, A. (1968). The Political Economy of Import-Substituting Industrialization in Latin America. *The Quarterly Journal of Economics*, 82(1), pp. 1–32.

Kaplinsky, R., and M. Morris. (2007). Do the Asian Drivers Undermine Export-oriented Industrialization in SSA? *World Development*, 36(2), pp. 254–273.

Litwack, J., et al. (2015). *Nigeria Economic Report*. Washington, DC: World Bank Group.

McKinsey Global Institute. (2012). *Manufacturing the Future: The Next Era of Global Growth and Innovation*. New York: McKinsey & Company.

McMillan, M., and K. Harttgen. (2014). What Is Driving the 'African Growth Miracle'? *NBER Working Paper No. 20077*. Cambridge, MA: NBER.

Mlambo, K. (2012). Zimbabwe: Returning From the Brink. In: E. Aryeetey, et al., eds., *The Oxford Companion to the Economics of Africa*. Oxford: Oxford University Press.

Newman, C., J. Page, J. Rand, A. Shimeles, M. Soderbom, and F. Tarp. (2016). *Made in Africa: Learning to Compete in Industry*. Washington, DC: Brookings Institution Press.

N'guessan, T. (2012). Cote d'Ivoire: Economic Reversibility. In: E. Aryeetey, et al., eds., *The Oxford Companion to the Economics of Africa*. Oxford: Oxford University Press.

Nti, K. (2015). *Diagnostic Study of Light Manufacturing in Ghana*. Accra: African Center for Economic Transformation, February.

Okonjo-Iweala, N. (2012). Nigeria: Managing Volatility and Fighting Corruption. In: E. Aryeetey, et al., eds., *The Oxford Companion to the Economics of Africa*. Oxford: Oxford University Press.

214 Africa's postcolonial experience

Oxford Business Group (OBG). (2012). *Ghana: Standing Behind Manufacturing.* Oxford: Oxford Business Group. Available at: www.oxfordbusinessgroup.com/news/ghana-standing-behind-manufacturing.

Purfield, C.M., T. Farole, and F. Im. (2014). *South Africa Economic Update: Focus on Export Competitiveness.* Washington, DC: World Bank Group.

Reinhardt, N. (2000). Back to Basics in Malaysia and Thailand: The Role of Resource-based Exports in their Export-led Growth. *World Development*, 28(1), pp. 57–77.

Republic of Ghana. (2011). *Ghana's Industrial Policy*, Accra: MOTI.

Riddell, R. (1990). *Manufacturing Africa.* London: James Currey.

Roemer, M. (1979). Resource-based Industrialization in the Developing Countries: A Survey. *Journal of Development Economics*, 6(2), pp. 163–202.

Singer, H.W. (1950). The Distribution of Trade Between Investing and Borrowing Countries. *American Economic Review*, 40, pp. 531–548.

Söderbom, M., and F. Teal. (2002). *The Performance of Nigerian Manufacturing Firms: Report on the Nigerian Manufacturing Enterprise Survey 2001.* Oxford: Centre for the Study of African Economies.

Sutton, J., and B. Kpentey. (2012). *An Enterprise Map of Ghana.* London: International Growth Center.

Teal, F. (1996). The Size and Sources of Economic Rents in a Developing Country Manufacturing Labour Market. *Economic Journal*, 106, pp. 963–976.

Tsikata, Y.M. (2001). Owning Economic Reforms: A Comparative Study of Ghana and Tanzania. *UNU WIDER Discussion Paper No. 2001/53.* Helsinki: WIDER.

United Nations Industrial Development Programme (UNIDO). (2009). *Industrial Development Report 2009: Breaking In and Moving UP—New Industrial Challenges for the Bottom Billion and the Middle-Income Countries,* Oxford, Oxford University Press.

United Nations Industrial Development Organization (UNIDO). (2015). *Industrial Development Report 2009: Breaking in and Moving Up – New Industrial Challenges for the Bottom Billion and the Middle-Income Countries.* Oxford: Oxford University Press.

Vecatachellum, D. (2012). Mauritius: A Small Open Economy Fully Integrated Into World Markets. In: E. Aryeetey, et al., eds., *The Oxford Companion to the Economics of Africa.* Oxford: Oxford University Press.

Wignaraja, G. (2003). Competitiveness, Productivity Management and Job Creation in African Enterprises: Evidence From Mauritius and Kenya. *MCC Working Paper No. 5.* Geneva: ILO.

World Bank. (2007a). *Mauritius – Country Economic Memorandum: Managing Change in a Changing World.* Washington, DC: World Bank.

World Bank. (2007b). *Nigeria – Competitiveness and Growth: Country Economic Memorandum: Executive Summary.* Washington, DC: World Bank.

World Bank. (2012). *Cote d'Ivoire - The Growth Agenda: Building on Natural Resources and Exports.* Washington, DC: World Bank Group.

World Bank. (2013). *Ghana – Country Partnership Strategy for the Period FY2013–FY2016.* Washington, DC: World Bank.

World Bank. (2014). *Country Partnership Strategy for the Federal Republic of Nigeria, FY2014–2017.* Washington, DC: World Bank.

World Bank. (2015a). *The Economic Situation in Cote d'Ivoire – Summary.* Washington, DC: World Bank Group.

World Bank. (2015b). *South Africa Economic Update: Jobs and South Africa's Changing Demographics.* Issue no. 7. Washington, DC: World Bank Group.

Zakari, A., and A. Boly. (2013). The Industrial Policy Process in Ghana. *Development Policy, Statistics and Research Branch Working Paper 2/2013.* Geneva: UNIDO.

9
LABOR-BASED INDUSTRIALIZERS

This chapter profiles the manufacturing industries of the six labor-based African industrializers. We will take stock of the available evidence on institutions, the business environment, economic diversification, efficiency, employment generation, and international competitiveness.

Factor-based industrialization

The industrialization of countries with limited endowments of mineral and energy resources (Scandinavia, Ireland, Mediterranean Europe, and Northeast Asia) shows that a successful strategy can be anchored in the endowments of land, labor, and skills. Economic activities might accentuate labor and agricultural resources (cash crops and fiber) which lend themselves to labor-intensive industrial development. The outcome, in the absence of substantial resource rents, is an egalitarian and regionally dispersed development since the mobilization of labor and basic agricultural resources tends to be broad-based.

The factor-based industrializers, because of their reliance on diffused endowments and wide-ranging agro-climatic conditions, show an impressive diversity of investment climate, growth performance, income levels, and economic profiles.

Performance on the growth of GDP and per capita income shows a general pick up after 1990 along with high volatility. The two North African countries in the sample, Egypt and Tunisia, stand out in terms of per capita income, capital per worker, and worker productivity. Tunisia experienced a growth takeoff around 1970 that was sustained through 2009. Egypt's growth takeoff started around 1975 and ended about the same time as Tunisia's.

216 Africa's postcolonial experience

Kenya and Tunisia are underperformers but with less volatility. Ethiopia and Tanzania suffered growth collapses (because of political shocks in the case of the former) but recovered quite dramatically after 2001 with an impressive public-sector-led investment drive. Interestingly, the high-income members of this group (Egypt, Senegal, and Tunisia) are the slow growers (see Figures 9.1 and 9.2).

Tunisia and Egypt not only have the highest per capita incomes and manufacturing intensity but also the highest worker productivity. Tunisia caught up in this respect with South Africa around 2008. Tunisia holds the highest index of industrialization for this group with a $673 manufacturing value added per capita – right below Mauritius ($1,082) and South Africa ($891).

The factor-based industrializers are also a mixed bag concerning industrial capacity. Tunisia and Egypt (but also Morocco) stand out as having completed the easy phase of import substitution while Ethiopia and Tanzania are outliers located at the non-industrial end of the spectrum.

Finally, the factor-based industrializers are not outliers in terms of business climate and firm characteristics. We use the features of lower-middle-income developing economies as aspirational points of reference. According to the data from the World Bank's Enterprise Surveys (see Table 9.3), recurrent and universal complaints by businesses abound. This is especially so with respect to the scarcity of affordable

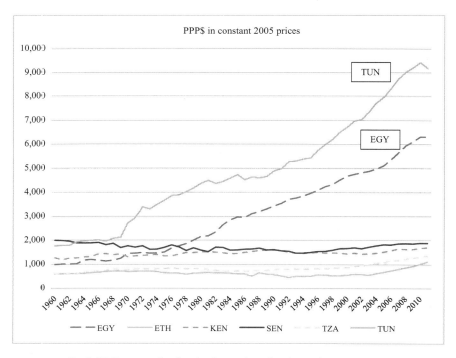

FIGURE 9.1 Real GDP per capita for the factor-based industrializers, 1960–2011
Source: PWT 8.1: www.ggdc.net/pwt.

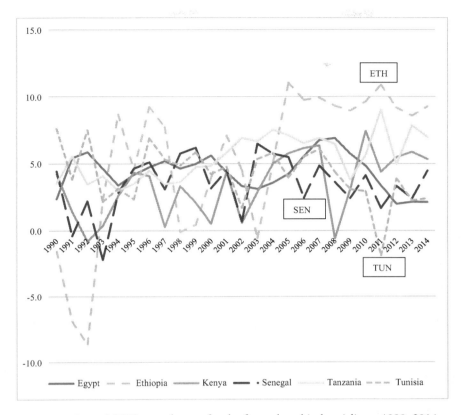

FIGURE 9.2 Annual GDP growth rates for the factor-based industrializers, 1990–2014
Source: The Conference Board database, May 2015. http://www.conference-board.org/data/economydatabase/

and reliable supply of electricity, inadequate finance for long-term investment, and political as well as policy instability. Data on global competitiveness show that the countries have comparable performance levels (see Table 9.4).

Indexes of structural change in manufacturing for 1970–2010 (Table 9.5 and 9.6) show that Egypt and Tunisia have more diversified manufacturing bases in terms of output structure. The structures of employment are, however, quite similar among the six economies.

Overall, Senegal stands out as having the highest-quality institutions and policies followed by Kenya and Tanzania. Concerning firm characteristics related to growth (greater access to finance, attractiveness for FDI, reliance on a permanent workforce, and a growing number of international quality certificates for manufactures), Kenya and Tunisia are by far the best countries. Egypt and Tanzania nonetheless have the least growth-friendly firm characteristics. We now turn to the economic and industrial profiles of each of the six labor-based economies.

TABLE 9.1 Economic profiles of factor-based industrializers, 1990–2014

Country	Series	1990	2000	2014
Egypt	GNI per capita, PPP$	3,790	6,050	10,260
Egypt	GCF (% of GDP)	29	20	14
Egypt	Industry (% of GDP)	29	33	40
Egypt	Population	56,397,273	68,334,905	89,579,670
Egypt	Services (% of GDP)	52	50	46
Ethiopia	GNI per capita, PPP$	420	490	1,500
Ethiopia	GCF (% of GDP)	0	0	38
Ethiopia	Industry (% of GDP)	10	12	15
Ethiopia	Population	48,057,094	66,443,603	96,958,732
Ethiopia	Services (% of GDP)	38	40	43
Kenya	GNI per capita, PPP$	1,470	1,690	2,940
Kenya	GCF (% of GDP)	24	17	21
Kenya	Industry (% of GDP)	19	17	19
Kenya	Population	23,446,229	31,065,820	44,863,583
Kenya	Services (% of GDP)	51	51	50
Senegal	GNI per capita, PPP$	1,160	1,500	2,300
Senegal	GCF (% of GDP)	9	20	26
Senegal	Industry (% of GDP)	22	23	24
Senegal	Population	7,514,201	9,860,578	14,672,557
Senegal	Services (% of GDP)	58	58	61
Tanzania	GNI per capita, PPP$	910	1,170	2,510
Tanzania	GCF (% of GDP)	26	17	31
Tanzania	Industry (% of GDP)	18	19	25
Tanzania	Population	25,458,208	33,991,590	51,822,621
Tanzania	Services (% of GDP)	36	47	44
Tunisia	GNI per capita, PPP$	3,550	5,830	11,020
Tunisia	GCF (% of GDP)	27	26	22
Tunisia	Industry (% of GDP)	34	30	29
Tunisia	Population	8,154,400	9,552,500	10,996,600
Tunisia	Services (% of GDP)	49	58	62

Sources and notes: World Development Indicators 2015.
GCF = gross capital formation

TABLE 9.2 Manufacturing in non-resource-based industrializers, 2014

Country	Profile (MVA in 2005 US$)
Egypt:	
MVA	20,376.0 million
MVA per capita	244
Share of MVA in GDP	16%
Biggest manufacturing activity	Coke, petroleum, nuclear fuel prdcts (31%)
Share of manufactured exports (2012)	73%
Ethiopia:	
MVA	1,350.3 million
MVA per capita	14
Share of MVA in GDP	5%
Biggest manufacturing activity	Food and beverages (41%)
Share of manufactured exports (2012)	18%
Kenya:	
MVA	2,827.3 million
MVA per capita	62
Share of MVA in GDP	10%
Biggest manufacturing activity	Food and beverages (31%)
Share of manufactured exports (2012)	. .
Senegal:	
MVA	1,444.8 million
MVA per capita	99
Share of MVA in GDP	12%
Biggest manufacturing activity	Food and beverages (33%)
Share of manufactured exports (2012)	91%
Tanzania:	
MVA	2,305.1 million
MVA per capita	45
Share of MVA in GDP	45%
Biggest manufacturing activity	Food and beverages (48%)
Share of manufactured exports (2012)	17%
Tunisia:	
MVA	27,481.1 million
MVA per capita	673
Share of MVA in GDP	17%
Biggest manufacturing activity	Recycling (46%)
Share of manufactured exports (2012)	86%

Source: UNIDO Industrial Briefs, June 2015. www.unido.org/Data1/IndStatBrief/

TABLE 9.3 Firm characteristics and business climate in factor-based industrializers

Indicator (survey year)	Egypt (2013)	Ethiopia (2011)	Kenya (2013)	Senegal (2014)	Tanzania (2013)	Tunisia (2013)	LMI (2013)
Business climate:							
Incidence of graft index	47.0	24.6	16.5	9.7	20.2	11.5	20.2
Days needed to obtain operating license	138.5	21.5	14.8	27.8	18.8	39.2	28.1
Management time spent dealing with regulations	3.1	7.8	7.4	3.0	2.0	46.5	10.5
Number of visits with tax officials	1.5	2.5	1.5	0.9	1.3	0.3	1.9
Firm characteristics:							
Firm age in years	14.2	12.9	20.3	16.6	13.4	19.6	16.6
% foreign-owned	5.5	10.6	5.7	8.7	2.9	7.7	7.5
% internal financing of investment	89.1	80.0	60.8	71.9	79.6	44.8	72.3
Collateral as % loan	272.5	181.1	187.7	271.7	240.2	251.5	210.1
% sales lost due to power outages	5.6	6.1	5.6	1.7	5.5	0.2	4.0
% of ind. firms importing foreign inputs	50.2	60.8	52.7	41.4	62.8	74.8	57.8
Days it takes to clear industrial imports	9.2	14.8	21.2	17.9	31.5	7.5	11.6
% firms trusting the courts	67.3	42.7	51.3	48.9	36.7	64.9	41.0
% internal quality certificate	8.6	12.6	21.8	9.3	17.6	16.8	15.5
Average number of full-time workers	35.5	31.5	41.8	37.5	18.1	48.0	37.6
% full-time female workers	11.8	22.2	29.1	20.7	44.0	30.4	27.8
Top three obstacles identified by firms	− Instability − Finance − Electricity	− Finance − Land − Electricity	− Informality − Corruption − Electricity	− Finance − Informality − Electricity	− Finance − Electricity − Tax rates	− Instability − Informality − Finance	

Sources and notes: Compiled from World Bank, Country Profiles; Enterprise Surveys. www.enterprisesurveys.org/reports. LMI = lower middle-income countries

Labor-based industrializers **221**

TABLE 9.4 Global competitiveness index for factor-based industrializers

	EGY	ETH	KEN	SEN	TZA	TUN
Global competitiveness index	**3.7**	**3.7**	**3.9**	**3.7**	**3.6**	**3.9**
(*Best GCI is 5.8, Switzerland*)						
A. Basic requirements:	**3.8**	**3.9**	**3.8**	**3.8**	**3.7**	**4.4**
Institutions	3.6	3.7	3.6	4.0	3.5	3.8
Infrastructure	3.4	2.6	3.2	3.0	2.4	3.7
Macroeconomic environ	2.8	4.7	3.6	4.2	4.5	4.3
Health and primary ed	5.3	4.8	4.6	4.0	4.3	5.9
B. Efficiency enhancers:	**3.6**	**3.5**	**4.0**	**3.6**	**3.4**	**3.7**
Higher ed and training	3.2	2.7	3.8	3.3	2.5	4.1
Goods market efficiency	4.0	4.1	4.2	4.3	3.9	3.9
Labor market efficiency	3.2	4.3	4.6	4.2	4.4	3.3
Financial markets	3.2	2.3	4.3	3.8	3.4	3.1
Technological readiness	3.2	3.5	3.3	3.1	2.5	3.6
Market size	5.1	3.9	3.8	3.0	3.8	3.9
C. Innovation & sophistication:	**3.2**	**3.4**	**3.9**	**3.8**	**3.2**	**3.3**
Business sophistication	3.7	3.5	4.2	4.0	3.4	3.6
Innovation	2.7	3.2	3.7	3.5	3.0	2.9

Source: World Economic Forum, the Global Competitiveness Report, 2015–2016.
http://reports.weforum.org/global-competitiveness-report-2015-2016/economies/.

Egypt (EGY)

Egypt is a densely populated country of some 90 million that straddles Africa and the Middle East. With a GDP of $287 billion in 2014, it had a GNI per capita of some $3,000 (or $10,260 in PPP terms). The headcount poverty rate was 42% in 2013 at $2.0 per day.

Egypt's respectable HDI score of 0.69 reflects the great strides made in educational attainment across the country. The mean years of schooling stood at 6.6 in 2014 while its Gini coefficient is one of the lowest in the world at 30.8% (Table 7.2).

Egypt has an unusual set of natural resource endowments. The silt and water of the Nile have historically supported highly productive agriculture in an otherwise barren moonscape. This endowment was rich enough to underwrite a hydraulic state and a world civilization (Handoussa, 2012). Egypt also has other endowments, one being its location in the passageway between the shipping-dense Mediterranean and the Red Sea. The other is its modest oil and gas deposits. Egypt is the largest non-OPEC oil producer and the second-largest dry natural gas producer in Africa although its high level of domestic consumption leaves little surplus gas for export (USEIA, 2015).

Compared with its latecomer peers such as Japan and India, a densely populated and spatially agglomerated Egypt (95% of the population resides almost entirely along the Nile or in the Nile Delta) enjoyed many favorable initial conditions in the inter-war decades. It built an extensive railway network starting in 1853, and the Suez Canal was completed in 1869. Both served to transport its irrigated and high-productivity export

TABLE 9.5 Structural change in manufacturing output for factor-based industrializers

Countries	EGY	EGY	ETH	ETH	KEN	KEN	SEN	SEN	TNZ	TNZ	TUN	TUN
Value added (%)	1970	2010	1990	2000	1970	2010	1980	2010	1970	2010	1970	2000
15 Food and beverages	11.9	13.0	49.5	49.5	31.4	30.0	27.3	17.2	26.7	48.5	25.7	18.0
16 Tobacco products	4.9	3.4	12.1	4.7	1.9	1.4	8.7	4.0	9.3	6.8	3.0	0.8
17 Textiles	32.3	3.3	11.1	6.2	4.8	1.1	23.5	9.5	23.6	5.5	9.5	6.4
18 Wearing apparel, fur	2.6	2.3	2.9	0.7	4.5	1.1	2.1	1.1	4.5	0.0	8.6	28.7
19 Leather and leather products	. .	0.2	7.0	4.7	. .	1.9	. .	. .	. .	0.2	. .	. .
20 Wood products (excl. furniture)	0.6	0.1	1.4	0.5	2.5	0.8	1.9	3.7	2.1	0.9	1.9	6.9
21 Paper and paper products	2.2	1.6	0.5	1.2	3.1	2.7	1.7	1.6	0.2	0.1	3.5	2.8
22 Printing and publishing	2.5	1.0	3.2	3.2	4.0	2.3	2.5	3.1	3.9	2.3	3.3	. .
36 Furniture; manufacturing n.e.c.	1.0	0.5	1.0	1.6	. .	2.2	1.4	2.9	4.5	10.0	2.1	. .
23 Coke and petroleum products	3.3	31.2	0.0	0.0	4.2	6.4	8.4	3.2	6.3	. .	4.4	8.0
25 Rubber and plastics products	2.6	1.9	2.7	4.5	1.1	2.7	5.3	5.1	0.6	3.6	2.6	2.8
26 Non-metallic mineral products	4.8	12.0	2.8	7.9	7.3	17.7	3.0	4.6	4.2	10.6	11.2	9.3
27 Basic metals	5.3	5.4	1.1	2.1	0.0	4.2	0.1	1.5	0.8	1.7	4.9	4.6
28 Fabricated metal products	4.6	1.7	1.2	1.4	8.0	. .	6.4	5.8	3.7	1.1	2.6	. .
24 Chemicals and chemical products	11.7	14.9	2.4	4.7	8.6	5.9	6.2	12.2	4.2	7.2	13.0	10.2
29 Machinery and equipment n.e.c.	2.1	1.1	0.1	0.1	1.0	1.2	0.2	1.0	1.7	0.3	0.1	0.4
30 Office and computing machinery	. .	0.7	0.0	0.0	. .	. .	. .	. .	. .	. .	. .	. .
31 Electrical machinery and apparat	3.6	3.4	0.1	0.0	6.5	. .	1.0	1.9	0.9	1.0	2.0	6.1
32 Communication equipment	. .	. .	0.0	0.0	. .	. .	. .	. .	. .	. .	. .	. .
33 Medical and optical instruments	0.1	. .	0.0	0.0	2.5	. .	0.0	0.0	0.0	. .	0.0	. .
34 Motor vehicles and trailers	3.8	2.0	0.9	6.9	8.3	1.3	0.3	21.7	2.7	0.0	1.5	2.8
35 Other transport equipment	. .	0.5	0.0	0.0	. .	. .	. .	. .	. .	0.0	. .	. .
D Total manufacturing (mill 2005$)	**695**	**5,997**	**584**	**466**	**131**	**3,182**	**553**	**8,984**	**74**	**1,408**	**130**	**3,498**

Source: Based on UNIDO, Indstat 2 database, 2015.

TABLE 9.6 Structural change in manufacturing employment of factor-based industrializers

Countries	EGY	EGY	ETH	ETH	KEN	KEN	SEN	SEN	TZA	TNZ	TUN	TUN
Employment	1970	2010	1970	2009	1970	1990	1980	2000	1970	2010	1970	2000
15 Food and beverages	14.0	20.5	14.0	20.5	14.0	20.5	14.0	20.5	14.0	20.5	14.0	20.5
16 Tobacco products	1.7	1.6	1.7	1.6	1.7	1.6	1.7	1.6	1.7	1.6	1.7	1.6
17 Textiles	19.4	20.5	19.4	20.5	19.4	20.5	19.4	20.5	19.4	20.5	19.4	20.5
18 Wearing apparel, fur	7.8	4.0	7.8	4.0	7.8	4.0	7.8	4.0	7.8	4.0	7.8	4.0
19 Leather and leather products	..	..	..	..	..	..	..	..	..	..	..	..
20 Wood products (excl. Furniture)	22.3	19.7	22.3	19.7	22.3	19.7	22.3	19.7	22.3	19.7	22.3	19.7
21 Paper and paper products	1.3	0.7	1.3	0.7	1.3	0.7	1.3	0.7	1.3	0.7	1.3	0.7
22 Printing and publishing	5.4	6.0	5.4	6.0	5.4	6.0	5.4	6.0	5.4	6.0	5.4	6.0
36 Furniture; manufacturing	3.5	2.2	3.5	2.2	3.5	2.2	3.5	2.2	3.5	2.2	3.5	2.2
23 Coke and petroleum products	0.7	0.8	0.7	0.8	0.7	0.8	0.7	0.8	0.7	0.8	0.7	0.8
24 Chemicals and chemical products	4.2	5.0	4.2	5.0	4.2	5.0	4.2	5.0	4.2	5.0	4.2	5.0
25 Rubber and plastics products	3.0	3.1	3.0	3.1	3.0	3.1	3.0	3.1	3.0	3.1	3.0	3.1
26 Non-metallic mineral products	3.6	3.1	3.6	3.1	3.6	3.1	3.6	3.1	3.6	3.1	3.6	3.1
27 Basic metals	4.5	3.5	4.5	3.5	4.5	3.5	4.5	3.5	4.5	3.5	4.5	3.5
28 Fabricated metal products	4.4	4.3	4.4	4.3	4.4	4.3	4.4	4.3	4.4	4.3	4.4	4.3
24 Chemicals and chemical products	4.2	5.0	4.2	5.0	4.2	5.0	4.2	5.0	4.2	5.0	4.2	5.0
29 Machinery and equipment	0.2	0.1	0.2	0.1	0.2	0.1	0.2	0.1	0.2	0.1	0.2	0.1
30 Office and computing mach.	..	..	..	..	..	..	..	..	..	..	..	..
31 Electrical machinery	3.4	2.5	3.4	2.5	3.4	2.5	3.4	2.5	3.4	2.5	3.4	2.5
32 Communication equipment	..	..	..	..	..	..	..	..	..	..	..	..
33 Medical and optical instruments	0.0	0.8	0.0	0.8	0.0	0.8	0.0	0.8	0.0	0.8	0.0	0.8
34 Motor vehicles and trailers	0.0	0.8	0.0	0.8	0.0	0.8	0.0	0.8	0.0	0.8	0.0	0.8
35 Other transport equipment	..	..	..	..	..	..	..	..	..	..	..	..
D Total manufact. employment	595,300	1,059,176	82,379	95,007	64,350	187,683	31,650	32,476	48,314	127,295	54,350	342,480

Source: Based on UNIDO, Indstat 2 database, 2015.

224 Africa's postcolonial experience

crops (mainly high-quality cotton but also rice) and bulky imports (such as coal and building materials as well as machinery). Just as gold had been the defining factor in the modern South African racialized political economy, "cotton" defined Egypt's class-based political economy. It did so through primitive accumulation under a big-landlord system (before the mid-1950s) and its progressive integration into the world economy.

Egypt's industrial efforts began in the nineteenth century with Muhammad Ali promoting import substitution industrialization in the hope of preserving Egypt's autonomy from the Ottomans and Europeans (Issawi, 1980; Owen and Pamuk, 1998). Panza and Williamson (2013) argue that his industrial policies (implicit export taxes on cotton and wheat, building irrigation canals, cheap inputs for domestic textiles, and non-tariff barriers) were reasonably successful. However, a vigorous industrialization drive was initiated only in the 1930s when, as in Latin America, import substitution was forced upon it by the collapse of primary export markets during the Great Depression.

Following the coup d'état by the Egyptian young officers, a state- and the native-dominated industrial sector was nurtured. During 1952–1973, import substitution and nationalization defined the public-sector-led industrialization drive focused on iron, steel, and chemical industries (Handoussa et al., 1986). By the end of the 1970s, Egypt completed the primary stage of import substitution to produce a proletarianized peasantry (Mabro and Radwan, 1976; Bent, 2015).

Egypt has a small and anemic formal private sector (World Bank, 2015a, 2015b). One reason for this is that Egypt has a much lower rate of firm entry than its peers. Young firms in Egypt tend to age without scaling up. Another is the decline of gross capital formation from a respectable 29% of GDP in 1990 to a dismal 14% in 2014 (see Tables 9.1 and 9.2).

Egypt's growth has recently been driven by the manufacturing sector, despite energy shortages and changes to the energy-subsidy scheme. Oil's share in the economy stood at 16%. Current transfers, official aid, and private remittances are another set of growth drivers. Together, they provide the equivalent to half of the export revenues in the 2000s (AEO-EGY, 2015).

To gauge the relationship between economic structure and growth, we have compiled internationally comparable data on the structures of Egyptian employment, output, and productivity at the one-digit ISIC level (Table 9.7). During the 40-year period (1970–2010), the structure of its economy was such that agriculture accounted for 14% of GDP while industry and services claim 40% and 46%, respectively. The "productive" sectors (agriculture, mining, and manufacturing) collectively lost 60% of their 1970 output share (of 70%) to the service sectors which accounted for half of the economy in 2010. Finally, the change in the employment structure was just as dramatic, with the service sectors increasing their share from 23% in 1970 to just over 50% in 2010.[1]

Egypt's manufacturing value added rose from some $0.7 billion in 1970 (in 2005 international dollars) to $6 billion in 2010. At market prices, manufacturing value added stood at $20 billion (or 16% of GDP) in 2014. Interestingly, coke and petroleum products accounted for 31% of production while chemicals and food processing add another 28% together making up some 60% of Egyptian MVA. Manufacturing also accounted for over 70% of Egypt's merchandise exports.

TABLE 9.7 Egypt: changes in sectoral economic structure, 1970–2010

	1970	1980	1990	2000	2010	Diff: 2010–1970
Employment structure:	%	%	%	%	%	%
Agriculture	51.3	42.8	34.6	30.1	23.6	−27.6
Mining	0.3	0.4	0.4	0.2	0.1	−0.2
Manufacturing	14.2	13.0	13.4	13.6	11.1	−3.2
Utilities	0.8	0.7	1.0	1.1	1.4	0.6
Construction	2.7	6.1	8.0	8.6	12.4	9.7
Trade and hotels	7.9	9.0	8.6	11.3	13.5	5.6
Transport-storage-comm.	2.6	6.5	6.4	6.3	9.0	6.5
Finance and business srvcs.	0.9	1.5	2.5	3.4	3.6	2.7
Govt + community services	19.3	20.1	25.3	25.4	25.2	5.9
Total employment[a]	7,549	10,251	12,771	16,815	22,020	14,471
Output structure:	%	%	%	%	%	%
Agriculture	28.0	19.2	14.6	15.9	12.8	−15.2
Mining	18.8	26.3	19.6	12.9	13.3	−5.5
Manufacturing	22.9	18.2	22.0	18.6	16.4	−6.5
Utilities	1.1	0.9	1.5	1.5	1.5	0.4
Construction	1.4	1.7	3.5	4.7	5.8	4.4
Trade and hotels	13.2	12.9	13.2	13.5	15.1	1.9
Transport-storage-comm.	3.0	9.6	10.4	8.6	14.3	11.3
Finance and business srvcs.	3.1	4.4	4.6	10.8	7.8	4.7
Govt + community services	8.3	6.8	10.6	13.4	12.9	4.5
Gross value added[b]	71,706	180,478	282,064	414,954	703,510	631,804
Productivity structure[c]*:*	$	$	$	$	$	Ratio: 2010/1970
Agriculture	5,191	7,880	9,304	12,989	17,335	3.34
Mining	530,574	1,070,680	1,215,697	1,386,675	3,230,709	6.09
Manufacturing	15,284	24,636	36,408	33,755	47,419	3.10
Utilities	13,702	23,567	32,361	33,368	34,260	2.50
Construction	4,996	5,024	9,694	13,498	15,055	3.01
Trade and hotels	15,956	25,281	33,919	29,594	35,704	2.24
Transport-storage-comm.	11,014	26,098	35,805	33,762	50,439	4.58
Finance and business srvcs.	31,449	53,053	41,222	79,258	68,614	2.18
Govt + community services	4,119	5,975	9,280	13,038	16,369	3.97
Economy-wide	9,499	17,606	22,086	24,678	31,949	3.36

Sources and notes: Calculations are based on the 2014 version of the GGDC 10-sector database: www.rug.nl/research/ggdc/data/10-sector-database which is documented in M.P. Timmer, G.J. de Vries, and K. de Vries, "Patterns of Structural Change in Developing Countries," *GGDC Research Memorandum 149*, Groningen Growth and Development Centre, 2014.

a Economy-wide persons engaged, in thousands.

b Gross value added in millions of 2005 international dollars.

c Gross value added per person engaged in 2005 international dollars.

226 Africa's postcolonial experience

The private sector accounts for just a quarter of Egypt's manufacturing sector output and employment, and about half of its exports. The relatively small group of entrepreneurs with good connections to the regime benefitted handsomely from a combination of tax holidays, subsidized utilities, and domestic market protection. Diwan et al. (2015), in their study of politically connected private businesses in Egypt, conclude that the entry of politically connected firms into new, modern, and previously unconnected sectors slows down aggregate employment growth and skews the distribution of employment toward less productive, smaller firms.

Internationally comparable data on changes in the structures of Egyptian employment, output, and productivity in manufacturing industries are presented in Table 9.8. They show that, during the 40-year period (1970–2010), manufacturing

TABLE 9.8 Egypt: growth performance of three-digit manufacturing industries, 1965–2004

Industry	ISIC3	Index of production (1995 = 100)				
		1965	1975	1985	1995	2004
Food products	311	27	35	91	100	106
Beverages	313	18	32	91	100	106
Tobacco	314	17	35	91	100	139
Textiles	321	66	100	133	100	60
Wearing apparel, except footwear	322	10	19	52	100	141
Leather products	323	77	156	235	100	78
Footwear, except rubber or plastic	324	57	106	235	100	78
Wood products, except furniture	331	93	49	146	100	22
Furniture, except metal	332	27	19	112	100	71
Paper and products	341	65	76	70	100	227
Printing and publishing	342	464	405	235	100	227
Other manufactured products	390	48	44	54	100	251
Petroleum refineries	353	17	35	138	100	91
Misc. petroleum and coal	354	17	35	138	100	91
Rubber products	355	54	58	109	100	142
Plastic Products	356	40	43	82	100	. .
Pottery, china, earthenware	361	28	48	46	100	131
Glass and products	362	28	48	46	100	131
Other non-metallic mineral	369	28	48	46	100	131
Iron and steel	371	29	35	73	100	183
Non-ferrous metals	372	29	35	73	100	183
Fabricated metal products	381	14	41	100	100	106
Industrial chemicals	351	14	30	96	100	202
Other chemicals	352	14	30	96	100	202
Machinery, except electrical	382	16	28	111	100	209
Machinery, electric	383	7	22	146	100	217
Transport equipment	384	49	94	219	100	335
Professional and scientific equipment	385	49	46	94	100	111

Source: Based on UNIDO, Indstat database, various years.

value added increased by a factor of 8.6 along with an unusual compositional shift. Light industry lost over half of its share largely to the mid-tech and capital-intensive branches. Assuming the data are reliable, the changes were most dramatic for textiles (falling from 32.3% to just 3.3%) and for coke and petroleum products (rising from 3.3% to 31.2%).

It is interesting to note in this regard that, around 1980, textile manufacturing, the oldest industrial sector in the Egyptian economy, was the largest subsector with 20% and 27% respectively of manufacturing value added and employment. The textile industry grew rapidly as it substituted for imports and developed a significant export trade especially in yarn and fabrics (World Bank, 1983).

The data also show that, while Egypt increased its manufacturing workforce by 78% to just over 1 million by 2010, the employment share of the labor-intensive and low-tech sectors remained just over 70% during the four decades under review. Finally, the data suggest that a dramatic increase in the productivity of the highly capital-intensive petroleum and gas industries is the driving force behind this localized structural transformation.

We present a battery of indexes for the industrial efficiency and the international competitiveness of Egypt (Tables 9.9 and 9.10). It is useful to note here that

TABLE 9.9 Egypt: efficiency of three-digit manufacturing industries, 1967–2006

Three-digit manufacturing industry	ISIC	(Y-V)/Y	W/V	K/L	V/L	W/L
	Code	%	%	$	$	$
Food products	311	78	38	2,587	4,239	1,590
Beverages	313	66	33	3,666	6,299	2,076
Tobacco	314	81	30	3,167	7,500	2,249
Textiles	321	68	59	1,271	2,451	1,456
Wearing apparel, except footwear	322	64	34	2,058	3,260	1,105
Leather products	323	76	50	1,319	2,945	1,477
Footwear, except rubber or plastic	324	63	48	2,013	2,707	1,308
Wood products, except furniture	331	71	60	1,832	2,749	1,649
Furniture, except metal	332	68	49	1,544	3,014	1,487
Paper and products	341	74	33	6,136	5,104	1,686
Other manufactured products	390	78	49	1,675	3,018	1,467
Printing and publishing	342	70	64	2,480	4,073	2,618
Petroleum refineries	353	71	18	28,332	28,691	5,034
Misc. petroleum and coal products	354	74	27	4,414	11,991	3,269
Rubber products	355	71	42	5,017	4,929	2,067
Plastic Products	356	72	36	2,520	5,267	1,882
Pottery, china, earthenware	361	60	38	862	5,313	1,996
Glass and products	362	60	50	3,250	3,325	1,666
Other non-metallic mineral products	369	62	29	10,750	7,096	2,075
Iron and steel	371	77	53	10,249	5,008	2,666

(*Continued*)

TABLE 9.9 (Continued)

Three-digit manufacturing industry	ISIC	(Y-V)/Y	W/V	K/L	V/L	W/L
	Code	%	%	$	$	$
Non-ferrous metals	372	76	33	9,118	8,333	2,752
Fabricated metal products	381	66	42	2,499	4,457	1,884
Industrial chemicals	351	64	43	7,986	6,175	2,655
Other chemicals	352	69	31	4,247	8,029	2,516
Machinery, except electrical	382	70	48	1,713	5,112	2,450
Machinery, electric	383	70	35	4,348	7,412	2,601
Transport equipment	384	70	47	2,085	4,877	2,307
Professional and scientific equipment	385	64	75	2,771	3,819	2,859
Manufacturing	300	72	40	3,905	4,842	1,929

Source: Based on UNIDO, Industrial Database, various years.

Definitions: Y = gross output, V = value added, K = fixed capital, L = employment, W = total wage bill. *Indexes of Efficiency:* Share of Purchased [(Y-V)/Y], Unit Labor Cost (W/V), Productivity of Capital (V/K), Productivity of Labor (V/L), Capital Intensity (K/L), Average Wage (W/L).

TABLE 9.10 Egypt: competitive industrial performance, 1990–2012

Year	MVA per capita	M Exports per capita	MHM in MVA	MHX in MX	MVA in GDP	M Exports in Exports	Industrialization intensity index
	$	$	%	%	%	%	
1990	116	32	23	11	13	56	0.25
1991	120	32	22	11	14	56	0.27
1992	120	32	17	11	14	56	0.25
1993	121	32	19	11	14	56	0.27
1994	124	32	27	11	14	56	0.40
1995	132	32	25	14	14	57	0.38
1996	139	32	28	10	14	57	0.41
1997	148	41	30	10	15	67	0.42
1998	157	34	36	12	15	69	0.47
1999	169	36	36	13	16	67	0.48
2000	179	52	36	19	16	74	0.48
2001	183	40	32	12	16	67	0.45
2002	187	43	32	11	16	64	0.45
2003	186	60	32	11	16	70	0.44
2004	188	72	28	10	16	68	0.40
2005	193	82	29	12	16	57	0.40
2006	200	91	22	14	16	50	0.36
2007	212	103	26	11	16	49	0.38
2008	225	205	26	24	16	62	0.38
2009	230	178	23	28	16	59	0.38
2010	238	202	22	26	16	62	0.36
2011	232	239	23	28	16	62	0.37
2012	234	219	23	31	16	62	0.35

Sources and notes: UNIDO, Competitive Industrial Performance (CIP) database, 2014.
MHM = medium- and high-technology manufacturing production
MHX = medium- and high-technology manufacturing exports
MX = manufacturing exports
MVA = manufacturing (M) value added

measures based on gross value added, while useful for gauging the efficiency with which intermediates are transformed into final output, are bedeviled by a high correlation between intermediate inputs and fixed capital stock which confound the effects of each on output. On the other hand, efficiency measures based on value added, while good at identifying capital's productivity, tend to inflate the effects of capital and labor on output (Söderbom and Teal, 2000, 2003).

If we use the share of purchased inputs as an index of the intensity of intersectoral linkages (or dependence), several agro-processing branches (food, tobacco, and leather) and mineral-processing branches (petroleum-related products and primary metals) of manufacturing show input purchases more than 70% of value added. Using the ratio of wages to value-added as a measure of unit labor per dollar of net output, we find that labor cost exceeds half of value added in the low-tech industries of textiles, wood products, and printing as well as in such mid-tech industries as glass, iron and steel, and (perhaps due to the high cost of skilled labor) in professional and scientific instruments.

The data suggest that there is a high correlation between investment levels and labor productivity in beverages, tobacco, paper, chemicals, machinery, petroleum, and iron and steel. Except for paper and plastics (wage levels lower than expected) and in printing and publishing as well as in non-ferrous metals (wages higher than expected), the imperatives of profitability must ensure that productivity and wages are intimately linked.

Quality aside, supply-push investment in higher education (some 3.5 million students enrolled in tertiary institutions) puts Egypt in the league of the developed countries. The combination of substantial brain drain, youth unrest, and worrisome skill-job mismatches in the domestic economy continue to frustrate the cause of shared growth through private-sector-led job creation, spatial and sectoral integration, and inclusiveness especially of women and the Upper Nile region (World Bank, 2015b).

Finally, the measures of international competitiveness paint the picture that some of the industrial deepening that began in the 1980s petered out especially after 2010. While Egypt has managed to develop a broad-based manufacturing sector, the kind of technological transformation achieved by its peers (Turkey, South Korea, Malaysia, and Indonesia) continues to elude it.

Ethiopia (ETH)

Ethiopia, with over 95 million people in 2014, surpassed Egypt for the second most populous African country after Nigeria. The country's real per capita income, $550 in terms of market prices (GDP of $57.5 billion) or $1,500 of GNI per capita in PPP terms, is substantially below the average for Africa. This lackluster record is reflected in one of the highest poverty rates in Africa – over three-quarters of Ethiopians subsist on less than $3.10 per day.

Ethiopia has a low HDI index of 0.44 which captures important features of its economic and social landscapes. For example, life expectancy in 2014 was 64 years, and its mean years of schooling was a dismal 2.4 years. The egalitarian 1975 land

230 Africa's postcolonial experience

reform favoring use-rights to land has, however, produced one of the lowest Gini coefficients in the world at 33.6%.

Economic growth was respectable in 1960–1972, meager in 1973–1992, and moderate in 1993–2002. Following the African trend, the economy recovered subsequently to attain an 8–9% average annual growth through 2015. This surge was driven by public investment which was funded by a mix of aid, remittances, expanded exports, and FDI. Over the past two decades, the country has made significant progress on key human development indicators. Primary school enrollments have quadrupled to approach universal coverage. Child mortality has been halved. Furthermore, the number of people with access to clean water and electricity has more than doubled, albeit from very low initial levels.

The structure of Ethiopia's economy is such that agriculture accounts for a substantial 42% of GDP while industry and services claim 15% and 43%, respectively. Its gross capital formation doubled to the Chinese level of 38% by 2014 (see Tables 9.1 and 9.2).

Ethiopia's economy is as non-industrial as it gets with manufacturing accounting for less than 5% of GDP. The internationally comparable data on changes in the structures of Ethiopian employment, output, and productivity of the economy at the one-digit ISIC level are presented in Table 9.11. During the 40-year period (1970–2009), agriculture lost a significant share of its output (falling from 74% to 42%) while the service sector almost doubled its share to 28%. While manufacturing also gained output share during the period, it remained a minor player. The change in employment structure was less dramatic for agriculture since its low and falling productivity caused a less dramatic drop in its share from 93% to 75% for the period since 1970.

The data also show that the productive sectors of the economy (agriculture, mining, and manufacturing) experienced a decline of labor productivity while the service sectors surprisingly gained significantly. This means the Ethiopian economy is far from being technologically dynamic.

Ethiopia's manufacturing value added rose from a mere $0.6 billion in 1970 (in 2005 international dollars) to $1.4 billion (and 150,000 jobs) in 2009. Manufacturing value added amounted to a paltry $2.8 billion or 5% of GDP in 2014. Food and beverages accounted for a whopping 40% of manufacturing production as well as for 20% of its merchandise exports.

We lack good data on growth rates at the two- or three-digit levels even for the post-1990 period. However, the aggregate figures make it clear that food processing and beverages as well as non-metallic products, which constituted 55% of total MVA, were the branches spearheading growth. Textiles and garments are just beginning to make a significant inroad along with leather products when compared to the pre-1990 levels (Abegaz, 1994). Cut flowers, leather products, garment, and sugar are currently spearheading an export-oriented, state-led industrialization drive (Gebreyesus, 2016; Oqubay, 2015).

Business entry regulations and processes are consistently highlighted by the private sector as burdensome and obstructive of firm entry and dynamism. The importance of promoting linkages and spillovers with domestic firms and the role of services in developing value chains is key. Additional policy measures are needed in

TABLE 9.11 Ethiopia: changes in sectoral economic structure, 1970–2010

	1970	1980	1990	2000	2010	Diff: 2010–1970
Employment structure:	%	%	%	%	%	%
Agriculture	92.5	89.3	89.4	84.9	75.1	−17.3
Mining	0.0	0.0	0.1	0.2	0.5	0.5
Manufacturing	1.9	1.7	1.8	3.1	6.2	4.4
Utilities	0.0	0.1	0.1	0.1	0.1	0.1
Construction	0.3	0.2	0.3	0.5	2.0	1.7
Trade and hotels	2.6	3.4	3.7	4.7	10.2	7.6
Transport-storage-comm.	0.3	0.4	0.4	0.4	0.5	0.2
Finance and business srvcs.	0.1	0.1	0.1	0.1	0.4	0.3
Government services	1.1	2.3	2.1	3.2	2.5	1.4
Community services	1.1	2.5	2.1	2.6	2.4	1.3
Total employment[a]	11,584	15,580	21,354	27,711	39,081	27,497
Output structure:	%	%	%	%	%	%
Agriculture	73.9	69.3	63.3	49.0	42.4	−31.5
Mining	0.2	0.1	0.3	0.5	0.6	0.3
Manufacturing	3.2	3.9	4.6	5.6	5.2	1.9
Utilities	1.0	1.3	2.2	2.1	1.8	0.9
Construction	4.4	4.2	3.8	4.1	5.7	1.3
Trade and hotels	11.6	11.9	13.0	14.7	18.8	7.1
Transport-storage-comm.	1.9	2.5	3.8	4.5	5.7	3.8
Finance and business srvcs.	0.9	2.0	2.7	4.2	6.1	5.2
Government services	1.8	3.1	4.4	12.0	11.0	9.3
Community services	1.1	1.8	1.9	3.4	2.9	1.7
Gross value added[b]	38,154	46,091	51,099	70,589	155,759	117,605
Productivity structure[c]:	$	$	$	$	$	Ratio: 2010/1970
Agriculture	2,631	2,297	1,694	1,469	2,248	0.85
Mining	61,830	12,968	6,359	5,493	4,745	0.08
Manufacturing	5,680	6,920	6,199	4,523	3,301	0.58
Utilities	70,381	63,238	63,192	67,782	72,706	1.03
Construction	48,581	49,666	35,485	19,966	11,234	0.23
Trade and hotels	14,570	10,253	8,514	7,895	7,321	0.50
Transport-storage-comm.	18,546	18,281	22,333	31,479	44,370	2.39
Finance and business srvcs.	25,253	62,710	67,787	72,201	54,805	2.17
Government services	5,221	3,929	5,090	9,471	17,621	3.37
Community services	3,499	2,134	2,212	3,264	4,819	1.38
Economy-wide	3,294	2,958	2,393	2,547	3,986	1.21

Sources and notes: Calculations are based on the 2014 version of the GGDC 10-sector database: www.rug.nl/research/ggdc/data/10-sector-database which is documented in M.P. Timmer, G. J. de Vries, and K. de Vries, "Patterns of Structural Change in Developing Countries," GGDC Research Memorandum 149, Groningen Growth and Development Centre, 2014.

a Economy-wide persons engaged, in thousands.

b Gross value added in millions of 2005 international dollars.

c Gross value added per person engaged in 2005 international dollars.

232 Africa's postcolonial experience

the areas of access to land and access to electricity, improvements in tax administrations and trade logistics, and appropriate provision of infrastructure.

We present a battery of measures of industrial efficiency and international competitiveness for Ethiopia in Table 9.12. Using the share of purchased inputs as an index of the intensity of intersectoral linkages or dependence, it becomes clear that many agro-processing sectors (leather, textiles, and apparel) and mineral-processing sectors (iron and steel) depend on input purchases equivalent to two-thirds of value

TABLE 9.12 Ethiopia: efficiency of three-digit manufacturing industries, 1990–2009

Three-digit manufacturing industry	ISIC	(Y-V)/Y	W/V	K/L	V/L	W/L
	Code	%	%	$	$	$
Food products	311	55	16	639	6,092	997
Beverages	313	35	11	1,835	13,473	1,472
Tobacco	314	29	6	912	35,576	2,091
Textiles	321	63	49	275	1,488	732
Wearing apparel, except footwear	322	65	53	330	1,336	712
Leather products	323	74	25	906	5,107	1,278
Footwear, except rubber or plastic	324	63	31	674	2,673	835
Wood products, except furniture	331	42	36	101	2,329	839
Furniture, except metal	332	54	34	356	2,177	730
Paper and products	341	63	23	689	4,999	1,164
Printing and publishing	342	49	29	564	4,214	1,204
Other manufactured products	390	..	..	..	..	..
Petroleum refineries	353	..	..	..	..	..
Misc. petroleum and coal products	354	..	..	..	..	..
Rubber products	355	56	18	2,836	9,402	1,736
Plastic products	356	62	14	5,635	4,886	694
Pottery, china, earthenware	361	..	..	..	..	..
Glass and products	362	40	22	775	4,589	996
Other non-metallic mineral products	369	50	13	1,039	7,320	921
Iron and steel	371	71	12	2,145	13,261	1,535
Non-ferrous metals	372	..	..	..	..	..
Fabricated metal products	381	61	21	694	4,958	1,043
Industrial chemicals	351	−4	6	331	17,525	1,027
Other chemicals	352	65	14	908	7,142	1,016
Machinery, except electrical	382	63	29	436	2,843	817
Machinery, electric	383	62	48	74	2,318	1,123
Transport equipment	384	73	15	1,440	9,044	1,319
Professional and scientific equipment	385	..	..	..	..	..
Manufacturing	**300**	**55**	**18**	**999**	**5,461**	**981**

Source. Based on UNIDO, Industrial Database, various years.

Definitions: Y = gross output, V = value added, K = fixed capital, L = employment, W = total wage bill. *Indexes of Efficiency*: Share of Purchased [(Y-V)/Y], Unit Labor Cost (W/V), Productivity of Capital (V/K), Productivity of Labor (V/L), Capital Intensity (K/L), Average Wage (W/L).

added. Transport equipment also has high (imported) input content indicating perhaps that it is an entirely assembly activity.

Using the ratio of wages to value-added as a measure of unit labor cost per dollar of net output, we find that labor cost is about half of value added in the low-tech industries of apparel and leather as well as in such skill-intensive industries as electrical machinery. One set of clues for these patterns is provided by the high correlation between capital intensity, labor productivity, and average wage. The data suggest that, except for plastic products, there is a strong positive correlation between capital per worker and output per worker, especially in transport equipment, rubber products, beverages, and iron and steel.

Finally, Table 9.13 presents other measures of productivity that capture international competitiveness. The overall picture is that Ethiopia is at the very beginning of an industrial drive.

TABLE 9.13 Ethiopia: competitive industrial performance, 1990–2012

Year	MVA per capita	M Exports per capita	MHM in MVA	MHX in MX	MVA in GDP	M Exports in exports	Industrialization intensity index
	$	$	%	%	%	%	
1990	9	1	4	0	6	14	0.07
1991	5	1	3	0	4	14	0.04
1992	4	1	4	0	3	14	0.03
1993	5	1	6	0	4	14	0.06
1994	6	1	6	0	5	14	0.09
1995	6	1	6	0	5	14	0.09
1996	6	1	6	0	4	14	0.08
1997	6	1	6	0	4	11	0.08
1998	6	1	8	1	5	8	0.10
1999	6	1	8	1	5	9	0.09
2000	6	1	12	1	5	13	0.14
2001	7	1	9	3	5	17	0.11
2002	6	1	7	1	5	21	0.10
2003	6	1	7	0	5	16	0.09
2004	7	1	8	10	4	6	0.09
2005	7	1	6	2	4	9	0.08
2006	8	1	7	3	4	7	0.09
2007	8	2	10	23	4	13	0.10
2008	9	2	8	23	4	11	0.09
2009	10	2	9	34	4	11	0.11
2010	10	3	9	32	4	10	0.11
2011	11	4	9	13	4	12	0.11
2012	11	3	9	18	4	10	0.11

Sources and notes: UNIDO, Competitive Industrial Performance (CIP) database, 2014.
MHM = medium- and high-technology manufacturing production
MHX = medium- and high-technology manufacturing exports
MX = manufacturing exports
MVA = manufacturing (M) value added

234 Africa's postcolonial experience

The lack of a level playing field between state-owned industrial enterprises, party- or military-affiliated firms, and unaffiliated private firms is also a hindrance to impactful competition. The pervasive presence of state- and party-owned businesses continues to shape the autonomous private sector's perception of the security of property rights and erodes policy credibility (AEO-ETH, 2015; Abegaz, 2013). Low skills, underdeveloped markets, inadequate and unreliable public services, and limited managerial experience together constitute binding constraints on the rapid transformation of merchant capital into industrial capital.

Ethiopia's extremely low labor productivity (about a third of China's and half of India's) partially nullifies its low wages. The Ethiopian urban economy, with about a sixth of the labor force, contributed 70% of growth between 1993–2005 and will remain the center of gravity for industrial development (World Bank, 2007, 2010).

Ethiopia's grandiose vision for bumping up the share of MVA from 5% to 25% of GDP includes a debt-financed public investment in infrastructure (especially highways and rails) and industrial parks. The Ethiopian Industrial Parks Development Corporation (IPDC), established in 2014, has plans to oversee the construction of 17 primarily Chinese FDI-financed Ethiopia plans to construct 17 integrated agro-industrial parks in at least four regional states. Ethiopia opened a giant industrial park in 2016 in Hawassa (Awassa) designed for the export-oriented manufacturing of textiles, garments, and agro-processing. The Hawassa Industrial Park, which cost some $275 million, has 35 factories with clients from the U.S.A., China, India, and Sri Lanka as well as six local companies. The rather optimistic expectation is that the park will create 140,000 jobs by the end of 2017.

The national plan calls for building 12 such industrial parks across the country, especially in Dire-Dawa, Kombolcha, Adama (Nazreth), Jimma, and Mekelle to join the likes of Bole Lemi which has created some 11,000 jobs already. Connectivity of these parks to ports in Djibouti is crucial for their success. The 750-km (460-mile) railway, built by two Chinese companies, has linked Addis Ababa and its industrial outskirts to the Red Sea port city of Djibouti at a substantial saving in transportation costs of imports and exports. Some 1,500 trucks a day currently lumber along the road, which carries 90% of imports and exports from landlocked Ethiopia to the port.[2]

This strategy is, however, bedeviled by the political fragility of minority rule and deeply institutionalized political capture of the state and the modern economy. The current rule by emergency decree in several regions of the country does not bode well for such a long-term debt- and FDI-driven strategy of industrialization.[3]

Kenya (KEN)

Kenya, with over 45 million people in 2014 has a GNI per capita of $2,940 in PPP terms. With a respectable average-years of schooling of 6.7, its HDI index stood at 0.55 (just below Ghana), and its Gini index was rather high at 47.7% (just below Nigeria).

Some 46% of Kenya's population lived on less than $3.10 per day in 2014, and yet its life expectancy stood at 61.6 years in 2014. These indicators capture important features of its economic landscape (Table 7.2).

Kenya was a quasi-settler colonial economy with a cadre of British farmers controlling the best land in the cool highlands. The medium-to-large-scale industrial and commercial sectors were long dominated by South Asians. Political independence brought the Kenyanization of the economy along with rampant corruption.

Kenya today is a multiethnic society where political ethnicity (especially among Kikuyu, Luhya, Luo, Kalenjin, and Kamba) has taken deep roots as was shown by the electoral violence of 2008 which exposed the structural fragility of the postcolonial state (Kirigai, 2012). It is also home to innovative cellphone-based business services and a large eco-tourist industry.

The structure of its economy is such that agriculture accounts for a substantial 31% of GDP while industry and services claim 19% (half of which is manufacturing) and 50%, respectively. Its gross capital formation, at 21%, needs to rise by one-half to finance a robust growth (see Tables 9.1 and 9.2).

The 1990s were a decade of low growth and little structural change. GDP started to grow steadily after 2002 with a dip in 2008 following electoral violence (Figure 9.1). However, real per capita income has been rising since 1995.

In the mid-1960s, Kenya launched an import substitution industrialization strategy that soon exhausted its potentials. In the early 1980s, it introduced import liberalization measures emphasizing private sector-led exports (Wignaraja, 2003).

Kenya is by far the most industrially developed country in East Africa, although the share of manufacturing in GDP has virtually remained at the level it was at independence in 1963 (UNIDO, 2013). Industrial activity is understandably concentrated around the three largest urban centers of Nairobi, Mombasa, and Kisumu.

MVA was just a tenth of that of Tunisia in 2014, and MVA per head increased modestly from $36 to $62 between 1998 and 2014. Food and beverages account for nearly a third of total value added (see Table 9.2). The value added per worker in Kenyan manufacturing firms has also declined steadily since the 1970s, and productivity differences across firms are very high (de Vries et al., 2013).

The formal manufacturing sector contributed just 12% of GDP in 2014 and employed 13% of the labor force in line with comparator countries. Value added per worker in 2010 was just half of what it was in 1970, and below the economy-wide average (see Table 9.14).

Kenya has some peculiar features worth noting. Some 60% of MVA is in the food processing and clothing industries. Moreover, Asians own two-thirds of medium and large-scale manufacturing firms (N'gui et al., 2016).

Manufacturing accounted for 26% of Kenya's merchandise exports, facing acute competition from China and India. Some 40% of Kenya's exports go to the East African Community.

The rate of structural transformation is partially captured by the differential growth rates of manufacturing at the three-digit level (see Table 9.15). Non-metallic

TABLE 9.14 Kenya: changes in sectoral economic structure, 1970–2010

	1970	1980	1990	2000	2010	Diff: 2010–1970
Employment structure:	%	%	%	%	%	%
Agriculture	81.0	78.0	71.2	56.1	48.3	−32.7
Mining	0.1	0.2	0.1	0.5	0.6	0.5
Manufacturing	3.8	3.5	5.3	10.0	12.8	9.0
Utilities	0.1	0.2	0.3	0.3	0.2	0.1
Construction	0.8	1.0	1.4	2.3	2.8	2.0
Trade and hotels	5.0	4.8	8.4	12.3	16.4	11.4
Transport-storage-comm.	1.4	2.2	1.5	3.6	3.4	2.0
Finance and business srvcs.	0.9	0.8	1.0	1.6	1.2	0.4
Government services	3.4	4.7	5.4	6.5	6.1	2.7
Community services	3.4	4.7	5.4	6.8	8.2	4.8
Total employment[a]	3,888	5,457	7,567	11,568	15,289	11,401
Output structure:	%	%	%	%	%	%
Agriculture	38.1	31.8	30.0	28.1	23.8	−14.3
Mining	0.6	0.7	0.6	0.6	0.6	−0.1
Manufacturing	7.0	12.6	13.3	12.2	12.1	5.0
Utilities	1.7	2.7	2.6	1.9	2.3	0.6
Construction	8.7	5.9	5.3	4.7	5.3	−3.3
Trade and hotels	10.7	11.7	11.5	12.0	14.1	3.4
Transport-storage-comm.	8.5	9.7	9.1	9.4	14.2	5.7
Finance and business srvcs.	3.4	3.9	4.5	8.2	8.1	4.7
Government services	12.8	17.7	18.8	18.0	15.0	2.2
Community services	8.4	3.3	4.4	5.0	4.5	−3.9
Gross value added[b]	397,538.5	554,886.3	837,929.0	1,037,243.2	1,527,992.6	1,130,454
Productivity structure[c]:	$	$	$	$	$	Ratio: 2010/1970
Agriculture	48,116	41,535	46,699	44,891	49,324	1.03
Mining	522,146	400,634	921,401	102,262	92,826	0.18
Manufacturing	190,040	368,305	275,449	108,963	94,652	0.50
Utilities	1,331,560	1,413,163	901,618	621,689	1,177,570	0.88
Construction	1,047,554	588,849	412,697	180,164	188,768	0.18
Trade and hotels	217,804	247,535	150,601	87,591	85,710	0.39
Transport-storage-comm.	623,818	444,516	685,380	231,270	413,289	0.66
Finance and business srvcs.	412,488	480,834	513,023	449,655	665,757	1.61
Government services	384,267	385,392	386,116	248,772	248,194	0.65
Community services	251,657	71,815	90,380	66,360	55,003	0.22
Economy-wide	102,245	101,689	110,739	89,669	99,942	0.98

Sources and notes: Calculations are based on the 2014 version of the GGDC 10-sector database: www.rug.nl/research/ggdc/data/10-sector-database which is documented in M.P. Timmer, G. J. de Vries, and K. de Vries, "Patterns of Structural Change in Developing Countries," *GGDC Research Memorandum 149*, Groningen Growth and Development Centre, 2014.

a Economy-wide persons engaged, in thousands.

b Gross value added in millions of 2005 international dollars.

c Gross value added per person engaged in 2005 international dollars.

Labor-based industrializers **237**

TABLE 9.15 Kenya: growth performance of three-digit manufacturing industries, 1965–2004

Industry	ISIC3	Index of production (1995=100)				
		1965	1975	1985	1995	2004
Food products	311	21	40	70	100	119
Beverages	313	12	41	59	100	85
Tobacco	314	26	45	71	100	67
Textiles	321	30	83	127	100	70
Wearing apparel, except footwear	322	47	52	231	100	116
Leather products	323	22	86	121	100	125
Footwear, except rubber or plastic	324	22	86	121	100	125
Wood products, except furniture	331	73	144	90	100	62
Furniture, except metal	332	71	195	136	100	108
Paper and products	341	21	39	96	100	218
Printing and publishing	342	10	23	73	100	95
Other manufactured products	390	5	17	43	100	226
Petroleum refineries	353	11	18	53	100	165
Misc. petroleum and coal	354	..	..	..	100	..
Rubber products	355	3	11	40	100	125
Plastic products	356	..	..	..	100	..
Pottery, china, earthenware	361	3	6	14	100	54
Glass and products	362	3	6	14	100	54
Other non-metallic mineral	369	30	52	57	100	94
Iron and steel	371	..	..	..	100	..
Non-ferrous metals	372	..	..	..	100	..
Fabricated metal products	381	14	34	46	100	123
Industrial chemicals	351	29	51	79	100	68
Other chemicals	352	12	22	53	100	165
Machinery, except electrical	382	133	175	141	100	113
Machinery, electric	383	13	34	61	100	101
Transport equipment	384	12	17	127	100	210
Professional and scientific equipment	385	..	..	..	100	..

Source: Based on UNIDO, Indstat database, various years.

products, textiles, and wood products lost out while paper, petroleum, and transport equipment gained significant output shares.

We present many measures of industrial efficiency and international competitiveness for Kenya (see Tables 9.16 and 9.17). Using the share of purchased inputs as an index of the intensity of intersectoral linkages, processing in nearly every branch of manufacturing relies on purchased inputs in a proportion that exceeds two-thirds of value added – beverages and glass products being the exceptions with half the value added.

Using the ratio of wages to value-added as a measure of unit labor per dollar of net output, we can see that labor cost is about half of MVA in the low-tech

238 Africa's postcolonial experience

TABLE 9.16 Kenya: efficiency of three-digit manufacturing industries, 1967–2002

Three-digit manufacturing industry	ISIC	(Y-V)/Y	W/V	K/L	V/L	W/L
	Code	%	%	$	$	$
Food products	311	92	33	406	4,635	1,515
Beverages	313	54	30	638	11,212	3,398
Tobacco	314	90	26	1,179	10,515	2,693
Textiles	321	68	56	113	2,154	1,215
Wearing apparel, except footwear	322	80	54	89	2,587	1,399
Leather products	323	78	54	130	2,285	1,226
Footwear, except rubber or plastic	324	71	49	225	3,789	1,846
Wood products, except furniture	331	72	61	59	1,531	928
Furniture, except metal	332	66	62	94	2,588	1,602
Paper and products	341	72	40	235	5,468	2,175
Printing and publishing	342	69	53	114	4,232	2,236
Other manufactured products	390	69	30	110	5,673	1,676
Petroleum refineries	353	98	20	3,271	32,121	6,532
Misc. petroleum and coal products	354	. .	. .	. .	. .	. .
Rubber products	355	71	28	953	11,249	3,160
Plastic products	356	72	26	598	6,764	1,729
Pottery, china, earthenware	361	62	51	7,088	3,777	1,913
Glass and products	362	51	50	36	3,044	1,518
Other non-metallic mineral products	369	78	42	895	5,677	2,375
Iron and steel	371	89	57	3,020	2,838	1,613
Non-ferrous metals	372	. .	. .	. .	. .	. .
Fabricated metal products	381	79	47	300	4,196	1,980
Industrial chemicals	351	83	45	281	5,986	2,689
Other chemicals	352	90	46	270	6,283	2,904
Machinery, except electrical	382	79	52	61	3,481	1,813
Machinery, electric	383	84	37	167	7,626	2,786
Transport equipment	384	86	67	81	2,317	1,552
Professional and scientific equipment	385	73	30	225	6,696	2,041
Manufacturing	**300**	**87**	**41**	**331**	**4,377**	**1,781**

Source: Based on UNIDO, Industrial Database, various years.

Definitions: Y = gross output, V = value added, K = fixed capital, L = employment, W = total wage bill.
Indexes of Efficiency: Share of Purchased [(Y-V)/Y], Unit Labor Cost (W/V), Productivity of Capital (V/K), Productivity of Labor (V/L), Capital Intensity (K/L), Average Wage (W/L).

industries of textiles, wood products, and transport equipment. Interestingly, food, beverages, and tobacco are rather capital intensive even though they account for over a third of output and employment. One giveaway is the high positive correlation among capital intensity, labor productivity, and the average wage in light industries. This correlation does not exist, or it is reversed for the resource-intensive and tech-intensive sectors.

Labor-based industrializers **239**

TABLE 9.17 Kenya: competitive industrial performance, 1990–2012

Year	MVA per capita	M Exports per capita	MHM in MVA	MHX in MX	MVA in GDP	M Exports in exports	Industrialization intensity index
	$	$	%	%	%	%	
1990	64	22	19	28	12	51	0.21
1991	64	21	19	8	12	44	0.22
1992	63	29	19	6	12	55	0.23
1993	62	24	18	10	12	46	0.24
1994	61	27	19	16	12	44	0.31
1995	62	31	18	17	12	47	0.29
1996	63	32	13	16	12	46	0.26
1997	61	32	18	14	12	47	0.29
1998	58	29	18	16	11	44	0.28
1999	55	22	23	16	11	41	0.31
2000	54	19	23	15	11	37	0.31
2001	53	16	25	19	10	34	0.31
2002	52	26	26	14	10	60	0.31
2003	53	38	28	16	11	50	0.32
2004	54	22	29	18	11	38	0.33
2005	55	56	26	15	11	58	0.30
2006	57	50	25	18	11	53	0.29
2007	59	56	24	21	10	52	0.29
2008	60	60	24	18	11	50	0.29
2009	59	56	26	26	11	50	0.32
2010	60	62	26	25	10	49	0.31
2011	61	62	26	25	10	49	0.31
2012	61	62	7	25	10	49	0.18

Sources and notes: UNIDO, Competitive Industrial Performance (CIP) database, 2014.
MHM = medium- and high-technology manufacturing production
MHX = medium- and high-technology manufacturing exports
MX = manufacturing exports
MVA = manufacturing (M) value added

Inefficiencies in the ability to allocate resources from low-productivity to high-productivity firms are also evident from the weak relationship between firm size and productivity (World Bank, 2014b). In Kenya, contrary to the African norm, firms with fewer employees appear to be more productive than firms with more employees. Despite some variance across sectors, large differences in productivity are prevalent across subsectors.

Kenyan manufacturing firms are constrained by inadequate access to capital for their long-term investments, infrastructure to import inputs and to export and distribute finished products, affordable and reliable electricity, relevantly skilled labor to man their operations, and fair and streamlined regulations that would compel

240 Africa's postcolonial experience

them to compete. In 2013, firms in Kenya reported that the obstacles that most constrained them were unreliable electricity, inadequate access to finance, difficulties in trading across borders, competition from the informal sector, and crime, theft.

Despite the significant challenges, Kenya does offer many attractions for domestic industrial investors and FDI. First, there is a large workforce with rapidly rising levels of educational attainment. Second, English is the main business language (along with Swahili as a regional language) which facilitates business relations internationally. Third, Kenya's geographical location is such that it serves a major hub for the export of goods from Ethiopia, Rwanda, South Sudan, Uganda, and Eastern Congo (UNIDO, 2013). Kenya also has a relatively market-friendly business environment in which small businesses are very dynamic, due in no small part to strong financial inclusion and good access to credit (AEO-KEN, 2015).

The disappointing industrial competitiveness and employment record of Kenya since the 1980s is attributable to three things (see Table 9.3): informal enterprises undercutting formal ones, rampant corruption in the registered sector, and the unreliability of power supply. Inefficiency and corruption, by raising transaction costs so onerously, erode Kenya's comparative advantage in financial services, tourism, and port services. Corruption remains the top concern of the business community along with poor basic public services precisely because it is so pervasive. In 2010, for example, the Ministry of Finance surmised that corruption costs over $4 billion per year in lost revenue.

The overall picture is that Kenya has made some inroads toward building a manufacturing base and exports. However, it has yet to record a viable trajectory of industrial sophistication with robust growth (World Bank, 2014b).

Senegal (SEN)

Senegal, with a population of some 15 million, had an economy of $15 billion in 2014. With a GNI in PPP terms of $2,300, its poverty and social indicators are at about the average for Africa.

Senegal's rather low HDI score of 0.47 reflects its low mean years of schooling (2.5), high Gini index (40.3%), and yet a respectable life expectancy of 66.5 years. Some 78% of its people subsist on less than $3.10 per day (see Tables 7.1 and 7.2).

Senegal managed to attain an average GDP growth rate of 5% per annum since 1995. This record brought a modest reversal of the decade-and-half-long secular decline in per capita income since 1980 (see Figures 9.1 and 9.2). The growth drivers were non-agricultural and non-manufacturing activities. The validity of the picture painted by the available statistics is uncertain. For one, the informal sector accounts for a whopping 60% of GDP and 80% of employment (Mbaye, 2012).

Much like its African peers, Senegal has had a lackluster performance in industrial development. During 1970–2010, the share of agricultural output in GDP declined by 11 percentage points to 18%. The share of agricultural employment fell even faster to 51% of the national labor force. More disturbingly, as shown in Table 9.18, labor productivity at the one-digit industry level fell significantly across the board (except for utilities).

TABLE 9.18 Senegal: changes in sectoral economic structure, 1970–2010

	1970	1980	1990	2000	2010	Diff: 2010–1970
Employment structure:	%	%	%	%	%	%
Agriculture	73.3	70.3	65.8	58.2	51.4	−21.8
Mining	0.2	0.1	0.1	0.1	0.2	0.0
Manufacturing	5.6	5.4	5.8	8.0	9.9	4.3
Utilities	0.3	0.5	0.7	0.2	0.0	−0.3
Construction	1.3	1.5	1.6	2.8	3.8	2.5
Trade and hotels	7.3	9.2	13.5	18.3	21.1	13.8
Transport-storage-comm.	1.8	1.7	2.1	2.0	3.4	1.6
Finance and business srvcs.	0.2	0.2	0.2	0.4	0.5	0.3
Government services	5.0	5.8	5.1	4.8	5.2	0.2
Community services	5.0	5.2	5.0	5.1	4.4	−0.5
Total employment[a]	1,001	1,612	2,602	3,229	4,342	3,341
Output structure:	%	%	%	%	%	%
Agriculture	29.0	22.7	20.9	20.9	17.7	−11.3
Mining	1.6	1.6	1.5	1.4	1.3	−0.3
Manufacturing	14.6	15.1	16.6	16.5	14.6	−0.1
Utilities	2.0	2.1	2.1	2.3	2.7	0.8
Construction	1.5	2.2	2.8	4.3	5.2	3.7
Trade and hotels	22.8	21.8	23.0	23.2	20.1	−2.7
Transport-storage-comm.	8.0	7.2	7.9	7.9	15.0	7.0
Finance and business srvcs.	2.0	5.5	6.3	7.1	8.2	6.2
Government services	16.3	19.4	16.6	13.9	13.1	−3.3
Community services	2.2	2.4	2.3	2.4	2.2	0.0
Gross value added[b]	1,469,563	1,770,299	2,246,515	3,050,261	4,589,566	3,120,003
Productivity structure[c]:	$	$	$	$	$	Ratio: 2010/1970
Agriculture	580	355	275	338	363	0.63
Mining	11,522	13,863	16,679	10,440	6,077	0.53
Manufacturing	3,812	3,061	2,458	1,957	1,557	0.41
Utilities	8,482	4,690	2,593	11,768	67,471	7.95
Construction	1,738	1,607	1,487	1,466	1,457	0.84
Trade and hotels	4,603	2,599	1,467	1,193	1,011	0.22
Transport-storage-comm.	6,492	4,549	3,187	3,730	4,622	0.71
Finance and business srvcs.	15,165	28,949	23,092	18,219	16,991	1.12
Government services	4,770	3,685	2,846	2,723	2,668	0.56
Community services	638	505	399	445	516	0.81
Economy-wide	1,468	1,099	863	945	1,057	0.72

Sources and notes: Calculations are based on the 2014 version of the GGDC 10-sector database: www.rug. nl/research/ggdc/data/10-sector-database which is documented in M.P. Timmer, G.J. de Vries, and K. de Vries, "Patterns of Structural Change in Developing Countries," *GGDC Research Memorandum 149*, Groningen Growth and Development Centre, 2014.

a Economy-wide persons engaged, in thousands.

b Gross value added in millions of 2005 international dollars.

c Gross value added per person engaged in 2005 international dollars.

242 Africa's postcolonial experience

While it is true that MVA rose by a factor of 15 during 1980–2010, manufacturing employment did not grow correspondingly (see Tables 9.5 and 9.6). Senegal's formal industrial sector mustered just 4,350 manufacturing jobs by 2010. About half of MVA is accounted for by the informal sector (Cisse et al., 2016: Table 7.2).

The country's gross capital formation rose slightly and stood at a respectable 24% of GDP in 2014 as did its overall industrial output. Manufacturing accounted for over a third of industrial output, with food and beverages claiming a third of MVA and 90% of exports. Although, as shown in Table 9.19, food and beverages grew rapidly during 1965–2004, the technology-intensive branches of metal products and machinery fell. This suggests little or no industrial deepening taking place.

TABLE 9.19 Senegal: growth performance of three-digit manufacturing industries, 1965–2004

Industry	Index of production (1995=100)					
	ISIC3	1965	1975	1985	1995	2004
Food products	311	78	86	99	100	132
Beverages	313	29	72	99	100	132
Tobacco	314	90	160	153	100	103
Textiles	321	70	135	194	100	57
Wearing apparel, except footwear	322	251	326	194	100	57
Leather products	323	. .	. .	. .	100	. .
Footwear, except rubber or plastic	324	. .	. .	. .	100	. .
Wood products, except furniture	331	95	105	124	100	112
Furniture, except metal	332	95	105	124	100	112
Paper and products	341	75	96	136	100	116
Printing and publishing	342	73	95	136	100	116
Other manufactured products	390	. .	. .	. .	100	. .
Petroleum refineries	353	0	0	83	100	117
Misc. petroleum and coal	354	0	0	83	100	117
Rubber products	355	0	0	83	100	117
Plastic products	356	. .	. .	. .	100	. .
Pottery, china, earthenware	361	. .	. .	. .	100	. .
Glass and products	362	. .	. .	. .	100	. .
Other non-metallic mineral	369	30	57	62	100	305
Iron and steel	371	. .	. .	. .	100	. .
Non-ferrous metals	372	. .	. .	. .	100	. .
Industrial chemicals	351	49	111	83	100	117
Other chemicals	352	0	0	83	100	117
Fabricated metal products	381	44	61	92	100	70
Machinery, except electrical	382	. .	. .	44	100	91
Machinery, electric	383	. .	. .	. .	100	91
Transport equipment	384	. .	. .	90	100	85
Professional and scientific equipment	385	. .	. .	. .	100	. .

Source: Based on UNIDO Indstat database, various years.

Labor-based industrializers **243**

Senegal's global competitive index is the average of its peer group (Table 9.4). Its CPIA scores are, however, above-average across all three dimensions – economic management, public-sector management, and structural policies (Table 9.4).

When we look at several indirect measures of manufacturing efficiency for 1970–2009 (Table 9.20), several interesting patterns emerge. Based on the share of

TABLE 9.20 Senegal: efficiency of three-digit manufacturing industries, 1970–2009

Three-digit manufacturing industry	ISIC	(Y-V)/Y	W/V	K/L	V/L	W/L
	Code	%	%	$	$	$
Food products	311	79	37	3,061	8,791	3,278
Beverages	313	74	28	7,479	14,014	3,905
Tobacco	314	74	26	2,964	25,400	6,668
Textiles	321	75	60	2,967	5,677	3,383
Wearing apparel, except footwear	322	70	59	752	4,399	2,597
Leather products	323	69	76	1,945	4,475	3,423
Footwear, except rubber or plastic	324	69	54	. .	5,355	2,888
Wood products, except furniture	331	77	58	1,876	4,054	2,333
Furniture, except metal	332	80	45	77	5,197	2,330
Paper and products	341	78	28	1,874	14,182	4,011
Printing and publishing	342	68	37	1,571	11,993	4,386
Other manufactured products	390	67	33	4,739	17,776	5,814
Petroleum refineries	353	93	26	616	21,800	5,595
Misc. petroleum and coal products	354	92	26	2,534	22,187	5,862
Rubber products	355	86	40	110	5,349	2,165
Plastic products	356	80	23	2,970	9,960	2,300
Pottery, china, earthenware	361	. .	. .	. .	. .	. .
Glass and products	362	86	58	. .	18,939	11,067
Other non-metallic mineral products	369	69	10	3,685	53,030	5,197
Iron and steel	371	. .	. .	. .	. .	. .
Non-ferrous metals	372	84	34	. .	9,330	3,216
Fabricated metal products	381	73	50	3,200	7,181	3,600
Industrial chemicals	351	80	28	8,575	20,362	5,767
Other chemicals	352	78	22	3,078	20,596	4,549
Machinery, except electrical	382	74	60	491	5,740	3,438
Machinery, electric	383	82	36	2,917	11,588	4,209
Transport equipment	384	56	77	836	6,931	5,310
Professional and scientific equipment	385	72	17	. .	12,770	2,108
Manufacturing	**300**	**79**	**34**	**4,405**	**10,948**	**3,732**

Source: Based on UNIDO, Industrial Database, various years.

Definitions: Y = gross output, V = value added, K = fixed capital, L = employment, W = total wage bill. *Indexes of Efficiency:* Share of Purchased [(Y-V)/Y], Unit Labor Cost (W/V), Productivity of Capital (V/K), Productivity of Labor (V/L), Capital Intensity (K/L), Average Wage (W/L).

244 Africa's postcolonial experience

purchased inputs as an index of the intensity of intersectoral linkages, it is evident that almost all branches of manufacturing rely on domestically sourced or imported intermediates at levels that exceed two-thirds of the values of their net output.

Using the ratio of wages to value-added as a measure of unit labor cost per dollar of net output, we find that wages and benefits constituted a third of the total cost of manufacturing. Labor-intensive industries, some resource-intensive branches (textiles, apparel, wood products, glass, and fabricated metals) and skill- and tech-intensive branches (non-electrical machinery and transport equipment), all report wage bills more than half of value added. The latter is, along with capital-intensive branches (such as tobacco, petroleum refinery, and glass products), among the highest paying sectors. In summary, Senegal has yet to complete the first phase of import substitution industrialization.

Tanzania (TZA)

Tanzania, with a population of some 52 million in 2014, had an economy of $48 billion at current market prices. Its GNI per capita stood at $2,500 in PPP terms.

Tanzania's HDI stood at 0.51 in 2014, reflecting its mixed bag of economic and social indicators. The mean years of schooling was 5 (Tables 7.1 and 7.2).

Life expectancy was a respectable 65 years, and its Ujaama-socialist legacy has yielded a low Gini index of 37.6%. Using an international poverty line of $3.10 per day, its poverty rate of 78% vies with Nigeria for the worst performance in the sample.

After a prolonged stagnation, real per capita income started to rise after the mid-1990s. By 2014, GNI per capita has nearly tripled over its 1990 level while gross capital formation rose from 26% to a high of 31% of national output during 1990–2014. GDP started to grow at a rate of over 5% per annum only after 1996 (Figures 9.1 and 9.2).

The structure of Tanzania's economy suggests that manufacturing is still in its infancy. Agriculture accounts for 72% of GDP but only for 30% of employment. Agriculture was understandably the only sector with significant gains in labor productivity during 1970–2010 while the rest of the economy appears to have deteriorated (see Table 9.21). Manufacturing contributed just 3% of national employment and 9% of economy-wide value added in 2014.

During 1960–1980, the Tanzanian government pursued an import substitution strategy to kick-start industrialization. The combination of an internally regimented quasi-socialist economy, donor pressure, and recurrent external shocks elicited structural adjustment in the subsequent 15 years. The import-dependent and inefficient infant industries shrank as a result while the overall economy recovered. Though facing stiff competition from newly industrialized countries, macroeconomic stability and regulatory reform brought about industrial recovery after 2000 (Msami and Wangwe, 2016).

Manufacturing value added remains highly concentrated (Sutton and Olomi, 2012). Food and beverages alone account for nearly half of total manufacturing

TABLE 9.21 Tanzania: changes in sectoral economic structure, 1970–2010

	1970	1980	1990	2000	2010	Diff: 2010–1970
Employment structure:	%	%	%	%	%	%
Agriculture	91.4	87.4	86.1	83.5	71.7	−19.7
Mining	0.1	0.6	0.4	0.5	0.8	0.7
Manufacturing	1.7	1.6	1.4	1.7	3.2	1.5
Utilities	0.1	0.1	0.1	0.2	0.5	0.4
Construction	0.6	0.7	0.8	0.8	1.4	0.8
Trade and hotels	1.9	4.4	5.4	6.8	9.8	7.8
Transport-storage-comm.	0.9	0.8	0.8	0.8	1.9	1.0
Finance and business srvcs.	0.1	0.2	0.2	0.2	0.7	0.5
Government services	2.0	2.7	3.3	3.5	8.2	6.3
Community services	1.2	1.6	1.5	2.0	1.9	0.7
Total employment[a]	5,816	8,028	10,723	13,516	19,413	13,597
Output structure:	%	%	%	%	%	%
Agriculture	36.0	31.3	36.4	38.4	29.9	−6.1
Mining	1.5	0.9	0.6	2.3	3.3	1.9
Manufacturing	11.5	11.6	7.8	8.9	10.2	−1.3
Utilities	1.2	2.3	2.3	2.6	2.5	1.3
Construction	9.9	8.2	11.0	7.6	10.4	0.5
Trade and hotels	19.4	15.3	15.0	16.0	17.0	−2.4
Transport-storage-comm.	8.4	9.1	7.0	7.1	8.5	0.1
Finance and business srvcs.	3.4	4.5	5.5	4.6	4.7	1.3
Government services	8.3	16.0	13.6	11.6	12.8	4.5
Community services	0.5	1.0	0.9	1.0	0.7	0.0
Gross value added[b]	3,936,895	5,545,159	7,129,847	9,636,316	18,808,033	14,871,139
Productivity structure[c]:	$	$	$	$	$	Ratio: 2010/1970
Agriculture	266,807	247,656	280,897	327,523	403,846	1.51
Mining	10,213	960	945	3,200	4,089	0.40
Manufacturing	4,533	5,104	3,793	3,797	3,046	0.67
Utilities	9,754	6,031	4,823	6,696	7,112	0.73
Construction	10,855	8,430	9,632	6,633	7,316	0.67
Trade and hotels	6,735	2,412	1,839	1,690	1,687	0.25
Transport-storage-comm.	6,408	7,702	5,753	6,579	4,296	0.67
Finance and business srvcs.	16,688	14,390	14,727	16,308	6,874	0.41
Government services	2,864	4,123	2,708	2,358	1,508	0.53
Community services	2,696	1,447	1,157	659	496	0.18
Economy-wide	676,954	690,701	664,920	712,967	968,833	1.43

Sources and notes: Calculations are based on the 2014 version of the GGDC 10-sector database: www.rug.nl/research/ggdc/data/10-sector-database which is documented in M.P. Timmer, G.J. de Vries, and K. de Vries, "Patterns of Structural Change in Developing Countries," *GGDC Research Memorandum 149*, Groningen Growth and Development Centre, 2014.
a Economy-wide persons engaged, in thousands.
b Gross value added in millions of 2005 international dollars.
c Gross value added per person engaged in 2005 international dollars.

246 Africa's postcolonial experience

value added. Four other labor- and resource-intensive branches (tobacco, textiles, non-metallic products, and furniture) account for another third of output. Although manufacturing employment rose 2.5 times during 1970–2010 to 127,000, more than half of the manufacturing labor force was employed in apparel, wood products, and food processing (Tables 9.5 and 9.6).

Industrial activity is also spatially concentrated in the primate port city of Dar-es-Salaam. Accounting for 91% of all manufacturing establishments, private-owned companies dominate the manufacturing sector. Tanzania lacks a critical mass of firms in a variety of industrial activities for manufacturing to be an innovative and job creating engine of the economy (UNIDO and GOT, 2012).

A combination of inward orientation, inadequate investment, and insufficient skill supply has frustrated industrial deepening in Tanzania despite signs of improvement after 2007 (see Table 9.22). The quality of institutions and policies

TABLE 9.22 Tanzania: competitive industrial performance, 1990–2012

Year	MVA per capita	M Exports per capita	MHM in MVA	MHX in MX	MVA in GDP	M Exports in exports	Industrialization intensity index
1990	23	3	18	9	8	17	0.15
1991	22	3	24	9	8	17	0.18
1992	21	3	11	9	7	17	0.12
1993	20	3	13	9	7	17	0.14
1994	20	3	12	9	7	17	0.17
1995	19	3	12	9	7	17	0.17
1996	20	3	12	9	7	17	0.17
1997	20	3	12	9	7	17	0.17
1998	21	5	12	30	8	26	0.17
1999	22	4	12	31	8	22	0.17
2000	22	4	9	7	8	20	0.17
2001	23	5	9	6	8	21	0.16
2002	24	6	8	4	8	23	0.15
2003	25	6	8	7	8	18	0.15
2004	27	7	5	8	8	21	0.12
2005	29	7	4	10	8	19	0.12
2006	31	11	4	11	8	26	0.12
2007	32	16	4	13	8	34	0.12
2008	34	31	3	23	8	42	0.12
2009	36	27	3	20	9	39	0.13
2010	38	42	3	14	9	49	0.13
2011	40	43	3	17	9	42	0.14
2012	42	43	3	23	9	37	0.10

Sources and notes: UNIDO, Competitive Industrial Performance (CIP) database, 2014.
MHM = medium- and high-technology manufacturing production
MHX = medium- and high-technology manufacturing exports
MX = manufacturing exports
MVA = manufacturing (M) value added

is respectable – especially in economic management. However, firms continue to complain about the inadequate availability of finance (a 240% collateral being one indicator), an unreliable supply of electricity, and high tax rates as the top three constraints.

Tunisia (TUN)

Tunisia, a densely populated coastal country of some 11 million, had a GDP of $49 billion in 2014. Its GNI per capita stood at a respectable $11,000 in PPP terms.

Tunisia had the second highest HDI of 0.72. This reflects its impressive life expectancy of 75 years, middling mean years of schooling of 6.8 years, and low inequality (Gini coefficient of 36.1%). Its poverty rate is also a low 13% at $3.10 per day.

Tunisia has a culturally homogenous population. Development is, however, bifurcated between the coastal and the hinterland regions.

Its strong state has long been committed to high-minded regulation but also to high public investment in human and physical capital. Tunisia's development performance has been impressive, thanks to robust growth, openness to foreign trade, and high investment in its offshore sector. The peculiar semi-liberal *infitah* policy of openness produced respectable outcomes in job creation, health, education, poverty reduction, and gender equality (OECD, 2015; Ayadi and Mattoussi, 2016).

As shown in Figures 9.1 and 9.2, Tunisia's real per capita income started its remarkable climb around 1970 with a significant acceleration after 1990. The GDP growth performance after 1990 was, however, too lackluster (roughly 4% per annum) to sustain the acceleration. The rather low 1% rate of growth of the population also boosted the real income per head.

During the 1970s and 1980s, this state-led onshore-offshore dual-economy model was successful at producing a structural transformation of the economy. As a result, Tunisia experienced rapid increases in exports as well as in industrial diversification. Public investment and **state-owned enterprises** (SOEs) built up the foundations of economic transformation of the country (World Bank, 2014b).

Despite the much-heralded success of the Tunisian model of economic development, several fundamental problems set the stage for the January 2011 revolution. Although Tunisia's real GDP per capita growth since the 1990s was respectable, it has remained far below the growth rates observed in other upper-middle-income countries over the same period. Furthermore, Tunisia has been plagued by persistently high unemployment. The rate of job creation was simply insufficient, and the quality of the jobs created remained too low to meet the aspirations of the increasingly large number of university graduates (World Bank, 2014b). Corruption at the highest political level did not help, either.

The economic structure of semi-arid Tunisia is such that agriculture accounts for just 8% of GDP while industry and services claim 29% (half of which comprised manufacturing) and 62%, respectively. Its gross capital formation declined from a healthy 27% of GDP in 1990 to 22% in 2014 (see Tables 9.1 and 9.2).

248 Africa's postcolonial experience

Much like other African economies, Tunisia's industrialization drive started with import substitution. Since the early 1970s, the authorities pursued an industrial policy aimed at boosting the competitiveness of exports beginning with low value-added activities such as textiles. Tax incentives attracted mostly subsidy-seeking foreign firms in the export-oriented offshore sector which accounted for 60% of exports. The result, as shown in Table 9.23, is a broad-based MVA growth during 1965–2004.

Tunisia has also taken advantage of its well-functioning transport, logistics, finance, and other business services to integrate well into global value chains. This

TABLE 9.23 Tunisia: growth performance of three-digit manufacturing industries, 1965–2004

Industry	ISIC3	Index of production (1995=100)				
		1965	1975	1985	1995	2004
Food products	311	47	47	72	100	155
Beverages	313	47	47	72	100	155
Tobacco	314	52	52	80	100	187
Textiles	321	27	44	62	100	141
Wearing apparel, except footwear	322	5	7	59	100	122
Leather products	323	54	76	56	100	179
Footwear, except rubber or plastic	324	29	26	32	100	179
Wood products, except furniture	331	47	45	87	100	176
Furniture, except metal	332	18	26	82	100	117
Paper and products	341	31	49	80	100	99
Printing and publishing	342	29	47	76	100	157
Other manufactured products	390	. .	. .	. .	100	117
Petroleum refineries	353	25	54	84	100	94
Misc. petroleum and coal	354	. .	. .	. .	100	. .
Rubber products	355	6	16	46	100	185
Plastic products	356	8	20	57	124	
Pottery, china, earthenware	361	20	34	69	100	143
Glass and products	362	12	20	45	100	143
Other non-metallic mineral	369	18	27	73	100	143
Iron and steel	371	. .	63	93	100	65
Non-ferrous metals	372	35	63	93	100	65
Fabricated metal products	381	11	59	104	100	107
Industrial chemicals	351	11	21	49	100	133
Other chemicals	352	12	21	49	100	133
Machinery, except electrical	382	52	148	135	100	167
Machinery, electric	383	9	23	59	100	233
Transport equipment	384	16	56	213	100	198
Professional and scientific equipment	385	. .	. .	. .	100	160

Source. Based on UNIDO Indstat database, various years.

Labor-based industrializers **249**

TABLE 9.24 Tunisia: competitive industrial performance, 1990–2012

Year	MVA per capita	M Exports per capita	MHM in MVA	MHX in MX	MVA in GDP	M Exports in exports	Industrialization intensity index
	$	$	%	%	%	%	
1990	314	329	9	24	16	77	0.24
1991	320	361	11	21	16	82	0.26
1992	334	386	11	21	16	81	0.26
1993	345	367	12	21	16	84	0.28
1994	369	451	13	19	17	87	0.34
1995	379	539	17	20	17	88	0.37
1996	385	528	17	21	16	87	0.36
1997	409	538	18	21	17	89	0.37
1998	428	558	19	23	17	90	0.38
1999	453	552	20	23	17	89	0.39
2000	475	528	20	25	17	85	0.39
2001	502	607	20	27	18	88	0.39
2002	506	624	21	27	18	87	0.39
2003	507	736	10	28	17	89	0.3
2004	507	866	10	30	16	88	0.28
2005	510	901	10	31	16	85	0.28
2006	521	1,002	9	32	15	86	0.27
2007	553	1,188	26	34	15	79	0.37
2008	565	1,544	19	39	15	82	0.33
2009	540	1,179	18	40	14	85	0.32
2010	596	1,294	20	45	16	83	0.34
2011	597	1,381	22	46	16	82	0.37
2012	616	1,337	22	45	16	84	0.35

Sources and notes: UNIDO, Competitive Industrial Performance (CIP) database, 2014.
MHM = medium- and high-technology manufacturing production
MHX = medium- and high-technology manufacturing exports
MX = manufacturing exports
MVA = manufacturing (M) value added

was especially the case with textile products, leather, and footwear; food, beverages, and tobacco; and electrical and optical equipment (OECD, 2015).

CPIA data are not available for Tunisia, but the World Bank's enterprise surveys (reported in Table 9.3) show that the country's business climate is quite good. Tunisian firms nonetheless complain about political uncertainty, unfair competition from the informal sector, and high collaterals (over 250% of the loan amount).

Tunisia is competitive in labor-intensive exports, mainly to the nearby European and Middle Eastern markets. It switched in a timely manner to export promotion. Manufactures eventually accounted for an impressive 86% of exports in 2014 (Nabli, 2012).

250 Africa's postcolonial experience

While the growth rates of skill-intensive and tech-intensive sectors are comparable to those of traditional branches of manufacturing, industrial deepening has yet to be achieved commensurate with the per capita income of the country (see Table 9.24). Tunisia's public-led industrialization still suffers from inadequate technological upgrading. Despite its impressive achievements so far, Tunisia does not yet have high-value-added industrial activities that one would expect from its level of human capital and infrastructure.

Notes

1 Agriculture, which employed half of the labor force in 1970, lost just over half of its employment share during the period. Currently, the formal industrial sector employs around 2.4 million workers, with an estimated 1.5 million in informal establishments.
2 Africa received some 58% or $46 billion of Chinese global official development assistance (ODA) during 2000–2014. Some 80% of Chinese official financial flows come in the form of non-concessionary loans concentrated in the energy and transport sectors. The biggest African recipients of Chinese development aid and loans-for-resources (in 2009 U.S. dollars) are Angola with $16.6 billion, Ethiopia with $14.8 billion, and Sudan with $10.6 billion. The two biggest Chinese-financed infrastructure projects in Ethiopia are the $3.3 billion Addis-Djibouti railway initiated in 2013 and completed in 2017, and the $2.4 billion Sebeta-Adama railway project approved in 2011 (Dreher et al., 2017).
3 Euler Hermes, for example, notes the following: "The ruling Ethiopia People's Revolutionary Democratic Front is dominated by the minority Tigrayan ethnic group (6% of the population). The Amhara (30% of the population), and even more so the historically oppressed Oromo (32% of population), feel excluded from the political process. Recent protests highlighted the government's inability to control dissent: demonstrators were killed, foreign investments were targeted. Critics dismissed [a] recent cabinet reshuffle, which brought in technocrats and members of the Oromo. Calls for broader inclusiveness will continue to affect the political stability and economic growth prospects." See: www.eulerhermes.com/economic-research/country-reports/Pages/Ethiopia.aspx.

References

Abegaz, B. (1994). A Late-industrialization Perspective on Ethiopian Manufacturing. In: B. Abegaz, ed., *Essays on Ethiopian Economic Development*. Aldershot: Ashgate, Avebury Press, pp. 159–224.

Abegaz, B. B. (2013). Political Parties in Business: Rent-seekers, Developmentalists, or Both? *Journal of Development Studies*, 49(11), pp. 1467–1483.

Africa Economic Outlook (AEO-EGY). (2015). *Egypt 2015*. Abidjan: AfDB, OECD, UNDP.

Africa Economic Outlook (AEO-ETH). (2015). *Ethiopia 2015*. Abidjan: AfDB, OECD, UNDP.

Africa Economic Outlook (AEO-KEN). (2015). *Kenya 2015*. Abidjan: AfDB, OECD, UNDP.

Ayadi, M., and W. Mattoussi. (2016). Disentangling the Pattern of Geographic Concentration in Tunisian Manufacturing Industries. *Learning to Compete Working Paper No 15*. Washington, DC: Brookings Institution.

Bent, P. (2015). *Agrarian Change and Industrialization in Egypt, 1800–1950*. [pdf].

Cisse, F., J. Choi, and M. Maurel. (2016). Industrial Policy in Senegal: Then and Now. In: C. Newman, et al., eds., *Manufacturing Transformation: Comparative Studies of Industrial Development in Africa and Emerging Asia*. Oxford: Oxford University Press, pp. 136–154.

de Vries, G., M. Timmer, and K. de Vries. (2013). *Structural Transformation in Africa: Static Gains, Dynamic Losses.* GGDC Research Memorandum 136. Groningen, Netherlands: Groningen Growth and Development Centre, University of Groningen.

Diwan, I., P. Keefer, and M. Schiffbauer. (July 2015). Pyramid Capitalism: Political Connections, Regulation, and Firm Productivity in Egypt. *World Bank Policy Research Working Paper 7354.* Washington, DC: World Bank.

Dreher, A., A. Fuchs, B. Parks, A. Strange, and M. Tierney. (2017). Aid, China, and Growth: Evidence from a New Global Development Finance Dataset. *Aid Data Working Paper 46,* Williamsburg: College of William and Mary, October.

Gebreyesus, M. (2016). Industrial Policy and Development in Ethiopia. In: C. Newman, et al., eds., *Manufacturing Transformation: Comparative Studies of Industrial Development in Africa and Emerging Asia.* Oxford: Oxford University Press, pp. 27–49.

Handoussa, H. (2012). Egypt: The Changing Role of the State. In: E. Aryeetey, et al., *The Oxford Companion of the Economics of Africa.* Oxford: Oxford University Press.

Handoussa, H., M. Nishimizu, and J. Page. (1986). Productivity Change in Egyptian Public-Sector Industries After 'The Opening,' 1973–197. *Journal of Development Economics,* 20, pp. 53–73.

Issawi, C. (1980). De-Industrialization and Re-Industrialization in the Middle East Since 1800. *International Journal of Middle East Studies,* 12(4), pp. 469–479.

Kirigai, J. (2012). Kenya: A Structural Transformation Paradox and Challenges for the Current Decade. In: E. Aryeetey, et al., eds., *The Oxford Companion of the Economics of Africa.* Oxford: Oxford University Press.

Mabro, R., and S. Radwan. (1976). *The Industrialization of Egypt, 1939–1973: Policy and Performance.* Oxford: Clarendon Press.

Mbaye, A. (2012). Senegal: After Devaluation, Improving Signals. In: E. Aryeetey, et al., eds., *The Oxford Companion of the Economics of Africa.* Oxford: Oxford University Press.

Msami, J., and S. Wangwe. (2016). Industrial Development in Tanzania. In: C. Newman, et al., eds., *Manufacturing Transformation: Comparative Studies of Industrial Development in Africa and Emerging Asia.* Oxford: Oxford University Press, pp. 155–173.

Nabli, M. (2012). Tunisia: Top Performance in Africa and the Middle East (But Less than Stellar Globally). In: E. Aryeetey, et al., eds., *The Oxford Companion of the Economics of Africa.* Oxford: Oxford University Press.

N'gui, D., J. Chege, and P. Kimuyu. (2016). Kenya's Industrial Development: Policies, Performance, and Prospects. In: C. Newman, et al., eds., *Manufacturing Transformation: Comparative Studies of Industrial Development in Africa and Emerging Asia.* Oxford: Oxford University Press, pp. 72–91.

Oqubay, A. (2015). *Made in Africa: Industrial Policy in Ethiopia.* Oxford: Oxford University Press.

Organization for Economic Cooperation and Development (OECD). (2015). *Tunisia: A Reform Agenda to Support Competitiveness and Inclusive Growth.* Paris: OECD.

Owen, R., and S. Pamuk. (1998). *A History of Middle East Economies in the Twentieth Century.* New York: I.B. Tauris.

Panza, L., and J. Williamson. (2013). Did Muhammad Ali Foster Industrialization in Early 19th Century Egypt? *CEPR Discussion Paper No. DP9363.* Washington, DC: Center for Economic and Policy Research.

Söderbom, M., and F. Teal. (2000). Skills, Investment, and Exports From Manufacturing Firms in Africa. *Journal of Development Studies,* 37, pp. 13–43.

Söderbom, M., and F. Teal. (2003). Are Manufacturing Exports the Key to Economic Success in Africa? *Journal of African Economies,* 12(1), pp. 1–29.

Sutton, J., and D. Olomi. (2012). *An Enterprise Map of Tanzania.* London: International Growth Center.

United Nations Industrial Development Organization (UNIDO). (2013). *Industrial Development Report 2013. Sustaining Employment Growth: The Role of Manufacturing and Structural Change*. Oxford: Oxford University Press.

United Nations Industrial Development Organization (UNIDO) and the Government of Tanzania (UNIDO and GOT). (2012). *Tanzania Industrial Competitiveness Report 2012*. Geneva: UNIDO.

U.S. Energy Information Administration (USEIA). (2015). *Egypt: International Energy Data and Analysis*. Washington, DC: USEIA.

Wignaraja, G. (2003). Competitiveness, Productivity Management and Job Creation in African Enterprises: Evidence From Mauritius and Kenya. *MCC Working Paper No. 5*. Geneva: ILO.

World Bank. (1983). *Egypt: A Program for the Development of Manufactured Exports*, vol. 1–3. Washington, DC: World Bank.

World Bank. (2007). *Ethiopia: Accelerating Equitable Growth*, part I, report no. 38662. Washington, DC: World Bank.

World Bank. (2010). *Industrial Clusters and Micro and Small Enterprises in Africa: From Survival to Growth*. Washington, DC: World Bank.

World Bank. (2014a). *Kenya Economic Update: Anchoring High Growth*. Washington, DC: World Bank.

World Bank. (2014b). *The Unfinished Revolution Bringing Opportunity, Good Jobs and Greater Wealth to All Tunisians*. Washington, DC: World Bank.

World Bank. (2015a). *Country Partnership Framework for the Arab Republic of Egypt for the Period, FY 2015–2019*, report no. 94554-EG. Washington, DC: World Bank.

World Bank. (2015b). *Egypt: Promoting Poverty Reduction and Shared Prosperity, a Systematic Country Diagnostic*, report no. 9972. Washington, DC: World Bank.

PART V
Rethinking industrial strategy

10

NEW INDUSTRIAL POLICY FOR AFRICA

This chapter explores the conditions under which an activist **industrial policy** (IP) might improve market outcomes in an industrializing African economy. A central argument of this chapter is that the fundamental question is not so much whether to engage in IP or whether IP has costs; it is instead about how to design and implement appropriate IP with better net social payoffs in an enabling institutional-policy space that is inclusive, adaptive, and accountable.

We provide here a thoroughgoing critical synthesis of the contentious literature on soft and hard IP in the hope of teasing out the relevant lessons for reimagining an African industrial policy in the age of neo-globalization. We will also survey long-term industrial development plans from selected African countries and review the politics of industrial policymaking in Africa to see if they are attuned to current thinking about smart industrial policy.

The debates on industrial strategy and policy

Industrial Policy may be usefully defined as *government activism that is intended to intensify or to modify the trajectory of an otherwise market-directed industrial development.* As an integral part of a country's overall development strategy,[1] IP may focus on interventions that selectively favor some industries, firms, products, or tasks over others to encourage specialization or diversification. It may focus on positive incentives for assimilating new ideas to enhance technological or managerial capability or negative incentives to discourage misallocation of scarce resources. More generally, it may introduce generic or sector-wide smart regulations and judicious openness to foster the discipline, and the emulation can maximize the benefits of deep global engagement.

256 Rethinking industrial strategy

These considerations raise several questions about policymaking. Are there novel and customizable policies that will help Africa traverse deep-veined pathways as well as telescope the catchup process under current country circumstances and the prevailing phase of globalization? How demanding are such policies in terms of government capability and discipline?

A useful framework that distils postwar development thinking regarding the elements of a successful growth strategy is provided in Figure 10.1. Distilled mainly from the East Asian experience (much of which is replicable), it underscores the importance of three sets of interdependent growth pillars that must be synchronized (World Bank, 1993: Figure 2.1): economic fundamentals (macro stability, competition, and good-enough governance), strategic policies (safety nets and industrial), and growth drivers (allocational efficiency and technological diffusion synchronized with adequate demand for late entrants) in order to generate the desired economic outcomes (growth rates, and poverty and inequality levels).

Economic fundamentals are, therefore, necessary but not sufficient. Selective interventions, if done in the right sequence and with appropriate design and full implementation, can accelerate growth and make it as widely shared as possible. The role of a responsible government is crucial in several respects, including ensuring macro stability through fiscal discipline, a competitive environment, livelihoods

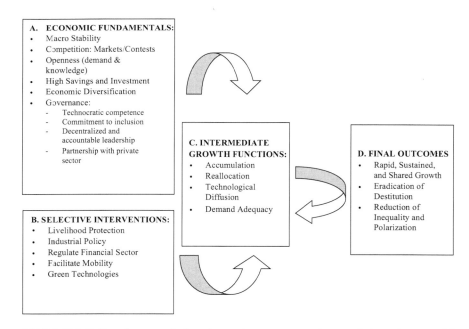

FIGURE 10.1 Policy framework based on the common characteristics of successful developers

Sources and notes: Adapted from World Bank (1993: Figure 2.1).
I added "Demand Adequacy" and elaborated on the governance dimension.

protection, prudential supervision and regulation of financial markets, and provision of key public services. The combination of good economic fundamentals, selective interventions, and bureaucratic effectiveness lead to high investment rates, enhanced allocational efficiency, gains in productivity, and adequate demand.

The boundaries between a market-based selection mechanism and non-market forms of economic organization are always shifting, and markets themselves are embedded in non-market governance institutions. Where the political settlement is stable, governments can learn to formulate and implement industrial policies that can facilitate entry into high value-adding activities by overcoming the disadvantages of late coming.

Where all these considerations come to a head is in the justly famous "infant industry argument" which emerged out of early debates on catchup industrialization by the likes of Hamilton, List, Mill, and Bastable. It addresses the puzzling fact that nearly every late industrializer (from Germany and the U.S.A. to Japan and Brazil) protected their fledgling industries. The simple answer, of course, is that judicious protection gives latecomers a fighting chance to mature and compete successfully against well-established first-movers.

Policy design must then take several considerations into account, including the initial level of industrial development, the endowment structure, and the political alignment of powerful elites who might support an integrationist or a nationalist mode of industrialization. IP must, therefore, be both a process and a product of collective deliberation.

Objectives and instruments of IP

The goals of IP might include boosting domestic production and income, exports, technological diffusion, shared and productivity-driven growth, generating employment, moderating inequality, and environmental sustainability. A good IP relaxes bottlenecks to stimulate private investment, domestic as well as foreign, through better infrastructure, risk-sharing schemes for projects with high spillovers, and state support for the skilling of the labor force and rapid technological diffusion to domestic firms. For this to be effective, state and corporate governance structures must embed accountability for results; and a pragmatic mindset must prevail to improve upon the market process where state action is clearly warranted, and to pilot novel initiatives with appropriate metrics for evaluation and policy learning (Lall, 2004; Levy, 2014; Lin and Monga, 2011).

Cimoli et al. (2009) identify five notable features common to good industrial policies. They are:

1 emulation of frontier technologies with high demand elasticity and great scope for learning to help reduce absolute disadvantage (technological gaps), which is what matters for income;
2 accentuation of the complementarity between purposeful technological learning and production capacity building via learning by doing;

3   countering unnecessarily restrictive WTO rules which force premature exposure to international competition before the requisite domestic capability is in place;
4   reliance on both carrots and sticks to balance support for infant industries with reciprocal obligations; and
5   avoidance of the natural resource curse by opting for resource-based industrialization, sovereign funds, venture funds, and the like.

A good IP then is less about picking winners or producing national champions than about nurturing high-potential infant industries or young firms and ensuring a robust competitive discipline as a filter. It is about identifying and cultivating rich linkages, which is why closing key infrastructure gaps or relaxing multi-purpose skills bottlenecks is so important. IP catalyzes knowledge spillovers and overcomes coordination failures rather than coddles beneficiaries. It avoids white elephants, does not rely on past success or the wrong models, and minimizes avoidable distributional conflicts. It is well-targeted, engages foreign and domestic stakeholders, and prioritizes dynamic learning to catalyze growth throughout the economy (Taglioni and Winkler, 2016).

The instruments for policy activism include macroeconomic and exchange rate policies, technology policies, and trade and foreign investment policies that target workforce education and training. Forms of selective policy activism in support of infant industries and fledgling firms include incubation-motivated state enterprises, selective credit allocation, favorable tax treatment, quotas, tariffs, production subsidies, various forms of export-import taxes and subsidies, and the provision of the right mix of physical and social overhead, reciprocity-guided FDI, limiting entry to ensure adequate market size for growing domestic firms, and avoiding coordination failures among fledgling local firms when it comes to the diffusion of new industrial technologies and managerial know-how. These policies are often labeled either vertical or horizontal.

Vertical IP refers to a narrowly targeted policy aimed at promoting a specific branch with high potentials for productivity gain, or even at picking individual firms within a branch. The focus here is on enhancing the key drivers of the vertical scope of productive capabilities and governance capabilities. Vertical IP, however, faces three sets of problems: cognitive limitations in picking winners when the technological or economic environment is fast moving, limited capability on the part of policymakers in poor countries to make optimal long-term choices in a world of uncertainty, and the ever-present risk of capture by entrenched legacy interests (Pack, 1988, 2000; Little et al., 1970).

Horizontal IP, on the other hand, provides generic or industry-wide support that is designed to enhance market connectivity, skill formation, and private investment. It may serve as a facilitator of self-discovery by focusing on the incubation of entrepreneurship and the nurturing of a business ecosystem with dense positive externalities. The litmus test here is that, in the absence of intervention, specialization in low-productivity activities is likely to take longer than it should.[2]

New industrial policy for Africa **259**

Another important dimension of IP, especially of great concern for a developing economy, is the gap between planning and implementation. The potential gulf between the need for IP and the prospects for its effective implementation can be wide. It turns out that the countries with the greatest need for IP (such as those in South Asia and Sub-Saharan Africa) also have the lowest technocratic capacity or a lack of political will.

To ensure implementation, effective mechanisms must be in place, including deliberation councils, supplier development forums, investment advisory councils, sectoral roundtables, private-public venture funds, and collaborations designed to elicit information about investment opportunities and critical bottlenecks. In other words, policy space must complement market space with ample room for bureaucratic actors and private industrialists to agree on socially beneficial policies to ensure society-wide "ownership" of IP.

Being low income, African economies lack well-established modern private and public institutions to implement first-best policies which can pass the **Mill-Bastable Test.** That is, infant industries must be protected but only temporarily on the condition that the net social benefits are measurably positive. More broadly, since the lack of deep financial markets and skill pools limits market-based options, governments should encourage pragmatic and cost-effective searches to identify and rectify weak markets and to supply key missing public inputs (Hausmann et al., 2007).

If a well-designed IP can bring significant improvements in the selection mechanisms of an underdeveloped market, the inevitable question is how to do industrial policy right. It is also clear that the "how" question also turns on the twin pillars of policy design and implementational capacity. We now turn to a review of the debate on practical IP.

Competing perspectives on IP

Economists like to engage in acrimonious theoretical debates on whether the optimal form and pace of industrialization are a product of *market-revealed comparative advantage* or *policy-driven infant industry* support. Lately, a third perspective has emerged that melds key elements of the two – *productive capabilities.*

IP skeptics who favor a market-directed approach implicitly assume that demand often creates its own supply. If there were profits to be made, existing firms or new entrants would eventually take advantage of these latent opportunities. All that is needed is the removal of obstacles to firm entry and exit.

Policy activists, on the other hand, operate under the presumption of pervasive market failure and tend to assume that supply can sometimes create its own demand. The market is presumed to fail to induce an optimal incubation of firms in poor economies. Proponents of the infant-industry argument highlight the role of the time- and resource-costs of mastering new technologies by laggards. To shift to a productivity-driven growth, they underscore the indispensability of judicious support for the most promising infant industries.

260 Rethinking industrial strategy

The productive-capabilities argument, the one we favor, seeks instead to identify the Goldilocks conditions by taking the long-term view that endowments can be altered and policies can go wrong. Switching from market-driven and endowment-dependent industrial development to a productivity-driven one requires credible government partnership with the private sector to build up high-risk and learning-intensive capabilities. The right mindset then is one that objectively assesses constraints (costs) and opportunities (benefits) to formulate implementable strategies tailored to each industry and stage of development.

Where and how government should intervene fundamentally depends not only on a good grasp of the nature of the context-specific capabilities and endowments but also on the prevailing international environment. As noted above, rapid and profound technological change, the globalization of production systems, and the emergence of formidable Asian competitors have created a radically new context for the industrialization of Africa.

We are now ready to take a closer look at the two competing perspectives regarding the design of IP in the hope of drawing instructive lessons. The first *conforms* to existing (often derided as static) comparative advantage (CA) while the latter *defies* existing comparative advantage to nurture a superior one.

CA-conforming IP: Market-fundamentalist thinking on the effectiveness of IP has focused on cautionary tales of how the cure (policy intervention) is often worse than the disease (Pack, 2000). This warning is important since no one benefits from an IP that can easily degenerate into a contest for rent creation and rent dissipation.

Justin Lin (2012) argues, in this vein, that structural differences among countries are largely endowment driven and that there is a better way to recognize non-linearity in development. This viewpoint pays attention to the efficiency of transition from the distorted world of mismanaged economies to an open and competitive one. It purports to offer a gradualist, pragmatic exit by opting for a phase-out of protection for pampered "infants that did not grow up."

In this view, the global market is the best disciplining mechanism for effective resource allocation, which may from time to time be usefully supplemented by Pareto-improving policy measures. This market-plus version also accepts the proposition that a country's revealed comparative advantage should be construed dynamically, that is, latent comparative advantage must be discovered by looking at extant factor endowments, emulation capabilities, and the characteristics of industries that can realistically be mastered with extra effort (Lin and Monga, 2011; Reinert, 2009).

It is hard to resist the temptation to come up with a recipe, even if it risks "looking backward" at successful developers under meaningfully different global circumstances (COGD, 2008; Lin, 2012). One such recipe, a market-driven but government-assisted "growth identification and facilitation," has been proposed by Lin and Monga (2011). It is a distillation of the lessons of experiences from East Asian industrialization.

Its advice for ambitious latecomers (and African industrializers) involves six inter-related, if not sequential, steps:

First, the government of an industrializing country must identify industries that have been successfully established for about 20 years in a middle-income comparator country. The model country must have a comparable endowment structure and a per capita income that is about 100% higher than the imitator's own.

Second, among the industries in that list (such as apparel and footwear), the government may give priority to those in which domestic private firms have already entered because of their market discovery efforts. The government should then remove the most binding obstacles that are preventing these firms from upgrading the quality of their products or from scaling up justifiably. Parenthetically, the growth diagnostic framework proposed by Hausmann et al. (2008) fits here quite well.[3]

Third, some of these industries in the list may be completely new to domestic firms. In such cases, the government should adopt specific measures to encourage FDI inflows directed at these industries. The government may also set up incubation programs to catalyze the entry of domestic private firms into these sunrise industries.

Fourth, in addition to the industries identified in step 1, developing-country governments should pay close attention to successful self-discoveries by domestic manufacturers.

Fifth, a reform-minded government must invest in industrial parks and export processing zones with the aim of encouraging industrial clustering. Policies about clusters, if well designed, can be important conduits for technological diffusion and ease of entry into export markets.

Sixth, the government may also provide limited incentives for domestic pioneer firms or foreign investors that are willing to work on the list of high-priority industries identified in step 1. It makes good sense to grant pioneers time-limited tax incentives, co-financing of investment, and preferential access to foreign exchange to internalize the positive externalities.

What this recipe adds up to is a risk-averse and prudently incrementalist industrial policy in which the state spots winners and supports them rather than tries to create them de novo. The Lin (2012, 2013) version of the new-structuralist economic perspective also takes for granted that this kind of IP works where the state already possesses an efficient and politically insulated bureaucracy which can discipline the fledgling industrial class.

CA-defying IP: The CA-defying perspective takes seriously the notion that the market does not maximize technological learning,[4] especially in a poor developing economy. Market failures matter more for new activities than for existing activities because of externalities, complementarities, high fixed costs of entry in an economy with shallow financial markets, and informational failures. The historical pattern of protect first and then disprotect reflects this reality (Chang, 2002).

Hausmann and Rodrik (2003) as well as Greenwald and Stiglitz (2006) notably underscore that the process of discovery (of new markets, new products, or new processes) is rarely automatic, and a weak private sector and shallow markets are

262 Rethinking industrial strategy

ill-suited for supplying it on their own (UNECA, 2016). This means, as noted by Hausmann, Rodrik, and Sabel (2007: 542), that

> globalization is by itself no recipe for some sort of natural catchup in technological capabilities and for easy convergence in incomes. On the contrary, more interdependent economies are likely to require *more and more sophisticated* measures of policy intervention by the weakest countries.

Furthermore, the heightened significance of thresholds of capabilities accentuates economies of scope over economies of scale that were the primary concern of high development economics. The implication for industrial policy then is that IP should shift its traditional focus less on complementarities to exploit economies of scale than to expanding economies of scope (Hausmann and Hidalgo, 2011).

The process of technological diffusion requires congruence between national technological capability and market opportunity. As Lall (1997: 129) aptly puts it,

> the process of becoming efficient in industry is slow, risky, costly and often prolonged, and faces a range of market failures that may call for interventions in both factor and product markets. In product markets, it may call for infant-industry protection. In factor markets, it may call for interventions to direct resources to particularly selected activities, selective as well as functional interventions in skill creation, the promotion of local technological activity rather than a passive dependence on imported technologies, and the setting up of a variety of supporting institutions.[5]

CA-defying IP focuses on those externalities associated with learning by doing.[6] Industrial policies that are appropriately designed to maximize **learning, industrial, and technology (LIT)** entail creating and allocating "rents," socializing the risks of private investment, embracing reciprocal control mechanisms with credible sunset clauses, privileging measures that transform rather than restrain ambition, and focusing on externalities and knowledge spillovers (Noman and Stiglitz, 2012). Wade (2012) notes in this vein that, since there is no policy package that fits all sizes, some IPs inevitably require government leadership of the market while others require government followership of the market.

Spectacular stories of successful IP from the developing world include South Korea's POSCO, possibly the world's most productive steel firm, and Dubai's Jebel Ali port, one of the world's largest and most successful ports – both established by public money and widely derided as uneconomic at the outset. In the 1970s, Korea had neither the skill nor the raw material for developing a world-class shipbuilding industry but decided to follow this path (Amsden, 1989; Wade, 1990). Today, South Korea is one of the three largest shipbuilding nations. Vietnam replicated this strategy quite successfully (UNECA, 2016).

Other well-known examples include the Chilean salmon industry – the creation of a public venture fund (Fundación Chile) – which stands in sharp contrast to the free-market brush with which Chile's economic success is so frequently painted. If pressed further, proponents of IP add to the list Brazil's aircraft industry, Taiwan's and Singapore's electronics industries, China's auto and auto components industries, and South Korea's chaebol-originated multinationals such as Luck Gold Star, Hyundai, and Samsung (Stiglitz et al., 2009; Amsden, 2001; UNECA, 2016).

A schematic view nicely illustrates the modalities of initiating and sustaining an industrialization drive by limiting non-Schumpeterian rents and facilitating the optimal allocation of economic rents and profits to productive investment (Noman, 2013). The progressive relaxation of the constraints on industrial development in a typical African country naturally begins with the initial level of investment (I) and founding entrepreneurship (E, C). It ends with a mature capitalist class (C'), the causal chain involving a two-phased transition (T):

$$E[E1, E2, I] \rightarrow T1 \rightarrow C(E1, C1, C2) \rightarrow T2 \rightarrow C'(E0, C2)$$

where:
E = state-linked actors
E0 = state regulator (separation of state office from officeholder)
E1 = state-centered entrepreneurs (rent-creating state enterprises, party enterprises, and military enterprises)
E2 = political entrepreneurs (rent-seeking enterprises in the politically connected private sector)
C1 = politically linked but profit-seeking private businesses
C2 = bona fide private businesses
C = immature capitalist class (mostly in commerce and services)
C' = mature capitalist class (industrialist or financier)
I = initial investible surplus (state as well as private)
T1 = first-stage transition
T2 = second-stage transition

The reasoning for the dynamics runs as follows. A combination of public and private investment and entrepreneurship kick-starts the industrialization process. As the existing potential gets exhausted and the comparative capabilities of the state and the private actors change markedly, new phases of opportunities and conflicts inevitably emerge. Industrial development progressively becomes private-owned and market-led.

A good IP can then be re-conceptualized as one that would ensure efficient inter-stage transitions (T1, T2). These transitions, though poorly understood, are fraught with traps − political traps as well as growth traps. As the World Bank's World Development Report (2017: 9–10) aptly puts it:

> With few exceptions, policy advice for these countries has focused on the proximate causes of transition, such as the efficiency of resource allocation or industrial upgrading. The real problem, however, may be rooted in the

264 Rethinking industrial strategy

distribution especially of political power. Powerful actors who gained during an earlier or current growth phase (such as the factor-intensive growth phase) may resist the switch to another growth model (such as one based on firm entry, competition, and innovation in a process of "creative destruction").

Realistically speaking, the transition for Africa is bedeviled by the capture of the state (thereby making the IP space non-contestable) by maximalist elites with weak incentives to offer meaningful bargains with "outsider elites." Sensible African IP may uncomfortably have to rely on self-restraint by benevolent developmentalist-authoritarian regimes and forward-looking industrial entrepreneurs who must coordinate to protect their enlightened self-interests by going against the grain of short-termism, patrimonialism, and clientelism.

Having examined the objectives, instruments, and modalities of IP, we are now ready to apply these ideas to the specific African circumstances. We will first look at the industrial plans and strategies of a selected number of countries, and then distil the lessons for African IP that is ideally centered on building domestic capability.

Recent African industrial development plans

In the context of development planning, national ownership of IP matters. Most African countries have industrial development plans that encapsulate their strategic visions and long-term commitments. The typical African country contemplating an ambitious industrialization drive badly needs money to invest in basic capacity building (infrastructure, social overhead, sharpened linkages with agriculture, trade facilitation, and the like), and to provide technical and long-term financing support for broad-based light manufacturing in the private sector.

The initial investment can, of course, come from the mobilization of state revenues and the savings of the commercial class and natural-resource owners, provided licit and illicit capital outflows can be stemmed. The cumulative value of illicit outflows from Africa since 1970, for example, exceeds $2 trillion (Kar and Cartwright-Smith, 2015). FDI, some 80% of which flows to just ten developing countries that have already achieved threshold levels of industrial development, is beginning to discover opportunities in Africa in the manufacturing, commercial agriculture, and business-services sectors.

Africa also needs commercializable ideas and globally minded entrepreneurs to identify and exploit latent production and trade opportunities at home and abroad (Noman, 2013). Industrial entrepreneurship can certainly come from the state-enterprise sector as well as from the non-industrial business class which is generally averse to entering manufacturing given the highly demanding financial, technical, and managerial capabilities. Joining GVCs even at the lowest, labor-intensive, rungs also requires some manufacturing experience.

Half of the African countries have formulated industrial plans (AfDB et al., 2017) with two complementary visions about the modality of industrialization: continent-wide and country-specific. Regional and international development organizations have been providing guidance and inspiration by formulating roadmaps for economic transformation through industrial development (UNIDO, 2015; UNIDO and UNCTAD, 2011). African continental institutions responded to the Washington Consensus earlier than most critics are willing to concede by offering alternatives of their own (Mebratu, 2000; UNECA, 2015). The most notable example is the Africa-centered development strategy put forward by the Organization of African Unity (OAU) in the form of the prescient Lagos Plan of Action (LPA) which covered the period 1980–2000. LPA advocated moving away from a self-limiting reliance on primary exports by building domestic and regional industrial capability under the motto of a self-sustained and self-reliant African industrialization drive.

The other continent-wide initiative is the new economic policy for African development (NEPAD) by the successor to the OAU – the African Union. These moves are in parallel with initiatives by UNIDO to cheerlead for an industrial Africa by annually celebrating an African Industrialization Day.

The Plan of Action for the Accelerated Industrial Development of Africa (AIDA), developed by the AU, ECA, AfDB, and NEPAD, also harps on the mutually constitutive nature of industrialization and structural transformation (Lopes, 2015). AIDA is based on three pillars: investing resource rents on infrastructure, promoting R & D and technological diffusion, and promoting private sector development – especially recognizing the critical role of small and medium scale enterprises.

We now profile the most recent industrial plans of five countries: Egypt, Ethiopia, Ghana, South Africa, and Tanzania. The time horizon and the main objectives of the industrial development plans are summarized in Table 10.1. While they show

TABLE 10.1 African industrial development plans, 1990–2030

Industrial plan country	Plan	Major targets
Egypt (2012)	Industrial Development Strategy, 2015–2025 www.tralac.org/ files/2012/12/Egypt-National-Industrial-Development-Strategy_EN.pdf	• Achieving higher growth in industrial production through aggressive export development and FDI attraction • Effecting a leapfrog in industrial productivity • Achieving a gradual shift from resource-based and low-tech activities to medium- and high-tech industries
Ethiopia (2015)	Growth and Transformation Plan II (2015–2020) www.africaintelligence.com/c/dc/LOI/1415/GTP-II.pdf	• Reach the economy's productive possibility frontier in agriculture and urban-based manufacturing • Enhance the transformation of the domestic private sector • Build the capacity of the domestic construction industry to close critical infrastructure gaps • Accelerate human development and technological capacity building

(*Continued*)

266 Rethinking industrial strategy

TABLE 10.1 (Continued)

Industrial plan country	Plan	Major targets
Ghana (2016)	Ghana's Industrial Policy, 2016–2020 https://s3.amazonaws.com/ndpc-static/CACHES/PUBLICATIONS/2016/04/16/Ghana+Industrial+Policy.pdf	• Expand productive employment in the manufacturing sector • Expand technological capacity in the manufacturing sector • Promote agro-based industrial development • Promote spatial location of industries to reduce poverty and inequality
South Africa (2014)	A National Industrial Policy Framework (NIPF)(Vision 2030) www.thedti.gov.za/industrial_development/docs/niPF-3aug.pdf	• Linkage with mining • SOE-private manufacturing interface • Manufacturing exports • Making growth inclusive • Develop key capabilities
Tanzania (2011)	Integrated Industrial Development Strategy 2025 www.tzdpg.or.tz/fileadmin/_migrated/content_uploads/IIDS_Main_Report.pdf	• Develop industrial clusters and the requisite infrastructure • Extend and improve the development corridors toward an industrial and logistics hub of East and Central Africa • Promote rural industrialization through an "Agricultural Development Led Industrialization" strategy with a target of MVA/GDP at 23%. • Provide growth opportunities for all growth-oriented SMEs and entrepreneurs
Pan-African: AU (2063) SADC (2063) EAC (2032)	• Action Plan for the Accelerated Industrial Development of Africa (2007); Agenda 2063 • SADC Industrial Development Policy Framework (2013) • East African Community Industrialization Strategy (2012)	• Export diversification • Infrastructure development • Human capital formation • Regional linkages • Support for SMEs • Self-sufficiency • Diversification for value creation

Source: Author.

recognition of the onset of GVCs, the focus is still on developing domestic supply chains for whole products and exportables.

Egypt's IDS

From the standpoint of Egyptian postwar industrial policy, Loewe (2013) identifies the following three distinctive periods: Nasser's statist experiments (1952–1970),

Sadat's open-door policies (1970–1981), and Mubarak's hesitant adjustment and privatization (1981–2004). Despite the treadmill of reforms, however, many features of the Egyptian industrial environment endure. Industrialization is at the center of economic policy with emphasis on selective and centrally directed IP. Public industrial enterprises are given a prominent role, especially before 1989. Domestic private capitalists are exceptionally risk-averse, preferring to invest in commercial and real estate investments rather than in much riskier long-term industrial or agro-industrial activities.

Egypt recently has launched an ambitious Industrial Development Strategy (IDS) covering the period 2015–2025. It is anchored in three pillars: (1) achieving higher growth in industrial production through aggressive export promotion and FDI attraction, (2) boosting industrial productivity through a carefully designed set of policies and programs aimed at leveraging industrial competitiveness, and (3) achieving a gradual shift in the industrial structure from resource-based and low-tech activities to medium- and high-tech activities.

At the beginning of the plan period, the industrial sector was reasonably diversified; it enjoyed an abundant supply of cheap labor; it had access to a relatively well-developed infrastructure; and it benefitted from low energy and utility costs. Egypt also enjoyed sizeable FDI inflows from the Gulf States and preferential access to the European market. On the other hand, the country faced several weaknesses and threats, including low productivity, a high resource- and labor-intensity of exports, inadequate supply of specialized skills, low quality-standards, an unfavorable business climate for SMEs, and stiff competition from China and India.

The ambition embedded in IDS is to turn the industrial sector into an engine of growth and job creation. At its launch date, manufacturing accounted for some 20% of formal-sector GDP. There were 26,000 formally registered establishments employing nearly 2.4 million workers. Also, manufactured exports accounted for 3% of GDP, 40% of non-oil export proceeds, and 11% of total current account receipts.

The first building block of Egypt's latest industrial plan is intended to boost industrial capabilities in six critical areas: human resources and entrepreneurship, the national innovation system, the national quality system, financing needs, infrastructure, and enterprises-based competitiveness programs. The second block strengthens integration with global markets and value chains. The third block enhances the resiliency of industrialization by making it inclusive and environmentally sustainable.

Technology-transfer centers will also be expanded, and the share of public-sector investment will decline significantly (from its current one-third share) with increases in domestic private investment and FDI. The latter will be especially tied to several new industrial parks and smaller industrial clusters.

An indicator of the centrality of industrial parks is the new Damietta Echo Industrial Park and a Russian-financed project along the Suez Canal. New industrial complexes are also expected to follow, including a newly announced plastic industry complex in the Sorghum district in Alexandria. Investors are also considering a

268 Rethinking industrial strategy

new Textile City in Upper Egypt where yarn, fabrics, dyeing, and finishing can be fully integrated. In the chemicals sector, the Petrochemicals Holding Company is planning 24 projects to transform Egypt into a regional petrochemical hub. A new industrial zone in Rubik, commonly called "leather city," offers new investment opportunities using its proximity to tanned leather facilities for targeting export markets. All these projects are designed to enhance the technological content of Egypt's manufactured exports as well as well-paying employment.

The newly expanded Suez Canal, at the cost of $8.2 billion, will be followed by plans to create new special economic zones. The new industrial zones will stretch 460 km, covering six ports and 1,000 factories. Because of the zones' development, there will be 18 industrial projects with a combined value of $40 billion to investors. The plans are expected to be executed over three to five years and envisage the Suez Canal corridor as the new industrial engine of the country (Oxford, 2016).

The government has also rolled out a broad strategy focused on small and medium-size enterprise (SME) development, value-adding industries, and improved financing channels. These include improved alignment between the skills of young graduates and the demands of the industrial workplace. The IDS has set an annual growth target of 9% for manufacturing, increasing its share of GDP above 25% by 2025. If fully implemented, the manufacturing sector is expected to create at least 1 million jobs by the end of the plan period.

One binding constraint has been the shortage of power, a challenge common to many emerging markets. The country's peak demand was 27,700 MW in 2014, 20% above the capacity of the national grid. Although the industrial sector accounts for no more than 30% of power use, the difficulties across the energy sector have had a sizeable negative impact on a range of industries. Relaxing this constraint is, therefore, one of the goals of IDS.

Ethiopia's GTP 2 and IDS

Ethiopia's post-1990 long-term development strategy, dubbed Agricultural Development-Led Industrialization (ADLI), seeks to integrate the demand side and the supply side of industrial development (E-MEDAC, 1993). It is better described as a politically expedient rural poverty reduction program than a full-fledged plan.

Ethiopia has also formulated a more focused Industrial Development Strategy (IDS) since 2002. The uptick of manufacturing development since 2005 reflects the centrality of industrial development in the government's five-year growth and transformation plans.

In the past few years, IP has been folded into five-year plans known as growth and transformation plans (GTPs). The strategic pillars of GTP 1 (2011–2015) included sustaining rapid and equitable economic growth, maintaining agriculture as a major source of economic growth, creating conditions for industry to play a key role in the economy, and an ambitious program of infrastructure expansion. The most notable achievements of GTP 1 include rapid and broad-based economic growth in the 8–10% range with construction, manufacturing, and services growing at double-digit levels, and remarkable gains in physical infrastructure – especially roads, power generation, and telecommunications. The rate of investment, led by the public sector and significant external debt-financing, exceeded one-third of GDP during the five years.

GTP 1, however, fell far short of ensuring food security with some 8 million people suffering chronic food deficit. Nor did it raise the share of manufacturing in GDP to more than the paltry 5% – this despite boosting the domestic financing of investment to levels above 40% (E-NPC, 2015).

ADLI, however, failed to deliver on its lofty promises for many reasons. It ignored the fact that subsistence agriculture cannot finance its own growth, let alone the growth of an industrial sector. A grudging acknowledgment of this reality is that all three post-war Ethiopian governments resorted to large-scale state farms and large privately owned commercial farms to raise food crops and cash crops to feed the cities, the factories, and the export market. The most recent incarnation is FDI-driven mega farms and foreign-owned industrial parks (ten so far), which, though promising, have yet to deliver the expected results (Oqubay, 2015).

The strategic pillars of GTP 2 (2016–2020) include achieving a rapid, climate-resilient, and broad-based economic growth; increasing the productivity and competitiveness of the productive sectors of the economy; enhancing the capability of the domestic private sector; closing critical infrastructure gaps, especially in the urban sector; and building up the requisite human capital to undergird technological upgrading. More specifically, the share of manufacturing is over-ambitiously targeted to rise from 4.6% of GDP in 2015 to 8%. Manufacturing exports are slated to double to 26% of merchandise exports by 2020 (E-NPC, 2015).

Ethiopia's IDPs are built around selective import substitution and selective export promotion – the latter aimed at leather and products, textiles and garments, sugar, electricity, and floriculture. GTP 2 institutionalizes *kaizen* as a productivity tool, commits to promoting micro and small enterprise development, expands formal vocational education (but without a school-to-work transition program), and envisages the establishment of FDI-funded industrial zones and industrial parks (JICA, 2011; World Bank, 2015; Oqubay, 2015).

Net FDI, whose stock stood at US$6 billion in 2014, rose from an annual average inflow of $300 million in 1996–2004 to $500 million in 2005–2014 and is projected to bring $1.0–$1.5 billion annually in 2015–2019 (World Bank, 2015). Examples of FDI going to manufacturing include Ayka Addis (Turkish, shoes), George (Taiwanese, shoes), and Huajian (China, shoes and leather products). However, illicit outflows (mainly through trade mis-invoicing) have amounted to a whopping $20 billion since 1980.

In the garment and leather products industries, Ethiopian workers (with an average of 6.0 years of schooling) are about half as productive as workers in the same industries in China (with an average of 10.0 years of schooling). And yet, Ethiopian wages are a fifth to a tenth of the rapidly rising Chinese wages. This productivity-adjusted cost advantage is eroded a bit when one considers the higher costs associated with transportation, energy, trade logistics, and regulation and taxation. Furthermore, productivity performance is heterogeneous among firms, with foreign-owned, publicly owned, and older firms being more productive than young domestic private firms (Dinh, 2012; World Bank, 2015; Abebe and Schaefer, 2016).

Dinh et al. (2012) also suggest rather optimistically that Ethiopia can become globally competitive in the apparel, leather product, and agribusiness industries and compete with imports in the wood and metal products industries. They offer five good reasons: (1) very low wages combined with high trainability of workers, (2) potential access to competitive sources of key inputs, (3) access to a state-of-the-art container port in Djibouti, (4) a large and growing domestic market and proximity to large export markets, and (5) duty-free access to EU and U.S.A. markets. Ethiopia thus shares many characteristics with Vietnam, where millions of productive jobs were created in light manufacturing over the past 20 years.

Ethiopia's IP features strong country ownership which was overly dependent on a strongman in the late Meles Zenawi (JICA, 2011; Shimada, 2015). This state leadership concomitantly produced a weak private sector despite the professed commitments to accelerating managerial learning and policy learning.

According to the cadre of Japanese advisors on industrial policy, Ethiopia certainly meets many of the ingredients of a successful IP. These include a strong leadership with the personal commitment of the top leader, a central organization with full authority and responsibility to draw up and implement sensible national strategies, nationwide campaigns to sensitize and mobilize citizens to support the national industrial plan, and appropriate training for leaders, instructors, entrepreneurs, and workers. This statist model, however, was judged to lack two key elements – supporting institutions at central and local levels, and neglect of private-sector capacity building (Shimada, 2015).

Ghana's GIP

Ghana's Industrial Policy (2016–2020) is set within the context of Ghana's long-term strategic vision of achieving middle-income status by 2020. It is to be achieved through a transition into an industry-driven economy that can deliver decent jobs with equitable and sustainable growth and development. The instruments and measures in GIP are also fully aligned with Ghana's Trade Policy, thereby reinforcing each other.

Ghana enjoys a few latent advantages in manufacturing, including access to a regional market of 300 million people, and an ample supply of raw materials and labor. However, manufacturing suffers recurrent power shortages, limited access to credit, and high overhead costs. The GIP framework is aimed at creating an industrial architecture based on a value-adding processing of the country's natural resource endowments through a private sector-led industrial development strategy.

The GIP pays special attention to growth, diversification, and upgrading the competitiveness of Ghana's manufacturing sector. The key development objectives of Ghana's IP include expanding well-paying jobs in the manufacturing sector, creating a modern productive economy with high levels of value-addition, expanding technological capacity in the manufacturing sector, promoting agro-based industrial development and spatial distribution of industries to reduce poverty and income inequalities, providing consumers with fairly priced and better quality products, and making industrial firms competitive in both the domestic and international markets.

Overall, the GIP represents the set of specific policy instruments and measures to be applied to improving access to competitive factors of production within the economy and enhancing productivity and efficiency for Ghana's industrial sector, especially the manufacturing subsector. The full spectrum of industrial policy initiatives cuts across four thematic policy areas, namely, production and distribution, technology and innovation, incentives and regulatory regime, and cross-cutting issues.

Ackah et al. (2016) note that the vital issues that must inform Ghana's IP are empowering the private sector, supporting for agro-based industries, and ensuring optimal spatial distribution of industrial activity. Implementation of plans, however, remains a big challenge.

South Africa's NIPF

One of the top manufacturing powerhouses in the continent, South Africa has a strong tradition of industrial planning. Furthermore, it has a reputation for aggressively pursuing a dual strategy of mineral exports and import substitution. The past few decades have however posed a serious challenge to the manufacturing industry, with both external and domestic factors weighing heavily on the sector's growth prospects.

Dubbed "Vision 2030," the National Industrial Policy Framework (NIPF) has four core objectives. The first is diversification beyond the current reliance on traditional commodities and non-readable services into higher value-added tradables. The second is long-term intensification and technological upgrading. The third is promotion of a job-rich and linkage-rich industrial development. And the fourth is achieving an inclusionary and balanced industrial development.

The intermediate goals of the NIPF include strong linkages between manufacturing and mining as well as between state enterprises and private enterprises. The plan also puts a high premium on developing key capabilities to boost manufacturing exports.

South Africa does have a significant domestic market for industrial goods. NIPF, therefore, puts forth such supportive policies as a stable macroeconomic and regulatory environment, appropriate skills development to reverse the damaging neglect of the Black and Colored education in the decades of Apartheid, and the provision of sufficient, reliable, and competitively priced modern infrastructure.

The policy framework also identifies low hanging fruits, namely, primarily relatively low-skill and exportable or import-competitive industries. They also include nontraditional tradable goods and services in the manufacturing and modern services sectors. Finally, the industrial policymaking process also values close

272 Rethinking industrial strategy

coordination across a range of government departments as well as regularized consultations with important private stakeholders.

Tanzania's IIDS

Tanzania's main industrial policy initiatives and development strategies include the Tanzania Development Vision (TDV) which aims to make Tanzania a "self-sustaining and semi-industrial economy" by 2025 (UNIDO and GOT, 2012). To fast-track the implementation of TDV, the Tanzania Mini-Tiger Plan 2020 was introduced with the goal of replicating the experiences of the Asian Tigers.

Within this framework, the Tanzanian Government has formulated an Integrated Industrial Development Strategy (IIDS), 2011–2025, to enable the realization of the objectives and targets stipulated in the TDV 2025. One objective of IIDS 2025 is to build an internationally competitive business environment through industrial accumulation, to strengthen the institutional framework, bringing about concentrated infrastructure development, and promoting competitive industries and enterprises.

Another objective is to make Tanzania the industrial and logistics hub of the Eastern and Central African region through the extension and improvement of existing development corridors and the establishment of an export and import platform at the waterfront of Dar-es-Salaam. Another objective is to promote rural industrialization through an agricultural development-led industrialization strategy.

One important policy instrument is the incubation of promising industrial firms through cluster development. Three waterfront SEZs are planned. The first is for Dar-es-Salaam, which is linked to the Central Railway Line to constitute the "Logistics Corridor." The second, the Mtwara SEZ, is being developed as the "Minerals Corridor." The third, the Tanga corridor, is intended to serve the areas of northern and north-western Tanzania up to and including Uganda, Rwanda, and the Great Lakes. TAZARA is intended to constitute the pillar of an "Agricultural Corridor."

The broader context for Tanzania's industrial development strategy (which targets chemicals, iron and steel, agro-processing, and textiles) is nicely encased in a long-term or a perspective plan covering the same period (UNIDO and GOT, 2012). As is often the case with its African peers, consistent and efficient implementation of such ambitious industrial policies remains a big challenge for Tanzanian industrial planning (Msami and Wangwe, 2016).

Toward a capability-focused African IP

An over-arching conceptual framework is provided in Figure 10.2 for making sense of the peculiarities of an African economic transformation. It depicts the major linkages among industrial capability, economic opportunity, and economic performance that we call the capability, opportunity, and performance (COP) framework.

The COP framework presupposes three things. They are (1) the existence of a political system that can ensure a durable social order along with the accountability

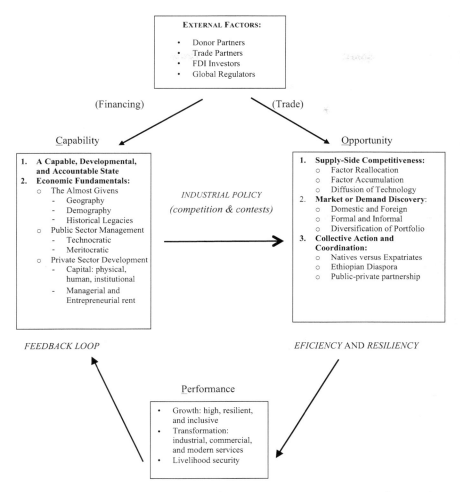

FIGURE 10.2 A capability-opportunity-performance (COP) perspective on African industrial development

Source: Author.

of state and business elites to ordinary citizens, (2) the existence of state capability to provide basic infrastructure, an appropriate regulatory framework, and social services, and (3) a private sector that can efficiently aggregate and advance its interests in the policy space.

Capability without opportunity is likely to be wasted, and opportunity cannot be exploited in the absence of domestic capability. Sufficiency is provided by exploiting market opportunities at home and abroad through sensible industrial policies.

The preceding review of past industrial policy experiments in Sub-Saharan Africa makes evident several difficulties of design and implementation. The

274 Rethinking industrial strategy

all-too-common reference to imitating the disciplined East Asian experience becomes rather inapt (Levy, 2014; Stein, 2012; Jomo, 1997). As Soludo (2014: 15) puts it:

> The impossibility of the replication of the East Asian experience in Africa was hinged primarily on such arguments as the "softness" of the African state, its "capture" by special interests, its lack of "embeddedness," its technical and analytic deficiencies, its weak administrative capacities, and the suggestions that the countries of the continent are hemmed in by "weak states" and "weak markets."[7]

What we need to know now is how to identify the key elements of an appropriately differentiated and implementable African industrial policy by facilitating effective coalitions of major stakeholders.

Newman et al. (2016) note in this respect that African IP must, first, seek to ensure adequate provision of basic public goods (especially reliable power supply, transport cost that is in line with the global average, and adequate skills through formal education and on-the-job training), and strong enough supporting and regulatory institutions. Beyond these, openness must be cultivated (via free-trade regimes for exporters of task and components, improved trade logistics, and adequate regional infrastructures). Industrial capabilities must be boosted (via FDI, linkages with GVCs, and enhanced managerial skills). Selective clusters must be nurtured. Finally, the policy must focus on a meaningful engagement of the private sector by identifying its needs and by including its associations in the policy dialog (UNECA, 2016).

Overall, African IP should focus on the most binding constraints and deploy readily available instruments that are targeted appropriately based on a country's most pressing needs, tied to performance criteria anchored in efficient learning, and formulated and implemented by a consultative government. Let us now take a closer look at the two illustrative concerns of African IP – financing and clustering.

Long-term Financing Needs: Whether a country wishes to grow by reshuffling existing resources or by boosting sustainable productivity growth, it needs a substantial level of patient capital undergirded by various mobilizable savings – public, private, or foreign. A major constraint on Africa's industrial drive is predictably an inadequate supply of long-term finance.

Although the need for capital investment is relatively small in light manufacturing, firms still rely on retained earnings which restrain graduation into medium and large-scale levels where employment generation is the highest. Banks understandably prefer heavily collateralized short-term financing and working capital. The much-needed but riskier long-term and lumpy investment in technology, improved buildings, and land remain underfinanced. This financing gap is substantial precisely because the risks associated with operating a light manufacturing business in Africa are very high because of weak asset markets and low saving rates. When added to poor trade logistics, market segmentation, and a slow winnowing out of inefficient firms, the large variation in productivity among heterogeneous firms is quite understandable (Dinh et al., 2012; Shiferaw, 2007).

There are several potential sources of financing, some mobilizable with reasonable positive incentives (interest rates, tax rates, profits, guarantees, etc.) while others require negative incentives (manipulation of prices, confiscatory taxes, or even confiscation of private property).[8] They include tax and non-tax revenues, profit remissions of state enterprises, domestic private investment, private savings in formal institutions, exports, FDI, development aid, portfolio investment from abroad, and remittances. External financial flows in 2017 (one-third each for FDI, remittances, and ODA) accounted for one-third of some $600 billion of total public revenue mobilization in Africa (AfDB et al., 2017).

The mobilization of large financial resources presupposes the existence of a well-designed investment strategy, a development-friendly government, and a domestic financial system that is both efficient and accessible to all on a competitive basis. Table 10.2 shows that only South Africa, Mauritius, Egypt, and Tunisia have a modern financial system in terms of both accessibility and depth.

Industrial policy in Africa would arguably require more external support, technical as well as financial, than was the case in Northeast Asia in the 1960s and the

TABLE 10.2 Measures of financial depth for the case-study countries, 1980–2010

Code[b]	DD/ GDP	DD/ GDP	DD/ GDP	DD/ GDP	DCP/ GDP	DCP/ GDP	DCP/ GDP	DCP/ GDP	BC/ Bd	BC/ Bd	BC/ Bd	BC/ Bd
(%)	1980	1990	2000	2010	1980	1990	2000	2010	1980	1990	2000	2010
CIV	40	39	19	21	41	36	15	18	232	185	112	81
EGY	43	51	74	65	13	25	52	33	36	36	80	48
ETH[a]	14	20	28	25	..	14	23	18	25	10	66	66
GHA	6	6	24	24	2	5	14	15	24	54	84	64
KEN	29	24	34	46	29	33	28	34	87	77	87	75
MUS	32	48	67	106	22	33	57	88	61	59	78	94
NGA	16	12	16	42	12	9	12	25	63	64	78	85
SEN	36	29	20	29	36	26	19	26	220	163	101	83
TUN	..	60	59	64	46	55	60	69	120	134	129	122
TZA	..	6	9	23		14	4	16	9	107	33	57
ZAF	46	54	71	82	56	81	134	154	84	104	134	119
ZWE	..	17	24	..	8	23	27	..	..	60	90	..

Sources and notes: World Bank, *Global Financial Development Database (GFDD)*, November 2013.
DD = demand deposits
DCP = domestic credit to the private sector
BC = bank credit
BD = bank deposits
a The figures under 2010 for Ethiopia are actually for 2008.
b For the translation of the country codes, see Table 10.4 below.

276 Rethinking industrial strategy

1970s. This should take largely the form of co-financing public investment in social overhead. Since 1980, official development assistance has instead focused on funding *structural adjustment* rather than *structural transformation*, namely, industrialization. Most of the money was directed at social spending to alleviate poverty rather than to eradicate mass poverty by generating adequate gainful employment in a modernized agriculture, services, and industry.

Official development assistance (ODA) has been an important source of financing for social development programs and some infrastructure, but not for the productive sectors or the private sector *directly*. As can be gleaned from Table 10.3, global disbursements of ODA from all sources amounted to $3.8 trillion during 1980–2014 (in 2013 prices) or $100 billion per year. Of this amount, Africa received its fair share of 30% or $1.3 trillion – $36 billion annually. To put this in perspective, in 2013, Africa's export receipts were $308 billion, and ODA receipts were $46 billion – or about 15% of export revenues.

Global ODA commitments from all sources were slightly higher at $4.0 trillion for the 35-year period. Of this, only one-third went to economic infrastructure and the productive sectors (of which manufacturing received just 13% of the allocation for agriculture and industry). Social and humanitarian spending absorbed over 60% of ODA in 1980–2014.

The data show also that ODA disbursements rose dramatically for a decade with the introduction of structural adjustment programs beginning in 1982, fell during 1992–2002, and rose dramatically after the 2007 global financial crisis. Development aid tends to be more crisis-induced and policy-conditioned than fused with the long-term development plans of the recipients. Some African countries (Egypt, Kenya, and Tanzania) are quite adept at attracting ODA in terms of overall size and in per capita terms. Others (Mauritius, South Africa, Egypt, and Tunisia) are strong exporters of a diversified basket of goods and increasingly services (see Table 10.4).

For middle-income countries, FDI is a major source of industrial financing, and the FDI-manufacturing link has intensified with the booming of GVCs. During 2005–2014, for example, global FDI flows averaged $1.5 trillion with about 40% going to a handful of developing countries (China, Russia, Hong Kong, Brazil, Singapore, Mexico, and India). Interestingly, nine of the 20 largest investor countries were from developing market economies or post-socialist economies which points to the growing scope for South-South investment and trade.

The increasing tradability of services and the growth of global value chains in which business services play an important role have meant that, in 2012, services accounted for 63% of global FDI stock, more than twice the share of manufacturing. The primary sectors claimed less than 10% of the total. Overall, globalized production by multinationals generated a value added of approximately $7.9 trillion (UNCTAD, 2015).

FDI inflows to Africa stood at $54 billion in 2012 (compared to $124 billion for China) with services accounting for about half of the total FDI stock in the region or more than twice the share of manufacturing (21%). The FDI stock in the primary sector, on the other hand, was 31% of the total (UNIDO, 2015).

TABLE 10.3 Disbursement of ODA to Africa, 1980–2014

Year	NAF	SSA	Africa	World	NAF/ Africa (%)	Africa/ World (%)
1980	7,189	18,563	26,126	92,090	27.5	28.4
1981	6,784	19,396	26,591	89,567	25.5	29.7
1982	6,856	21,010	28,296	88,791	24.2	31.9
1983	5,390	20,556	26,445	85,173	20.4	31.0
1984	5,758	22,467	30,084	90,472	19.1	33.3
1985	7,149	25,159	33,303	89,753	21.5	37.1
1986	5,043	24,697	30,481	91,794	16.5	33.2
1987	4,922	24,408	30,124	86,642	16.3	34.8
1988	4,337	26,051	30,939	91,363	14.0	33.9
1989	4,568	27,856	33,287	89,225	13.7	37.3
1990	12,636	28,440	41,627	101,984	30.4	40.8
1991	11,381	27,355	39,468	100,812	28.8	39.2
1992	7,927	28,007	36,623	99,382	21.6	36.9
1993	5,763	26,455	32,732	92,190	17.6	35.5
1994	5,686	27,730	34,382	93,200	16.5	36.9
1995	3,919	24,279	28,928	84,314	13.5	34.3
1996	4,458	21,943	27,159	84,290	16.4	32.2
1997	4,276	21,325	26,801	80,684	16.0	33.2
1998	4,522	21,022	26,638	87,140	17.0	30.6
1999	4,047	19,187	24,166	87,015	16.7	27.8
2000	3,448	19,996	24,442	91,201	14.1	26.8
2001	3,748	23,048	27,425	95,084	13.7	28.8
2002	3,114	29,451	33,346	102,986	9.3	32.4
2003	2,965	33,182	36,884	107,324	8.0	34.4
2004	3,821	32,041	36,654	112,433	10.4	32.6
2005	3,189	38,332	42,509	143,085	7.5	29.7
2006	3,307	46,745	51,075	139,286	6.5	36.7
2007	3,564	37,007	42,150	131,001	8.5	32.2
2008	4,223	40,248	45,797	146,933	9.2	31.2
2009	3,202	44,523	50,227	147,112	6.4	34.1
2010	2,735	45,425	49,817	154,133	5.5	32.3
2011	4,007	44,958	50,924	158,523	7.9	32.1
2012	4,897	44,972	51,889	152,139	9.4	34.1
2013	8,782	45,984	56,636	167,175	15.5	33.9
2014	7,313	43,950	53,789	177,579	13.6	30.3

Sources and notes: OECD, International Development Finance, 2016.
NAF = North Africa
SSA = Sub-Saharan Africa
Disbursements of ODA from all donors in 2013$.

278 Rethinking industrial strategy

TABLE 10.4 Foreign exchange receipts from exports and official aid, 1980–2013

Country	Code	Variable	1980	1990	2000	2013	2013/ 1980
Cote d'Ivoire	CIV	EXP	..	..	..	..	..
Egypt	EGY	EXP	6,231	9,989	14,527	45,325	7.3
Ethiopia	ETH	EXP	..	..	..	..	..
Ghana	GHA	EXP	..	..	..	..	..
Kenya	KEN	EXP	1,966	3,156	3,646	6,706	3.4
Mauritius	MUS	EXP	915	2,111	3,491	4,907	5.4
Nigeria	NGA	EXP	..	23,794	28,505	60,961	2.6[a]
Senegal	SEN	EXP	987	1,455	1,927	3,029	3.1
South Africa	ZAF	EXP	31,065	35,404	58,986	78,331	2.5
Tanzania	TZA	EXP	..	602	1,747	5,544	9.2[a]
Tunisia	TUN	EXP	4,547	7,444	12,161	29,488	6.5
Zimbabwe	ZWE	EXP	1,622	2,534	3,118	2,325	1.4
Cote d'Ivoire	CIV	ODA	475	1,061	568	1,241	2.6
Egypt	EGY	ODA	3,349	9,507	2,009	5,467	1.6
Ethiopia	ETH	ODA	504	1,596	1,070	3,827	7.6
Ghana	GHA	ODA	454	884	883	1,331	2.9
Kenya	KEN	ODA	959	1,852	760	3,252	3.4
Mauritius	MUS	ODA	80	136	35	142	1.8
Nigeria	NGA	ODA	82	397	256	2,515	30.8
Senegal	SEN	ODA	609	1,268	689	973	1.6
South Africa	ZAF	ODA	..	..	779	1,261	1.6[b]
Tanzania	TZA	ODA	1,644	1,890	1,631	3,438	2.1
Tunisia	TUN	ODA	528	608	348	675	1.3
Zimbabwe	ZWE	ODA	374	544	271	803	2.1
SSA	**SSF**	**EXP**	**..**	**116,311**	**172,312**	**307,886**	**2.6[a]**
SSA	**SSF**	**ODA**	**18,413**	**28,182**	**20,513**	**46,471**	**2.5**

Sources and notes: World Bank, World Development Indicators, as updated February 2016.
ODA = net official development assistance, in millions of 2012 U.S. dollars
EXP = export revenue, in millions of 2005 U.S. dollars
SSA = total for Sub-Saharan Africa
a 2013/1990.
b 2013/2000.

FDI intensity (its share of GDP) is in the 1–2% range for most African countries (Ghana, Tanzania, and Zimbabwe being the exceptions). For some countries (notably Egypt, Nigeria, and Tunisia), remittances account for well above 4% of GDP (see Table 10.5).

The statistics are notoriously unreliable, but China alone boasts an FDI stock in Africa of well over $100 billion with annual inflows accelerating to over $15 billion

New industrial policy for Africa **279**

TABLE 10.5 Foreign exchange receipts from FDI and remittances, 1980–2013

Country	Code	Variable	1980	1990	2000	2013	2013/ 1980
			%	%	%	%	Ratio
Cote d'Ivoire	CIV	FDI/GDP	0.9	0.4	2.2	1.3	1.4
Egypt	EGY	FDI/GDP	2.4	1.7	1.2	1.5	0.6
Ethiopia	ETH	FDI/GDP	. .	. .	1.6	2.0	. .
Ghana	GHA	FDI/GDP	0.4	0.3	3.3	6.8	19.2
Kenya	KEN	FDI/GDP	1.1	0.7	0.9	0.7	0.6
Mauritius	MUS	FDI/GDP	0.1	1.5	5.8	2.2	21.0
Nigeria	NGA	FDI/GDP	−1.2	1.9	2.5	1.1	−0.9
Senegal	SEN	FDI/GDP	0.4	1.0	1.3	2.1	5.0
South Africa	ZAF	FDI/GDP	0.0	-0.1	0.7	2.2	175.8
Tanzania	TZA	FDI/GDP	. .	0.0	4.5	4.7	. .
Tunisia	TUN	FDI/GDP	2.7	0.6	3.5	2.3	0.8
Zimbabwe	ZWE	FDI/GDP	0.0	-0.1	0.3	3.0	127.8
Cote d'Ivoire	CIV	REMIT/GDP	0.3	0.4	1.1	1.2	3.9
Egypt	EGY	REMIT/GDP	11.8	9.9	2.9	6.6	0.6
Ethiopia	ETH	REMIT/GDP	. .	0.0	0.6	. .	. .
Ghana	GHA	REMIT/GDP	0.0	0.1	0.7	1.9	92.0
Kenya	KEN	REMIT/GDP	0.4	1.6	4.2	2.4	6.2
Mauritius	MUS	REMIT/GDP	. .	. .	3.9	0.0	. .
Nigeria	NGA	REMIT/GDP	0.0	0.0	3.0	4.0	117.9
Senegal	SEN	REMIT/GDP	2.2	2.5	5.0	. .	. .
South Africa	ZAF	REMIT/GDP	0.1	0.1	0.3	0.3	3.2
Tanzania	TZA	REMIT/GDP	. .	. .	0.1	0.9	. .
Tunisia	TUN	REMIT/GDP	3.6	4.5	3.7	4.9	1.3
Zimbabwe	ZWE	REMIT/GDP	0.3	0.0	. .	. .	. .
SSA	**SSF**	**FDI/GDP**	**0.1**	**0.4**	**1.9**	**2.3**	**26.4**
SSA	**SSF**	**REMIT/GDP**	**0.6**	**0.7**	**1.5**	**2.2**	**3.7**

Sources and notes: World Bank, World Development Indicators, as updated February 2016.
FDI = foreign direct investment, as % of Gross Domestic Product
REMIT = personal remittances, as % of Gross Domestic Product
SSA = total for Sub-Saharan Africa

(or $40 billion if portfolio investments are included). The forecast is that the BRICS economies are growing fast enough to overtake the world leaders by 2030 in the size of their home economies: China will surpass the U.S.A., Russia will be bigger than France, India will match Japan, and Brazil is haltingly catching up with Germany.

Africa certainly cannot offer the high technology China seeks, but it can help satisfy some of its needs for fuel, fiber, and cheap labor. Secondarily, it offers markets

280 Rethinking industrial strategy

for Chinese trinkets, electronics, and cellphones – 3 out of 4 households or over 400 million Africans already own cellphones, a penetration rate equal to that of China and India. Going from voice to data is the next challenge. In this respect, Chinese investment in infrastructure, and lately in manufacturing, is a huge differentiator from the longstanding Western and Japanese forms of arms-length economic engagement with Africa.

One domestic solution for the paucity of large long-term financing of development projects is to establish general and sector-specific development banks owned largely or wholly by the state. Such banks, if politically insulated, can mobilize sizeable funds and package loans with technical assistance. They can coordinate with regional (the African Development Bank) and international (the World Bank and the Asian International Infrastructure Bank) development banks to crowd-in private domestic as well as foreign investment. Almost every successfully industrializing economy has employed such novel and hybrid institutions (Amsden, 2001; Ferraz et al., 2015; Abebe and Schaefer, 2016).

Industrial Clusters: As we saw above, the world economy has changed structurally since the 1980s. Major developments include financial globalization in all its forms, the reintegration of the post-socialist countries, the full industrialization of China, the emergence of East Asia as a purchasing power that matches both the EU and North America, and a financial-fiscal crisis that has engulfed the entire world economy.

Rising wages in East Asia are expected to release an estimated 85 million low-paying jobs for Africa, Indo-China, and South Asia to scramble over (Dinh et al., 2012). Higher domestic income from resource exports at home and a rising middle class in Asia have expanded markets for cultural and labor-intensive products. On the supply side, the quality of infrastructure and human capital in Africa is rising quite remarkably, albeit from a low base.

As Kaplinsky (2013) notes, industrial development in Africa is bounded by two critical framing dynamics: the exclusionary characteristics of global growth paths, and, perhaps less convincingly, the likely persistence of the commodity boom. The global industrial landscape is certainly being shaped by four sources of disruption: an emerging middle class in developing countries, the continual introduction of disruptive technologies, the global diffusion of innovative capabilities, and the emergence of new forms of entrepreneurship.

Industrial parks have played a catalytic role in facilitating industrial upgrading and export-led growth in East Asia, but also in Latin America and parts of South Asia. The African experience with industrial parks over the past two decades, which has mostly involved traditional export-processing zones, has been less spectacular as a vehicle for promoting exports and for generating well-paying jobs. Only Mauritius has used industrial parks as an effective vehicle for economic transformation.

With respect to trade, a typical list of policy advice for Africa includes the need to de-monopolize trade, streamline the import regime, allow exporters duty-free access to imported inputs, refrain from large doses of anti-export bias (just for the ease of taxability and to cater to urban interests), make trade reform credible and effective (including uniform tariffization and streamlined customs procedures),

New industrial policy for Africa **281**

mainstream regionalism in an open way, and insist on national ownership of development programs.

Several factors have been invoked to explain the limited success of industrial parks across Africa (Farole, 2016; Dinh et al., 2016). Poor strategic planning took the form of a mismatch of FDI with comparative advantage which resulted in few takers across a wide range of manufacturing sectors. Poor locational choices were made that were driven by political considerations in the vain hope of benefitting laggard regions rather than the regional growth engines with gateway infrastructures. China-like infrastructural services in the special economic zones were less than world-class. Poor implementation capacity and lack of authority bedeviled the technocracy. Finally, the lack of high-level support and policy stability manifested in a half-hearted commitment to a cluster-based strategy. These include passing zone laws but failing to implement paper-perfect regulations and providing inadequate resources for management, infrastructure, and promotional activities.

Regional integration and FDI flows within Africa itself can serve as stepping stones for a full-throated global engagement. Intra-African investment has, since 2007, been growing at a 32.5% compound rate. South Africa has been leading with $18 billion invested across several sectors, followed closely by Morocco and Nigeria. In 2011, the rate of return on inward FDI in Africa (9.3%) was the highest compared to other regions of the world – 8.8% in Asia and 4.8% in developed economies. FDI stands at around US$50 billion, an all-time high (Lopes, 2015).

Smart Industrial Policies: As in the case of aid effectiveness, need and capability rarely go together in developing countries. Nurturing the capability to design and implement effective IP is an integral part of building up industrial capability.

Global value chains are FDI-dependent, loose-footed, and producer driven while others are buyer driven. AfDB-OECD-UNDP (2014) emphasizes five key considerations for GVC-oriented IPs: they must be value-chain specific, tradeoff is involved in favoring on activity line over another, collaboration between public and private sectors can be crucial, who controls the vertical chain matters for upward mobility of component providers upstream and assemblers downstream, and low-road strategies risk "race to the bottom."

The policy implications are that IP must focus on lead firms to enter new value chains, capture higher-value tasks in existing chains, foster local sourcing, and focus on cultivating resilient linkages (Milberg et al., 2014; Taglioni and Winkler, 2016). While a shrinkage in policy space has occurred between GATT and WTO, there nonetheless remains some space for experimentation under the latter (UNECA, 2016). Finally, economic knowledge, theoretical and empirical, plays an important role in fostering non-conventional and yet sensible policy design and implementation.

Coming very late to the game, Africa is compelled to trail-blaze its own path of industrial catchup. The new African industrial strategy will not be about choosing between whole products or components. It will have to produce both while prioritizing based on gestation lags in capacity building and current market opportunities (Altenburg and Lutkenhorst, 2015).

282 Rethinking industrial strategy

To recapitulate, a smart African IP must, therefore:

1 Be a product of a robust policy dialog between key stakeholders on both the private side and the public side of the industrial economy.
2 Facilitate the transition of informal industrial firms to formal ones as well as the scaling up of the most promising SMEs.
3 Favor the domestic (nationalist) industrial class over the comprador and expatriate classes where economically sensible.
4 Nurture national value chains to meet domestic demand as well as to enter the higher niches of global value chains.
5 Invest in infrastructure, green technologies, and appropriate human capital to continually upgrade technological capability.
6 Support key agricultural and service subsectors that can anchor a broad-based industrial development.
7 Design public investments with the aim of crowding-in private investments in priority sectors.
8 Synchronize macroeconomic policies and industrial policies to make both efficient and sustainable.
9 Stem excessive inequality of income to ensure a socially inclusive and buoyant domestic demand for homemade manufactures and to incentivize low-skilled workers to invest in upgrading their skills.

The new African IP, in its soft or hard form, is clearly no longer about processing resources per se. It is about helping set the direction of the economy away from dead-ends. It is about building multifaceted platforms for the design, production, and marketing of high-demand industrial goods and services.

Finally, smart African IP must be a joint effort of a responsible state and a wealth-creating private sector by eliminating any measurable mismatch between the capabilities of the private industrial sector and the market opportunities open to it. IP is ultimately all about a careful search for fruitful pathways rather than for a magic bullet to an industrial utopia.

Notes

1 Strategy and policy are often used interchangeably. I use (development) 'strategy' to refer to the overall thrust of development while industrial policy is a component of the former, and it is industry-focused and instrument-specific. I also use the following untenable distinctions rather loosely because they are prevalent in the literature: selective IP versus general IP, market-directed versus IP-directed. We do not know of a country, including the United Kingdom and especially the U.S.A., which did not engage in activist IP in the early stages of its industrialization.
2 An eclectic approach, one that combines elements of the two but transcends them in some respects, pragmatically focuses on the discovery process rather than on the outcomes. It recommends high-power incentives to encourage private risk-taking to undertake deep-veined innovative ventures and to empower forward-looking entrepreneurs running the state enterprises. Finally, it is experimental-minded as it seeks effective ways of connecting isolated pockets of innovation and continually monitoring progress (Rodrik, 2014).

3 Growth diagnostics seeks to establish a practicable decision-tree framework for policy focus on the most binding constraints on growth at a given point in time. The idea is that the most binding constraints on growth (such as financing, infrastructure, or penetrating a thick market) are best removed sequentially (Hausmann and Rodrik, 2003; Hirschman, 1958). Growth diagnostics, a kind of clinical analysis, presumes that we have good measures of the relative prices and marginal contributions of various constraints on growth. Obtaining such metrics is, however, a rather hard task in developing economies where multiple binding constraints are the norm, and the kind of data needed to identify them in the circumstances of each country at a given stage or point in time are rather scarce.

4 Greenwald and Stiglitz (2013: 7), in fact, define economic development starkly as "the process of technological diffusion and industrial upgrading."

5 This is, of course, not an argument for poor interventions whether in the form of a poorly implemented IS or a mercantilist EP. As Lall (1997: 130) again notes, "The larger East Asian NIEs show that selective interventions in an export-oriented setting, carried out by well-trained technocrats and backed by investments in human capital, can be extremely effective in creating a dynamic set of competitive industries, with considerable domestic linkages and indigenous technological content. Without such interventions, industrial development is likely to end up with less dynamism and depth."

6 Learning by doing refers to productivity increases over time as employees learn either from experience, each other, or via training. Technology may be thought of as two distinct types of creative activity. One is innovation, mainly by firms in developed countries where the major policy concern is one of appropriability. The other is imitation, mainly in developing countries where the issue is earning rent via adaptation. Learning is statically inefficient (current profits are low) but dynamically efficient (future profits are high) which means many things. Learning to learn and the effective ability to learn determines the rate of adoption and adaptation of future technology; imitation may be country-wide (balanced growth among latecomers) or industry-specific; externalities abound since entrepreneurship needs nurturing (social returns being unequal to private returns) and arises from domestic production interlinkages; and venture capital is hard to find due to the prevalence of poor credit markets.

7 The literature offers a litany of errors of commission and errors of omission from past African experiences with IP (Aryeetey and Moyo, 2012; Lall and Wangwe, 1998; Maio, 2009; Whitfield et al., 2015). As Soludo et al. (2004: 30) once again rightly put it: "The central question for the political economy of policy-making relates to how, in a poor society with a weak leadership and poor institutions, good leadership that is committed to good policies emerges, especially given that both good leadership and policies are endogenous to other fundamental characteristics of the society."

8 At the conclusion of the infamous Soviet Industrialization Debates of the late 1920s, the brutal solution for the industry-financing problem was for the peasantry to forcibly give up its surplus via Stalin's collectivization drive of 1928–1932 – a strategy China pursued with the mechanism of rural communes and the Great Leap Forward which were operative during 1955–1978. Japan, South Korea, and Taiwan pursued a different strategy – one of smallholder ownership, support for agricultural development, and manipulation of the terms of trade between industry and agriculture to siphon off a portion of the productivity gains. Other late industrializers relied on diverting resource rents to industry (South Africa, Indonesia, and Iran), attracting FDI (Thailand, Ireland, and Malaysia), or both (Mexico, Brazil, and Indonesia).

References

Abebe, G., and F. Schaefer. (2016). Review of Industrial Policies in Ethiopia: A Perspective From the Leather and Cut Flower Industries. In: A. Noman and J. Stiglitz, eds., *Industrial Policy and Economic Transformation in Africa*, 1st ed. New York: Columbia University Press, pp. 123–161.

284 Rethinking industrial strategy

Ackah, C., C. Adjasi, and F. Turkson. (2016). Industrial Policy in Ghana: Its Evolution and Impact. In: C. Newman et al., eds., *Manufacturing Transformation: Comparative Studies of Industrial Development in Africa and Emerging Asia*, 1st ed. Oxford: Oxford University Press, pp. 50–71.

AfDB, OECD, and UNDP. (2014). *Global Value Chains and African Industrialization*. Geneva: UNDP.

African Development Bank (AfDB), Organisation for Economic Co-operation and Development (OECD), and United Nations Industrial Organization (UNIDO). (2017). *African Economic Outlook: Entrepreneurship and Industrialisation*. Abidjan: AfDB.

Altenburg, T., and W. Lutkenhorst. (2015). *Industrial Policy in Developing Countries: Failing Markets, Weak States*. Cheltenham: Edward Elgar.

Amsden, A. (1989). *Asia's Next Giant: South Korea and Late Industrialization*. Oxford: Oxford University Press.

Amsden, A. (2001). *The Rise of 'The Rest': Challenges to the West From Late Industrializing Economies*. New York: Oxford University Press.

Aryeetey, E., and N. Moyo. (2012). Industrialization for Structural Transformation in Africa: Appropriate Roles for the State. *Journal of African Economies*, 21(2), pp. 55–85.

Chang, H.J. (2002). *Kicking Away the Ladder: Development Strategy in Historical Perspective*. London: Anthem Press.

Cimoli, M., et al. (2009). *Industrial Policy and Development: The Political Economy of Capabilities Accumulation*. Oxford: Oxford University Press.

Commission on Growth and Development (COGD). (2008). *The Growth Report: Strategies for Sustained Growth and Development*. Washington, DC: World Bank.

Dinh, H., et al. (2012). *Light Manufacturing in Africa: Targeted Policies to Enhance Private Investment and Create Jobs*. Washington, DC: World Bank.

Dinh, H., et al. (2016). The Binding Constraint on the Growth of Firms in Developing Countries. In: H. Dinh and G. Clarke, eds., *Performance of Manufacturing Firms in Africa An Empirical Analysis*. Washington, DC: World Bank, Chapter 4.

Ethiopia: Ministry of Economic Cooperation and Development (E-MEDAC). (1993). *An Economic Strategy for Ethiopia*. Addis Ababa: E-MEDAC.

Ethiopia: National Planning Commission (E-NPC). (2015). *The Second Growth and Transformation Plan (GTP II) (2015/16–2019/20)*. Addis Ababa: E-NPC.

Farole, T. (2016). *Factory Southern Africa?: SACU in Global Value Chains – Summary Report*. Washington, DC: World Bank Group.

Ferraz, J., C. Leal, F. Marques, and M. Miterhof. (2015). Financing Development: The Case of BNDES. In: J. Stiglitz and J.Y. Lin, eds., *The Industrial Policy Revolution I*. New York: Palgrave Macmillan, pp. 143–157.

Greenwald, B., and J. Stiglitz. (2006). Helping Infant Economies Grow: Foundations of Trade Policies for Developing Countries. *American Economic Review*, 96(2), pp. 141–146.

Greenwald, B., and J. Stiglitz. (2013). Learning and Industrial Policy: Implications for Africa. In: J. Stiglitz, J.Y. Lin, and E. Patel, eds., *The Industrial Policy Revolution II: Africa in the 21st Century*. New York: Palgrave Macmillan, pp. 1–24.

Hausmann, R., D. Rodrik, and C. Sabel. (2007). Reconfiguring Industrial Policy: A Framework with an Application to South Africa. http://citeseerx.ist.psu.edu/viewdoc/download?doi=10.1.1.450.8623&rep=rep1&type=pdfUnpublished manuscript.

Hausmann, R. and C. Hidalgo. (2011). The Network Structure of Economic Output. *Journal of Economic Growth*, 16 (4), pp. 309–342.

Hausmann, R., J. Hwang, and D. Rodrik. (2007). What You Export Matters. *Journal of Economics Growth*, 12, pp. 1–25.

Hausmann, R., and D. Rodrik. (2003). Economic Development as Self-Discovery. *Journal of Development Economics*, 72(2), pp. 704–723.

Hausmann, R., D. Rodrik, and C. Sabel. (2008). Reconfiguring Industrial Policy: A Framework With an Application to South Africa. *Harvard Kennedy School Working Paper No. 08–031*. Cambridge, MA.

Hirschman, A.O. (1958). *The Strategy of Economic Development*. New Haven, CT: Yale University Press.

Japan International Cooperation Agency (JICA). (2011). *Ethiopia's Industrialization Drive Under the Growth and Transformation Plan*. Tokyo: JICA and GRIPS Development Forum.

Jomo, K.S. (1997). *Southeast Asia's Misunderstood Miracle: Industrial Policy and Economic Development in Thailand, Malaysia, and Indonesia*. Boulder: Westview.

Kaplinsky, R. (2013). Walking (Stumbling) on Two Legs: Meeting SSA's Industrialization Challenge. In: J. Stiglitz, J.Y. Lin, and E. Patel, eds., *The Industrial Policy Revolution II: Africa in the 21st Century*. New York: Palgrave Macmillan, pp. 173–200.

Kar, D., and D. Cartwright-Smith. (2015). *Illicit Financial Flows From Africa: Hidden Resource for Development*. [online] Global Financial Integrity. Available at: www.gfintegrity.org/storage/gfip/documents/reports/gfi_africareport_web.pdf.

Lall, S. (1997). *Learning From the Asian Tigers: Studies in Technology and Industrial Policy*. New York: St. Martin's Press.

Lall, S. (2004). Selective Industrial and Trade Policies in Developing Countries: Theoretical and Empirical Issues. In: C. Soludo, O. Ogbu, and H. Chang, eds., *The Politics of Trade and Industrial Policy in Africa*. Trenton: Africa World Press, Inc.

Lall, S., and S. Wangwe. (1998). Industrial Policy and Industrialisation in Sub-Saharan Africa. *Journal of African Economies*, 7(Supplement 1), pp. 70–107.

Levy, B. (2014). *Working With the Grain: Integrating Governance and Growth in Development Strategies*. New York: Oxford University Press.

Lin, J.Y. (2012). *New Structural Economics: A Framework for Rethinking Development Policy*. Washington, DC: World Bank.

Lin, J.Y. (2013). From Flying Geese to Leading Dragons: New Opportunities and Strategies for Structural Transformation in Developing Countries. In: J. Stiglitz, J.Y. Lin, and E. Patel, eds., *The Industrial Policy Revolution II: Africa in the 21st Century*. New York: Palgrave Macmillan, pp. 50–72.

Lin, J.Y., and C. Monga. (2011). Growth Identification and Facilitation: The Role of the State in the Dynamics of Structural Change. *Development Policy Review*, 29(3), pp. 264–290.

Little, I., et al. (1970). *Industry and Trade in Some Developing Countries*. London and New York: Oxford University Press.

Loewe, M. (2013). *Industrial Policy in Egypt 2004–2011*. Bonn: German Development Institute.

Lopes, C. (2015). Agriculture as Part of Africa's Structural Transformation. *Journal of African Transformation*, 1(1), pp. 43–61.

Maio, M. (2009). Industrial Policies in Developing Countries: History and Perspectives. In: M. Cimoli, G. Dosi, and J. Stiglitz, eds., *Industrial Policy and Development: The Political Economy of Capabilities Accumulation*. Oxford: Oxford University Press, pp. 107–143.

Mebratu, D. (2000). *Strategy Framework for Sustainable Industrial Development in SSA*. PhD thesis, Lund University.

Milberg, W., X. Jiang, and G. Gereffi. (2014). Industrial Policy in the Era of Vertically Specialized Industrialization. In: J. Salasar-Xirinachs, I. Nubler, and R. Kozul-Wright, eds., *Transforming Economies: Making Industrial Policy Work for Growth, Jobs and Development*. Geneva: UNCTAD and ILO.

Msami, J., and S. Wangwe. (2016). Industrial Development in Tanzania. In: C. Newman, et al., eds., *Manufacturing Transformation: Comparative Studies of Industrial Development in Africa and Emerging Asia*. Oxford: Oxford University Press, pp. 155–173.

Newman, C., J. Page, J. Rand, A. Shimeles, M. Soderbom, and F. Tarp. (2016). *Made in Africa: Learning to Compete in Industry*. Washington, DC: Brookings Institution Press.

Noman, A. (2013). Infant Capitalists, Infant Industries and Infant Economies: Trade and Industrial Policies at Early Stages of Industrialization in Africa and Elsewhere. In: J. Stiglitz, J.Y. Lin, and E. Patel, eds., *The Industrial Policy Revolution II: Africa in the 21st Century*. New York: Palgrave Macmillan, pp. 281–292.

Noman, A., and J. Stiglitz. (2012). Strategies for African Development. In: A. Noman, K. Botchwey, H. Stein, and J. Stiglitz, eds., *Good Growth and Governance in Africa*. Oxford: Oxford University Press, pp. 3–50.

Oqubay, A. (2015). *Made in Africa: Industrial Policy in Ethiopia*. Oxford: Oxford University Press.

Oxford Business Group (OBG). (2016). *Egypt*. Oxford: Oxford Business Group.

Pack, H. (1988). Industrialization and Trade. In: H. Chenery and T.N. Srinivasan, eds., *Handbook of Development Economics*, vol. 1. Amsterdam: North-Holland, pp. 334–380.

Pack, H. (2000). Industrial Policy: Growth Elixir or Poison? *World Bank Research Observer*, 15(1), pp. 47–67.

Reinert, E. (2009). Emulation Versus Comparative Advantage: Competing and Complementary Principles in the History of Economic Policy. In: M. Cimoli, G. Dosi, and J.E. Stiglitz, eds., *Industrial Policy and Development*. Oxford: Oxford University Press, pp. 79–106.

Rodrik, D. (2014). An African Growth Miracle? *NBER Working Paper No. 20188*. Cambridge, MA: NBER.

Shiferaw, A. (2007). Firm Heterogeneity and Market Selection in Sub-Saharan Africa: Does It Spur Industrial Progress. *Economic Development and Cultural Change*, 55(2), pp. 393–423.

Shimada, G. (2015). The Economic Implications of a Comprehensive Approach to Learning on Industrial Policy: The Case of Ethiopia. In: A. Noman and J. Stiglitz, eds., *Industrial Policy and Economic Transformation in Africa*. New York: Columbia University Press, pp. 102–122.

Soludo, C. (2014). A Synthesis of Major Themes in the Political Economy of Trade and Industrialization in Africa. In: C. Soludo, M. Ogbu and H.J. Chang, eds., *The Politics of Trade and Industrial Policy in Africa: Forced Consensus?* Trenton, NJ: Africa World Press, pp. 1–40.

Stein, H. (2012). Africa, Industrial Policy, and Export Processing Zones: Lessons From Asia. In: A. Noman, K. Botchwey, H. Stein, and J. Stiglitz, eds., *Good Growth and Governance in Africa*. Oxford: Oxford University Press, pp. 322–344.

Stiglitz, et al. (2009). *Report by the Commission on the Measurement of Economic Performance and Social Progress*. United Nations. Available at: www.stiglitz-sen-fitussi.fr.

Taglioni, D., and D. Winkler. (2016). *Making Global Value Chains Work for Development*. Washington, DC: World Bank Group.

UNCTAD. (2015). *World Investment Report 2015*. New York: United Nations Conference on Trade and Development.

United Nations Economic Commission for Africa (UNECA). (2015). *Economic Report on Africa 2015*. Addis Ababa: UNECA.

United Nations Economic Commission for Africa (UNECA). (2016). *Transformative Industrial Policy for Africa*. Addis Ababa: UNECA.

United Nations Industrial Development Organization (UNIDO) and the Government of Tanzania (UNIDO and GOT). (2012). *Tanzania Industrial Competitiveness Report 2012*. Geneva: UNIDO.

United Nations Industrial Organization (UNIDO). (2015). Industrial Development Report 2016: The Role of Technology and Innovation in Inclusive and Sustainable Industrial Development. Geneva: UNIDO.

United Nations Industrial Organization (UNIDO) and United Nations Conference on Trade and Development (UNCTAD). (2011). *Africa Report 2011: Fostering Industrial Development in Africa in the New Global Development*. Geneva: UNIDO.

Wade, R. (1990). *Governing the Market: Economic Theory and the Role of Government in East Asian Industrialization*, Princeton: Princeton University Press.

Wade, R. (2012). How Can Low-Income Countries Accelerate their Catchup With High-Income Countries? The Case for Open-Economy Industrial Policy. In: A. Noman, K. Botchwey, H. Stein, and J. Stiglitz, eds., *Good Growth and Governance in Africa*. Oxford: Oxford University Press, pp. 243–272.

Whitfield, L., O. Therkildsen, L. Buur, and A.M. Kjær. (2015). *The Politics of African Industrial Policy: A Comparative Perspective*. New York: Cambridge University Press.

World Bank. (1993). *The East Asian Miracle: Economic Growth and Public Policy*. Washington, DC: World Bank.

World Bank. (2015). *4th Ethiopia Update: Overcoming Constraints in the Manufacturing Sector*. Washington, DC: World Bank Group.

World Bank. (2017). *World Development Report 2017: Governance and the Law*. Washington, DC: World Bank.

11

AFRICA'S INDUSTRIAL FUTURE

Industrialization redux

The central theme of this book is that the hallmark of successful economic development is structural transformation, the core feature of which is the diversification and upgrading of the structures of production and trade through industrialization. The accumulation of industrial capabilities in a competitive environment has many advantages for a developing economy. It affords a wider choice set for dealing more effectively with market shifts and volatility. It facilitates the discovery of new profitable activities; and it often provides high-wage employment for many. It paves the way for the emergence of inclusive and innovative institutions.

Countries with diversified economies grow faster and are more resilient. Economic diversification away from primary commodities towards a knowledge-based economy goes on rapidly until per capita gross domestic product exceeds $10,000 or so (Alcorta et al., 2013; de Vries et al., 2013).

Africa entered the twenty-first century with two institutional handicaps born of its deep-seated poverty and colonial legacies: the twinning of pervasive market failures and government failures. But, it can overcome these handicaps with massive investments in infrastructure (roads, railways, communication networks, and power supplies) and a favorable policy environment. To stem significant capital and skill flight and to accelerate inward foreign investment, African countries must also find effective ways to boost their bureaucratic capability and political accountability to favor wealth-creation over rent-redistribution.

Africa is certainly the biggest remaining challenge to development economists and policymakers alike. South Korea and Taiwan were, after all, widely considered some of the most unpromising places compared to Egypt or Ghana as late as the 1960s. The metaphor "leaping leopard" is chosen here over the predictable alternatives (lion, cheetah, or elephant), since the leopard is strong enough to defend its turf against all but the most formidable predators, and can run fast when it must but prefers to pounce on its prey after a patient weighing of its options. The lynchpin of an African industrial strategy must be "thinking big while starting small" – building pragmatically on existing capabilities while upgrading them and synchronizing the built-up capabilities with deep-veined domestic and global opportunities with the help of smart policies.

One can reasonably wonder, as we did earlier, whether Africa should ever bother with ambitious industrial policies at all. The skeptics point to the fact that Africa is too isolated and has undergone lackluster structural change since the 1980s. This means it may already have foregone growth emanating from structural shifts from low-productivity to high-productivity activities (Page, 2013).

Outside of South Africa, Mauritius, and Tunisia, Africa's industrial base is certainly puny. With some exceptions, it lacks Asia's rich history of proto-industrial activity on which to build. Few foreign residents or foreign companies moved into manufacturing until very recently to serve as pioneer industrialists as was the case of East Asia and Latin America. There are no agro-industrial pioneers comparable to China's township and village enterprises or urban cooperatives in those countries (Ethiopia, Ghana, and Tanzania) that seriously flirted with African socialism.

In the heydays of the 1960s and the 1970s, newly independent Africa emulated other regions of the world in undertaking import-substituting industrialization rather indiscriminately. This led to short-lived but remarkable progress until the pre-existing potential was exhausted. Absent a tenacious and pragmatic cultivation of new linkages and technological upgrading, the model proved to be self-limiting.

Much has been learned from this grand experiment, and the world economy itself has changed rather markedly. Dinh et al. (2012) and Newman et al. (2016) argue that Africa can expand into light manufacturing. To compete with the relatively better-positioned competitors in Indo-China, South Asia, and Central America, Africa will have to concentrate its limited resources in a multipronged effort to progressively remove the most binding constraints on productivity growth.

Recent empirical studies on African industrialization (Newman et al., 2016; Dinh et al., 2012) do offer the advice that Africa should imitate East Asia in focusing on three closely related drivers of firm-level productivity – exports, agglomeration, and firm capabilities. By starting out as low-wage "factory economies," African economies must cultivate upstream and downstream linkages to segments of modern agriculture, services, and mining. They must expand secondary education (especially technical) beyond the current 40% coverage, offer practical training to school leavers by building model offices, factories and farms, and incubation programs for greenfield SMEs with clear paths for upscaling, and modernize infrastructural (roads, rails, power, and water), ICT, and financial services. This is a tall order, indeed.

The question, therefore, is no longer about *whether* Africa must industrialize, but about *how fast* it could or *how best* it should industrialize. To answer the how question satisfactorily, one must take full account of the existing capabilities of each country, the prospects for closing major skill and technological gaps, and the opportunities that are available in the national economy, regional economies, and the global economy. Synchronizing the built-up capabilities with the right opportunities is where sensible industrial policy comes in.

Smart industrial policy for Africa

At this point, we can only recapitulate rather than parse the relevant lessons from the historical experiences of other regions that successfully managed catchup industrialization albeit under different global circumstances. A typical catalog of historical lessons underscores many useful ideas which means policymakers must think and act strategically taking all these into account. Political cohesion and a sense of national mission matter; so, does a threshold of pre-existing capability (especially a rich craft culture and an effective mechanism for graduating from informal activity). There is such a thing as the manufacturing learning curve. Latecomers compete based on total unit cost, not just unit labor cost, which depends on wage levels, productivity levels, and other costs of doing business in the country.

We now know a lot about what works and what does not when it comes to industrial policy, and it makes life easier if the impediments of African industrial takeoff are the product of policy mistakes rather than manifestations of structural forces. Macro stability and openness are good as are selective industrial policies that focus on efficient technological learning. Broad-based and equitable taxes and expenditures are good as are quality public services. Where market failures and government failures are pervasive, a partnership model between the state and the private sector is the right way to go. The logic of partnership also applies between rich-country governments and poor-country governments (World Bank, 2017).

Furthermore, supply must forge ahead of demand for at least some pioneering activities, given an incubation lag. This is unavoidably so because, in an underdeveloped economy, demand cannot be fully relied upon to create its own supply. Takeoff occurs when all the necessary ingredients are in place on the supply side and when they are synchronized with demand. Technological and business upgrading of medium and small-scale enterprises is the key to boosting the national value added of exports and economic flexibility to meet ever-changing market demand.

It must also be noted, however, that both the internal circumstances and the international environment under which Africa is mounting an industrialization drive do not lend themselves to an easy comparison with forerunners. Africa is clearly not China in terms of the massive investment in industrial development under the era of import substitution, a large enough domestic market, the township and village enterprises that spearheaded agro-industrial activities and massive investment in human and physical capital, and the nationalism that undergirded developmentalism. It also does not lend itself to an easy comparison with India again in terms of a rich manufacturing heritage and extensive import substitution to build on as well as high state capability. Africa opened much earlier, but it lacked the built-up capability to be globally competitive. Openness or capability alone may be necessary but not sufficient – together, they meet the sufficiency condition with

Africa's industrial future **291**

the help of sensible policy (Baldwin, 2016; Dicken, 2015; Hallward-Driemmeir and Nayyar, 2017).

It would, therefore, be safe to conclude that Africa can and must industrialize – and do it optimally. To telescope the process, African industrial strategies must be country-specific, forward-looking in taking account of ever-changing global opportunities and constraints, supportive of worthy local firms, able to leverage new opportunities in South-South investment and trade, and focused on creating more well-paying jobs for the large pool of working-age youth.

Telescoping, of course, has it disadvantages as China clearly demonstrated. Societies need time to adapt to economic transformation lest they suffer social anomie. One way or another, Africans must soon figure out an effective way to turn around the alarmingly accelerating and crisis-induced brain drain and capital drain into a growth miracle by ensuring a reasonably free society for citizens to bet on the continent's great promise.

This is what it would take for Africa's industries to leapfrog, and its economies to take a great lurch forward, much like the modus operandi of the pouncing African leopard. With a good knowledge of the dynamics of industrializing late, political and economic elites will hopefully master the art of cooperation if only out of enlightened self-interest.

References

Alcorta, L., N. Haraguchi, and G. Rezonja. (2013). Industrial Structural Change, Growth Patterns, and Industry. In: J. Stiglitz, J.Y. Lin, and E. Patel, eds., *The Industrial Policy Revolution II: Africa in the 21st Century*, 1st ed. New York: Palgrave Macmillan, pp. 457–491.

Baldwin, R. (2016). *The Great Convergence: Information Technology and the New Globalization.* Cambridge: Belknap-Harvard Press.

de Vries, G., M. Timmer, and K. de Vries. (2013). *Structural Transformation in Africa: Static Gains, Dynamic Losses.* GGDC Research Memorandum 136. Groningen, Netherlands: Groningen Growth and Development Centre, University of Groningen.

Dicken, P. (2015). *Global Shift: Mapping the Changing Contours of the World Economy.* New York: The Guilford Press.

Dinh, H., et al. (2012). *Light Manufacturing in Africa: Targeted Policies to Enhance Private Investment and Create Jobs.* Washington, DC: World Bank.

Hallward-Driemmeir, M., and G. Nayyar. (2017). *Trouble in the Making? The Future of Manufacturing-led Development.* Washington, DC: World Bank Group.

Newman, C., J. Page, J. Rand, A. Shimeles, M. Soderbom, and F. Tarp. (2016). *Made in Africa: Learning to Compete in Industry.* Washington, DC: Brookings Institution Press.

Page, J. (2013). Should Africa Industrialize? In: A. Szirmai, W. Naude, and L. Alcorta, eds., *Pathways to Industrialization in the Twenty-First Century.* New York: Oxford University Press, pp. 244–268.

World Bank. (2017). *World Development Report 2017: Governance and the Law.* Washington, DC: World Bank.

APPENDIX ON DATA SOURCES

An ever-expanding, internationally comparable database now exists for the study of modern economic growth and industrialization. Table A.1 highlights the notable features of selected sources. The key sources describing the development and basic descriptions of the datasets are appended to the table.

A. Sponsoring organizations

1   WDI: The World Bank currently makes available economy-wide, industry-level, and enterprise-level data for over 200 countries since 1960 embracing a wide variety of economic and social indicators. Data in the World Development Indicators (WDI) and Enterprise Surveys are especially valuable.

2   Maddison: Angus Maddison has pieced together time series data on national product going back to two centuries for 56 developed and less developed nations. See www.ggdc.net/maddison/maddison-project/data.htm.

3   PWT: Under the name of *Penn World Tables*, Robert Summers, Irving Kravis, and Alan Heston have developed data since 1950 for 152 countries on national product and its components carefully adjusted for international differences in purchasing power.

4   UNIDO: The most extensive data, some going back to 1960, on industrial production and employment. Data for manufacturing, based on standardized national surveys for formal-sector enterprises, is available at the three-digit ISIC level for most countries while data at the four-digit levels are available for far fewer countries.

5   OECD: The Organisation for Economic Co-operation and Development provides data on financial flows, net value added in GVCs, and various economic data for member states.

6   UNCTAD: The United Nations Conference on Trade and Development provides cross-country data on trade and investment.

Appendix on data sources **293**

7   RPED: The World Bank launched the Regional Program on Enterprise Development (RPED) in the early 1990s to collect survey data on manufacturing enterprises in several African countries. The variables include African business environment, employment, credit, exports, and imports.

TABLE A.1 Data sources on industrial development

Dataset	Brief description	Key references
Groningen Growth & Dev. Centre (GGDC)	The GGDC 10-Sector database provides a long-run internationally comparable dataset on sectoral productivity for Africa, Asia, and Latin America. Source: www.rug.nl/research/ggdc/data/10-sector-database	Timmer, de Vries, and de Vries
Key Ind. Labor Market (KILM)	The KILM Database is a comprehensive database of country-level data on 18 key indicators of the labor market from 1980 to the latest available year. Source: www.ilo.org/empelm/what/WCMS_1142/lang-en/index.htm	ILO
Global Mat. Flows Database	The Global Material Flows Database comprises data for than 200 countries for 1980–2011, and for more than 300 different materials aggregated into 12 categories of material flows. Source: www.materialflows.net/home	SERI and WU Vienna (2015)
Industrial Pay Inequality Database	The UTIP-UNIDO Industrial Pay Inequality Database provides Theil measures of inequality in wages and earning for 167 countries covering the period, 1963–2008. Source: www.edac.eu/indicators_desc.cfm?v_id=209	University of Texas and UNIDO (2015)
World Bank: (WDI) and ES	World Development Indicators (WDI) presents the most comprehensive and up-to-date economic and social data. Enterprise Surveys (ES) provides economic data for 135 countries, 100 indicators, and 130,000 firms since 2005. Sources: http://data.worldbank.org/data-catalog/	World Bank (2016)
World Input–Output DB (WIOD)	WIOD provides time series data on input-output tables for 40 countries covering the period, 1995–2011. Source: www.wiod.org/new_site/home.htm	Timmer, et al. (2015)
World Integrated Trade System (WITS)	WITS database is a compilation of data on trade and tariffs from various relevant databases, mainly from the Comtrade database of the United Nations Statistical Division. Source: http://wits.worldbank.org/about_wits.html	World Bank (2015)
Labor Cont. of Exports (LACEX); Job Cont. Exports (JOCEX)	LACEX was developed by Calì et al. (2015) based on a panel of global input-output tables and exports from the Global Trade Analysis Project (GTAP) and employment data from the ILO. The database measures the contribution of labor to a given country's exports – measured as employees' compensation or wages (LACEX) or the number of jobs (JOCEX). LACEX covers a maximum of 120 countries and JOCEX 88 countries. Source: http://data.worldbank.org/data-catalog/lacex	Calì, et al. (2015)

(Continued)

294 Appendix on data sources

TABLE A.1 (Continued)

Dataset	Brief description	Key references
RPED	The World Bank is undertaking a large cross-country study of manufacturing enterprise development in Africa. Participating countries include Cameroon, Ghana, Kenya, Nigeria, Tanzania, Malawi, Zambia, and Zimbabwe. Source: http://documents.worldbank.org/ curated/ en/980771468193748295/pdf/568910NWP0RPED10Box 353743B01PUBLIC1.pdf	Biggs and Srivastava (1996)
Global Financial Development Database (GFDD)	The Global Financial Development Database is an extensive dataset of financial system characteristics for 203 economies. It contains annual data, starting from 1960 through 2013 for 109 indicators. Source: www. worldbank.org/en/publication/gfdr/data/global-financial-development-database	
International Development Statistics (IDS)	IDS are the depository of CRS data on official development assistance from DAC and non-DAC donors, managed by the OECD. Sources: www.oecd.org/ development/stats/idsonline.htm	
OECD	The TiVA database provides data on services, exports, imports, and supply chains related to GVCs. Source: http:// data.worldbank.org/data-catalog/export-value-added	Baldwin (2016); Taglioni and Wenkler (2016)

B. Key references about cross-country data

1   Biggs, Tyler, and Pradeep Srivastava. (1996). *Structural Aspects of Manufacturing in Sub-Saharan Africa: Findings from a Seven-Country Enterprise Survey*. World Bank.
2   Calì, M., J. Francois, M. Manchin, D. Oberdabernig, H. Rojas-Romagosa, and P. Tomberger. (2015). *The Labor Content of Exports*. Mimeo, The World Bank.
3   Cihak, Martin, et al. (2012). Benchmarking Financial Systems Around the World. *World Bank Policy Research Paper 6175*. Washington, DC: World Bank.
4   International Labor Organization (ILO). *ILOSTAT Database*. Geneva.
5   Maddison, Angus. (1995). *Monitoring the World Economy, 1820–1992*. Paris: OECD.
6   Summers, Robert, and Alan Heston. (1991). The Penn World Table (Mark 5): An Expanded Set of International Comparisons, 1950–1988. *Quarterly Journal of Economics* 106(2) (May), pp. 327–368.
7   Sustainable Europe Research Institute (SERI) and Vienna University of Economics and Business (WU Vienna). (2015). *Global Material Flow Database*. Vienna.
8   Timmer, M.P., and G. de Vries. (2014). Patterns of Structural Change in Developing Countries. *GGDC Research Memorandum 149*. Groningen: University of Groningen.
9   Timmer, M.P., and Others. (2015). An Illustrated User Guide to the World Input-Output Database: The Case of Global Automotive Production. *Review of International Economics*, 23(3), pp. 575–605.

Appendix on data sources **295**

10 United Nations Industrial Development Organization (UNIDO). *Industrial Statistics: Guidelines and Methodology*. Vienna: UNIDO.

11 University of Texas and UNIDO. (2015). *UTIP-UNIDO Industrial Pay Inequality Dataset*. Austin: University of Texas at Austin.

12 World Bank. (2015). *WITS Dataset*, Available online.

13 World Bank. (2016). *World Development Indicators 2016*. Washington, DC.

14 Overseas Development Institute (ODI). *Supporting Economic Transformation*. Available at: http://set.odi.org/data-portal/.

15 U.N.U. World Institute for Development Economics Research (WIDER). (2015). *Learning to Compete*.

16 Organisation for Economic Co-operation and Development (OECD). Trade in Value Added (TiVA) database: www.oecd.org/sti/ind/whatcantivdatabasetellus.htm. Baldwin (2016). *The Great Convergence*. Cambridge: Belknap Press of Harvard University Press.

17 Taglioni, D., and D. Winkler. (2016). *Making Global Value Chains Work for Development*. Washington, DC.

GLOSSARY

Big Push. Given ever-present indivisibilities and external economies, synchronized investments in many complementary and lumpy activities are needed to make them all profitable.

Capabilities Escalator. The conceptual framework of a presumed sequential ladder or escalator involving the stages of acquisition of managerial, technological, and then technology-generation capabilities through a combination of public and private investment.

Capability. The freedom (range of choices) at the disposal of individuals, firms, or communities to achieve valued forms (functionings) of economic well-being (see Box 4.1).

Clientelism. An advanced form of patrimonialism whereby politicians in semi-democratic states strategically distribute public resources to individual supporters or voters.

Comparative Advantage. An "industry-based" notion which asserts that trade is mutually beneficial when each trading nation focuses on delivering those goods and services in which it enjoys the lowest *relative* cost of production.

Competitive Advantage. A "firm-based" notion which asserts that firms maximize profits when they deploy their capabilities (input costs, technology, and management) to the production and delivery of those goods and services in which they enjoy the lowest cost for a given quality level.

Containerization. Shipping freight in relatively uniform, sealed, and moveable containers whose contents do not get unloaded at each point of transfer. This intermodal interchange with standardized handling equipment is much more efficient than the break-bulk system with modality-specific deliveries marked for individual consigners.

Convergence (of Income or Productivity). Income convergence refers to the progressive equalization of per capita income because poorer countries grow faster than richer countries as they approach the common steady state level of income per capita. Productivity convergence refers to a reduction in the dispersion of factor productivities or TFP among sectors or firms across countries.

Convergence, Structural. Structural transformation within manufacturing (or across the entire economy) which results in a reduction in the cross-country dispersion in the composition of production, consumption, employment, and trade as an economy manages to catchup with those in the technological frontier. Alternatively, it refers to the

Glossary **297**

attainment of broad similarities in the structures of manufacturing (or the composition of the entire economy) as a low-income economy manages to technologically catch up with an advanced economy.

Deindustrialization. The long-term decline in the share of manufacturing in national value added and in national employment leading to rising dependence on import.

Demographic Dividend. A stage in the demographic transition where the dependency ratio falls and releases investible resources that would raise income.

Developmental State. A state controlled by a vanguard ruling party that is committed to boosting growth through a combination of direct government investment (social and physical infrastructure and public enterprises) and support for the "best of the worst" in the often politically connected private sector (see Box 7.1).

Dualism. The coexistence of two distinct economic systems within the same country.

Dutch Disease. The appreciation of the real exchange rate that follows the discovery of tradable natural resources or commodity price booms, which by inducing sharp increases in the inflows of foreign currency as well as domestic wages across industries, render other sectors of the economy less competitive.

Dynamic Comparative Advantage. Sustained rather than episodic changes in the pattern of comparative advantage induced by significant changes in factor endowments or technology.

Economic Transformation. The process of involving significant reallocation of human and non-human resources from low-productivity activities to high-productivity activities within sectors or between sectors.

Economies of Agglomeration. Economic benefits from positive spillovers that emanate from geographic proximity to other competing or customer firms.

Economies of Scale. Increasing all inputs increases output disproportionately.

Economies of Scope. Average cost falls as product assortment increases.

Export Processing Zone (EPZ). A designated area receiving special support (fewer worker right, duty-free imports of inputs, tax breaks, and public services) to encourage production for export (see Box 6.1).

Export Substitution Industrialization (ESI). Promoting higher export volumes (export promotion) or greater value-added exports to enhance foreign exchange earnings and technological diffusion from abroad.

Extensive Growth. Growth through factor accumulation which, unlike productivity-driven intensive growth, does not alter output per unit of input (such as labor productivity or per capita income).

External Economies (diseconomies). Extra benefits (positive externality) generated by certain legitimate activities of firms or organizations that confer unrequited benefits to others within the industry. The market has no mechanism to equalize the private benefits and social benefits of such innovative but not fully internalizable activities.

Flying Geese Model (FGM). The metaphor that the diffusion of technology and the distribution of production from leaders to followers (firms or countries) follows an ordered, V-shaped formation rather than the metaphor of agglomerative (seemingly chaotic) formation of starlings.

Foreign Direct Investment (FDI). The acquisition, by non-resident firms, of physical capital and workforce in a foreign country with the intent of serving the domestic market and the export market.

Global Value Chain and Global Supply Chain. (see Box 6.2).

Green Industrialization. Low-carbon print, environmentally sustainable form of industrialization.

298 Glossary

Import Substitution Industrialization (ISI). Replacement of previously imported or likely importable manufactures by domestic production through multifaceted support for native-owned infant industries or foreign-invested industries to save on foreign exchange payments and to build up export capability in manufactures.

Industrial District. Marshallian clusters of small and medium-size companies forming a geographic network of competitors, specialized suppliers, service providers and users, a skilled labor force, and regional governments committed to providing the necessary public services to stem coordination failure. (see Box 6.1).

Industrialization (Late). Industrializing in a world where there are well-established leaders. It offers a broad scope for learning while also raising the threshold of competence for latecomers.

Industrialization (Very-late). The options open to laggard industrializers in the post-1990 age of global value chains and supply chains where China rather than the West is the center of global manufacturing.

Industrial Park. Enterprise zone that is has been granted special treatment to promote industrial investment. (see Box 6.1).

Industrial Policy. Government involvement (through state enterprises, preferential trade as well as fiscal policies, various forms of financial support for private firms, and support for entry into regional and global markets) which is intended to accelerate or alter the trajectory of industrial development. These incentives, often industry-specific or firm-specific, are designed to facilitate efficient and speedy structural transformation by removing obstacles toward well-functioning markets. The intermediate targets may be boosting production, exports, technological diffusion, productivity growth, employment generation, or environmental sustainability.

Infant Industry. Fledgling firms in a newly established industry that merit time-bound state support or protection provided that the productivity gains from learning or dynamic economies of scale far outweigh the resources devoted to its support.

Informal Sector. The portion of the economy that is populated by small, unregistered businesses (accounting for half of the businesses in Africa) with no legal protection and little access to financing from the formal sector.

Innovation. The introduction of a new or a significantly improved product, process, marketing, or organizational know-how.

Institutions. Well-established informal norms and practices as well as those formalized in laws and regulations which govern incentives and sanctions.

Intensive Growth. Growth through productivity gains, often linked to progress in research and development and human-capital accumulation, all of which will boost per capita income.

Intermediates. Produced (non-primary and non-capital) goods that are used as inputs in the production of final goods or services.

Kaizen. Kaizen is the Japanese practice of continuous improvement involving management and workers alike with an emphasis small but cumulative efficiency gains in the management of value chain and supply chain.

Lean Production (Manufacturing). A Japanese-pioneered organizational innovation in manufacturing processes that combines the flexibility and quality of the craftsman with the economies of scale of Fordist mass production. The factory floor is organized around optimally designed team stations with some control over the assembly line and just-in-time inventory to minimize input use without sacrificing quality or productivity.

Linkages (backward and forward). Interdependence among key economic activities, often in the form of spatial agglomeration, that defines a circular causality. A backward linkage of an investment in a project is one that stimulates input suppliers while a forward linkage is one that stimulates input users, the simultaneous operation of which benefits the economy the most.

LIT Policy. Learning, industrial, and technology (LIT) policies are a package of measures focused on diffusing superior technologies from leaders to laggards (firms or countries) via efficient learning strategies to telescope the catchup process.

Malthusian Trap (aka Low-Income Trap). A self-reinforcing poverty trap whereby increases in average living standards in low-income countries induces more rapid population growth which restores the previous equilibrium.

Middle-income Trap. The phenomenon of middle-income, semi-industrial countries experiencing prolonged stagnation usually attributed to the inability to master medium-to-high-technology activities that would ensure sustained productivity-driven growth.

Mill-Bastable Test. Infant industries must be protected but only temporarily on the condition that the net social benefits are positive due to the presence of dynamic learning-learning-by-doing effects for the protected industry and positive spillover effects to other firms within the industry to other industries.

Neopatrimonialism. The use of a Weberian rational-legal state bureaucracy to shroud patrimonial rule whereby the redistribution of budgetary resources and economic rent is widely used to cement a regime's constituency (usually ethnic, religious, or regional).

Non-manufacturing Industries. Activities that are usually included in a broad definition of "industry" such as modern mining, construction, and public utilities (electricity, gas, and water).

Official Development Assistance (ODA). Financial (grants and loans with at least 25% grant element) and technical assistance that come from governmental (official) donors and is intended to promote development in the recipient country.

Original Equipment Manufacturer (OEM). Offshore firms specializing in components or tasks used as intermediate inputs into designed and branded products that belong to other (headquarters) firms.

Political Order. A modern political order is built on three pillars whose simultaneous presence is considered a momentous achievement for a developing country: a strong and capable state, the state's subordination to the rule of law, and government accountability to all citizens.

Purchasing Power Parity. An exchange rate that, after adjustments for differences in costs across countries of both tradable and nontradable, measures the relative purchasing power of national currencies much better than the market exchange.

Rent (Economic). The difference between the price received and the opportunity cost (normal profit) incurred which may be legal (such as innovation rents and import quota license), or illegal.

Rent Seeking. Expenditure of real resources (in political activities or innovative activities) to secure a price premium or public largess (see Box 7.1).

Revealed Comparative Advantage. Comparative advantage judged on the basis actual performance rather than on (the hard to gauge) potential performance level.

Special Economic Zone (SEZ). A region, comprising losing industrial districts or centralized industrial and science parks, with regulations that are looser and infrastructures that are globally competitive – all designed to boost technological transfers and exports of manufactures especially with foreign direct investment taking the lead (see Box 6.1).

State-owned Enterprise. An enterprise owned and operated by state agencies usually for providing public goods and services, or private goods with high positive externalities.

300 Glossary

Structural Transformation.   A discernible pattern of radical changes in the composition and distribution of output, employment, and trade – usually toward high value-added and high-demand activities.

Technological Capabilities.   The ability to learn and exploit superior technologies from leading firms or countries to enhance one's productivity and competitiveness.

Technological Change.   The productivity- or quality-enhancing process of turning new or superior ideas into practice by moving from the stage of invention and proto-typing to the stage of application or commercialization.

Total Factor Productivity (TFP).   The joint product of all factor inputs (labor, skills, resources, and capital) as measured by total output divided by the composite inputs and its level is attributed to technological capability and institutional quality.

Unit Cost.   The total cost per unit of a product (aka average cost) which includes production, transportation, marketing, and transaction costs. Unit costs are a joint product of input cost and factor productivity.

Unit Labor Cost.   A partial measure calculated as the total compensation of employees per unit of output (or per dollar of output).

Value Chains versus Supply Chains.   (see Box 6.2).

INDEX

Abidjan 7, 185
Acemoglu, D. 31, 42nn6–7, 67, 73
Adelman, I. 100
Africa Centre for Economic Transformation (ACET) 160
Africa of the colonial trade economy 153
Africa of the labor reserves 154
African Development Bank (AfDB) 7, 42n8, 153, 265, 281
African Transformation Index (ATI) 160
agglomeration 34, 48, 51, 54, 66, 69, 72–73, 77, 90, 101, 112–113, 139–140, 147n3, 289, 297–298
aggregate convergence 25–27
agriculture-demand led (ADLI) 100
Agriculture Development-Led Industrialization 268–269
agriculture-led industrialization 98–101
agriculture supply 98
agriculture supply-led 100
A-I-S 34–35
Akamatsu, K. 74, 79n2
Alcorta, L. 116
Amin, S. 153
Amsden, A. 68, 72, 83–84, 92–93, 95, 114–115
Ansu, Y. 167
Argentina 50, 70, 83, 94

balanced industrialization 99, 101–103
Baldwin, R. 58, 66–68, 71–72, 78, 95, 111, 137, 143–146, 294
Bangalore 128

Commission on Growth and Development 19
comparative advantage 8, 10, 35, 40, 58, 70, 76–77, 87–88, 90–91, 94–95, 99, 103, 104n2, 112, 127–128, 135, 137, 145, 156, 197, 205, 240, 259–260, 281, 296–297, 299
competitive industrial performance 56, 189, 194, 197–198, 202, 209, 228, 233, 239, 246, 249
containerization 67, 83, 132, 296
convergence 18–19, 23, 25–27, 34–36, 43n11, 54, 58, 75, 77, 147n2, 159, 262, 296
COP framework 272
Cote d'Ivoire 18, 21, 27, 37–38, 156, 160, 162, 167, 169–170, 178–183, 184–190, 278–279
customization 66, 133–134, 137

Dahlman, C. 130n8, 175
demographic dividend 6, 29, 297
development accounting 20, 22
development banking 70, 72
developmental regime 129, 165–167
Developmental state 143, 166–167, 297
de Vries, J. 39, 192, 196, 201, 206, 225, 231, 236, 241, 245, 293
diffusion S-curve 69
Dinh, H. 7, 162, 270, 289
diversification 1–3, 18–19, 34–36, 53–54, 58, 73–74, 77–78, 86, 88, 91–92, 95–97, 102, 111–113, 119, 121, 129n1, 160, 168, 175, 191, 193, 215, 247, 255, 266, 270–271, 288
diversified business group 72, 92, 95–98

302 Index

diversify-and-then-specialize thesis 73
Dubai 262
Durlauf, S. 23
Dutch Disease 199, 297
dynamic 10, 20, 41, 42n2, 54, 59n5, 73–75,
77, 79n2, 87–88, 91–92, 94, 96, 104n2,
111, 120, 127–128, 135, 138–139, 144,
146, 147n4, 160, 176, 197, 205, 230,
240, 258, 260, 263, 280, 283nn5–6, 291,
297–299

East Asia 2, 8–9, 28, 52, 65, 67, 76, 78,
79n2, 84, 87, 93, 102–103, 129, 139, 141,
158, 161, 169, 195, 256, 260, 274, 280,
283n5, 289
Easterly, W. 23
economic institutions: exclusionary 15, 41, 163
economic rent 54, 75, 79n3, 166, 263, 299
Egypt 18, 21, 27, 37–38, 40, 50, 156,
167–170, 177, 203, 215–220, 221–229,
265, 267–268, 275–276, 278–279, 288
Egyptian 224, 226–227, 266–267
electrification 43n12
enclave 55, 114, 176
endogenous growth 19, 68, 73
Ethiopia 4, 7, 10, 21, 37–41, 50, 154, 160,
165, 167, 169–170, 182–183, 216–220,
229–234, 240, 250nn2–3, 265, 268–270,
273, 275, 278–279
Europe 2, 4, 16, 39, 49–50, 65, 67–68, 70,
76, 124, 126, 139, 162, 169, 203, 215
European Periphery 8, 19, 83
exogenous growth 19, 68
export diversification 35, 53, 121, 193, 266
Export Expansion 121
export processing zones 55, 113, 123,
129nn5–6, 139, 261, 280
export promotion 86, 100, 118–120, 122,
129n1, 155, 191, 249, 267, 269
export substitution 54, 113, 118–122,
143, 297
extensive growth 19, 297
external economies 53, 140, 143, 175,
296–297
externalities 19, 51, 54, 77, 113, 115,
127–128, 139–140, 147n5, 176, 258,
261–262, 283n6, 299

factor accumulation 19–20, 22–23, 42n2, 297
factor-based industrializers 184, 215–218,
220–223
factor endowments 42n2, 77, 112, 154n1,
260, 297
factory economies 66, 90–91, 123, 138, 289

Fei, J. 98
Feinstein, C. 204
financing gap 274
firm capabilities 25, 91, 289
First Global Century 65, 67
flying geese model 128, 297
foreign direct investment 68, 70, 72, 115,
127, 143, 189, 197, 211, 279, 297, 299
France 50, 279
free trade zones 139
fusion models 74

general purpose technologies 69, 97
Germany 21–22, 26, 70, 138, 279
Gerschenkron, A. 79n2, 163
Ghana 18, 21–22, 27, 37–38, 50, 158, 160,
165, 167, 169–170, 178–183, 190–194,
265–266, 270, 278–279, 288, 294
Gini coefficient 168, 170, 184, 190, 195,
203, 221
global supply chains 71, 99, 139–140
global value chains 7, 52, 71, 91, 97, 129,
132–141, 143–144, 147n1, 197, 248, 276,
281–282, 298
Gordon, R. 59n2, 67, 69–70, 133
great divergence 2, 48
green industrialization 145, 297
growth accounting 20, 22

Hausmann, R. 35, 88, 91, 261–262
Hawassa 234
headquarters economies 66, 90–91, 123,
137–138, 146
Heckscher-Ohlin-Samuelson 76
high technology 57–58, 103, 114, 189, 194,
198, 202, 209, 228, 233, 239, 246, 249,
279, 299
Hirschman, A. 79n2, 88, 98, 283n3
Hoffmann, W. 72
Hoffmann's Law 72
Hong Kong 58, 83, 87, 123, 125, 138
human development index 168, 170, 184,
190, 195, 199, 203, 210, 221, 229, 234,
240, 244, 247
Hungary 21–22

ICT 4, 66–68, 71–72, 90, 102, 111–112, 132
import penetration 120–121
import repression 114
import reproduction 114
import substitution 3, 54, 79n2, 86–87, 100,
113–118, 120–123, 125, 129n2, 143,
155–156, 189–191, 195, 199, 216, 224,
235, 244, 248, 269, 271, 290, 298

import substitution industrialization 155, 224, 235, 244, 298
income elasticity 51, 69, 119
India 3–5, 16, 18, 51, 54, 79n1, 102–103, 155, 162, 167, 205, 267, 279–280, 290
Indo-China 4, 140, 280, 289
Indonesia 21, 26, 50, 58, 94, 103, 138, 167
industrial capability 3, 56, 74, 83, 89–92, 113, 144, 265, 272, 281
industrial clusters 7, 90, 139–140, 266–267, 280–281
industrial competence 53
industrial deepening 10, 32, 55, 71, 96, 111, 113, 118, 123, 129, 141–145, 185–186, 191, 193, 229, 242, 246, 250
industrial districts 101, 139–140, 299
industrial park 4, 140, 234, 267, 298
industrial policies 9–11, 71, 138, 171, 224, 257, 262, 272–273, 281–282, 289–290
industrial revolution 1–2, 32, 41, 43n10, 65, 67–68, 71, 73
infant industries 99, 115, 143, 244, 258–259, 298–299
infitah policy 247
informal manufacturing 160–163
informational externalities 54, 128
innovative entrepreneurs 25
institutional quality 21, 23, 67, 300
intensive growth 24, 264, 297–298
intra-industry 53, 66, 90, 115, 121, 128
ISIC 35, 49, 58, 85, 115, 118, 120, 129n4, 168, 185, 205, 292

Jamaica 76
Jerven, M. 29

Kaldor, N. 52
Kaldor's Laws 51, 73
Kaplinsky, R. 280
Kelsall, T. 7
Kenya 21, 37–38, 50, 141, 158, 160, 167, 169–170, 216–219, 278–279, 294
knowledge-based 24, 92–94, 288
Krugman, P. 122
Kuznets, S. 31, 34, 72, 88

Lagos Plan of Action 265
Lall, S. 88, 104n2, 143, 145, 262, 283n5, 283n7
late industrialization 10–11, 41, 65, 83–105, 111
Latin America 8, 37, 40, 52, 65, 67, 84, 129, 160, 162, 169, 204, 224, 280, 289
lean production 71, 298
Lesotho 40, 168

Lewis, W.A. 34–36, 72, 75, 79n2, 98
Lewis model 75
Linder, S. 74
linkages 11n2, 19, 33–35, 39–41, 53, 55, 74, 98–100, 102, 104, 113, 139–140, 156, 161–162, 175, 258, 264, 266, 271–272, 274, 281, 283n5, 289, 298–299
low technology 58, 114, 127, 199

Maddison, A. 17, 292
manufacturing value added 2, 5, 10, 49, 52, 56–58, 58n1, 84, 121, 124, 168, 177, 178, 185, 195, 216, 224, 227, 230, 244
marketable surplus 75
marketed surplus 75
market failure 3, 18, 86, 88–89, 96, 259
market-led 28, 87, 94, 111, 118, 263
Marsh, P. 68, 72, 133–134
mass production 68–69, 83, 127, 133–134, 298
Matthews, J. 79n2, 97
Mauritius 3, 10, 37–38, 40, 50, 113, 125, 141, 154, 160, 165, 167–170, 177–180, 186, 193, 195–199, 202, 210, 216, 275, 278–280, 289
Mazumdar, D. 7
McMillan, M. 103
Mediterranean 154, 221
Mexico 50, 58, 70, 72, 83, 94, 126, 138, 199
Middle East 76, 139, 221
middle-income trap 197, 299
Millennium Development Goals 30
Mkandawire, T. 87
Mokyr, J. 67
Monga, C. 105n5, 260
multiple-equilibria 27

neopatrimonial 29, 163, 165–166, 172n4, 184
neopatrimonialism 165, 299
neo-structuralist 88–89
new globalization 6, 9–10, 66, 138, 144, 146
Newman, C. 7, 158–159, 171, 274, 289
Nigeria 21, 37–38, 41, 50, 116, 155, 160, 167, 169–170, 178–181, 200, 202–203, 229, 244, 278–279, 281, 294
Nipponian Model 123
non-manufacturing 48, 56, 73, 193, 240, 299
North, D. 67
Northern Italy 83, 139–140

OECD 24, 59n4, 127, 281, 292n5, 294
official development assistance 115, 250n1, 276, 278, 294, 299

304 Index

offshorability 71
Old Globalization 66
original equipment manufacturing 126, 130n7
own-brand manufacturer 126

Page, J. 7
Perez, C. 68, 72, 127
Polanyi, K. 11n1, 79
policy lock-ins 27
political failure 3, 26
political settlements 27, 164
Porter, M. 127, 136
poverty traps 29
Prebisch, R. 35, 79n2
primary products 18, 127
primary stage 120, 224
primitive accumulation 41, 153, 224
product cycle model 126
production function 20
production-oriented 74–76
productivity-driven 8, 24–25, 31–32, 35, 69, 76, 86, 91, 127, 155, 160, 257, 259–260, 297, 299
purchasing power parity 39–40, 156, 169, 299

Ranis, G. 98
ready-made garment 4, 129, 129n6
regional growth engines 281
rentier states 49
rent seeking 49, 96, 103, 112, 117, 154, 164–165, 167–168, 172n4, 175, 199, 299
replicative entrepreneurs 25
resource-based industrializers 10, 168, 175–212, 219
Riddell, R. 7
Rodrik, D. 88, 103, 116, 118, 147n2, 261–262
Roemer, M. 175
Rosenberg, N. 67
Russia 4, 26–27, 67–68, 83, 279

scale elasticity 20
scale-sensitive assets 112
Schumpeterian 20, 68, 263
Second Global Century 65, 67
second unbundling 112, 132–147, 159
self-discovery 35, 53, 88, 147n5, 258
self-selection 53, 159, 162
self-sufficiency 116, 119, 121, 210, 266
Sen, A. 15, 18
Senegal 21–22, 37–38, 50, 160, 167, 169–170, 182–183, 217–220, 240–244, 278–279
separation costs 111
Sigma-convergence 26

Silicon Valley 128, 140
Singapore 26, 50, 58, 83, 94, 113, 123, 138, 195
Singer, H.W. 35
SMEs 140, 266–267, 282, 289
Soderbom, M. 7, 158, 162
Solow model 51, 73
Soludo, C. 274, 283n7
Sonobe, T. 7
South Africa 4, 10, 21–22, 37–38, 40, 50, 129, 141, 155, 160, 165, 167, 169–170, 177–180, 193, 197, 199, 203–209, 265–266, 271, 275, 278–279, 281, 289
South Asia 3–4, 8, 37–38, 52, 55, 139, 280, 289
Southeast Asia 138, 141
South Korea 4, 18, 21–23, 27, 56, 58, 94, 123–124, 129, 146, 262, 283n8, 288
Soviet industrialization debates 3, 41, 86, 99, 283n8
special economic zones 139–140, 268, 281
specialization 3, 35–36, 51, 53, 69, 72, 75–77, 86, 96, 133, 135, 156, 255, 258
specialized industrial 139–140
Spence, M. 24, 33
state-led 28, 70, 76, 97, 195, 230, 247
state-owned 234, 247, 299
static efficiency 24–25
structural adjustment 87, 155, 244, 276
structural homogeneity 35
structuralist 10, 74, 87–89, 92, 104n2, 261
Sub-Saharan Africa 4–5, 7, 22, 28–29, 37–38, 40, 55, 140, 157, 161, 171n3, 207, 211, 259, 273, 277–279
supply chains 67, 71–72, 91, 99, 135–139, 266, 294, 298, 300
Sutcliffe, R. 55
Sutton, J. 143

Taglioni, D. 66, 72, 147n4, 294
Taiwan 8, 26, 39, 50, 58, 83, 94, 123, 126, 138, 146, 167, 283n8, 288
Tanzania 18, 21–22, 27, 37–38, 41, 50, 160, 167, 169–170, 171n2, 182–183, 216–220, 244–247, 265–266, 272, 276, 278–279, 294
task-based 119, 135, 138, 143
Teal, F. 193
technological capabilities 2, 26, 30–31, 78, 84, 120, 262, 300
tertiary stage 120
Thailand 21, 26, 39, 50, 56–58, 94, 123, 126, 138, 167
third global century 66–67, 71
total factor productivity 16, 20–22, 26, 31, 67, 70, 118, 141, 159–160, 190, 296, 300

trade-oriented 74, 76–78, 89
tropics 26, 48
Tunisia 3, 21, 37–38, 40, 55, 57, 141, 167, 169–170, 186, 215–220, 235, 247–250, 275–276, 278–279, 289
Turkey 4, 21–22, 58, 83, 94, 138, 205

unbundling 3, 66–67, 71, 111–130, 132–147, 159
UNCTAD 7, 156, 292
UNECA 7, 11n2, 104, 105n6, 146, 155, 171n1
UNIDO 7, 84, 104, 105n3, 116, 147n3, 180, 185, 187–189, 194, 198, 202, 207–209, 212n1, 219, 222–223, 226, 228, 232–233, 237–239, 242–243, 246, 248–249, 265, 292–293
unit cost 87, 92, 105n5, 136, 145, 158–159, 290, 300
United States 21, 33, 50, 59n2
unit labor cost 35, 68, 72, 105n5, 115, 138, 158–159, 208, 228, 232–233, 238, 243–244, 290, 300

value chains 7, 52, 71, 78, 97, 132–136, 141, 143, 145, 171, 185, 197, 210, 230, 248, 267, 276, 281–282, 298, 300
Vernon, R. 127
vertical disintegration 54
vertical integration 54
very-late 3, 8, 52, 55, 65, 71–72, 75, 83–105, 132, 145, 298
Vietnam 3, 26, 41, 94, 142, 167, 191, 262, 270
Vogel, S. 100

Wade, R. 88, 166, 262
Wangwe, Samuel 7, 283n7
Washington Consensus 89, 265
West Africa 153, 161, 184, 186, 193
Whitfield, L. 7, 165
Williamson, J. 18, 65, 67–70, 224

Young, A 29, 79n2

Zimbabwe 21, 37–38, 40, 158, 161, 169–170, 178–183, 210–212, 278–279, 294